Alan Sorrell, 'Falling Tower', date uncertain. Sorrell (1904–74) was a neo-Romantic artist known both for his 'reconstruction' drawings of archaeological sites and depictions of past cultural life, and for his 'imaginative' work, which was characteristically inspired by the monuments and images of the past.

For Jo,
who learnt to love theory

Archaeological Theory

An Introduction
2nd Edition

Matthew Johnson

WILEY-BLACKWELL

A John Wiley & Sons, Ltd., Publication

Library of Congress Cataloging-in-Publication Data

Johnson, Matthew, 1962–
    Archaeological theory : an introduction / Matthew Johnson. – 2nd ed.
       p.   cm.
    Includes bibliographical references and index.
    ISBN 978-1-4051-0014-4 (hardcover : alk. paper) – ISBN 978-1-4051-0015-1 (pbk. : alk. paper) 1.   Archaeology–Philosophy. I.   Title.
CC72.J65 2010
930.1–dc22

                                                                    2009039202

A catalogue record for this book is available from the British Library.

Set in 10/12pt Sabon by SPi Publisher Services, Pondicherry, India
Printed in Singapore by Ho Printing Singapore Pte Ltd

01   2010

Contents

List of Figures

Acknowledgements

The author and publishers gratefully acknowledge the following for permission to reproduce copyright material:
Acknowledgements

Preface cartoon © Anthony Hadon-Guest; figure 2.2 from Childe, V. G., *The Danube in Prehistory* (Oxford University Press, 1929); figure 2.4 copyright © 2010 by Transaction Publishers. Reprinted by permission of the publisher; figure 2.5 from Clarke, D., *Analytical Archaeology* (second revised edition) (Routledge, London, 1976); figure 2.6 from Daniel, G. E., 'The dual nature of the megalithic colonisation of prehistoric Europe', *Proceedings of the Prehistoric Society* 7, 1941, courtesy of The Prehistoric Society, Salisbury; figure 2.7 from *Before Civilisation: A Radiocarbon Revolution and Prehistoric Europe* by A. C. Renfrew, published by Century. Reprinted by permission of The Random House Group Ltd.; figure 3.1 © The Kobal Collection; figure 4.3 from Hillman, G., 'Interpretation of archaeological plant remains', reprinted from Lone, F. A., Khan, M. and Buth, G. M., *Palaeoethnobotany – Plants and Ancient Man in Kashmir* (A A Balkema, Rotterdam, 1993); figure 5.1 from Clarke, D., *Analytical Archaeology* (second revised edition) (Routledge, London, 1976); figure 7.1 from Hodder, I. and Orton, C., *Spatial Analysis in Archaeology* (Cambridge University Press, 1976); figure 7.3 from Tilley, C., *Material Culture and Text: The Art of Ambiguity* (Routledge, London, 1991, © Dr Christopher Tilley); figure 8.1 from Unstead, R. J., *Looking at History 1: From Cavemen to Vikings* (Black, London, 1953); figure 8.2 © Klammers and the University of Minnesota Collections; figure 8.3 © Minnesota Historical Society; figure 9.1 http://commons.wikimedia.org/wiki/File:St_George_and_the_Dragon-altar_wing-NG-Praha.jpg; figure 9.2 © The British Museum, London; figure 9.3 © The British Museum, London; figure 9.4 from Clarke, D., *Analytical Archaeology* (Routledge, London, 1976); figure 10.1 Private collection/The Bridgeman Art Library

Nationalaity; figure 10.2 © Crown copyright, RCHME; figure 10.3 © Royal Geographical Society, London/The Bridgeman Art Library; figure 11.2 © Crown copyright NMR.

The publishers apologize for any errors or omissions in the above list and would be grateful to be notified of any corrections that should be incorporated in the next edition or reprint of this book.

Preface: The Contradictions of Theory

This book is an introductory essay on archaeological theory. It tries to explain something of what 'theory' is, its relationship to archaeological practice, how it has developed within archaeology over the last few decades, and how archaeological thought relates to theory in the human sciences and the intellectual world generally.

To many, 'theory' is a dirty word both within and outside archaeology. Prince Charles earned almost universal approbation when he condemned 'trendy theorists' in education; nobody however, including the Prince himself, seemed to be very clear precisely who he meant. When visiting an archaeological site a few years ago a suggestion of mine met with laughter and the response 'that's a typical suggestion of a theorist'. I don't recall anyone telling me exactly why my suggestion was so absurd, and when I visited the site the following year the strategy had been adopted. For the meat-and-potatoes Anglo-Saxon world in particular, theory is an object of profound suspicion. It is a popular saying that for the English, to be called an intellectual is to be suspected of wanting to steal someone's wife (sexism in the original). Theory, 'political correctness' and being 'foreign' stand together in the dock as traits to be regarded with hostility in the English-speaking world – and beyond; there is even a word for hostility to theory in German – *Theorifeindlichkeit*. I shall look at some of the reasons why this is so in chapter 1.

At the same time, however, theory is increasingly popular, and seen as increasingly important, both within and outside archaeology. Valentine Cunningham commented in *The Times Higher Education Supplement* that theorists in academia are 'a surging band, cocky, confident in academic credentials, job security and intellectual prestige', inspiring the columnist Laurie Taylor to write a memorable account of a bunch of theorists intellectually roughing up a more empirical colleague at a seminar before departing to the local bar. His account was fictitious but contained much truth.

Anthony Haden-Guest

'You're a terrorist? Thank God. I understood Meg to say you were a *theorist*.'
From Culler (1997: 16)

There are various indices of the 'success' of an explicitly defined archaeological theory; one might cite the frequency of 'theoretical' symposia at
major conferences such as the Society for American Archaeology or the
European Association of Archaeology, or the incidence of 'theory' articles in
the major journals. One particularly telling index is the rise and rise of the
British Theoretical Archaeology Group conference (TAG). This was formed
as a small talking-shop for British archaeological theorists in the late 1970s,
but since then has become the largest annual archaeological conference in
Britain with substantial participation from North America and Europe.
There are now similar organizations in North America, Scandinavia (Nordic-
TAG) and Germany (*Arbeitsgemeinschaft Theorie*).

It is true that a lot of papers delivered at TAG scarcely merit the term
'theoretical', and even more true that many only come for the infamous
TAG party in any case. It must also be conceded that the degree of impact
of TAGs and 'theory's' influence on the 'real world' of archaeological practice, and the cultural and legislative framework of archaeology, is debatable.
The theorist often feels like Cassandra, constantly giving what he or she sees
as profound predictions and insight and constantly being ignored by the
decision makers.

This book is written to give the student an introduction to a few of the
strands of current thinking in archaeological theory. It is deliberately written

as an introduction, in as clear and jargon-free a fashion as the author can manage (though as we shall see, criteria of clarity and of what constitutes jargon are riddled with problems).

It is intended as a 'route map' for the student. That is, it seeks to point out prominent landmarks on the terrain of theory, comment on relationships between different bodies of thought, and to clarify the intellectual underpinnings of certain views. As such, it is anything but an encyclopaedia; it is hardly one-tenth of a comprehensive guide to the field, if such a guide could be written. The text should be read with reference to the Further Reading and Glossary sections, and over-generalization, oversimplification and caricatures of viewpoints are necessary evils.

Above all, I remind all readers of the fourth word in the title of this book. I have tried to write an *Introduction*. The book, and its different chapters, are meant to be a starting-point for the student on a range of issues, which she or he can then explore in greater depth through the Further Reading sections. Many of the comments and criticisms made of the first edition of this book focused on an alleged over- or under-emphasis of a particular theoretical viewpoint, or lack of coverage. Many of these criticisms were valid, and I have tried to deal with them in this second edition; but many evaluated the text as a position statement with which they happened to agree or disagree, rather than on its pedagogical intention, that is as an introductory route-map to the issues. Additionally, students need to be reminded that this book should be the start, not the end, of their reading and thinking, a point I will return to in the Conclusion. A route-map is not an encyclopaedia.

To pursue the route map analogy, the route followed here is one of several that could be taken through the terrain of archaeological theory. I could have devoted a chapter each to different thematic areas: Landscape, The Household, Trade and Exchange, Cultures and Style, Agency, and so on. In each case, a variety of approaches to that theme could be given to show how different theories contradict or complement each other and produce different sorts of explanation of the archaeological record. Alternatively, a tour could be taken through different 'isms': positivism, functionalism, Marxism, structuralism, poststructuralism, feminism. These would be reasonable paths, and ones moreover that have been taken by other authors.

This book, however, tries above all to bring out the relationship between archaeological thought and wider strands of theory in intellectual and cultural life as a whole. It seeks to show how specific theoretical positions taken by individual archaeologists 'make sense' within a wider context, cultural, social and political as well as academic. This book also seeks to bring out the relationship between archaeological theory and archaeological practice more clearly than has been done in the past. The structure adopted here, of a historical approach focusing initially on the New Archaeology and reactions to it before moving on to current debates, fitted this purpose best.

I have written above that this book is a guide for 'the student'; I mean the student in the broadest sense. Many practising archaeologists employed outside the academic world have told me that they are interested in current theoretical debates, and see such debates as of potential relevance to their work. Nevertheless many feel alienated by what they see as the unnecessary obscurity and pretentiousness that is central to the theoretical scene. I don't subscribe to such an analysis, but I have to acknowledge that it is widespread. Right or wrong, I hope that they may find that what follows is of some help.

In trying to survey many different theoretical strands, I have been torn between trying to write a 'neutral', 'objective' survey of different currents of thought on the one hand, and a committed polemic advancing my own views on the other. The end product lies, perhaps a little unhappily, somewhere between these extremes. On the one hand, the construction of a completely objective survey simply isn't intellectually possible; the most biased and partial views on any academic subject consistently come from those who overtly proclaim that their own position is neutral, detached and value-free. In addition, it would be disingenuous to claim that the book is written from a disinterested viewpoint – that it is a guide pure and simple. Obviously an interest in theory goes hand-in-hand with a passionate belief in its importance, and an attachment to certain more or less controversial views within the field.

On the other hand, if we want to understand why theory is where it is today, any account of a wide diversity of intellectual positions must endeavour to be reasonably sympathetic to all parties. A survey can never be neutral, but it can make some attempt to be *fair*. As R.G. Collingwood pointed out in relation to the history of philosophy, most theoretical positions arise out of the perceived importance of certain contexts or issues; that is, philosophical beliefs are in part responses to particular sets of problems, and have to be understood as such rather than given an intellectual mugging. One's intellectual opponents are never all morons or charlatans to the last man and woman and one's bedfellows are rarely all exciting, first-rate scholars. Before we get carried away with such piety it must be remembered that this does not mean that certain positions are not therefore immune from criticism. An intellectual relativism in which 'all viewpoints are equally valid' or in which 'every theory is possible' is not a rigorous or tenable position. We can see historically that some theoretical positions have been abandoned as dead ends, for example the extreme logical positivism of the 1970s.

I have also been torn between writing a historical account of the development of theory, and of giving a 'snapshot' of theory in the present. On the one hand, it might be held that my re-telling of the origins of the New Archaeology of the 1960s, and more arguably the processual/postprocessual 'wars' of the 1980s and 1990s, is now out of date. On the other hand, I feel that in order for the student to understand where theory is today, it is necessary to look at its development over the last few decades, and indeed to look at the deeper intellectual roots of many views and positions in the more remote past, for example in the thinking of figures like Charles Darwin and Karl Marx. Much of traditional cultural evolutionary theory, and much of the early postprocessual critique, may appear to be passé to some; but I do not think that the modern student can understand current thinking without reference back to this literature. Archaeology would be a strange field of study if it asserted that it could understand the way the discipline thinks in the present, without reference back to the way it thought in the past.

For this second edition of the book, I have made a number of changes. I give a more extended account of these and reflection on them in the Further Reading section, but two stand out. First, there has been an explosion in archaeological discussion of Darwinian evolution, and I have therefore divided the chapter on 'Evolution' into two. Second, the first edition concentrated on theory in the Anglo-American world, in part reflecting my own background and limitations. This concentration was rightly criticized by many non-Anglo scholars. I have tried in this second edition to write a more inclusive text, giving more attention to Indigenous and postcolonial perspectives as well as drawing more attention to theoretical contributions from across the world. I have nevertheless retained the original structure of the book, and have run the risk of 'fitting in' material around this organizing structure; but the alternatives, for example of having a separate chapter on non-Anglo theory, or of a country-by-country survey, seemed to me to be greater evils and to do greater violence to the very subtle texture of theoretical debate.

The adoption of an informal tone and omission of detailed referencing from the text is deliberate. It is to help, I hope, the clarity of its arguments and the ease with which it can be read. Many 'academic' writers have often been taught to forsake the use of the 'I' word, to attempt to render our writing neutral and distant, to avoid a conversational or informal tone, all in the name of scientific or scholarly detachment. This may or may not be a valid project. The aim here however is educational rather than scholarly in the narrow sense.

One of my central points, particularly in the first chapter, is that all practising archaeologists use theory whether they like it or not. To make this point clear and to furnish examples I have often quoted passages from avowedly 'atheoretical' writers and commented upon them, to draw out the theories and assumptions that lie implicit within those passages. In most cases the passages come from the first suitable book to hand. I want to stress that critiques of these examples are not personal attacks on the writers concerned. Here, the need to use practical examples to make a theoretical point clear clashes with the desire to avoid a perception of unfair, personalized criticism.

The text is based in part on lecture notes for various undergraduate courses I have taught at Sheffield, Lampeter, Durham and Southampton. The students at all four institutions are thanked for their constructive and helpful responses. Some students may recognize themselves in the dialogues in some of the chapters, and I ask their forgiveness for this. The first edition of the book was partly conceived while I was a Research Fellow at the University of California at Berkeley in the spring of 1995. I would like to thank Meg Conkey, Christine Hastorf, Marcia Ann Dobres, Margot Winer and many others too numerous to mention for their hospitality during that time and for making my stay so enjoyable and profitable. I also thank Durham University for giving me study leave for that term. A number of reviewers, some anonymous, made a string of invaluable comments without which the book would have been much more opinionated and parochial and much less comprehensible. These include especially Randy McGuire, Jim Hill, Chris Tilley and Elizabeth Brumfiel. Robert Preucel and Ian Hodder reviewed the final draft extensively. Tim Earle, Clive Gamble and Cynthia Robin kindly corrected my misconceptions for the second edition. Dominic McNamara drew my attention to the Foucault quotation in chapter 6. Within the Department of Archaeology at Durham, Helena Hamerow, Colin Haselgrove, Anthony Harding, Simon James, Sam Lucy and Martin Millett read and made invaluable comments on the first draft. Brian Boyd, Zoe Crossland, Jim Brown and John McNabb helped with illustrations. William R. Iseminger kindly supplied figure 9.5 and Francis Wenban-Smith kindly supplied figure 10.4. Collaboration with staff of the History, Classics and Archaeology Subject Centre, particularly Annie Grant, Tom Dowson and Anthony Sinclair, influenced my thinking on the pedagogical framing and impact of the second edition. Conversations on the philosophy of science with my late father C. David Johnson clarified many points.

I moved to Southampton in 2004; I thank an outstanding group of colleagues and students there for their advice and support over the last five years. I prepared revisions for the second edition while a visiting scholar at the University of Pennsylvania in the autumn of 2008. I thank Bob Preucel and Richard Hodges for making that visit possible, and the students of Bob's theory class for their input and hospitality. I also thank Clare Smith, Heather Burke and Matt Spriggs for organizing a stimulating visit to Australia in 2003/4, and Prof Joseph Maran, Ulrich Thaler and the staff and students of Heidelberg University for four wonderful months discussing theory and practice in spring 2005.

More broadly, can I thank everyone who has taken the time to speak or write to me over the last ten years to express their appreciation for this book. Students, teachers and practicing archaeologists have given me some very kind compliments, for which I am flattered and grateful, from the Berkeley feminist who said that I wrote like a woman to the Flinders student who sent me a picture of her Matthew Johnson Theory Action Doll.

Conversations with Chris Taylor, Paul Everson, Casper Johnson and David Stocker informed the discussion of Bodiam in chapter 10, though errors and misconceptions in this discussion remain my responsibility. John Davey, Tessa Harvey, Jane Huber, Rosalie Robertson and Julia Kirk at Blackwell were always patient, encouraging and ready with practical help when needed. My wife Becky made comments on successive drafts; proof-read the final manuscript; and most importantly, provided emotional and intellectual support without which this book would never have been written. In return, I hope this book explains to her why archaeologists are such a peculiar bunch of human beings, though I know she has her own theories in this respect. My thanks to everybody.

1

Common Sense is Not Enough

Archaeology can be very boring, distressing and physically uncomfortable. Every year we excavate thousands of sites, some with painstaking and mind-numbing patience, some in a great and undignified hurry. Every year we get chilled to the marrow or bitten half to death by mosquitoes while visiting some unprepossessing, grassy mound in the middle of nowhere. Miles from a decent restaurant or even a warm bath, we try to look interested while the rain comes down in sheets and some great professor whose best work was 20 years ago witters on in a monotone about what was found in Trench 4B. Every year we churn out thousands of interminable, stultifyingly dull site reports, fretting over the accuracy of plans and diagrams, collating lists of grubby artefacts to publish that few will ever consult or use again.

Why?

We could spend the money on hospitals. Alternatively we could quietly pocket the cash and write a much more entertaining, fictitious version of what the past was like while we sat on a sun-kissed terrace somewhere in southern California. If we were feeling ideologically sound we could raise an International Brigade for a liberation struggle somewhere. Each of these alternatives has its attractions, but we don't do any of these things. We go on as we have done before.

One reason we don't do these things is because *archaeology is very important*. The past is dead and gone, but it is also very powerful. It is so powerful that an entire nation (Zimbabwe) can name itself after an archaeological site. It is so powerful that archaeological sites are surrounded by police and are the subject of attempted occupations by New Age travellers. It is so powerful that even individual groups of artefacts like the Parthenon frieze are the subject of major international disputes.

The question 'why do we do archaeology?' is therefore bound up with the question 'why is archaeology – the study of the past through its material remains – so important to us?' And this again leads on to the question of 'us', of our identity – *who are we?* And these are all theoretical questions.

Definitions of Theory

'Theory' is a very difficult word to define. Indeed, I shall return to this topic in the final chapter, since different theoretical views define 'theory' in different ways. Different definitions cannot therefore be fully explored without prior explanation of those views.

For the time being, I propose to define theory as follows: theory is *the order we put facts in*. I will go on to discuss the extent to which 'facts' exist independently of theory, and how we might define 'facts'. We can also note that most archaeologists would include within the purview of theory *why we do archaeology* and the social and cultural context of archaeology. They would also refer to *issues of interpretation*. Most archaeologists would agree that the way we interpret the past has 'theoretical' aspects in the broad sense. For example, we could cite general theories such as cultural and biological evolution, issues of how we go about testing our ideas, debates over how we should think about stylistic or decorative change in artefacts.

There is disagreement over whether many concepts can be considered 'theoretical' or whether they are merely neutral techniques or methods outside the purview of theory. Stratigraphy, excavation and recording techniques, and the use of statistical methods are, for example, clearly all examples of putting facts in a certain order. However, they might be considered 'theoretical' by some but 'just practical' or 'simply techniques' by others. Theory and method are often confused by archaeologists. In this more restricted sense of theory, if theory covers the 'why' questions, method or methodology covers the 'how' questions. So theory covers *why* we selected this site to dig, method *how* we dig it. However, theory and method are obviously closely related, and many archaeologists including myself regard such a straightforward division as too simple.

To give an example of the relationship between theory and method, we might consider different methods of investigating social inequality in the archaeological record. Thus the method archaeologists might use would be to compare graves 'richly' endowed with lots of grave goods with poorer, unadorned graves. It is evident in this exercise that certain ideas or theories about the nature of social inequality are being assumed (that social status will be reflected in treatment of the body at death, that material goods are unequally distributed through society and that this has a direct relationship to social inequality, and so on). These ideas are themselves theoretical in nature.

Perhaps theory and method are one and the same thing and cannot be separated; perhaps they have to be separated if archaeology is to be a rigorous discipline that is capable of testing its theories against its data. This is a debate we shall return to in chapter 4.

> *I'm sorry to butt in, but all this discussion of theory and method clearly demonstrates just how sterile and boring theory really is. You're already lost in definitions and semantics, you haven't mentioned a single fact about the past, and I'm beginning to wish I hadn't bothered to start reading this and had turned my attention to that new book about the Hopewell culture instead. Theory is irrelevant to the practice of archaeology; we can just use our common sense.*

Ah, Roger, the eternal empiricist. (Roger Beefy is an undergraduate student at Northern University, England, though women and men like Roger can be found in any archaeological institution. Roger fell in love with archaeology when he was a child, scrambling up and down the ruins of local castles, churches, burial mounds and other sites. Roger spent a year after school before coming to Northern University digging and working in museums. Roger loves handling archaeological material, and is happiest when drawing a section or talking about seriation techniques over a beer. Now, in his second year at Northern University, Roger has found himself in the middle of a compulsory 'theory course'. Full of twaddle about middle-range theory, hermeneutics and postcoloniality, it seems to have nothing to do with the subject he loves.)

So, you want to know why theory is 'relevant' to archaeological practice. Perhaps you will bear with me while I discuss four possible reasons.

1 We need to justify what we do

Our audience (other archaeologists, people in other disciplines, the 'general public' or 'community' however defined) needs to have a clear idea from archaeologists of why our research is important, why it is worth paying for, why we are worth listening to. There are a hundred possible answers to this *challenge of justification*, for example:

- The past is intrinsically important, and we need to find out about it for its own sake.
- We need to know where we came from to know where we're going next. Knowledge of the past leads to better judgements about the future.

- Only archaeology has the time depth of many thousands of years needed to generate comparative observations about long-term culture processes.
- Archaeology is one medium of cultural revolution that will emancipate ordinary people from repressive ideologies.

The chances are that you disagree with at least one of these statements, and agree with at least one other. That doesn't change the fact that *each statement is a theoretical proposition* that needs justifying, arguing through, and debating before it can be accepted or rejected. None of the statements given above is obvious, self-evident or common-sensical when examined closely. Indeed, very little in the world is obvious or self-evident when examined closely, though our political leaders would have us think otherwise.

2 We need to evaluate one interpretation of the past against another, to decide which is the stronger

Archaeology relies in part for its intellectual credibility on being able to distinguish 'good' from 'bad' interpretations of the past. Were the people who lived on this site hunter-gatherers, or were they aliens from the planet Zog? Which is the stronger interpretation?

It's impossible to decide what is a strong archaeological interpretation on the basis of 'common sense' alone. Common sense might suggest, for example, that we accept the explanation that covers the greatest number of facts. There may be thousands of sherds of pottery dating from the first millennium BC on a site, all factual in their own way, but one other fact – a tree-ring date of AD 750, for example – may suggest that they might be all 'residual' or left over from an earlier period. In practice, every day of our working lives as archaeologists, *we decide on which order to put our facts in*, what degree of importance to place on different pieces of evidence. When we do this, we use theoretical criteria to decide which facts are important and which are not worth bothering with.

A good example of the inadequacy of common sense in deciding what is a strong or weak archaeological explanation is that of ley lines. Ley lines were 'discovered' by Alfred Watkins in the 1920s, when he noticed that many ancient archaeological sites in Britain could be linked up by straight lines. The idea that ancient sites lay on straight lines could be 'proved' easily by taking a map upon which such ancient monuments were marked and drawing such lines through them. Watkins suggested these lines represented prehistoric trackways. Nonsense, said the professional archaeological community. It was common sense that prehistoric peoples living thousands of years before literacy or formal geometry were far too primitive to lay out such geometrically sophisticated lines. Watkins had intended his book as a genuine contribution to archaeology, but his research, sincerely carried out, was laughed out of court and consigned to the ranks of lunatic 'fringe archaeology'. Other writers took his thesis up in succeeding decades but extended it by suggesting that the lines were of sacred significance or mystical power.

Now it is quite clear today that prehistoric peoples would have been quite capable of laying out such lines. The original, common-sensical criteria used by archaeologists for rejecting Watkins's thesis were completely invalid.

Ley lines do not exist. This was shown by Tom Williamson and Liz Bellamy in *Ley Lines in Question*, which analysed such lines statistically and showed that the density of archaeological sites in the British landscape is so great that a line drawn through virtually anywhere will 'clip' a number of sites. It took Williamson and Bellamy a book's worth of effort and statistical sophistication to prove this, however.

The moral of the debate over ley lines is that what is considered to constitute a strong or a weak explanation is not simply a matter of 'common sense'. I would argue that if we really want to understand what drove and continues to drive the ley line debate, we have to look, in part, at class divides in British archaeology. In his time Watkins was derided as a vulgar amateur, while today the tradition of ley line searchers continues strongly in 'alternative' or New Age circles. New Age travellers and others in their turn view middle-class professional archaeologists with suspicion. Others might dispute this social interpretation and suggest alternative reasons for the intellectual development of the issue. I might reply: we would then be having a theoretical debate.

3 We must be explicit in what we do as archaeologists

In other words, we must be as open as possible about our reasons, approaches and biases, rather than trying to conceal them or pretend that they do not exist. This is a basic rule of academic discourse, though it is not always followed. Lewis Binford, a character we shall meet properly in the next chapter, made the point that all scientists of all disciplines need to be aware of the assumptions they are making if they wish to be productive.

It goes without saying that we can never be completely explicit about our biases and preconceptions. This should not stop us trying.

4 We don't 'need' theory, we all use theory whether we like it or not

Put another way, *we are all theorists*. This is the most important point of all. The most lowly troweller, the most bored washer of ceramics, the most alienated finds assistant or lab technician, are all theoreticians in the sense that they all use theories, concepts, ideas, assumptions in their work. (The theory may have been imposed on them by the project director or funding body, but it is theory nevertheless.) Put another way, the driest, most descriptive text or site report is already theoretical. Somebody wielding a WHS or Marshalltown trowel relies on theories of soil colour change and stratigraphy in his or her work; editorial judgements about the relative weighting and order given to pottery and artefact reports in a site monograph depend on a judgement on what is 'significant' about that particular site which in turn rests on theoretical criteria.

Any archaeologist who therefore tells you that their work is 'atheoretical', that they are 'not interested in theory', or that they are doing 'real archaeology' as opposed to those 'trendy theorists' is not telling the whole truth. They are as much theorists as anyone else, though they might choose to mask their theoretical preconceptions by labelling them 'common sense' or derived from the 'real world'. In doing so, I would argue that they are bypassing their responsibility to make clear the intellectual basis of their work, trying to hide the theoretical assumptions and approaches that they are in fact using from critical scrutiny. They are indulging in an intellectual sleight of hand.

I would go further: pretending to be atheoretical is an attempt to impose a kind of *machismo* on to archaeological practice. As we shall see in chapter 8, archaeological practice is bound up with gendered notions of what is or is not valuable. There is, at least in the English-speaking world, always something vaguely effeminate (and therefore, it is implied, somehow secondary) about talking, reasoning, discussing, trying to think clearly and explicitly. It is difficult to see Vin Diesel at a philosophy discussion group. 'Real men' don't do isms and ologies; they just dig – preferably with a really large, heavy pickaxe.

> *I've listened long enough to this; you're descending into abuse now. I'm willing to concede that we all use theory in some sense, but at the end of the day it's the facts, the raw data, that count.*

I'm not going to argue now about whether 'raw data' really exist independently of theory – that will come later. Let's suppose for now that raw data really do exist. Where does that get us? There is an infinity of archaeological facts. They are piled in their millions in museum and laboratory storerooms, in microfiche lists and in tables of data. Here are some pretty undeniable 'facts':

The pot I am holding is 600 years old.

Cuzco is an Inca site in Peru.

Lepenski Vir is a Mesolithic site in Serbia.

Colono Ware pottery has been found in Virginia.

A skeleton was excavated at Maiden Castle, Dorset, England, with an iron projectile lodged in its spine.

Great Basin projectile points come in different sizes.

The Bronze Age preceded the Iron Age.

Tikal was a major ceremonial centre for the Ancient Maya.

There are usually lots of clay pipe fragments on post-1500 sites.

The Dordogne area of France is full of cave art.

The Great Wall of China is studded with towers.

In Chaco Canyon the ancient pueblos are built of stone.

Do the sentences above add up to a meaningful account of the past, a coherent archaeological narrative? No. Simply dredging up facts and waiting for them to cohere into an orderly account of the past is like putting a number of monkeys in front of typewriters and waiting for them to come up with the complete works of Shakespeare.

What makes us archaeologists as opposed to mindless collectors of old junk is *the set of rules we use to translate those facts into meaningful accounts of the past*, accounts that 'make sense' to us as archaeologists and (it is hoped) to those who read or engage with our work. And those rules, whether they are implicit or explicit, are theoretical in nature. Facts are important, but without theory they remain utterly silent.

Let's take the example of a distinguished Professor of Archaeology who claims to be writing in an atheoretical, factual manner using 'common sense', and see what he is really doing. I have selected this text more or less at random:

> It is worth stressing that Romano-British culture was based on a money economy. In south-eastern Britain coins were indeed in use before the conquest, but the Romans were responsible for spreading their circulation throughout the island. The extent to which currency permeated the whole commercial life of the country, down to the smallest transactions, may be gauged from the occurrence of coins on the humblest Romano-British sites and in the remotest part of the province. (Alcock 1976: 174)

One theoretical assumption being made here is that ideas like 'transaction' and 'commercial life', which only gain their modern meaning in the later eighteenth century and only arguably so even then, can easily be applied to Roman Britain without further explication. It follows that the writer must expect the reader to use his or her modern experience of transactions and commercial life – market oriented, largely unconnected with social relations, mediated by a common means of monetary exchange – to understand the meaning of the sentence. This and other assumptions may or may not be true, but they are theoretical in nature.

A second is a 'middle-range' assumption: that is, it connects particular facts on the one hand to general theories on the other (see chapter 4). Alcock assumes that the relative numbers of coins on different site types (note the use of an implicit site hierarchy that equates with a social hierarchy, assumed rather than demonstrated: 'the humblest sites') will accurately reflect the level of what Alcock has termed 'commercial activity'. Of course, we have already acknowledged that commercial activity is a much more theoretically complex beast. Again, this is a theoretical proposition.

Alcock's account may or may not be 'true', a 'fair picture' or 'valid'; that is a matter for debate among those specializing in this period. It is certainly deeply theoretical. I could go on analysing the passage for several more pages, but the point has been made that even the most apparently straightforward, transparent, 'clear' prose conceals theoretical depths.

> *All this is very plausible and convincing, but I still dislike theory intensely. Theorists seem constantly to use incomprehensible jargon, write in an impenetrable style, and never to get anywhere tangible. You might persuade me there is a point to theory, but you can't stop me being irritated and alienated by what theorists write.*

No, I can't. I get irritated by a lot of theoretical writing, just as I get irritated by all sorts of archaeological writing. But you've raised a lot of points here that are worth taking in turn.

First, why the 'jargon'? Long words with specialized meanings are not confined to archaeological theory. Every area within archaeology has its own specialist terms of reference; in this sense jargon is in the eye of the beholder. My familiar terms as a theorist or as a specialist in vernacular architecture may seem jargon to the environmental specialist, and those of the environmental specialist may equally seem jargon to me.

There is a deeper problem with the accusation of jargon, however. There seems to be an assumption behind such an accusation that we can always express what we want to say in 'clear, simple and easy' language. If only archaeology were so straightforward! If it were, we might have concluded the archaeological project with a perfect understanding of the past hundreds of years ago. Archaeology is, if nothing else, about new ideas about the past.

We express ideas in words, and it may be appropriate to use new words to lead the reader to think in new ways.

Human societies were and are very complex things. As part of the natural world they share its complexity, and also have a social and cultural complexity all of their own. We don't complain when the chemist or biologist uses technical language incomprehensible to the lay person, so why should we when the archaeologist does so?

The point I am making here is that archaeologists expect the finer techniques of archaeological practice to be difficult to comprehend and master; that is the nature of our discipline. We are prepared to put effort into mastering the language and practice of stratigraphy, Harris matrices, seriation, scientific dating techniques, even the half-intuitive practical skill of differentiating between layers by the feel of the soil under the trowel. But the 'theory' side of what we do – using the tiny scraps of information thus gained to tell us about the human past in all its richness and complexity – must be at least equally difficult as these 'practical' tasks. It fact, it must be one of the most intellectually demanding tasks we as a species have ever set ourselves.

> *I think you're missing the point. The suspicion is that jargon is being used to mystify, to create a language of exclusion where the outsider is made to feel small.*

There is some justice in this charge. Certain forms of academic rhetoric are used, intentionally or unintentionally, to set up in-groups and out-groups. I do not defend such a practice. But again, one hears the vague murmur of pots calling kettles black; all sectional interests within and outside archaeology do this. Read any article in *Vernacular Architecture* on the classification of scarf-joints with squinted and pegged abutments, or a medieval historian on enfeoffments and subinfeudation.

Finally, 'writing clearly' assumes that one is *writing about something else*. In other words, that there is a real, external world out there with certain essential, concrete features, features that language can describe in a more or less clear and neutral manner. Now whether one is describing the decoration on pots or suggesting what it might have been like to live in the Bronze Age, this is a highly debatable assumption. Certainly, in most traditions of Western thought, the past doesn't exist anywhere outside our own heads. I have never touched, kicked or felt the past.

Theory is difficult. If one accepts that all archaeologists are theorists, then logically it is no more or less difficult than any other branch of archaeology.

But archaeology itself is difficult. We have set ourselves an incredibly daunting task. We want to understand human societies that have been dead and gone for thousands of years, whose customs, values and attitudes were almost certainly utterly different from our own. We have to do this without talking to the people themselves. What is more, we want to understand how and why they changed in the way they did. And the only materials we have to achieve this immense task are a few paltry scraps of rubbish they left behind on the way, most of which have long since decayed into dust. Such a task is not a simple one; the wish that, for all its practical discomforts and difficulties, it be an intellectually easy one is quite understandable, but very naïve.

Theory is also difficult for reasons that have less to do with jargon as such and more to do with academic practice. Practitioners in theory will often say one thing and do quite another. A theoretical article will proclaim that it is tackling a problem from a new, exciting perspective and just churn out the same old approach thinly disguised. Another article will accuse a rival of a string of theoretical iniquities and then do exactly the same things itself using different language.

Which leads to my final point: theory is difficult, in the last analysis, because it requires one to think for oneself. When a student writes a term paper or essay on southwestern Native American pottery, he or she can churn out a series of 'facts' gleaned from the standard textbooks. Such a list of facts, or more accurately a repetition of the textbooks' narratives, may not get a particularly good mark in the absence of any critical analysis or independent thinking whatsoever, but the student will get by. Such an approach comes unstuck, however, in writing a theory essay. It's more difficult to regurgitate things copied out of books and not really deeply understood when one is dealing with abstract ideas, particularly when one writer disagrees so clearly and fundamentally with another. Though any crop of undergraduate essays will demonstrate that it is not impossible.

The literary theorist Jonathan Culler (1997, 16–17) points out that:

> theory makes you desire mastery: you hope that theoretical reading will give you the concepts to organize and understand the phenomena that concern you. But theory makes mastery impossible, not only because there is always more to know, but, more specifically and more painfully, because theory is itself the questioning of presumed results and the assumptions on which they are based.

Theory, then, involves pain. It involves the deliberate placing of oneself in a vulnerable position, where the need to think for oneself makes one's conclusions always provisional and always open to attack from others.

Thinking for oneself, however, is something every student of archaeology (or any other critical discipline for that matter) is (or should be) in the business of doing. Ultimately, critical evaluation with reference to evidence is the key-stone of a liberal education. In an age when education is increasingly seen as a commodity, in which knowledge can, it is implied, be bought and sold in the marketplace, the idea of an education as learning the skills of thinking critically and of evaluating the evidence for and against a particular view is more and more under attack. Perhaps it is this cultural context that has led to some of the sharpness of the ritualized denunciations of theory.

Understanding Theory

> *Well, I still feel pretty dubious about theory, but I'm prepared to go along with you for a bit. Where do we go from here?*

The rest of this book will try to illuminate some of the major trends in archaeological theory, starting with the 1960s and moving on from there. To try to make this book as clear as possible, I am going to adopt two strategies.

First, from time to time I shall talk at length about developments in associated disciplines and in intellectual thought as a whole. As a result, long passages and even sub-sections of chapters may seem utterly irrelevant to the practising archaeologist. The reason I do this is because archaeology has had a habit of picking up ideas second-hand from other disciplines. Ideas have been changed, even confused and distorted, in the process. As a result, it is necessary to go back 'to source' to explain them clearly and to understand precisely how they have been used and abused by archaeologists. So please bear with the text, plod through the 'irrelevant' material, and I will then try to explain its relevance to archaeological thought.

Second, I shall look at the development of theory historically, looking first at the origins of the New Archaeology, then at reactions to it. I suggest that by understanding the historical context of a set of ideas such as 'New Archaeology' or 'postprocessual archaeology', one may more easily sympathize with its aims and grasp some of its underlying principles and concerns. By understanding this context we can also put many of the features of contemporary archaeology in their historical surroundings rather than place them in a vacuum.

The next chapter will discuss the New Archaeology; the following three will look at the questions of 'science' and 'anthropology' that it raised. The New Archaeology is now over 40 years old, but the intellectual questions raised by New Archaeologists are, I will suggest, absolutely central to contemporary archaeological theory and practice.

2

The 'New Archaeology'

Most archaeologists fall in love with the subject by getting 'hooked' on things. The things vary from case to case – castles, Roman baths, flint or chert arrowheads, Neolithic pots, Maya temples – but in most cases the immediate appeal is of mystery and romance, of the past calling to us through its remains. This romantic appeal is often aesthetic and sensual as well as intellectual. Archaeologists love clambering round medieval ruins or handling pottery sherds. We try to persuade ourselves, however, that these ruins or sherds are mere 'data'. (One colleague told me that as a result of the acute boredom of his researches he now loathes Neolithic pottery to the depths of his soul, but I interpret this as another, rather twisted form of love.) Artefacts, whether as small as an arrowhead or as large as a royal palace, fascinate us.

This love of artefacts, in itself, has nothing to do with archaeology in the strict sense as the study of the past. Artefacts *tell us nothing about the past* in themselves. I have stood in the middle of countless ruins of castles and ancient palaces and listened very carefully, and not heard a single syllable. Colleagues tell me that they have had similar distressing experiences with pottery, bones, bags of seeds. They love handling and experiencing their material, but it remains silent. In and of itself, it tells them precisely nothing.

Artefacts can't tell us anything about the past because the past does not exist. We cannot touch the past, see it or feel it; it is utterly dead and gone. *Our beloved artefacts actually belong to the present.* They exist in the here and now. They may or may not have been made and used by real people thousands of years ago, but our assessment of the date of their manufacture and use is itself an assessment that we make, that is made in the present.

Until scientists invent a time machine, *the past exists only in the things we say about it.* Archaeologists choose to ask certain questions of our material: 'How many beads were found in this grave?' 'Do we see a shift to intensive exploitation of llamas in the Formative Period?' 'What was it like to live in the Bronze Age?' 'What degree of social inequality do we see in this period?' We make general or particular statements about the past: 'There was increased use of obsidian in Phase 3B of this site'; 'There were more elements of cultural continuity between Mesolithic and Neolithic populations than have hitherto been assumed'; 'Gender relations became less equal through time'; 'The Romans were a cruel and vicious people'. These are all statements made here, now, in the present, as I write and you read. They do not belong to the past.

It is only in works of fiction, or if you believe in ghosts, that past and present can really be made to collide and merge into each other. It is striking that many writers have used this collision with great effect to disturb and horrify the 'rational' Western mind (the novels of Peter Ackroyd are excellent examples of this). More critically, this collision of past and present is also possible within 'non-Western' schemes of thought, where living cultural traditions may be held to be embodiments of cultural memory and in which past and present are not so radically divided; hence in part the conflicts between different cultures over, for example, excavation and reburial of Native American human remains, where the belief that time moves in a cycle rather than in a line makes archaeological excavation a threat to the present through its 'desecration' of the past. 'Indigenous archaeology' does not, then, necessarily make this radical division between present and past, a point we will return to in chapter 12.

Now it is the task of archaeologists to find out about the past. We want to know what really happened back then. The source materials – stones, bones, pots – are in the present, and the past that we create is also in the present. We will never 'know' what the past was 'really like', but we all can and do try to write the 'best' account we can, an account that is informed by the evidence that we have and that tries to be coherent and satisfying to us.

One of the basic problems of archaeology, then, is summarized in figure 2.1. Somehow we have to take the archaeological materials that we have and through our questioning get them to give us information about the past. There is a gulf between past and present, a gulf that the archaeologist has to bridge somehow even if it can never be bridged securely or definitively. Otherwise we risk a descent into the mindless activity of simply assembling and collating old objects for their own sake, rather than as evidence for the past (an activity which has been derided as 'mere antiquarianism', though such a term fails to do justice to the methods of early antiquarians).

I am labouring this point because it is easy to fall into the trap of believing that the very physicality of archaeological material will in itself tell us what the past was like. It will not. Kick a megalith and it hurts; stand in a castle chamber and you see nothing but medieval fabric. But kicking the megalith or standing in that cold chamber will tell you nothing about what the Neolithic or the Middle Ages were 'really like', or what processes led to the

PRESENT   PAST

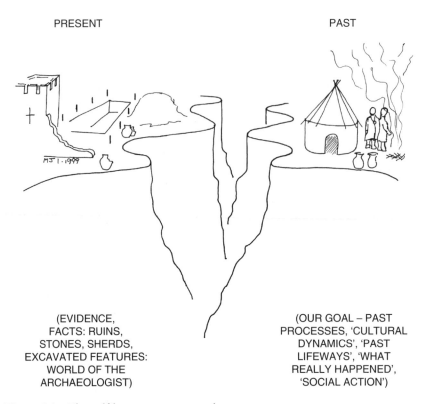

(EVIDENCE,   (OUR GOAL – PAST
FACTS: RUINS,   PROCESSES, 'CULTURAL
STONES, SHERDS,   DYNAMICS', 'PAST
EXCAVATED FEATURES: LIFEWAYS', 'WHAT
WORLD OF THE   REALLY HAPPENED',
ARCHAEOLOGIST)   'SOCIAL ACTION')

Figure 2.1   The gulf between present and past

construction and use of the megalith or castle. Archaeologists only see megalith and castle in the present, the here and now. This is a present that is
framed by contemporary ideas, attitudes and assumptions. We see megalith
and castle through our eyes, not the eyes of the prehistoric or medieval
observer.

The idea that there is some direct link is closely allied to a belief in 'common sense' discussed in the previous chapter and a naïve empiricism, in
which we do not need theory to translate between present and past. Such a
position, as we have seen, is simply not intellectually sustainable, but is is
nevertheless still widespread in areas of archaeology that have yet to feel the
full impact of explicit theory, and we will return to it again and again in the
chapters that follow.

I am also labouring this point because it can be seen as *the point of depar-
ture for very different views of archaeological theory*. One of the few areas
of common ground for most archaeological theorists is that we all want to
talk about the past, and we all use archaeological material in the present to

do so. But how do we do this? One possible suggestion is that we should use the methods of the natural sciences on our material, to try to test alternative hypotheses about past events and processes against that material and so expand and develop our understanding. Another possibility is to view artefacts like literary texts, to 'read' them as we would a piece of writing, and so begin to uncover the rich complexity of past cultural meanings.

There are a multiplicity of other views; and the problem has been perceived for some centuries. Indeed its origins can be traced directly to the genesis of modern archaeology in the work of Renaissance antiquarians. The English humanist Sir Thomas Browne centred his wonderful mid-seventeenth century essay *Hydriotaphia* around the discovery of cremation urns that we now believe to be of Anglo-Saxon origin, fifth to seventh century AD in date. Browne contrasted the physical solidity of the urns with the impossibility of understanding the religious beliefs that they expressed, or even the impossibility of assigning a date to them (he speculated that they might be Roman: figure 2.2).

The question of how to link present and past, however, surfaced in its most explicit form with the New Archaeology of the 1960s and 1970s. Though now over 40 years old, the New Archaeology raised foundational questions about the nature of archaeology that form the basis of many theoretical views today.

Culture History

There is an ongoing debate about the nature of archaeological theory before the New Archaeology. There is not space here to do this debate justice.

Some historians of archaeology maintain that the century before 1960 was the 'long sleep' of archaeological theory, in which very little explicit discussion of theory took place. They argue that archaeologists concentrated on collecting masses of archaeological material within an unquestioned, generally assumed framework. Others deny this, maintaining that this period did see lively theoretical debates of various kinds. They further maintain that the importance of the New Archaeology for the development of archaeological thought has been grossly overestimated. In particular, they point to New Archaeology's origins and impact in Britain and North America, and its much more limited impact in many other parts of the world.

I want to set this important historical debate aside, and stress here that one of the starting points of the so-called 'New Archaeology' lay in what I have discussed above, that is in the notion that *mere data collection* – the acquisition of more stuff – *does not in itself lead to a better understanding of the past*. David Clarke, one of the principal proponents of the New Archaeology, started his classic book *Analytical Archaeology* with a telling quote from Lewis Carroll:

En Sum quod digitis Quinque Levatur onus propert :

Figure 2.2 Illustration of burial urns from Sir Thomas Browne, *Hydriotaphia* (1658). The Latin tag is from the Latin poet Propertius: 'See, I am a burden which is lifted by five fingers'

Now here, you see, it takes all the running you can do, to keep in the same place. (The Queen to Alice, *Through the Looking-Glass*, Chapter 2, Lewis Carroll, 1832–98.)

Every year produces a fresh crop of archaeological excavations, a new harvest of prehistoric artefacts. ... The archaeologists come and go, new names and sites outshine the old, while hundreds of years of collected material overflows and submerges our museum storerooms. At the same time a relentless current of articles and books describe and label the new material so that the intrepid archaeologist, by dint of furious activity, can just maintain his [*sic*] status quo against the constant stream of data. However, the nebulous doubt arises in our minds that a modern empirical discipline ought to be able to aim at more rewarding results than the maintenance of a relative status quo and a steady flow of counterfeit history books. (Clarke 1978: 3)

Clarke, then, was not at all sure that the methods of archaeologists actually give us better and more reliable versions of the past. In his view, archaeologists seem to dig up more and more things but stay in the same place in terms of our ideas. Our knowledge of artefacts in the present grows better and better, but because we do not bridge the gulf with the past very well, progress in understanding that past does not follow.

What were the theories Clarke was dissatisfied with? In other words, how did archaeologists before the 1960s, and how do many archaeologists continuing to work in culture-historical traditions today, translate archaeological material into statements about the past? It is easy to over-generalize here, and exceptions can always be found. One of the basic building-blocks, however, was the idea of an archaeological culture and what it meant in terms of past human populations. In the words of Gordon Childe:

We find certain types of remains – pots, implements, ornaments, burial rites, and house forms – constantly recurring together. Such a complex of associated traits we shall term a 'cultural group' or just a 'culture'. We assume that such a complex is the material expression of what today would be called a 'people'. (Childe 1929: v–vi)

Such an idea of culture has been called *normative*. That is, it depends on two assumptions: first, that *artefacts are expressions of cultural norms*, ideas in people's heads, and second, that *those norms define what 'culture' is*. I will give two examples, one from the present and one from the past.

1   The English are the English because they drink tea, speak English, don't eat horse, and queue in an orderly fashion, often for hours without complaint. This distinguishes them from the French who drink coffee, speak French, eat horse and do not queue with such equanimity. (These are, of

course, all cultural norms, ideas about what is the right way to behave, and one can easily see that they are in fact ideals (in this case crude stereotypes) that don't necessarily correspond to reality in every case.)

2   The *Linearbandkeramik* (LBK) archaeological culture differs from the *Trichterbandkeramik* (TRB) in Neolithic Europe: in LBK areas we find rectangular house forms, pottery decorated with linear designs, a certain form of arable economy. In TRB areas house form, pottery decoration and economy are all different. (Again, this is an ideal: not every TRB or LBK site will share all the features of all the others.)

Such a concept of culture is also *polythetic*: that is, it depends on a number of different traits occurring together rather than on one trait alone. Drinking coffee does not make an English person French; a single rectangular house does not turn a TRB settlement into an LBK village. It is a number of traits occurring together, as Childe stressed, that defines culture. In North America, lists of traits were tabulated and added up from site to site.

So to summarize, in the traditional view we translate present into past by collecting artefacts into groups, and naming those groups as archaeological cultures. We then make the equation between an archaeological culture and a human culture by making the assumption that artefacts are expressions of cultural ideas or norms. (It is a tenable position, sometimes taken, to only go half-way with this process: in other words, to classify and name archaeological cultures, but to deny an equation with human cultures.)

This approach, which was termed 'culture history' by many, has several consequences. In the first place, it leads to a tendency to *particularize* what archaeologists say about the past rather than generalize. What this means is that instead of stressing the similarities between things, one stressed the differences and particularities between them.

One might, for example, want to generalize between the LBK and TRB, to stress that these different groups were at the same 'level' of social or economic development. They might both be classified as societies with a certain level of social ranking, for example, or with certain similar modes of subsistence economy, or exchange and trade. The culture-oriented approach, however, tends to direct attention away from such general features towards what makes the TRB and LBK distinctive, both from each other and from other cultures. It encourages us to stress their differences, their diagnostic and peculiar features, their particular forms of house type and burial rite, the contrast between the zigging of one form of pottery decoration and the zagging of another form, rather than those they have in common.

The second consequence of a normative view of culture is that cultures tend to be viewed as *unchanging*. To repeat, the normative approach sees artefacts as expressions of shared ideas. If people in the LBK all shared the same ideas on how to build houses, make pots and bury their dead, where

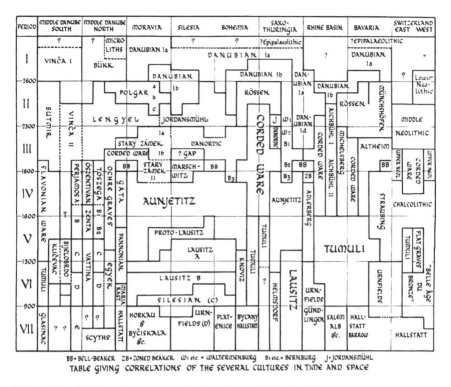

Figure 2.3   'Cultures' in space and time, from Childe (1929)

did change come from? The easiest way to explain change is to suggest that it was brought in from outside, from another human group. Such outside 'influence' can be of one of two forms: migration of peoples, or of *diffusion* – the spread of ideas through contact between groups.

Accounts of prehistory written using a culture-historical framework, then, tend to consist of two elements. The first is a chronological sequence of cultures, a sort of timetable with culture groups listed instead of trains. The second is a map full of arrows to indicate the migration and diffusion of ideas that marked change between cultures (see for example figures 2.3 and 2.4).

The whole synthesis thus produced tends to be *descriptive*. That is, it describes phases and areas of cultural change: this culture followed that culture, this innovation spread or diffused at that rate. Much traditional prehistory reads like much traditional history, that is like a chronicle of events held together by a narrative. Often, there is little explicit explanation of why this or that pottery style changed, why this or that culture spread or changed.

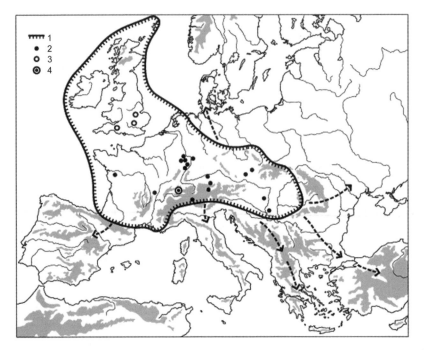

Figure 2.4   Piggott's (1968) view of culture. Piggott's caption reads: 'Distribution of mature La Téne culture and influences; 2, Sword scabbards in Swiss style; 3, British derivatives; 4, Many scabbards'

This descriptive emphasis is one reason why culture-historical approaches continue to be popular in Classical, medieval and historical archaeology: in these areas, underlying causes or reasons for change are often implicitly invoked not from the archaeological material itself, but from documents and wider historical narratives. Thus, a series of pieces of art or examples of tombs or architectural features will be described, with change then being ascribed to the 'influence of Rome' or the 'spread of Renaissance values' (see chapter 5).

In some regional and national traditions, for example in much central and eastern European work, a well-established and continuing approach is to use typologies and distribution maps to sort artefacts into archaeological groups and cultures in time and space, without then making the step of moving outwards to statements about human cultures. Rather, the archaeological entities thus defined can then be gathered together and synthesized with evidence from historical linguistics and historical ethnography to form an overarching discipline of 'prehistory', within which archaeology is one of several contributing techniques, alongside historical ethnography, historical linguistics and other disciplines such as folklife studies. In North America, the 'direct historical method' worked backwards from 'known' Native American groups from ethnography and history, mapping them in terms of archaeological cultures, and working backwards to a prehistoric origin point.

Lewis Binford called the culture-historical view of change 'an aquatic view of culture' (Binford 1964, 204). Binford's image was a caricature, but like all good caricatures it contained an essence of truth. What Binford meant was that the traditional archaeologists of his time saw the map of the prehistoric world as being a little like a large pool of water. When an innovation was made for whatever reason in a given place, it would tend to spread through the process of 'influence' or diffusion in all directions, like the ripples from a stone dropped in the pool. In any given location, then, one sees cross-cutting 'ripples' of influence.

I want to repeat that this characterization of culture-historical archaeology is far too brief, over-simplified and over-generalized. Suggestions for further accounts are given in the Further Reading section. In particular, it leans too heavily on what New Archaeologists such as David Clarke, Colin Renfrew and Lewis Binford said that traditional archaeology was like. Many have complained that the New Archaeology set up a distorted image of traditional thought for its own polemical purposes, a 'straw person' that could easily be knocked down. But if this is what New Archaeology thought traditional thinking was like, this was what New Archaeology was reacting against.

Origins of the New Archaeology

What, then, was the 'New Archaeology'? One thing is certain: it is no longer new. The term 'New Archaeology' is applied to a school of thought that swept through much of Anglo-American archaeology in the 1960s and early 1970s. It must be seen in the contexts of similar currents of thought in other disciplines – the New Geography in particular.

The 'New Archaeology' was also not a single set of beliefs or theories. One does not expect all members of a political party to have identical views on all policy matters; there are rather certain core ideas and values that inform the approach of any one party. Similarly, under the banner of the New Archaeology was a very diverse set of archaeologists with different approaches and beliefs. What united them all was a sense of dissatisfaction with the way archaeology was going, a sense that things had to change and that they, as a thrusting new generation of 'young Turks', were going to change it.

This dissatisfaction with traditional archaeology was crystallized in the phrase: 'we must be more *scientific* and more *anthropological*'. In this one phrase can be seen New Archaeology's source of disaffection with what went before, the foundations of its rise, and in my view the seeds of subsequent developments.

Why was culture history seen as unscientific? We must go back to David Clarke's comments on running harder and harder to stay in the same place. *More data do not automatically equate to better ideas about the past.* Archaeologists spend much of their time accumulating more and more information and presenting that information in ever more detail – what is sometimes called in German *Materialschlacht*, or literally 'war of the materials'. This does not automatically mean however a better and better idea of what the past was like, for all the reasons discussed above. Such studies simply fit more and more archaeological material into the same existing classification, for example an endless sequence of cultures. The end result is not necessarily a better or more accurate picture of the past in any way.

'Science', argued the New Archaeologists, uses its data to test hypotheses about the way the world works, and generalizes from these conclusions. 'Science' progresses; it does not simply collate its facts into orderly patterns, rather it confronts theory and data in such a way as to make larger and larger and deeper and deeper its understanding of the world. The natural sciences, in this view, have a proven record of developing better and better understandings of the world around us.

Why was culture history seen as not anthropological? Anthropology is the study of humanity. Traditional archaeologists, in the basic process of sorting artefacts into groups and cultures, often seemed to ignore human beings: pottery styles seemed to get up and march around with no reference to the humans that produced them. In this sense many forms of culture history can be seen as *fetishistic*. A fetish is a thing that comes to stand for something else such as a human or a human group: traditional archaeologists often seem to spend their time describing the movement of these things without thinking about the human beings, the cultural systems, behind them. In the shorthand of culture history, pottery styles and house types seem to develop little legs and run around without any help from human beings.

At a deeper level, traditional archaeology was not anthropological in the sense that there seemed to be no guarantee that the archaeological 'cultures' so lovingly produced by culture historians had any relationship to real human communities. Many New Archaeologists questioned the link between archaeological cultures – Childe's recurring assemblages of traits – and past peoples. Childe himself had come to doubt whether we really could equate archaeological cultures and past peoples:

> It would be rash to define precisely what sort of social group corresponds to the archaeologist's 'culture'. ... Culture and language need not coincide. (Childe 1942: 26–7)

This is why many New Archaeologists moved away from the normative conception of culture and looked for other ways to explain the things we dug up. Clarke's famous 1973 article claimed that archaeology experienced a 'loss of innocence'. The innocent equations archaeology had made between artefacts, cultures and peoples, or between data and interpretation more generally, had to be questioned.

To repeat, the New Archaeology must be understood as a movement or mood of dissatisfaction rather than as a specific set of beliefs. David Clarke called it 'a set of questions rather than a set of answers' (1973). It was certainly marked with revolutionary fervour. Lewis Binford, its most famous figure, tells a story that sums up both this fervour and its irritation with the particularism of traditional methods:

> I remember one day when one of the traditional Griffin students had returned from a field trip to the Upper Illinois valley. He had burst into the museum with the announcement that he had found a 'unique' item, a negative-painted sherd from the site. Griffin was obviously stimulated, and Papworth said, 'Let me see'. He took the sherd, looked at it and then threw it on the floor and ground it to pieces with the heel of his shoe. 'That's what I think of your "unique" sherd'. Griffin was in total shock, the student was practically in tears, and I was laughing inside. (Binford 1972: 130–1)

New Archaeology: Key Points

As the New Archaeology developed, certain key themes came to be repeated in the writings of its proponents. I will try to summarize these under seven points. If the descriptions seem brief and over-simplified, many of these themes will be discussed and developed further in future chapters. The important thing here is to get an overall sense of the spirit of the movement.

First, an emphasis on *cultural evolution*. The word 'evolution' has a series of different though related meanings stretching back to the work of Darwin in the nineteenth century (see chapters 9 and 10). For some within New Archaeology, it meant in part that societies could be classified on a scale from simple to complex. Cultures in this view evolved from one state to another, for example from 'band' societies to 'tribal' networks to 'chiefdoms'. This stress was in part a rejection of the aquatic view of culture, with its random ripples spreading across the map. Instead New Archaeologists wanted to look at the internal dynamics of a society, what was driving its general direction of social development (the phrase often used was 'cultural trajectory').

Evolution was also part of a conscious stress on generalities rather than particularities. Cultures might differ in their specific forms of jewellery and house type, one pottery style might zig and the other zag. But both societies

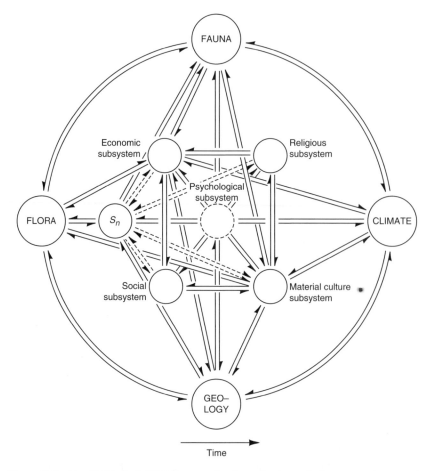

Figure 2.5   David Clarke's (1976) systemic view of culture. In language characteristic of the New Archaeology, Clark's caption reads: 'A static and schematic model of the dynamic equilibrium between the subsystem networks of a single sociocultural system and its total environmental system. S_n represents the summation of the effects of alien sociocultural systems connected to S by cultural 'coactions' (dashed lines) and to the environment by 'interactions' (solid lines). To set the model in motion all the components must oscillate randomly along intercorrelated trending trajectories'

might be comparable on the same level on an evolutionary scale. So we could generalize about, say, the evolution of state level societies from chiefdom level societies, without worrying too much about the different art styles or pottery decoration in each case.

Second, an emphasis on *systems thinking* (see figure 2.5 and chapter 5). Culture wasn't just a mixed bag of different randomly acquired norms, as culture history had implied; rather it was a system. Lewis Binford (1964) defined culture as 'man's extrasomatic means of adaptation'.

To clarify Binford's point, other animals are adapted to their environment through their bodies – the giraffe has a long neck to reach to the tops of trees in the savannah, polar bears have lots of fur to deal with the Arctic winter. Humans adapt through culture – the Inuit wear furs and live in igloos, the !Kung San have an extensive range of specialized hunting equipment. These cultural adaptations are all outside (*extra*) the body (*soma*), hence 'extrasomatic'.

So past cultures were:

(a) not just a bag of different, randomly acquired norms – the different parts of the system were related one to another as part of a functioning system;
(b) comparable to other kinds of system such as those found in the physical and animal worlds.

I will talk more about systemic approaches in chapter 5. But note here that it allowed New Archaeology to do two things. It firstly helped the stress on *generalization*. Different cultures may have had different pottery styles and burial rites, but the underlying social system could be shown to have underlying similarities (they were both more or less complex, practised similar systems of gift exchange even if the specific goods traded were different, and so on).

It secondly helped New Archaeologists to be more *optimistic* about what archaeology could achieve. One of the least attractive features of traditional archaeology was its implied pessimism: we can never reconstruct the religious or social life of past peoples, we can only build chronologies. Christopher Hawkes famously wrote of seven levels of inference in archaeology, ranging from technology and subsistence to the almost unknowable areas of society and religion. James Deetz questioned this:

> Stress on the essential interrelatedness of cultural systems allows us to reach understandings of many aspects from a relative few ... this certainty is at least a partial answer to the problems posed by the incompleteness of the archaeological record. (Deetz 1972: 112)

Third, if culture was adaptive, it was adaptive to an external environment. For the archaeologist Kent Flannery, we were not just looking at objects and trying to learn about human cultures through them; we were trying to reconstruct the whole ecological system behind both 'the Indian and the artefact' (1973b). This theoretical stress on the importance of the external environment led to interest in cultural materialism (in which the material world is seen as more important than the mental world), cultural ecology, and modelling of the subsistence economy. Here, new theoretical attitudes went hand-in-hand with the new *scientific techniques* that were developed in the postwar period: faunal analysis, palaeoethnobotany, carbon-14 dating, dendrochronology, and so on.

Fourth, there was stress on a *scientific approach*. New Archaeologists saw traditional archaeology as modelling itself on the techniques of traditional history, with cultures taking the place of historical actors and the aim being the reconstruction of individual events in time. This may not have been a fair characterization, either of what archaeologists actually did or what traditional historians actually do, but it led New Archaeologists in part to embrace Science as the way forward. According to Watson, Redman and LeBlanc in their *Explanation in Archaeology: An Explicitly Scientific Approach* (1971), one index of the progress of archaeology is the extent to which hypotheses are scientifically tested.

Fifth, there was stress on the idea of *culture process*. The idea of 'process' was central to New Archaeology and remains absolutely central to much of archaeological theory, but it is a difficult idea to grasp. It involves several related themes that have already been touched on: we want to explain rather than be merely descriptive – to ask 'why?' rather than merely 'when?'; we want to look at the underlying process rather than the 'noise' on top; we want to look at change in the long term. I will examine the concept of process in more detail in chapter 5.

Many New Archaeologists contrasted culture process to culture history. In this view, traditional history simply described a set of more or less random political events such as battles and births and deaths of monarchs without ever really explaining anything. By substituting process for history, the long-term trends or processes beneath the surface of such events became the important objects of study.

Sixth and more generally, there was a trend to attempt to become more explicit about one's biases. A good scientist, argued New Archaeologists, does not use unspoken and implicit assumptions; he or she makes clear their aims and interests. Much of the New Archaeology was concerned with making what had been unspoken formally outlined. A good example is the technique of typology, or the classification of objects according to their changing form. It has long been accepted that one could classify objects, and that this classification has something to do with chronological order: archaeologists make statements like 'pottery vessels get baggier through time', or 'this jewellery style goes out of fashion in this period' as a matter of course. But the criteria by which a typologist suggests one piece of jewellery or architectural style is 'early' and another one is 'late' are rarely clearly spelt out (in fact, they often tend to be implicitly derived from ideas and concepts developed by nineteenth-century art historians).

In his book *Analytical Archaeology*, David Clarke used many of the concepts of traditional archaeology – typology, assemblage and culture for example – but discussed openly, explicitly and at length how they should be defined. For Clarke, the need to be explicit and precise in one's terms to replace 'the murky exhalation that passes for "interpretative thinking" in archaeology' was one of the main thrusts of the New Archaeology.

A related aspect of making one's biases explicit was *problem orientation*, or the belief that one should survey and dig sites, or do research more generally, with clear research questions in mind. Again, this linked in with being scientific – the scientist tested specific hypotheses, he or she brought specific questions to the data. In chapter 3, we will see how asking specific questions or testing specific hypotheses was central to the idea of archaeology as a science.

A seventh and final concern of New Archaeology was the understanding of *variability*. What this meant was a basic understanding of our material in statistical terms. Previous archaeologists had often concentrated on the biggest and best sites, or the most beautiful artefacts. New Archaeologists pointed out that we couldn't understand, say, a major urban civilization without looking at its rural infrastructure (the importance of looking at the whole system again), and we couldn't understand the rural infrastructure without knowing just how many rural sites there were on the ground. So to really get to grips with understanding that civilization, the archaeologist might want to forgo digging yet another elite site with lots of pretty, exotic artefacts and instead concentrate on systematic survey of ordinary farmsteads. The finds might be less spectacular, but the understanding of the settlement system would be much greater.

To understand variability, New Archaeologists looked much more critically at sampling theory and techniques. To be sure of variability, at the very least we had to be sure we were looking at a representative sample of sites. Kent Flannery told a memorable parable of a Mesoamerican archaeologist who only stopped to record archaeological sites if he was forced to put his Jeep into first gear to get over the top of them. In response, New Archaeologists explored methods of sampling randomly or at least systematically.

Many of the worst aspects of the traditional attitudes the New Archaeology castigated still survive and indeed flourish today. A few years ago I remember asking a prominent, senior scholar who had written several influential books on traditional architecture how many houses of a certain date and type there were in a certain county of England. 'Oh', he said, 'an awful lot'. Yes, but how many? Tens, hundreds, thousands? 'Well, a lot, but I really couldn't put a figure to it' came the reply. And how many were there in an adjacent area? 'Oh, not many at all …'. And what, statistically, was the proportion of Type A houses to Type B houses in the two areas? 'Ah …'. And yet you are quite confident in saying that Type A houses are more frequently found than Type B houses in this area but not that, and we can indeed go on from this observation to draw conclusions about relative levels of wealth in the two areas? 'Oh yes, that's quite clear ...'. One does not have to be a paid-up New Archaeologist to see that such reasoning is an insecure foundation for any understanding of the archaeological record.

> *I'm a bit sceptical about all this. In the first place, archaeologists before New Archaeology were not the dry, traditional dullards that New Archaeologists made out. They did many of these things already. Look, for example, at Grahame Clark's work at Star Carr, where environmental analysis was used in the 1950s. Or Alfred Kidder's work in Mesoamerica and the American Southwest. And Gordon Childe can hardly be accused of many of the sins the New Archaeology tried to pin on culture historians. His books* Man Makes Himself *and* What Happened in History *are full of dynamic pictures – they try to explain things, they deal with underlying processes ...*

Your analysis contains a lot of truth. Traditional archaeology is not necessarily the narrowly descriptive, sterile pursuit that New Archaeology painted it. It can be argued, for example, that traditional accounts of migration and diffusion *do* address 'why?' questions rather than simply describe the data. There are ongoing debates within such traditions on the concept of ethnogenesis and the nature of historical change. Additionally, books like Childe's *The Prehistory of European Society* presented a model in which Indigenous cultures were seen as creative and dynamic and in which modified diffusion played a key role in explanation. Again, in North America the 'culture history' model was in part caricatured by New Archaeology.

Nevertheless New Archaeology's criticisms were pertinent. For our purposes in trying to understand where theory is today, it isn't of primary importance to ascertain whether New Archaeology was *accurate* in its criticisms; we want to understand why New Archaeology developed in the way it did. Our all-too-brief sketch serves for this purpose.

It is equally true that much of New Archaeology was not really new. Like so many theoretical movements in archaeology, it borrowed from other disciplines. The work of the cultural anthropologist Leslie White was especially influential. His 1949 book *The Science of Culture* stressed the need for a scientific approach and the idea of culture as a system. Again, another anthropologist, Julian Steward, had stressed cultural ecology and adaptation in his work. Binford's early work makes clear his profound debt to both

White and Steward. Finally, stress on systems thinking owed much to Walter Taylor's emphasis on what he called a 'conjunctive approach' in his 1948 *A Study of Archeology*. But don't forget that White, Steward and Taylor were in a minority within their own disciplines. White in particular was writing *against* the orthodox cultural anthropology of his time when his thinking was adopted by archaeologists.

The New Archaeology, particularly in its stress on anthropology, can be particularly associated with the New World. In Britain New Archaeologists such as Clarke and Renfrew had a great impact; Kristiansen, Randsborg and others applied New Archaeology to Scandinavian archaeology, and there was some take-up in other areas of Europe, for example Spain. Overall, however, the impact of the New Archaeology was not as revolutionary or as hard-hitting as in North America. I suggest there were several reasons for this.

One is the institutional set-up of archaeology. In North America, there are few Departments of Archaeology. The majority of academic archaeologists have posts within Departments of Anthropology, and form a 'minority' within those departments. Some archaeologists are hosted in Classics departments, but (with exceptions) these archaeologists are not always as engaged in theoretical discussion as their 'anthropological' counterparts. By contrast, in Britain Departments of Archaeology are largely separate institutions, or are more closely linked to Departments of History. In continental Europe, archaeologists again often find themselves within Institutes of Pre- and Proto-History rather than having primary links with anthropology, though links with ethnography and folklife of European peoples are often found.

Hence, North American graduate students intending to do their PhDs on an archaeological topic and go on to an academic career will generally be expected to read extensively and take courses in anthropological theory, where they will encounter many of the ideas of evolution and cross-cultural comparison discussed above. By contrast, a European graduate student will probably have less theoretical training in general and often very little encounter with anthropological method.

Underlying this institutional difference are different perceptions of the past. American archaeology is split between study of 'native' New World cultures and the Old World and the 'historical archaeology' of its colonies, to the extent that Native American archaeology is often spelt differently – 'archeology'. The anthropologist Franz Boas played a pivotal role in keeping archaeology within the ambit of anthropology in North America in the earlier twentieth century. Now anthropology has traditionally been concerned with 'other cultures' rather than with 'us'. As relatively few Native Americans were employed within American archaeology until very recently, New World cultures have been perceived very much as 'them'. In the past, archaeological remains such as burial mounds and cliff dwellings had been interpreted as evidence for the Lost Tribes of Israel or analogous groups, it being assumed that Native Americans were too 'primitive' to have produced such cultures; but such theories had been completely abandoned by the archaeological profession by the 1960s. This situation is changing, for example with increased recruitment and training of Native Americans as archaeologists and with a changing political and cultural context (see chapter 12), but this institutional and cultural history remains powerful in determining archaeology's position in North American cultural and intellectual life.

For British and other European archaeologists the situation is different. The prehistoric site of Stonehenge is used as a symbol of 'English Heritage', though it was built 2–3,000 years before the 'English', according to traditional history, arrived on what is now the English coast. The British, like Europeans generally, perceive prehistoric archaeology as part of 'their' past, part of their 'heritage'. Right or wrong, this perception has meant that both past and present archaeological interpretation has been thoroughly permeated with nationalist concerns, often of a politically unpleasant variety. Also, prehistory and history are seen as much more of a continuum: Neolithic Greece leads to the Minoans and Myceneans, and Iron Age studies blend into the Roman and early medieval periods. There is therefore not such a radical divide between prehistoric and historical archaeology.

So British archaeologists tend not to worry so much about the need to make explicitly theoretical generalizations in order to justify their work, and are much more comfortable with the idea of archaeology as the 'handmaiden of history'. New Archaeology had even less impact in continental Europe than it did in Britain, again for complex historical reasons. It also had less influence on the study of later periods: 'New Archaeology' had a major impact on the study of European prehistory, arguably most of all on the Palaeolithic, but less on Roman, medieval and post-medieval archaeology, to the extent that I would characterize the majority of European medieval and later archaeology as remaining culture-historical in method, tone and emphasis.

I think that there was also a practical element in the differential impact of New Archaeology in different areas of the globe. Stand in the middle of the Arizona desert and the need for sampling theory, understanding of variability, and so on is all too clear. By contrast, British and other European landscapes are cramped; they have been intensively settled for millennia, and intensively studied for centuries. Most of their basic units (administrative boundaries, patches of woodland) are irregular in shape and are themselves hundreds if not thousands of years old. As a result, many of the techniques of New Archaeology such as sampling theory make clear sense as practical strategy in the Arizona desert, but are counter-intuitive in the densely settled palimpsest that is Wessex.

Anyway, what happened to all this youthful enthusiasm? I bet it didn't get very far.

Many of the ways in which New Archaeology developed will be picked up in later chapters. One thing that inevitably happened is that New Archaeologists got older. From being pushy young research students intent on causing a fuss, they became tenured lecturers and professors with job security, positions on powerful committees and funding bodies and supervising pushy graduate students of their own. Indeed, many of the key youthful figures in New Archaeology fostered groups of students who are today's generation of senior academics.

As New Archaeology got older and developed as a body of thought it became known as *processualism*. Processualism is so called because of its stress on culture process (point five above); the term will be discussed further in chapter 5.

Case Study: The Enigma of the Megaliths

An excellent example of the way New Archaeology led to new ways of thinking about the past was that of megalithic tombs in Western Europe. These are burial monuments built with large stones, within which collective burials often took place.

Traditional studies of megaliths had concentrated on dating, typology and diffusion. Scholars such as Glyn Daniel and P. Bosch-Gimpera had defined megaliths into sub-groups based on their position around the Western Mediterranean and Atlantic seaboard (figure 2.6). They tried to date these groups in the absence of scientific dating techniques such as carbon-14; the only way of doing this was to look for similarities in the form of the monuments and assume that similarities had been produced through contact. Ultimately, then, megaliths could be dated by reference to their presumed ancestors in the Mediterranean such as the Maltese temples. These could then be cross-dated in turn with reference to the literate civilizations of the Eastern Mediterranean. There was a clear link here between theory (the importance of typology and the dominant idea of diffusion) and archaeological practice (the need to set up a working chronology, without which we couldn't really say anything at all).

Colin Renfrew questioned this work. He used the tree-ring calibration of radiocarbon dates to show that the megaliths on the Atlantic seaboard were

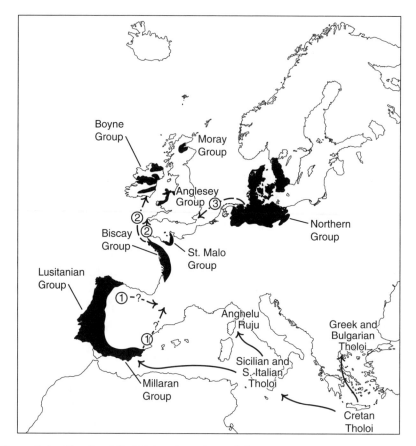

Figure 2.6   Glyn Daniel's (1941) view of megalith origins

in fact much older than their supposed 'origins' in the Mediterranean. Some scholars responded by simply reversing the arrows so that the 'influence' went in the opposite direction, but Renfrew suggested that instead of trying to prove or disprove diffusionary links, we should instead ask why the monuments were built in the first place. In short, *we should look less at chronology and diffusion and more at the underlying process involved.* Or to put it another way, we should not be content with dating and describing; we should try to explain the phenomenon of the megaliths.

Renfrew suggested that megaliths might be territorial markers. He pointed out that whereas early agricultural communities moving from east to west across Europe had plenty of land, being able to simply expand westwards into new territory when things got cramped, when such peoples reached the Atlantic coast there was nowhere left to go. Additionally, these areas also

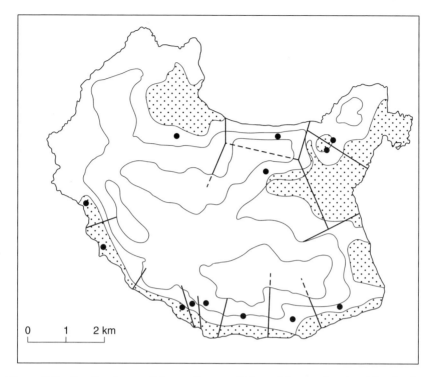

Figure 2.7 Renfrew's megaliths on Rousay, Orkney Islands, showing 'distribution of chambered tombs in relation to modern arable land (stippled), with hypothetical territorial boundaries' (Renfrew 1973a)

had a high population level in the preceding Mesolithic period, populations who would also be pressing for territory. In such a situation he suggested that different communities would be competing for land. The megalithic tombs, then, would mark out the land of particular groups, by reference to the ancestors buried within them.

So Renfrew's arguments:

1 explained rather than merely described the existence and distribution of megaliths;
2 used ethnographic analogies from societies assumed to be at a similar level of social development to strengthen his argument – monumental structures in Polynesia, linked to particular descent groups in competition over land;
3 stressed environmental factors and hence adaptation to the environment – the shortage of land;

4   saw megaliths not as one diagnostic trait to define cultures, but as one functional element of a total cultural system;

5   'tested' his model – by drawing hypothetical divisions between megaliths on the Scottish island of Orkney, Renfrew claimed to demonstrate that the megaliths were spaced at the centre of possible territories, each territory being of approximately equal size (figure 2.7).

Conclusion

If the New Archaeology was a revolution, it suffered the same fundamental problems of any revolution. New Archaeology had a double slogan: science and anthropology. But like many revolutionary slogans, discord and disagreement broke out when archaeologists tried to work out in practice what those slogans really meant. In many ways, the ongoing story of archaeological theory to the present day can be seen as the attempt to deepen our understanding of these slogans, and to 'roll out' the concerns of New Archaeology beyond their original applications.

The next three chapters will deal with these questions and bring the reader into the present. Chapter 3 will ask: What do we really mean by the term 'science'? Chapter 4 will ask: What do we really mean by the word 'testing' – how do we evaluate archaeological arguments? Chapter 5 will ask: How do societies work, what do we really mean by 'anthropology'?

We shall see in the process that debates within archaeological theory mirror debates in the human sciences such as history, sociology, cultural anthropology, politics and economics very closely. Questions of science, testing and how societies really work are central to the human sciences as a whole.

3

Archaeology as a Science

There are both positive and negative views of science. In the positive view, science is wonderful. It has given us modern medicine, transport, a level of material affluence few people would wish to give up. We know the way the world is because scientists tell us so. Scientists are so powerful, hold such a grip over our beliefs and sentiments, that we believe them even when our strongest intuitions tell us otherwise, when boarding an aeroplane for example. But in the negative view science can be disturbing and alarming. It can be dangerous, it can offend human sensibilities. Science has moral limits: look what happened to Doctor Frankenstein (figure 3.1).

Both positive and negative views of science are culturally loaded. To clarify, *Science is viewed in a certain way within Western culture*. The sociologist Auguste Comte suggested that science is a central institution of authority in the modern world, just as the Catholic Church acted as an authority for the people of medieval Europe.

Modern Western society is partly based on the idea of Science with a capital S. The term 'scientific' is used as a form of approbation, and that of 'unscientific' as one of abuse. But Westerners are often less sure what they actually mean by the term 'Science', which I have dignified here with a capital S to distinguish the image from the reality. What is Science, are there different forms of Science, and to which forms (if any) can or should archaeology strive to approximate?

This was one of the problems that faced the New Archaeology as it matured, and it is a problem which archaeology still faces today. As we have seen, 'we must be more scientific' was a good slogan, and concentrated (and continues to concentrate) appropriate criticism on limitations in the approaches and methods of culture historians. But New Archaeology found that deciding what it actually meant by its slogan was more difficult.

One of the ways in which archaeology has become more 'scientific' in the last 50 years is in its techniques. The period after the Second World War saw

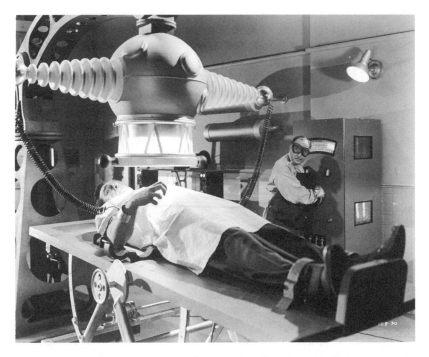

Figure 3.1 Lon Chaney, Jr (left) and Lionel Atwill in *Man Made Monster* (1941, Universal): still from Everson, W. K. 1974 *Classics of the Horror Film* (Secaucus, NJ, The Citadel Press), 152–3

an explosion in the number and range of 'science-based' techniques used in archaeology. These included the use of computers, the study of environmental remains, pollen diagrams, dating techniques such as carbon-14 and dendrochronology, soil geomorphology, paleopathology, and so on. Though I did not discuss these at any length in the last chapter, for many people, such as David Clarke, this development and growth in use of scientific techniques was a central part of the New Archaeology. In the last decade, advances in DNA research, chemical analysis of human and animal bones, advanced geophysical techniques, geographical information systems, virtual reality, and many other developments have continued to unfold.

This development of scientific techniques, and their place as an ever more important part of the discipline, has led to a problem of technical specialization. An archaeologist in 1950 had to have an understanding of some statistics, and the principles of geology. Sixty years later, she or he does not necessarily have to know the practical details of a technique, but does have to know how to use a pollen diagram, how to manipulate statistical packages on computers, how to interpret and understand the significance of a radiocarbon determination or a tree-ring date, and at the very least how to understand and use the findings of a range of other very complex and specialized techniques. As a result, it can be argued that archaeology is a much more fragmented discipline, and less of a unified and homogenous community, than it was 50 years ago.

In this sense the general atmosphere of the practice of archaeology has become more 'scientific'. Where archaeologists used to work in dusty back-rooms full of old junk, their offices are often now part of suites of laboratories (often taken over second-hand from other, more 'respectable' physicists, biologists or chemists who have moved into newer, smarter accommodation). In many universities, particularly in North America, smart white labcoats have succeeded frayed tweed jackets with elbow-patches as the uniform of the academic archaeologist. Perhaps more importantly, key career targets for many academics are now articles in peer-reviewed scientific journals as much as the more traditional synthetic monograph or site report.

The growth of 'science' has led to changes in the pattern of funding of academic archaeology. In the USA, archaeology is funded under the aegis of the National Science Foundation. In Britain and in much of the rest of Europe, funding is often predominantly 'humanistic' (for example, through the British Arts and Humanities Research Council) or tied to 'culture' or 'heritage', though the situation varies widely in different national contexts and is subject to rapid change.

In its essentials, however, *the use of scientific techniques does not in itself imply the use of 'science' as a distinctive approach to finding out about the past*. David Clarke wrote that the use of scientific techniques 'no more make archaeology into a science than a wooden leg turns a man into a tree' (Clarke, 1978: 465). For the traditional archaeologist Jacquetta Hawkes, archaeology remains essentially a humanistic, not a scientific, pursuit: 'however scientific the methods employed, the final aims are historical' (Hawkes, 1968: 257).

To clarify, archaeologists use an increasing battery of techniques to assist in dating, the environment, geophysical techniques, and so on. These techniques have given us more and more data of potential use in the study of the past. But we are still left with the gulf between present and past discussed in chapter 2 and presented in figure 2.1. 'Science-based' techniques accumulate even more data in the present. If that gulf between present and past remains unbridgeable, then the statements archaeologists make about the past remain 'unscientific' however clean their white coats are or how much money they spend on the many machines that go ping! in laboratories. If, on the other hand, the gulf can be bridged securely, using the methods of the natural sciences, then archaeology really can be called scientific, regardless of whether or not archaeologists wear white coats and use lots of expensive equipment.

Definitions of Science

New Archaeology suggested the use of 'science' as the solution to the *problem of inference*, discussed in the last chapter. If archaeologists have no reliable means of assessing how valid their arguments really were, it is only natural to look at how natural scientists do it. The natural sciences of physics, chemistry, biology, after all, appear in the view of many to have demonstrable and indeed spectacular success in terms of their ability to accurately describe and explain the world when compared for example to other forms of thought such as magic or mysticism.

Such an argument is reinforced by the disciplinary success of science in the 'real world'. Whatever one's views of science as a theory, there is no disputing its long-term success as a discipline. Scientists are often well funded compared to humanistic scholars, and often appear to have the ear of government and an influential role in setting public policy.

In one sense there is no argument about whether archaeologists should be scientific. If science is about the rational accumulation of knowledge, assessed in rigorous, systematic ways, then all archaeologists would consider themselves to be scientists. (At least, archaeologists would all claim to be scientists, though our opponents always seem to be lacking in rigour, system or method.) Science in this broad sense is often referred to by the German term *Wissenschaft*. Even the most fervent opponent of 'archaeology-as-science' would probably consider themselves scientists in this sense.

Positivism

There are, however, more narrow definitions of what science is (figure 3.2). One of these definitions is called *positivism*, which is another word with several meanings. Theorists confusingly use the word 'positivism' in different senses in different contexts. Here, I shall isolate two.

1 A set of beliefs about how we should conduct scientific enquiry

These beliefs include:

(a) The idea that scientists should *separate theory from method*, however method is defined. If we have two or more competing theories to explain a phenomenon, then we have to have some kind of independent and neutral method to judge which theory is the better. It is no good trying to conduct such an independent test if our method is not independent

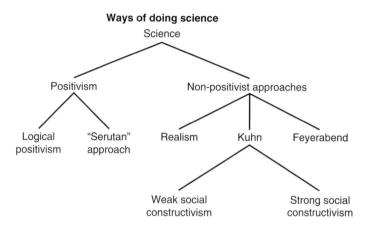

Ways of doing science

Figure 3.2   A selective diagram showing some schools within the philosophy of science

and neutral, but is predicated on one of the theories being true. This is why many archaeologists would vehemently oppose the very broad definition of theory I adopted in chapter 1 as 'the order you put facts in', as it does have the implication of making a clear and strict separation of this kind difficult if not impossible.

(b)   The separation of the *context of the discovery of an idea from the context of its evaluation*. It doesn't matter whether the law of gravity came to us sitting under an apple tree or in a book-lined office or in a drug-crazed hallucination; what is important is that the existence of such a law is evaluated scientifically separately from this context. Again, we might get some perfectly good ideas about processes in the prehistoric past from comparative ethnography or from a novel or a dream; what is important, in this view, is that we then test the ideas against the archaeological record to see whether they are valid or not.

Archaeologists will often claim, therefore, that they are using a particular idea or model only for *heuristic* or learning purposes; that is, they find the model of value in throwing up new hypotheses or possible interpretations. They might well insist that such hypotheses or interpretations need then to be formally tested or evaluated before they can be considered to be of lasting value.

(c)   *A generalizing explanation is the only valid form*. Here, generality is closely linked to the importance of predictability and testability. Results have to be predictable and repeated for scientific validity. Scientists can test the law of gravity by observing apples dropping from trees again and again and again. The law of gravity is framed as a general proposition that has predictable consequences, all other things being equal.

  If an explanation is not generalizing, if it cannot suggest a consistent pattern of results, it will not be predictable and therefore will not be amenable to testing again and again.

(d) *Untestable statements are outside the domain of science.* In less extreme forms of positivism, this does not mean that untestable statements are unimportant. For example, moral and metaphysical questions may be untestable but central to our lives. Whether God exists or whether slavery or child labour are morally wrong are clearly important issues for individuals to discuss and act upon as human beings and communities; but they are not scientifically testable one way or the other. Science therefore, in this view, has nothing to say about them.

(e) It follows from (d) that *scientific thought should be independent of value judgements* and political action. The threat to use nuclear weapons or investment in countries with repressive regimes may or may not be morally or politically wrong; we all, scientists or non-scientists, make value judgements concerning these matters as human beings living in the world today. But the scientist cannot bring these judgements into the methods of his or her work. She or he might comment on them in other spheres, even campaign against nuclear weapons or repressive regimes, but must draw a clear line between (morally neutral) scientific knowledge and moral judgement and action.

Positivism in this sense has tended to be linked with a specific method of testing propositions, called the *Hypothetico-deductive-nomological* model, or HDN for short. The HDN model suggests that one proceeds as a scientist by taking a specific hypothesis and testing it. The deductions one makes from the result of the test should then be used to produce generalizing explanations ('nomothetic' or 'nomological' means generalizing). The need to test specific hypotheses, rather than just dig sites because we might find something interesting or because they are particularly big or beautiful, was an issue discussed in the last chapter.

  But positivism also, confusingly, has a second set of meanings attached to it.

2 The belief that the social sciences, including archaeology, should try to follow the historical path of development of the natural sciences

This argument was advanced for sociology by the nineteenth century French social philosopher Auguste Comte, who was one of the key figures in the development of the human sciences in general. Comte looked to the example of biology. Before the eighteenth century, biology had, in Comte's view, been a speculative and unsystematic pursuit at a time when the scientific techniques and methods of physics and chemistry were already established. By model-ling its disciplinary rules on the 'hard sciences' of physics and chemistry, however, biology had freed itself from the shackles of prescientific beliefs and become a rigorous science. Comte suggested that social sciences like sociology could follow a similar route, moving from their present unscientific state to that of a natural science.

New and processual archaeology can clearly be identified with much of the agenda outlined above. New Archaeology tried to generalize; it tried to adopt a HDN model of testing; its whole project was that of Comte's, that of leading archaeology along an analogous path to that of the natural sci-ences to a mature, rigorous, self-critical discipline. For David Clarke (1973), this was part of archaeology's 'loss of innocence'.

Examples

For New Archaeology, then, and for much of 'processual archaeology' today, we should adopt a broadly positivist definition of what we do. We should be trying to test or evaluate hypotheses about the past, and to draw generalizations from those hypotheses.

Such a model might proceed as follows:

1   *Hypothesis*: early states involve differential access to resources, in other words that élites have greater access to basic goods (a hypothesis sug-gested maybe by political anthropologists).
2   *Test*: dig a cemetery from an early state society and chemically analyse the human bones.
3   *Deduction*: the élite ate more meat, so we deduce that they did indeed have greater access to nutrition.
4   *Generalization*: early states do have such differential access, subject to further testing, other examples from other cultures at the same phase of social development, etc.

Another example might be hunter-gatherers and social complexity:

1   *Hypothesis*: that hunter-gatherer groups adapt to marginal environments in part through greater economic specialization and social complexity (suggested perhaps by study of modern ethnographies).
2   *Test*: take a marginal environment such as Upper Palaeolithic Europe in the last Ice Age, and look for different types of site suggesting task differentiation, the presence or absence of trade goods suggesting social alliances, etc.

3 *Deduction*: that social alliance and logistical hunting strategies are responses to harsher climates.
4 *Generalization*: there is a positive correlation between increasingly marginal environments and greater social complexity.

Note that in both these examples there is a *tendency to generalize*. General statements tend to emerge from the discussion: for example, that increasing complexity of trading networks tends to be linked to élites and thus to development of social ranking, whether this is in late prehistoric Europe, Mesoamerica or Polynesia. Look at the titles of some typical edited volumes in the processual mould, in which different articles often based on data sets from around the world and different time periods focus on certain processes which are held to be general and cross-cultural: *Ranking, Resource and Exchange ... Specialisation, Exchange and Complex Societies ... Heterarchy and the Analysis of Complex Societies ...*

Such generalizations are what is meant by a 'softer' approach to covering laws than that taken in other areas of the natural sciences. In its first phases, some New Archaeologists searched for 'laws' of human behaviour, on the model of the hard sciences. It has proven to be very difficult to come up with 'laws' for past human behaviour akin to the law of gravity (we will discuss the attempt to create a unified field with biology, itself a 'softer' science than chemistry or physics, through the application of Darwinian ideas in chapter 10). This does not mean, however, that the production of generalizations about past human behaviour is necessarily an invalid or an unimportant goal – indeed, for the reasons discussed above, for a discipline that sees itself as a science in which propositions are testable, generalization or general theory has to be a central component of archaeology.

Objections to 'Science'

We noted that if part of the appeal of 'Science' comes from its cultural value in modern society, so opposition to 'Science' is similarly culturally loaded. For some, archaeology can never be scientific; rather, it is a humanistic discipline. Rather than being about white labcoats and generalizations, it is about what it means to be a civilized human being. Archaeology in this view is a noble, aesthetic, romantic pursuit into the essence of humanity and civilization, untainted by the vulgarities of labcoats and test-tubes. In some conceptions of this view, human beings are special because they are unique and unpredictable: they simply can not be generalized about or subsumed in statistics. Further, many of the things that are most 'distinctively human' and therefore most worthy of humanistic study (great art and literature, for example) are precisely those that in this view are least amenable to scientific enquiry.

Such a view is easy to ridicule, and it certainly does not stand up to more than a few seconds of critical thought (if humans really were unique and unpredictable, opinion polls would produce completely random results and any attempt at social or economic policy by government agencies would start and end in chaos), but is a very popular and emotionally powerful one. Human beings often like to think that they are unique, are beyond statistics; but wishing something does not make it true.

Such a view, or a more sophisticated version of it, is nevertheless foundational to many elements of modern archaeology. For example, Classical archaeology was in its historical origins an outgrowth of the study of the 'Classics'. The texts, history and monuments of Greece and Rome were studied because they were held to constitute the foundations of civilized and humane behaviour, for example in the origins of the idea of democracy in fifth century BC Athens. Further, for men of the upper classes in the Renaissance, Classical texts provided role models – how great men should act, what it meant to be civilized. Very few Classical archaeologists would subscribe to such an unmodified view of the rationale of their discipline today, but elements of such a view are nevertheless still very powerful, in that they are inscribed into the institutional set-up and identity of Classics and of Classical archaeology, for instance in the separation between centres of 'pre- and proto-history' and 'Classical archaeology' in many institutions in continental Europe.

A series of more intellectually powerful objections to the positivist conception of archaeology-as-science are commonly brought up. I shall deal with them in turn.

1   Science is based on testing and observation of results. The past, however, is dead and gone. We will never be able to directly observe it. *Can we ever test propositions about the past* as we can (it is argued) in science? Possibly not; this is a question I shall address below and more particularly in the next chapter. It is worth noting that archaeology in this respect shares some of the interpretative problems with other sciences that interpret phenomena observed now in terms of processes and events that occurred in the very distant past. Geology interprets data observed today (layers, sediments) in terms of processes that happened millions of years ago; astronomy observes phenomena many light-years away. In both cases, it is possible to argue that 'direct' observation of phenomena is problematic.

2   Atoms, chemicals and even biological organisms can be seen as objects, insensate things that behave in predictable ways. Human behaviour, however, can be seen as *purposive* or *intentional*. In other words, human actions can only be fully explained by reference to the ideas and intentions that humans have. Ideas and intentions do not have any physical

existence (except, arguably, as electronic traces in the brain); they only exist as thoughts, between our ears. They can not be directly observed or 'measured' by the archaeologist. Interpretation in archaeology is therefore, in this view, always *hermeneutic* (about ideas, meanings and symbols) in nature rather than scientific. This argument, or variants thereof, is one of the central planks of interpretive archaeology.

Kuhn and Feyerabend

The final and perhaps most serious objection to positivism is that it is not a theory but a myth. In other words, positivism is an ideal model of scientific philosophy, but is a bit of a fraud in practice: it gives a false idea of what scientists actually do. To ask archaeology to follow the rules of positivist science is therefore asking them to follow a chimera.

There is much confusion here over whether positivism describes *what scientists actually do*, or whether it is merely an *ideal statement of what they should do*. Some philosophers claim that it is merely an ideal statement. If positivism is only an ideal account, what do scientists actually get up to in their laboratories?. Many have argued that what counts as an 'observation' and 'fact' is decided at least in part by social rules, not by purely objective enquiry however defined. Instead, scientific debates are decided through processes that are thoroughly enmeshed in social relations, not disengaged from society.

Two philosophers of science are often cited in non-positivist accounts of science. The first is Thomas Kuhn. Kuhn argued that the history of science is not just a simple progressively upward success story of hypothesis testing leading to expanded knowledge. Rather, it is one of successive *paradigms*. A paradigm is much deeper than a single theory or proposition: it is a set of beliefs about the way the world works that underlies the whole everyday process of science very deeply, so deeply that it is rarely overtly put into words. During a period of 'normal science' in Kuhn's terms, one paradigm enjoys such undisputed sway over science that its assumptions are rarely even stated explicitly, let alone questioned or debated. Everyone just gets on with scientific labour within the assumptions of the paradigm.

Kuhn suggested that a paradigm will break down eventually. When it does, it is eventually replaced by a new paradigm in a 'paradigm shift'. Such a period of paradigm shift is intense, emotional, revolutionary, rather than cool and detached; a spirit of revolutionary fervour militates against 'rational' argument.

The story of science, then, is one of successive paradigms succeeding one another via revolutionary upheavals rather than of steady accumulation of better and better knowledge of the world around us. Colin Renfrew and others argued in the 1960s and 1970s that the New Archaeology represented a 'paradigm shift' and that we should therefore expect processual archaeology to settle down to a new period of 'normal science' (something that, as we shall see, has arguably not happened). There was an irony here, in that Renfrew was citing with approval a philosopher of science whose work actually tended to undermine many of the positivist assumptions of New Archaeology.

Kuhn himself repudiated the idea that science didn't progress; his view was that paradigms broke down under the steadily increasing weight of contradictory evidence, and that each paradigm was a successively better and more accurate way of looking at the world. Renfrew and others agree with him in this respect. Other scholars, however, took Kuhn's ideas and extended them in ways that Kuhn himself opposed. They drew different and more wide-ranging morals from his work: in particular, that:

1   What constituted valid 'facts' or 'observations' depended on the prevailing paradigm. In other words, what was relevant evidence, and what was ruled out of court, depended at least in part on one's initial paradigmatic assumptions. In this view, then, *facts are therefore always theory-dependent.*
2   Social and political forces, not just disinterested scientific enquiry, played a key part in prompting and shaping paradigm shifts.

Kuhn's main influence on the philosophy of science, therefore, has been in a move away from positivist assumptions about the nature of scientific progress, a questioning of the use of a single positivist method in scientific enquiry, and a scepticism towards the narrative of science as an unqualified success story.

The second key figure is Paul Feyerabend, whose description of the way science actually works is always popular since it consists of two words: *Anything Goes.* Feyerabend questioned whether science had a single method at all. He suggested that if we looked historically at the development of science, change in scientific beliefs had always been marked by a diversity of methods.

Feyerabend used the example of the astronomer Galileo, who, he argued, moved science forward by breaking all the rules, using political rhetoric and appeals to emotion and working within the social and political context of seventeenth-century Italy: 'Galileo prevails because of his style and his clever techniques of persuasion, because he writes in Italian rather than in Latin, and because he appeals to people who are temperamentally opposed to the old ideas and the standards of learning connected with them' (Feyerabend 1988: 13).

For Feyerabend, the lesson of the history of scientific ideas was that to achieve better results, scientists should reject the use of a single method. Rather, we should encourage an unlimited diversity of methods and groups within sciences, and to allow and even encourage 'unscientific' strategies such as appeals to emotion. Feyerabend stressed the social and political forces that, in his view, actively shape scientific enquiry. He pointed out that the relative merits of scientific ideas are not tested out on a level playing field. He stressed what he saw as the enormously powerful nature of scientific institutions and argued that they hid their partiality behind their 'objective' façade. Positivism in the form of a single method, in Feyerabend's view, masks 'institutional intimidation' by pretending to be neutral, hinders the development of science, and encourages scientism (the belief that Science is not simply different, but superior) and the 'cult of the expert'.

Social Constructivism

It is important to stress that Kuhn and Feyerabend saw their work as describing what scientists actually do, rather than as a prescription of what they should do. Their work encouraged the development of sociological studies of science – that is, ethnographic or historical examinations of what actually happens in the scientific process. In the 1990s, these studies coalesced into a school of thought calling itself *social constructivism* or *constructionism*: the belief that scientific knowledge is not purely objective, but is at least partly or entirely socially constructed. ('Weak social constructivism' holds that it is partly socially constructed; 'strong social constructivism' that it is entirely so.)

Examples from the natural sciences include:

1 *Quarks*. Andrew Pickering (1984) discussed the 'discovery' of this subatomic particle. He stressed that rather than quarks 'really existing' and waiting to be discovered, a full account of the scientific activity leading to the definition of quarks must look at such things as the decisions of funding bodies, personal and institutional relationships, university and state politics, and so on. Quarks in this view were not 'discovered'; rather, they were actively 'constructed' by the scientists involved. And this construction was a social one; it depended on the interaction of scientists, politicians, funding agencies, universities and the wider public.
2 *Races*. Scientific definitions of different races in physical anthropology are, it can be argued, impositions on a continuum of physical types across the globe. Where, then, do classifications by physical anthropologists into different races come from? It can be argued that scientific classifications of 'types' are not neutral devices for objective classification, but are in fact derived from the end points of trade routes from Europe to and from the 'colonies' in the nineteenth century, that is at precisely that time when the basic classifications of physical anthropology were being formed: Northern Europeans, West Africans, Hong Kong Chinese, American 'Indians'...

If social constructivism is a correct analysis of science, then the question 'should archaeology be a science or a humanity?' is rendered meaningless. Constructivism questions the claim of science to be a distinctive form of knowledge in the first place. It therefore denies any basic, *a priori* differences between science and non-science. It suggests that we should look at what human beings do in laboratories in the same way as we look at what they do in other walks of life.

Social constructivism unleashed what was often a very angry and bitter debate between different groups of scientists and others, often referred to retrospectively as the 'science wars'. 'Strong' social constructivists were seen by their opponents as threatening the very foundations of rationality and academic enquiry itself. Since the 1990s, the intensity and ferocity of this debate has subsided on both sides, though the issues at stake remain fundamental and we will return to them in future chapters.

> *All this is fine, but I find it difficult to understand how this might apply to archaeology. Which version of science do archaeologists currently prefer? Do they come down on one side or the other of the debate?*

There is no one answer to your question; you will have to read the literature, and then make up your own mind.

Different archaeologists advocate different forms of scientific philosophy. Shanks and Tilley argued in the late 1980s that positivism's stress on separating method from theory is fraudulent, because theory and method can never be separated. Like Feyerabend, they see positivism as a covert, underhand way of controlling what we can and cannot say and do in archaeology. Positivism for them is an archaeology of NO. They wrote in a spirit of sarcasm:

> It doesn't matter what you say as long as you say it in the right way; as long as you conform to the rules of positivist/empiricist discourse, rational method; as long as what you say is reasonable, not fantasy or extreme, is open to 'testing' against the data, is not overtly political, is not subjective. And if you transgress these laws of discourse, the epistemology … police are waiting. (Shanks and Tilley 1992: 23)

For Shanks and Tilley, the way we write about the past is largely about political rules. They want to unmask the political nature of these rules.

Opponents replied: if we abandon positivist criteria, what alternatives are there? If we accept such views, aren't beliefs in magic or in mystical forces just as 'scientific' as rational debate?

As a result of these debates spilling over into archaeology in the 1980s and 1990s, there has been a growing interest in philosophies or conceptions of scientific method that acknowledge that all archaeological data are socially constructed in some sense, but which try to move beyond a simple either/or position. The 'science wars' seemed to many to be based on a false choice, an unnecessary opposition or polarity – either Science had to be absolutely objective and untainted by cultural context, or it had to be nothing more than one more discourse among many, including magical and superstitious beliefs. Both of these views or positions are, in the view of many, including myself, unsatisfactory. For archaeologists this translates into the question: if we have to reject a crude or naïve positivism, can we nevertheless salvage something from the wreckage – keep hold of some idea of rigour and method?

For example, Alison Wylie has combined an insistence that science is inevitably value-laden in different ways, with an exploration of ways in which in practice, archaeologists do move back and forth in an empirically informed manner between data and interpretation. More broadly, there has I think been a subtle shift in the language and tone of different strands of processual and postprocessual archaeology. Fewer processualists talk of 'testing' their arguments, but they do insist on proper and rigorous 'evaluation'. Conversely, interpretive and 'postprocessual' archaeologists acknowledge and affirm that arguments do need to be evaluated with reference to the data, and that the data at the very least form a network of resistance.

At the same time, this theoretical position has been complemented and strengthened by practical developments. There has been a growing body of work that has used 'scientific' techniques however defined to look at interpretive questions. For example, archaeologists have used human skeletal material to explore issues of gender, the body and identity. Materials science has been deployed to examine the socially constrained choices that craftspeople made in the production of pottery and other artefacts. Techniques of archaeological computing such as geographical information systems have been used to explore the experience of place. These are all themes we will examine in later chapters.

But if you find the same range of views within archaeology, it is also worth pointing out that the debate over scientific method in archaeology is a re-run of a similar debate in virtually every other social science. Behavioural psychologists claim that thoughts are beyond the domain of science, so we should concentrate on people's behaviour. In sociology, Auguste Comte and Emile Durkheim laid out sociological method in a positivistic framework; their aim was to construct a science of society in which predictions and generalizations could be made about social phenomena in the same way as natural phenomena. The sociologist Anthony Giddens and others have, in opposition to Durkheim and Comte, argued for the impossibility of a neutral, value-free science of society. Similar debates occur within all those disciplines classified as social sciences: history, linguistics, economics, politics. Many feminists claim that Science is not merely political, but that it is moreover a male construct: the rules of 'rational method' mask male bias behind a cloak of objectivity.

Archaeologists can comfort themselves that their epistemological worries are at least shared across the domain of the social sciences. Whether this makes them easier to resolve is open to doubt.

4

Middle-range Theory, Ethnoarchaeology and Material Culture Studies

In this chapter, we return to figure 2.1 and the gap between present and past, 'data' and 'interpretation', but we take a rather different route from chapter 3 in asking how archaeologists bridge this gap. We have all this stuff, this archaeological material – pots, stones, bones. It exists here in the present; how do we get it to tell us about the past?

If any statement about the past is unavoidably made in the present, it is also unavoidably *an analogy*. An analogy is the use of information derived from one context, in this case usually the present, to explain data found in another context, in this case the past.

To clarify: all archaeologists of whatever theoretical stripe make a link between present and past by using analogies. We always make an assumption that things in the past were like – analogous to – the present. Analogy underpins even the most mundane interpretation. Consider, for example, the way archaeologists assign function to objects: 'this was a storage vessel'. We argue that it was a storage vessel in the past because its form (large, sturdy, undecorated) would make it seem 'natural' to us to use it in this way in the present. Further, we strengthen our argument through other analogies. The object was found with others of the same type in the room of an ancient palace adjacent to a food preparation area, which we label a 'kitchen' – another analogy with the present. Chemical analysis reveals the object contained food remains – again, by analogy with the present, we infer that the vessel was used to store food.

The more links we can make, the more we argue or assume that the two situations are analogous. This mode of analogical thinking is perhaps pretty obvious once it is spelt out in this manner, but nevertheless absolutely central to the way we write about the past. And like other such 'obvious' points, the issue of analogy needs further critical examination.

Binford and Middle-range Theory

Lewis Binford addressed this issue with great force in the 1970s. While the general arguments covered in the last chapter were raging over the grand theoretical issues of epistemology and positivism, Binford suggested that such debates were in many ways secondary to a more central issue. Binford insisted that archaeology's claim to be a science rested or fell on this issue of analogy. His argument, in brief, ran like this:

Archaeological data – stones, bones, potsherds – form a *static record* in the present. We carefully record stones, bones, potsherds and their position and arrangement in the ground in the here and now. But we are not interested in the here and now, we are interested in the past: our task is to ask questions of this material in the present, questions about the past. Specifically we are interested in the *dynamics* of past societies, that is the way past cultural systems functioned, developed, were transformed.

Further, since science is a discipline which seeks to generalize for the reasons discussed in the last chapter, we want to develop generalizing theories about past dynamics (figure 4.1, which is a different version of figure 2.1).

All archaeologists offer possible links between statics and dynamics, every time they put forward an interpretation of archaeological evidence. In practice, Binford argued, archaeologists do this by making assumptions about the *middle range*, that is, the 'space' between statics and dynamics. For example, we excavate a cemetery consisting of a few graves with lots of grave-goods and many graves with very little (static data); from this we infer a society characterized by wealth or social inequality (past dynamics). We do so by assuming a middle-range link between the number and/or value of grave goods and the social/economic status of the person buried. A second example: we excavate a pueblo in the American Southwest and discover that it increases in size and number of rooms through time. We infer population increase from this. Again, we make a middle-range assumption, namely that settlement size, measured in terms of the number of rooms in a settlement, correlates positively with population size.

Right or wrong (and however obvious they may look at first sight, the assumptions in both of the examples above can be debated), these statements can be called *middle-range* assumptions. Such middle-range assumptions guide archaeologists from observation of the static archaeological record (burials in excavated cemeteries, data on settlements derived from surveys) to general statements and theories about the past (social structure and ranking, population estimates, possible links between these variables, generalizing propositions about links between rank, population size, and social complexity: figure 4.1).

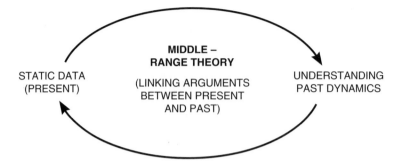

Figure 4.1   Present statics, past dynamics and middle-range theory

Such propositions are called middle-range by Binford because they link, in his words, statics to dynamics, and particular observations of the archaeological record to general theories about the past. In much of 'practical' archaeology, Binford argues, many propositions are often not theorized and remain implicit, as they have an apparently common-sensical, banal or trivial nature: 'the larger the settlement, the more people are likely to have lived there'.

Now many middle-range propositions may be banal or trivial, but *any good scientist should make his or her disciplinary assumptions formal and explicit* however obvious or common-sensical they might be. Many of the interpretive problems that arise within archaeological traditions that do not consider themselves to be 'theoretical' can be traced to a lack of clarity about middle-range assumptions, which are treated as 'common sense'. For example, villages in medieval Europe may be referred to as 'planned' because they are identified as of regular design and are further seen as evidence of 'lordship'. The implicit assumption that regularity (a static pattern, observable in the present) implies planning (a dynamic process in the past) and further implies 'lordship' (a social institution) needs to be critically examined. Similar comments might be made about the assignation of high or low status to buildings on the basis of their size and decoration, or something so mundane as the designation of features as 'roads' or 'trackways' on the basis of their size and appearance.

If such assumptions remain implicit, untested, taken-for-granted, then we can never do more than tell untestable stories about the past, because the criteria for deciding that *this* argument is good and *that* argument is bad are never made clear, let alone objective and rigorous. One scholar can assert (as 'atheoretical' archaeologists frequently do) that this argument is 'plausible' and that other argument 'wild', 'improbable' or a 'flight of fancy' by reference to an implicit common sense which is never evaluated. Binford therefore suggested that we should consciously develop an explicit 'middle-range theory' (MRT) to link present statics with past dynamics. (It is important to note in passing that this archaeological definition of the middle-range is subtly different from that used by sociologists such as Robert Merton, who developed the term 'theories of the middle range' to delineate theories that fell in the range between empirical generalizations and 'grand theory'.)

Now the only place that we can see a definite, certain, measurable link between a set of activity patterns or dynamics and what they look like archaeologically is in the present. We can never see a Neolithic farmer making a flint arrowhead with the debris flying in all directions, or a Palaeolithic hunter skinning and butchering an animal, leaving bones to kick around in the dust, be gnawed by dogs and finally be buried and enter the archaeological record. But what we can do is look at comparable activities – manufacturing of stone tools, hunting and butchering activities, the gathering, winnowing and sowing of seeds – in the present.

In the present, archaeologists can make a detailed and accurate record of how particular activities or systems of activities give rise to particular patterns of archaeological debris. We can look at how modern peasant societies prepare and process their grain and other foodstuffs, or how modern hunter-gatherers butcher their kills. We can observe and measure precisely what sort and how much debris then enters the archaeological record as a result of these activities, and what then happens to that debris as a result of attrition and decay. Archaeologists must therefore look at the *ethnographic present* for the source of an explicit middle-range theory. Binford wrote: 'My aim was to study the relation between statics and dynamics in a modern setting. If understood in great detail, it would give us a kind of Rosetta Stone: a way of "translating" the static, material stone tools found on an archaeological site into the vibrant life of a group of people who in fact left them there' (Binford 1983a: 24). In other words, just as the Rosetta Stone had the same inscription in three different ancient languages enabling the modern linguist to use the stone to translate from one language to another, so we should be trying to find things that enable us to translate from the observed archaeological record to the past.

Binford called such ethnographic studies *actualistic*; that is, observation and recording by archaeologists of ethnographic situations taking place in the actual, the here and now. He compared the archaeological record to that of a footprint in the forest. One might, seeing a particular size and shape of footprint, conjecture that it belonged to a large, heavy animal without having any clear idea of the animal concerned. Later, one observes a bear making that precise shape and form of a footprint; from that observation in the present, one can say with greater certainty that the previous footprint had been made by such an animal in the past.

One form of actualistic study that remains an enduring element of archaeological practice is *experimental archaeology*. For example, experimental studies have eludicated the manufacture and use of flaked and polished stone tools. The debris produced at each stage of experimental manufacture could be compared with the debris in the archaeological record; microscopic traces of wear on prehistoric tools could be compared with those on modern tools that had been used experimentally for butchering, scraping hides and so on. Actualistic study can also take the form of *ethnoarchaeology*, or the study of material culture in the present by archaeologists.

Archaeologists have always been interested in the study of modern peoples and their material culture, and have used ethnographic material as analogies for things they saw in the archaeological record. Long before David Clarke wrote about the Iron Age lake village of Glastonbury, the huts there had been compared to huts of 'natives' in East Africa. Indeed, such parallels were at the heart of the emergence of archaeology as a discipline. Nineteenth-century ideas of social evolution, in which all societies went through the same fundamental stages, carried the implication that we could use present day 'primitive' societies as analogies for the prehistoric past. Thus, for example, Lubbock's famous 1865 book *Prehistoric Times* was subtitled *As illustrated by ancient remains, and the manners and customs of modern savages*. It contained illustrations of artefacts from both prehistory and from contemporary groups such as the Inuit.

Binford and others, however, suggested that such 'ethnoarchaeological' work had to be done primarily not by ethnographers, but by archaeologists with a specific eye to the analogies between present and past. Archaeologists could not rely on ethnographers collecting relevant material, since their aims and purposes were different – ethnographers were concerned with a range of issues, and were not in Binford's view specifically interested in the link between human activities and archaeological material.

For Binford, the development of 'robust' middle-range theory was far more important than metaphysical debates about the status of archaeology as a science. While colleagues were arguing about the finer points of philosophy and epistemology, then, Binford set off for Alaska to study the Nunamiut 'Eskimo' hunters.

Interpreting the Mousterian

Binford's account of why he did so (related most accessibly in *In Pursuit of the Past*) is instructive. Binford had been interested in the 'Mousterian Question' for some time. The Mousterian period at the junction of the Middle and Upper Palaeolithic could be found in different contexts in the Old World, but had been most closely analysed in southern France; it was named after the French cave site of Le Moustier.

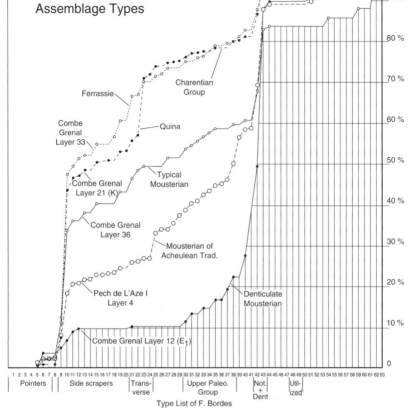

Figure 4.2 Bordes' Mousterian assemblage types, as redrawn by Binford (1983a)

The Mousterian was defined and characterized by certain distinctive types of stone tools, which had been classified by the French archaeologist François Bordes. Bordes had then looked at the different proportions of different stone tool types in different layers, and shown that these could be classified into different patterns or assemblages: 'typical Mousterian', 'Charentian', 'Mousterian of Acheulean tradition', 'denticulate Mousterian', and so on (figure 4.2).

How might we interpret this pattern found in the present in terms of past processes? Bordes had assumed that different stone tool assemblages reflected the presence of different cultural groups. That is, he followed the assumptions of other traditional or culture-historical archaeologists in assuming that certain artefact types and assemblages represented distinctive 'cultures'. Different stone tool types reflected different cultural norms, and assemblage variability therefore reflected cultural variability. Others disagreed in how this 'interassemblage variability' might be interpreted. Binford, for example, suggested that different assemblages were not the detritus of different cultures, but should be seen within an adaptive framework – as different 'tool-kits'.

Binford wanted to test his hypothesis. He collected huge numbers of statistics from Mousterian assemblages in France and put them on to a computer. (We see here the stress on grasping variability and on quantitative methods characteristic of New Archaeology.) He expended a huge amount of labour feeding the information in, and found that there were some interesting patterns in the material he had collected. But herein lay the central problem. Binford found that there was nothing he could do with them.

Binford had no secure idea what activities or processes might have created those patterns. Bordes's suggestion that different proportions of tool types were reflective of different cultural groups, Binford's argument that different groups of tools were different 'tool-kits', and reflected different kinds of cultural adaptation, and other Palaeolithic specialists' interpretations might all be appropriate explanations, all of which appeared to be 'satisfactory' explanations of the data, no matter how many statistics the computer churned out.

Using Binford's own terminology, he had lots of information about statics in the present, but lacked the means – the middle-range theory – to translate these into past dynamics. As a result his ideas of what his patterns meant could be contrasted with the ideas of others such as Bordes, without being able to test between the two. The arguments of Binford and Bordes remained just different stories, with no clear way to judge which was the more accurate.

Binford's work with the Nunamiut, then, was animated by a desire to produce middle-range information that would give him a 'handle' on this question. The Nunamiut, as a group who practised hunting of deer in an environment similar to that which pertained in southern France during the Mousterian period, offered a chance to attack the question of what these patterns might mean. Observation of the Nunamiut could answer the question: 'what kinds of hunter-gatherer activities give rise to what kinds of archaeological assemblages?'

Before we can consider whether Binford's Nunamiut work gave him this secure handle, we must consider its underlying theory a little more.

Uniformitarian Assumptions

Binford lays down two conditions that middle-range theory must satisfy. Middle-range theory must be:

1   Formally *independent from* our development of *general theory*.
    Remember that in the positivist view, science is about testing things, and
    the importance of keeping method separate from theory. How can
    archaeologists test between two general theories if our middle-range
    theory is based on one of them? This would give rise to the danger of a
    circular argument.
2   Based on a *uniformitarian assumption*. In other words, archaeologists
    have to assume that conditions in the past were like those in the present.
    If conditions in the past varied, all bets are off; anything could have hap-
    pened; actualistic studies in the present offer no secure guide to what
    might have happened in the past.

Consider this second assumption for a moment. Archaeologists can assume
that physical properties and processes (gravity, the structure of molecules,
geological processes such as soil formation and sedimentation) were the
same in the present as in the past. Indeed, it was this assumption that was
central to the development of modern geology, and hence stratigraphy in
archaeology, in the nineteenth century. The nineteenth-century geologist
Lyell had argued against ascribing geological features such as layers of sedi-
mentary rock to catastrophes and cataclysmic events such as the biblical
Flood, events that had no parallel in the present. Instead, we had to assume
that features such as layers of rock were created by processes observable in
the present (such as marine sedimentation). Of course, a few physical processes and conditions are demonstrably not uniform – the proportion of
carbon-14 in the atmosphere has varied over the millennia, for example,
which is why carbon-14 determinations have to be 'calibrated' against
dendrochnology in order to turn determinations into dates.
   Physical processes may have largely been the same in the past, but human
behaviour is much more diverse. Uniformitarian assumptions about human
behaviour are much more difficult to make. The law of gravity applies regardless of time and place, but different human cultures do things in very different
ways. This difficulty is particularly apparent for the Lower and Middle
Palaeolithic periods where archaeologists are dealing with extinct hominid
species that are not *Homo sapiens sapiens*. We can debate whether 'human
nature' or 'basic human needs' are constant for other periods, but at these early
times we are dealing with hominid species that are not our own. Archaeologists
cannot therefore assume that practices we might suppose common to all human
groups were even present at that time. Binford himself makes the point that
practices such as 'home-base behaviour' (regular return to a 'home' such as a
transitory camp) may be 'natural' or assumed for modern humans, but cannot
be assumed for the hominids of the Lower Palaeolithic.
   Somewhere in the middle, between the physical and human worlds, are
assumptions about the behaviour of animals and plants, resting in the

domain of ecology. Plant and animal ecology is not quite as 'hard' and invariate as the laws of physics and chemistry, but not as 'soft' and variable as cultural behaviour. For example, modern sheep will herd when threatened by a predator, whereas other species will scatter; in so far as this behaviour has a genetic basis, this has obvious implications for which species were easier to domesticate in the Neolithic (sheep being amenable to being herded by humans and dogs).

It follows that the development of middle-range theory may be relatively plausible for areas of the archaeological record that are governed by or dependent on physical or biological processes, but less so in other areas. Let's consider some examples:

1   The preparation of grain for human consumption can only be performed in certain ways: harvesting can only take place during certain times of the year, the wheat must be separated from the chaff, the grain must be dried, and so on. The different processes involved in the harvesting and processing of grain give rise to certain recognizable by-products like chaff or charred remains. The processing of crops can readily be explored through ethnoarchaeology and experimental archaeology (figure 4.3).

2   Ageing of animals. Archaeologists can assume that measures of animal age such as tooth eruption sequences did not vary in the past, and further assume that mating and breeding patterns took place in the same seasonal rhythm. It is therefore possible to take a collection of bones and determine not only age at death, but at what time in the year animals were being killed. This in turn might lead to secure inferences about whether animals were being bred for meat or dairy products, and so on.

3   As a more marginal example to explore the limits of the uniformitarian assumption, we can differentiate between 'kill sites' and 'residential sites' on the basis of the bones found at each site. Archaeologists can safely make the uniformitarian assumption that the ratio of meat to bone remains fairly constant for an animal's body part, and therefore reason that hunters will carry back the meat-bearing parts of the animal while leaving behind less 'meaty' parts of the animal (something often referred to as the 'Schlepp effect'). Whether a site is a kill site or a home base will therefore be reflected in the different kinds of bone left on site, and much ethnoarchaeological research has gone into establishing just how this might work. (But this might not work because of 'cultural' factors. A group might have cultural taboos against consuming a particular part of an animal, or conversely a part might be prized for its 'ritual' properties. A high cultural value placed on part of an animal that did not correspond to its calorific or protein value might confuse these signatures. I shall explore this problem further below.)

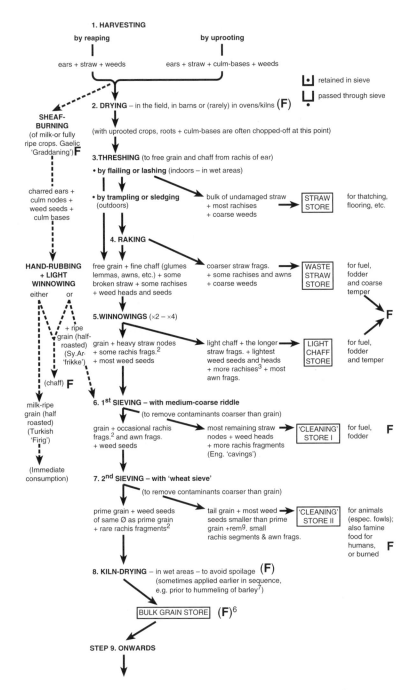

Figure 4.3 Part of Hillman's (1984) ethnoarchaeological model of grain processing, derived from ethnographic research in Turkey, with F indicating those points at which products are exposed to fire and therefore preservation by charring. After Hillman (1984: figure 2)

Many of these studies can be grouped under the heading of *taphonomy*. Taphonomy is the study of how the archaeological record is created from 'cultural' and 'natural' behaviour. It stresses how we cannot make easy connections between what we find in the archaeological record and past activities, and is most strongly developed in areas like botanical and faunal remains and animal behaviour.

To take one small example: the gnawing of bones by dogs. Sebastian Payne has shown how gnawed bones will more easily decay than complete bones. Sites, therefore, on which dogs are present may have many fewer bones, and perhaps different sorts of bones, than sites where no dogs are present. The negative conclusion of this is that we may misinterpret the very similar economy of sites whose only real difference is that dogs are present at one of them.

Case Study: Bones at Olduvai

To be successful, then, middle-range theory must not only develop propositions linking present statics and past dynamics. It must then take those propositions and use them in a formal way to judge between different interpretations of the same archaeological assemblage. Let us look at a case study to see whether such a judgement actually happens.

In the last chapter of his book *Bones: Ancient Men and Modern Myths*, Binford claims that 'my analysis will represent the application of a methodology developed from control information obtained in actualistic studies' (1981b: 253). In other words, he will use his ethnoarchaeological work to help determine which process gave rise to which pattern in the archaeological record. Does it?

Binford develops a series of propositions from his Nunamiut material, thereby predicting the static results of certain dynamics. For example, he proposes that if tool-using hominids were living in base camps, hunting and killing animals and transporting some parts of the kill, then one would expect a home-base assemblage similar to that of modern hunter-gatherer residences. Among other things, one would expect the hominids to be bringing back parts of the animal with lots of meat, and leaving behind parts with little meat. If, on the other hand, the hominids are only scavenging, other hunting animals will have taken off the high meat-bearing parts, leaving only low-utility parts for the hominids to pick over, resulting in an inverse situation.

Binford then looks at different sites, dividing them into sites where the animal caracasses have also been scavenged by other animals and sites where this has not happened ('ravaged' and 'non-ravaged'). He treats unravaged sites in detail, arguing against the association of hominids with the animal remains. He concludes that there are some less noticed assemblages 'consistent with the removal of essentially marrow-yielding bones from the already ravaged kills of other predator-scavengers', an interpretation reinforced by stone tool evidence.

In my view, this is an interesting and logical argument, but not a formal example of the application of middle-range theory. One would expect a series of formal propositions correlating statics with dynamics, then an observation of the statics, and finally a formal analogy with the dynamics. (To pursue Binford's own analogy, first we propose that bears leave certain prints, then see a print, and conclude that it was made by a bear.) But Binford does not do this. Instead, the evidence is explored *contextually*, with the Nunamiut work serving in a looser role than that of formal analogy. For example, the wolf-kill parallel is not even mentioned in the initial set of formal propositions. So Binford's use of ethnoarchaeological data is interesting and even rigorous, but not a formal use of middle-range theory if we adopt the strict criteria that Binford himself laid down.

We might extend these observations to the Mousterian case study outlined above. It might be expected after Binford's work that secure inferences could be drawn about how the Mousterian might be interpreted. But in fact the debate has simply gone on, or one might argue in more positive terms that it has progressed and expanded its terms of reference. The conclusion we can draw from this is that while middle-range research can help us think about the archaeological record in new and interesting ways, it is difficult to see it working in practice to formally judge between alternative hypotheses in a way that will 'prove' one theory and 'disprove' another. Rather, as Binford himself came to insist in his later work, middle-range research can act to expand and deepen our explanations by identifying ambiguity in the archaeological record, and by pointing towards avenues of further research to define and explore that ambiguity. What other reasons are there to be sceptical about the value of middle-range theory?

Middle-range Theory: Problems

In my view, Binford is quite accurate in suggesting that archaeology stands or falls as a positivist 'science' as conceived in the last chapter on the successful development of middle-range theory. If we can reliably relate present statics to past dynamics through the use of middle-range propositions, then we really can isolate archaeological reasoning from its social and political context and stop just telling stories about the past. If we cannot do so, then the aim of developing archaeology as a neutral science in the narrowly positivist sense might appear doomed.

Two issues can be raised with respect to the debate over analogy and middle-range theory:

(1) An analogy, whether based on the rubric of middle-range theory or not, doesn't prove or test anything. We can never know whether the uniformitarian asumption discussed above is in fact correct. If I interpret an excavated feature as a storage pit, and show that the feature shares 5, 10, 15 characteristics in common with ethnographically 'known' storage pits, there is still a possibility that the feature could be interpreted in some other way.

This criticism gets stronger the more sceptical one is about general theories of cultural evolution. If human cultures really do all go through the same stages, and cultures at each stage of cultural evolution are basically similar to one another, it follows that features from excavated, prehistoric contexts will probably be very like those known from ethnography. A uniformitarian assumption based on cultural similarity will therefore be very strong. To put it another way, if the Inuit really are just like all hunter-gatherer groups, then the use of their material culture and patterns of activity as an analogy for past hunter-gatherer groups is very plausible.

If on the other hand one believes that all cultures are historically unique, and cannot be compared one with another or lumped into evolutionary stages, then there is no reason to accept that this feature was a storage pit merely because it looks like one from another culture 2000 years later, 3000 miles away and from a completely different cultural context. Perhaps we should treat the Inuit as unique or at least distinctive, and if so, be very cautious about arguing that any patterns derived from their means of living can be used in any way as a template for any other hunter-gatherer group past or present. We might certainly point to the fact that groups such as the !Kung San are not 'pristine' hunting and gathering groups, but have complex histories of their own. Here is a case where it can be argued that middle-range assumptions are not in fact independent of general theory; on this argument, they are inextricably linked to general theories, in this case views of cultural evolution.

Advocates of middle-range theory would reply, following from the last chapter, that it does not matter where ideas come from – what matters is how they are tested. Of course we shall never be absolutely sure that this feature was a storage pit, but we can evaluate its plausibility against alternative hypotheses.

In his later work, Binford suggests that we don't absolutely test a proposition one way or the other, but we can focus on where the archaeological record is ambiguous. In other words, archaeologists should focus on the *lack* of fit between the data and what they expected to find, and the things in the archaeological record that we cannot easily explain. These elements of ambiguity and lack of fit, he argues, generate fresh research questions and prompt further research. Over time, then, a scientific archaeology will never provide a full, final explanation, but it can and does demonstrably move forward in its understanding of past processes, as in the wolf-kill example discussed above.

An analogy can be strengthened if some form of cultural continuity can be demonstrated between two groups. It has been argued for example that the modern Hopi tribe of the southwestern United States are the cultural descendants of what archaeologists have called 'Anasazi' populations. Now on 'Anasazi' sites archaeologists find semi-subterranean circular chambers, very similar to the ones found on modern Hopi pueblos. It is, therefore, plausible to refer to modern Hopi rituals in their own kivas. Again, such a link does not conclusively 'prove' anything, but it does derive interpretative strength from such a link because continuity in cultural ideas and practices is probable.

An important element of traditional archaeology in North America was the *direct historical method*, where one started by delineating groups of Native Americans in the present and then tried to trace their cultural antecedents to, effectively, prehistoric groups. Such a method has no direct parallel in European archaeology, though Christopher Hawkes once suggested we should write prehistory backwards, working from 'known' historical groups back to the Iron and Bronze Ages. Such an approach also underlies recent European interest in 'ethnogenesis', or the study of the creation of ethnic identities. Scholars work backwards from 'known' cultural or ethnic groups in the historical or folklife records, combining the evidence of linguistics, archaeology, and ethnography, to examine the 'genesis' of these groups in prehistory.

Both Alison Wylie and Ian Hodder have stressed a distinction between *formal* and *relational* analogies, suggesting that the latter are stronger. Formal analogies rest simply on the notion that if some elements of the two situations are similar, others must be also. Obviously such analogies are weak, though they tend to be stronger the more points of similarity that can be demonstrated between the two contexts. Relational analogies rest on a cultural or natural connection between the two contexts, as with the direct historical method, where connections based on cultural continuity can be suggested.

For example, we might interpret pits on African prehistoric sites as grain storage pits, citing a range of ethnographic examples. As it stands, such an analogy is pretty weak, though it might be strengthened with the number and range of parallels we might draw (are the pits of the same size and shape? Do we consider past and present societies to be at the 'same level of social development'? Do the ethnographic examples come from the same kind of environment, settlement type, economy?). An understanding of the relations between different variables would make the analogies still stronger.

Do the ethnographic examples come from African societies with direct historical links to the prehistoric culture we are studying? Can we ask *why* grain is stored in this way, citing 'natural' reasons (the most efficient way to keep grain dry in this type of climate) or 'cultural' factors?

In practice, of course, formal and relational analogies are two ends of a range of analogical arguments of lesser or greater strength.

(2) The issue of cultural continuity leads on to the second issue. It can be argued that people are influenced by cultural ideas in their behaviour. These ideas don't just affect obviously 'cultural' things like religious beliefs manifested in the manner of burial or other 'ritual' practices. They also affect apparently mundane activities such as the organization of household space and attitudes towards rubbish. They therefore affect archaeological deposition, and must be taken into account when considering the formation of the archaeological record.

Take for example Henrietta Moore's ethnoarchaeological study of the Marakwet in East Africa. Moore found that the way Marakwet houses and compounds were laid out related to their ideas of gender – what it meant, culturally, to be a man or to be a woman in Marakwet society. Different areas of domestic compounds were thought of as 'male' and 'female'. This set of cultural ideas affected where individual residences lay and how the compound was laid out. Again, Ian Hodder looked at the distribution of pig and cattle bones in different settlements of the Nuba. He found lots of pig bones in the compounds of one tribe, but very few in another. Hodder suggested that this was due to different cultural attitudes. In this culture, women were associated with pigs – women were responsible for the pigs' feeding and maintenance. In one area, there was a strong (male) belief that women were polluting: hence, by association, compounds were kept clean of pig bones and other debris. In another area, such pollution beliefs were weak, the people of that area seemed not to care that their compounds were left covered in refuse. Hodder argued that an archaeologist excavating different compounds would need to understand something of Nuba beliefs in order to interpret the faunal remains 'correctly'.

Much ethnoarchaeological and experimental work continues on the relationship between statics and dynamics. A particularly strong area is the taphonomy of bones, but other areas include the production of stone tools, plant remains and site economy in general. Such work tends to concentrate on problems raised by the archaeological record of the Palaeolithic and early farming communities – in other words, relatively early elements of the archaeological record. It tries to focus on quite specific archaeological questions, often relating to subsistence economy.

Behavioural Archaeology

Let's return to figure 2.1, the gap between present and past, and the issue of how to infer past processes from archaeological data in the present.

A second method to bridge this gap was outlined by Michael Schiffer, who coined the term *behavioural archaeology*. Behavioural archaeology began in the 1970s as the study of site formation processes – how artefacts move from their 'systemic context', that is, their use in actual human behaviour, to their 'archaeological context' in which they are excavated. Schiffer drew attention to the intervening factors between these two contexts: for example, 'depositional processes', 'reclamation processes', 'disturbance processes' and 'reuse processes'. In seeking to link up behaviour with patterning in the archaeological record, the project of behavioural archaeology obviously shares common ground with much of middle-range theory and taphonomy. Binford himself rejected this term and chose to attack much of Schiffer's philosophy in quite outspoken terms; but behavioural archaeology, taphonomy and middle-range theory can be considered as closely related bodies of thinking.

Behavioural archaeology, however, goes on from this point to encompass a much broader set of interests, and to define itself as a distinctive approach to archaeology as a whole. Skibo and Schiffer (2008, 6) have stated:

> the core component of this approach is the redefinition of archaeology as a discipline that studies relationships between people and things in all times and all places ... The relationships between people and artifacts are discussed in terms of regularities discerned in processes of manufacture, use, and disposal that make up the life histories of material things, as in flow models and behavioural chains.

The most famous example of behavioural archaeology is the Tucson Garbage Project initiated by Bill Rathje, where the link between behaviour and material debris is examined in the present through study of the garbage the modern people of Tucson throw away.

In other words, behavioural archaeology looks for regularities in the relations between people and objects in all times and places. In this way, it brings together study of the prehistoric past with studies of much more recent artefacts, including objects in the present. Some of Schiffer's most fascinating work has been on objects such as the early electric car, the lighthouse, and the portable radio, which sits alongside that of his and colleagues' studies of more 'traditional' topics such as pottery manufacture and the discard and reuse of objects.

Material Culture Studies

Behavioural archaeology has also come to share a set of interests with 'material culture studies' in general. Ethnoarchaeological work such as Henrietta Moore's and Ian Hodder's, mentioned above, led to the proposition that to understand material culture, one had to look at cultural meanings. The way was thus laid open to a range of studies which looked at material objects, buildings and landscapes in both the prehistoric and recent past and present, in which the methods of archaeology, ethnography and related areas were combined.

It is often difficult to see any distinction in this work between archaeology and anthropology – whether, that is, scholars are looking archaeologically at material culture in its social context, or anthropologically at society with a theoretical emphasis on the importance of materiality and material things. Indeed, an interdisciplinary journal edited by this 'school' (the *Journal of Material Culture*) brings together different disciplines in this very way, and includes work by art and design historians, scholars from cultural studies, archaeologists, cultural anthropologists, and many other areas.

It can also be argued that these interests have very deep historical roots – they go back to the importance attached to the collection of material culture by early ethnographers, giving rise to many of the great collections of artefacts found in museums like the Pitt Rivers or the great North American collections such as the Smithsonian. They also go back to the origins of archaeology in early modern antiquarianism and its emphasis on the close study and discussion of monuments and artefacts from a wide range of areas and periods.

A particularly important element of recent work in material culture studies has been the archaeology of the recent past. Scholars have looked, for example, at the material traces of the Second World War and of the Cold War, combining written history, the testimony of participants, and archaeological study of surviving structures and artefacts. Much of this work brings together interdisciplinary interests such as a concern with how people's memories and accounts of the past are embedded in material objects and landscapes.

As a result of this convergence of approaches and interests, the study of material culture in the present, allied to a recasting of archaeology as not simply about the past but about the relationship of people and things, is one of the most important and vibrant areas of archaeological theory today. There are a diversity of approaches drawing theoretical inspiration from a diversity of sources, from a continuing tradition of middle-range research through to studies of modern material culture informed by postmodern and interpretive theories. I will come back to these approaches again and again in future chapters, and try to pull them together at the end of the book under the general banner of 'materiality'.

Which approach to material objects offers the most convincing way forward depends, in part, on the general theory of society that one finds convincing. Can one generalize between societies? Are societies to be seen as systems fundamentally adapted to their environment, or is symbolic meaning important? These are questions we will examine in the next chapter.

5

Culture and Process

In the last two chapters, we have seen how different forms of archaeological theory differ in their approach to questions of epistemology (the nature of knowledge claims) and questions of testing or evaluation (analogy and middle-range theory). We will now look at how theories differ in their approach to cultural forms and social change.

How do human societies work? How do human beings relate to one another? How can any human being have the power of command over a hundred, let alone a thousand or a million, others? Were social groups in the past formed through consent and cooperation, or through conflict and power? Is social change a gradual, cumulative process, or does it arise violently through the clash of ideas and groups, through conflict and contradiction? How do the day-to-day actions of ordinary individuals making pots or feeding children relate or add up to long-term, large-scale changes like the origins of agriculture or the rise of modern capitalism? These are some of the core questions within disciplines that deal with humans and the relations between them, not just archaeology but particularly sociology, cultural anthropology, and history.

All these questions can arguably be re-phrased as: what is culture, and how and why does it change? The definition of 'culture' was a core concern of anthropology, most obviously in the achievement of Franz Boas in making the idea of 'culture' the centrepiece of the fourfield approach in North America at the end of the nineteenth century.

The word 'culture' appears simple at first sight, but it is desperately complex and difficult to define. One group of meanings clusters around what it means to be 'cultured' or 'civilized', and are value-laden; it is an insult to call someone 'uncultured'. This general use of the term bleeds into much of humanistic archaeology – as we have seen, the genesis of Classical archaeology depended on a notion of what it meant to be cultured, and the term 'civilization' and adjective 'civilized' are also ambiguous in this respect.

Franz Boas rejected this view. For Boas, culture was not something which one person or group had and others did not. He insisted that all human groups have cultures, in the sense of systems of ideas and symbols, cultures which make sense in themselves. Boas established what anthropologists now regard as commonplace: that culture cannot be equated to or directly derived from race, and nor can it be judged on an ethnocentric yardstick. Further, 'culture' is not some kind of add-on to human existence, something which humans only have time for once they have satisfied their other needs such as subsistence.

Archaeologists try to talk about ancient cultures and societies, and attempt to understand how and why they existed and changed as they did. They are thus immediately locked into the sociological and anthropological questions raised above. Yet again, we cannot choose to avoid theory in this regard. 'Atheoretical' archaeologists, for example, will not address such questions explicitly, but they do use metaphors that imply a particular view of how societies work.

We have already seen one such metaphor in action: the aquatic view of culture, in which ripples of diffusion spread across the cultural lake, cross-cutting one another. Another popular metaphor is that of society as a body. For example, we might talk about societies or social stages reaching 'maturity' or use other bodily metaphors, of social 'sickness' or 'disease'. (Supposedly descriptive and atheoretical accounts of the rise and fall of the Roman Empire are full of such metaphors.) The bodily metaphor often involves organic rhythms of 'youth', 'maturity' and 'decline'. Works of traditional history speak of 'the birthpangs of Protestantism'. Architectural metaphors are also popular: a society 'collapses from within', or a particular archaeological phase or event 'lays the foundations for' certain subsequent changes.

The different metaphors used by 'atheoretical' archaeologists to characterize societies in this way are more than just words. Consciously or unconsciously, they refer back to theoretical ideas that are part of a common intellectual currency. Many relate, for example, to nineteenth-century European conceptions of history and art history. German Romantic philosophers, in particular Hegel, talked of a *zeitgeist* or essential spirit. Such a spirit might be characteristic of a historical period or stage of world history, or a people or race. Such a spirit might then be used to explain a particular art style or aesthetic preference; so for example Classical columns and proportions used in Greek and Roman architecture were held to be expressions of some underlying system of humanist rationality.

An underlying conception of *zeitgeist* profoundly influenced European art and architectural history and its applications to archaeology, for example of the Classical, medieval and Renaissance periods. Mediated by this tradition, theoretical ideas of a culture being defined and characterized by some essential or inner spirit were implicitly translated into everyday words and phrases often used by archaeologists, particularly in popular texts: 'the spirit of the Bronze Age', 'the ethic of *Romanitas* still held sway', 'the inner essence of the Celtic peoples', 'the medieval mind'.

To repeat, all these ideas, whether implicit or explicit, and whether right or wrong, are theoretical ideas and need to be examined and criticized as such. The idea of *zeitgeist* in particular is morally questionable (as well as intellectually unsustainable) when applied in racial terms: it may sound innocent enough to talk of 'the Celtic spirit', but reference to 'the Indo-European spirit' would rightly be viewed with suspicion. These ideas continue nevertheless to stand in as substitutes for more developed and explicitly theorized concepts in many traditional narratives, and to be uncritically deployed in popular debates over an 'essence' of cultural identity which often descend into questionable stereotypes ('typical English reserve', 'natural Latino exuberance', 'Gallic flair').

Culture History

You will recall from chapter 2 that more traditional forms of archaeology have a *normative view of culture* in which a culture is defined as a set of shared ideas. These ideas are imperfectly expressed in material culture; the varied forms of artefacts imperfectly reflect different norms (figure 5.1). In this view, one tends to stress the *particularity* of cultures – why and how they are different from the adjacent group. Culture history can also be seen as an *idealist* view, in that it is ideas and norms that are seen as being important in the definition of cultural identity.

There are two problems with the culture-historical view of how human societies work. The first problem is that it tends to be *mentalist*. That is, it explains why a culture is the way it is primarily by reference to what people are thinking. The identification and criticism of mentalist explanation can be found time and again in archaeology and the human sciences generally. The fatal objection to a mentalist explanation is as follows: a culture decorates its houses this way because of its cultural norms. But why does it have these cultural norms? Why not a different set of norms? Again, why is this pottery decorated in this way? Because of the norms inside the potter's head; the potter wanted it to look that way. Why did the chicken cross the road? Because of what was inside its head: it wanted to get to the other side.

Culture-historical archaeology is full of arguments that can be criticized as being mentalist. They are especially prevalent and pernicious where religion is involved, since here the author can implicitly appeal to an unspecified inner spiritual need that the reader is lulled into assuming is 'natural':

> No system such as [the minster system], being designed to economise both in buildings and clergy [*why was it designed this way? Because clerics wanted*

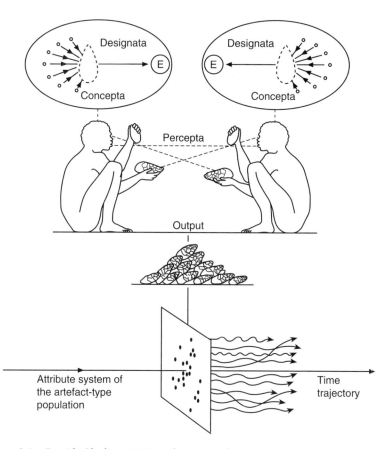

Figure 5.1 David Clarke's (1976) diagram of the normative view of culture. Members of a group produce handaxes. Each has an idea of what a handaxe should look like; by observing others and communication this idea approximates to the group idea or norm. Individual handaxes are imperfect representations of this norm, being flawed, or made with more or less skill

it to be this way?], could hope to meet the needs of every Christian believer [*why not? What are these needs? Are these needs really self-evident if one is not a fundamentalist Christian?*] And it was inevitable that, alongside these centres, a network of private chapels, or oratories, should very quickly have developed [*why was it inevitable?*]. (Platt 1981: 1; comments mine)

The answers to the questions in italics can only follow if the 'need' for churches is taken as self-evident, in need of no further explanation. Why did people have certain ideas inside their heads that led them to 'need' more churches? Why were the old belief systems, pagan or otherwise, now deemed inadequate? And who deemed them inadequate – why did the religious élite assume that the common people 'needed' these ideas? Were changing 'needs' of this kind anything to do with contemporary socio-economic changes, and if so, what were those changes?

In short, to explain an archaeological feature or historical phenomenon by reference to a untheorized need or intention in someone's head is to explain nothing at all. Mentalist arguments of this kind can be found lurking implicitly within many traditional archaeological and historical syntheses: they can even be built into the core of their assumptions.

The second objection raised by New Archaeologists to the normative approach to culture is that culture is just treated as a rag-tag assemblage of ideas. Why do ideas fit together in a certain way? What, if anything, does the zigging versus the zagging on the pottery have to do with varying settlement and house types? Why, in short, do certain things fit together in the way they do?

The New Archaeology's definition of culture was therefore very different. For New Archaeology, culture was a *system* (figure 2.5). A system was defined by David Clarke as 'an intercommunicating network of attributes or entities forming a complex whole' (Clarke 1978: 495). For Flannery and Marcus, systems were characterized by exchanges of matter, energy and information among their components.

This is a very different view of culture. Instead of looking for shared norms, systems thinkers looked for different elements or *subsystems* and studied the relations between them. Instead of looking 'inside' at what people thought, what was going on inside their heads, at centre stage, they often prefer to look 'outside', at how their cultural system was adapted, to an outside environment.

Cultural Systems: Summary

There are six aspects of thinking about cultural systems that it is important to grasp.

(1)   Cultures are, at least in part, the way they are because they are *adapted to an external environment*, whether that is the surrounding natural environment or that of neighbouring, competing social systems. We have seen how Lewis Binford defined culture as 'Man's extrasomatic means of adaptation'. Much thinking on cultural systems thus tends to have close intellectual ties to Darwinian ideas of adaptation. Many thinkers have moved away from this stress on adaptation to the external environment in recent years, as we shall see.

(2)   Elements of culture, in this view, are more or less *observable*. Obviously you cannot dig a cultural system up directly – you will never see a 'trade' or

'subsistence' subsystem in the archaeological record. You can argue that they are observable, however, in the sense that they depend on systems of energy and information flow rather than on thoughts or norms.

To clarify: you can't see 'norms' inside the mind of the potter; it's difficult to think of a way of 'testing' what was going on inside his or her head, particularly if he or she has been dead for several thousands of years. On the other hand, you can think of possible ways to measure the incidence and importance of 'trade' for a given archaeological group. You might, for example, look at the presence and proportion of non-locally made pottery from excavated contexts. Again, you can't dig up 'subsistence', but you can measure and quantify the area of land suitable for arable cultivation round a site, or the meat weight and calorific value represented by the data gleaned from a faunal assemblage. So one can see how an archaeologist might begin to construct and measure a link between, in this example, subsistence economy and trade – and might then 'test' this hypothesized link by reference to the archaeological record.

(3)   Such systems can be modelled and are amenable to being compared from culture to culture. In this way, they can lead to comparative observations and generalizations about cultural processes.

(4)   Elements of cultural systems are interdependent; subsistence, trade, ritual, social subsystems are related one to another. As a result, change in one part of the system will affect the whole leading to *positive* or *negative feedback, homeostasis* or transformation. What do these terms mean?

Many systems thinkers have suggested that cultural systems can be seen in fundamentally similar terms to other kinds of system in the natural world. Natural systems in ecology, for example, tend towards a state of balance. When they are affected by some external change, such as a change in climate or the introduction of a new predator, the whole system will, after a period of fluctuation, tend to reach a new state of overall balance through modifications in the relations between the subsystems.

So, by analogy, an environmental change (say an improvement of the climate) will affect subsistence (making farming more productive). This will enable farmers to produce more agricultural surplus, and to use that surplus to engage in more trade in luxuries or prestige goods, thus changing the trade subsystem. The new prestige goods may also affect the social subsystem; accumulation of such prestige items might bolster the position of élites, increasing the social distance between élites and commoners. The changed social and trade subsystems will then of course react back on subsistence – newly powerful élites might encourage or insist on further agricultural intensification, or initiate large-scale projects like irrigation. With negative feedback, the system reaches a new balance; this tendency towards a new equilibrium is called homeostasis. On the other hand, positive feedback might occur – for example, the new flow of prestige goods produces a transformation in the social system, new forms of ranking that are unstable, which reacts back proportionally on trade and farming as new social groups demand more surplus and trade goods.

(5)   Different elements of cultural systems are linked to one another and explained by *function*. For example, if you want to explain ritual elaboration in a particular period, it might be explained in terms of the *function* of religious systems in giving legitimization to social ranking ('we are of high status because only we have access to the gods'). Again, an intensification in agricultural production (that is, producing more food) might be linked to the need to produce a surplus for prestige purposes – again one subsystem is explained by reference to its function in terms of others.

This is important because it suggests that we can look at the significance of certain practices in the archaeological record without necessarily having to make assumptions about their symbolic meaning, which for many taking this view, is untestable. In this case, we see ritual elaboration, say through the size and form of temples and religious paraphernalia, and interpret it as legitimating an élite. We don't need to worry about what this or that religious practice 'meant', what the form of the temples symbolized.

(6)   Archaeologists can examine the links between subsystems in terms of *correlation rather than simple causes*. We might observe, for example, that over time in a particular context intensification of subsistence agriculture goes hand-in-hand with population rise. Arguing about which 'caused' the other is pretty fruitless, being a chicken-and-egg argument. In delineating a cultural system, however, one can note the correlation between the two and build it in within a larger model of systemic change or stability.

The Idea of Process

Closely related to the idea of culture as a system is the idea of cultural process. We have seen that New Archaeology sought to replace 'culture history' with 'culture process'. Since that move, the idea of process has remained central to much of archaeological thinking.

Like so many terms in archaeological thought, 'process' is important and habitually used, but it remains a difficult term to define. It refers to a cluster of interconnected propositions:

(a)   Process is about the 'why?' questions – it is about explanation, not simply narrative description. Archaeologists want to ask 'why?' rather than merely 'when?' or 'who?'. A traditional culture sequence such as that of Childe's (figure 2.3) may be valuable in describing a sequence, but it tells us nothing about why one culture succeeded another, or why, for example, innovations like agriculture or metallurgy spread quickly or slowly. The idea of process, then, relates closely to ideas of cultural evolution.

(b) Archaeologists want to look at the underlying process rather than the 'noise' on top. Why pottery decoration zigs or zags is unimportant in this view; instead, what is important is to look at pottery as one artefact of trade or of craft specialization, and to chart the process by which, for example, the long-term development of market networks relates to such specialization. Particular phenomena will always vary: as with economics or sociology, what may be important is the underlying trend.

(c) Archaeologists want to look at change in the long term. Many archaeologists would argue that if you want to do anthropology, the obvious place to start is in the present. Archaeology's great, possibly its only, contribution to the wider study of human beings had to be through its long-term perspective which cultural anthropologists, working only in the present or recent past, do not have.

In this sense, processual thinking shares many of the concerns with the rhythms of long-term history as discussed by *Annales* historians such as Fernand Braudel, though at the time these parallels in thinking were little noted and it fell to a later generation of theorists writing in the 1980s to point out the similarities (see chapter 11).

Example: Cultural Process around the North Sea

In his book *Dark Age Economics* Richard Hodges developed a processual interpretation of the rise of towns, trade and social complexity in post-Roman northwest Europe. Again, Hodges's arguments must be seen in context. Hodges was working against a backdrop of traditional archaeological thought that had spent a great deal of time excavating early medieval trading sites and analysing documentary evidence. Much ink had been spilt trying to determine the exact date of settlements, very often in an attempt to prove that this or that settlement was 'the first' and that urban life spread outwards from that centre. This work, however, had done almost nothing in *explaining* the re-emergence of towns and trade before AD 850, had treated the evidence in a particularistic manner and in ways that were riddled with questionable mentalist and essentialist arguments (reference to innate 'rekindling of the spirit of trade' or 'the trading spirit of the Frisian peoples').

Hodges suggested that the whole of the North Sea area should be seen as a cultural system, within which social complexity, the rise of urbanism and the growth of trade were linked. Drawing on ethnographic parallels such as the Kula exchange network, he suggested that as with chiefdom societies in general, the position of the chief or king at the apex of society depended on his ability to control the production and circulation of luxury or 'prestige' goods. The more successful the chief was at controlling this flow, the more he could reward his followers with gifts that in turn created reciprocal obligations.

The rise of a limited number of towns in the seventh to ninth century AD could be seen as an attempt to control this production and flow; Hodges drew attention to the planned nature of these settlements, suggesting that planning reflected central control and their royal origin. He also pointed out their location: on estuarine or riverine sites suitable for long-distance trade, away from existing centres of authority.

Note that this explanation *generalizes*. It puts early medieval Europe within a general classification of 'chiefdom societies' and seeks to understand them in that light. Now 'chiefdom societies' can be seen in Polynesia, the Americas, the Bronze Age in the Aegean; that is, in a variety of ethnographic, ethnohistoric and prehistoric situations spanning the globe. In all these areas other scholars have drawn attention to the importance of the flow of prestige goods, the links between prestige and chiefly power, the processes leading to greater social complexity. Citing this literature, Hodges criticized traditional scholars who had emphasized the uniqueness of northwestern Europe, suggesting memorably that we should not consider the underlying processes of cultural change to be any different in this context just because a few Northern European monks took it into their heads to write down what they thought of current events.

Such an evolving social system is more or less *observable* in the archaeological record. We cannot directly see trade or urbanism, but we can develop archaeological indexes of trade through statistical studies of artefacts. We cannot see social ranking directly, but we can develop an index of it in terms of burial practices, the richness or paucity of grave goods.

Cultural Process: Strengths

It has been argued by some writers that all archaeologists think in terms of cultural systems and processes. We all think of societies as functioning units, and as we have seen many 'traditional' writers use the metaphor of bodily systems implicitly. Much thinking in these terms is implicit within explanations, even if the writer does not use the appropriate jargon or is even consciously aware of the intellectual background to what he or she is doing.

There are three strengths of thinking in terms of systems and process which are worth outlining:

(1)   It avoids the problems of mentalism discussed above. Hodges tries to explain the rise of towns and trade; he does not take the easy and fallacious route of ascribing it in mentalistic fashion to some indefinable 'Viking spirit'; it is linked to other processes within a total picture of an evolving social system.

(2)   It avoids *monocausal explanations*, in other words explanations that try to single out one or other cause for an event. In so doing processual thinking can combine the strengths of such explanations and avoid their weaknesses.

One example is the study of the collapse of civilizations. In studying why civilizations suddenly collapse, much fruitless academic argument has been spent in arguing over single, specific causes. The eruption of Santorini and its relation to the collapse of the Minoan civilization, the 'Classic Maya collapse', or the convenient attribution of collapses to sudden invasions of vast hordes of barbarian peoples, are obvious examples.

Processual thinking directs our attention back to 'why?' questions. It points away from sudden invasions and disasters towards an understanding of *why* certain stresses or events were or were not critical (figure 5.2). For example:

(a)   The fall of the Roman Empire. Traditional accounts are often consumed in endless detail on this or that barbarian invasion. A processual thinker asks: Why was this barbarian invasion a fatal blow rather than easily repulsed? What internal factors lessened the ability of the Empire to respond? Conversely, what systemic or structural factors underlay the barbarian invasions – population rise, territorial stress, changes in political structure?

(b)   The collapse of the Minoan civilization. In the past, many looked to specific causes, such as chance invasions of barbarians or the eruption of the volcano of Santorini. In all these cases, practical arguments raged back and forth – for example, Spyridon Marinatos's suggestion that the Santorini eruption was primarily responsible was brought into question by new dating evidence. But thinking more broadly, pointing to particular events does not help us understand the underlying process. Why should particular events like invasion or natural disaster lead to irrecoverable decline rather than rapid regeneration?

(c)   The 'Classic Maya collapse'. Many of the great monuments of the Maya civilization of Central America were suddenly abandoned, apparently almost overnight. Again, traditional explanations looked to specific historical causes such as earthquake, invasion or natural catastrophe to explain this 'collapse'. Processual thinkers redirect attention to what they saw as more fundamental underlying factors – the relationship between population rise and agricultural productivity, for

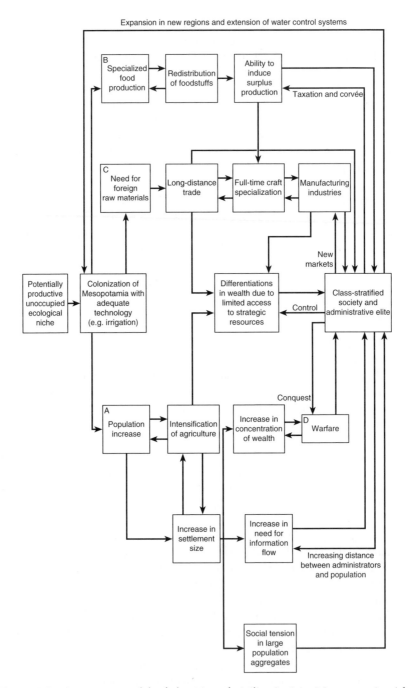

Figure 5.2 A systems model of the 'rise of civilization' in Mesopotamia. After Redman (1978: figure 7.7)

example. By modelling the Maya civilization as a system, they draw attention to relationships between changing 'variables'. Analysis of these variables makes an apparently sudden collapse explicable as the culmination of certain long-term processes.

(3) Cultural process is a potential source of *optimism* for archaeology. If all aspects of a culture are functionally linked one to another, we need not be restricted in what we talk about as archaeologists. Indeed, there is no reason why we cannot infer the rest of society from the meagre archaeological record. This is what I call the fairycake argument (with apologies to Douglas Adams): if all parts of the universe are linked to one another, the argument goes, we can infer the entirety of the universe from one small piece of fairycake. Binford used this argument when he wrote: 'granted we cannot excavate a kinship terminology or a philosophy, but we can and do excavate the material items which functioned together with these. ... The formal structure of artefact assemblages together with the between-element contextual relationships should and do present a systematic and understandable picture of the *total extinct* cultural system' (Binford 1964; his emphasis)

The Context of Cultural Systems

So far I have described processual thinking in isolation. However, it is important to place systems thinking in its context. As with so many archaeological theories, a lot of the intellectual background to systems thinking lies in associated disciplines sharing the same fundamental intellectual issues.

As we saw earlier, the links between different cultural elements or subsystems are *functional* ones. In functional explanation, culture is seen as comparable to an organism such as the human body or any other complex organism – there is an *organic analogy*, to use a common piece of jargon. Biologists explain different parts of an organism by reference to their function within the system as a whole. For example, the form of the heart – a powerful pump – is explained by reference to its function in pumping blood which takes oxygen around the body. Sociologists explain subsystems within modern social systems by reference to their functions. For example, the form of the modern state – an administrative bureaucracy – is explained by reference to its economic, social and political function(s). Processual thinkers similarly explain elements of past cultures by reference to their function; for example, religious practices and institutions are seen in terms of their function in legitimating social hierarchies, or the presence of élites is explained with reference to their function in managing complex activities such as irrigation agriculture.

Functionalism, as a theory of culture, has been defined as the proposition that cultures are like organisms, so that the part is explained in terms of its function in relation to the whole. Cohen defines it as 'the notion that all of the institutions, beliefs and morals of a society are interrelated as a whole, so that the method of explaining the existence of any one item in the whole is to discover the law which prescribes how this system coexists with all the others' (Cohen 1968: 34). Functionalism developed in the later nineteenth century with the rise of the human sciences as a whole. Different versions were expounded by Auguste Comte, Herbert Spencer, Emile Durkheim, Radcliffe-Brown and Malinowski (note that many of these thinkers were also associated with early attempts to fashion anthropology and sociology in a positivist mould).

We can understand functionalism better if we think about its intellectual and social context. British social anthropology in particular went hand-in-hand with the training of administrators for the Empire. Thus the one very powerful implication of functional thought was that the apparently irrational, weird and wonderful customs of 'native' peoples, such as belief in magic and witchcraft or elaborate rules surrounding exchange systems, were functionally connected to the workings of the group as a whole. Would-be administrators were taught to think about the customs of their subjects in context and not to apply a simplistic moral or evolutionary scale. Customs should not therefore be thought of as simply irrational, relics from a previous stage of social evolution, or as the perversions of 'savage' life.

If customs were not irrational, neither could they be satisfactorily explained as relics of previous societies. Evolutionists had often suggested that certain customs were 'hangovers' from previous stages of the evolution of a society. Functional thinking was *synchronic* – that is, it examined how different elements of society fitted together at one particular slice of time. In other words, it said 'Never mind about historical origins. How does this or that institution or custom function here and now, at this particular moment in time?'

Processual Thinking: Drawbacks

Thinking in terms of cultural processes therefore appears to be a very strong way of thinking about cultures in the past. It avoids many problems of traditional approaches, provides convincing explanations, and allows us to develop generalizing and comparative arguments. Yet in many theoretical circles, particularly in Britain, many of the ideas outlined above have been either abandoned or at least heavily qualified. Why?

First, there is a series of well-rehearsed criticisms of functionalism. These criticisms, some argue, can equally be applied to theories of cultural process. They include the following:

(1)   There is, it is argued, a flaw at the heart of functional explanation. If we explain something by reference to its function in keeping a total system going, this does not explain where it came from historically. An over-simplified example: we explain the rise of élites in state societies by reference to their managerial functions in coordinating agricultural activities. But where did these élites come from?

One possible answer is that it was a conscious decision; but it is difficult to see a cultural group sitting down round the hearth and saying 'OK, we're having problems coordinating large-scale irrigation agriculture, so we'll invent an élite and believe in them as gods. They will then function in the following ways to keep our system in equilibrium …'

A more plausible answer is to link functional with adaptive explanations; that is, to say that societies that happen to have developed such élites, for example through historical accident, are better adapted and compete more effectively within their environments. In the long run therefore they tend to be 'selected for' in the Darwinian sense, and in the long run they are the ones we will find in the archaeological record. *Processual arguments are therefore often closely related to adaptive explanations*, in terms of the way they are expressed and the sort of archaeologists who put them forward. This is a point to which we will return in chapter 10.

(2)   Processual arguments depend on functional linkages. But these links are always open to doubt in specific terms. There may be alternative strategies available to individuals and cultures that are not considered.

For example, one of the classic functional linkages is that made between increasingly marginal environments and agricultural intensification. As an environment becomes more difficult to live in, it is argued, human groups will elaborate and intensify their efforts to cultivate food. At Chaco Canyon in northwestern New Mexico, archaeologists have found that in the period AD 700–800 there is an upsurge in the building of ceremonial monuments, and a transition from pithouses to stone pueblos. This activity is taken as indicative of the development of a higher level of social complexity. This level of complexity often has been understood in systemic terms. The environmental record suggests that at this time the climate at Chaco was getting drier. A drier climate, it is argued, meant that if agriculture was to be successful crops had to be irrigated rather than rely on rainfall. The large-scale coordination of labour needed to run such systems required a managerial élite.

However, alternative strategies were available: why not simply abandon the area? Or adopt population control? Why adopt this form of agriculture rather than that form? Why, specifically, does the management of irrigation agriculture require an élite; can it not be run through egalitarian cooperation between groups? It has recently been argued that reorganization, rather than collapse, is the most common human response to climatic or environmental change.

It is objected, then, that alternatives are always available: that the forms of processual thinking outlined above fail to explore why this particular strategy was adopted rather than that particular strategy. Such choices between particular adaptive strategies may depend on the particularity of cultural groups, or on cultural preferences.

(3)   Functionalism cannot, it is objected, explain *change* adequately. A functional or systemic model can explain why a system remains stable. However, why do societies become increasingly complex?

For example, Kent Flannery wrote a classic early study of the origins of agriculture in Mexico, explaining the transition from a hunting and gathering way of life as part of a wider systemic change. He treated 'Man and the southern highlands of Mexico ... as a single complex system, composed of many subsystems, which mutually caused each other'. Culture being adaptive in this view, change was seen in terms of 'gradual change in procurement mechanisms', regulated by seasonality. The strengths of this argument were (a) it directed attention away from the rather tedious search for the earliest example of agriculture in the form of 'the first corncob'; (b) it thus tried to explain the origins of agriculture merely than describe its diffusion; (c) it directed attention to agriculture as part of a gradual change in culture rather than a sudden invention; and (d) the important role of a changing environment could be stressed. One weakness, however, was the assumption that 'without external change, [the development of agriculture] might never have occurred' (Flannery 1973a).

It can be argued, then, that models of cultural process often require an external 'kick' to start them off. Again, this has led to an interest on the part of many archaeologists, particularly those working on the origins of early states, to explore how change and conflict might be 'built in' to processual models. I will explore this interest further in chapter 9 and below.

(4)   The political implications of thinking about cultural systems can be seen as objectionable. Suppose for a moment that systems thinking in its more inflexible forms were 'true'. What would its lessons be for us today?

(a)   That the nature of social stability and transformation is inflexible, composed of long-term processes beyond the consciousness or control of mere individuals, who are only pawns in the game. These long-term processes are very complex and can only be understood with lots of impenetrable jargon (mutual causal deviation amplifying processes). However, such processes are scientifically understandable. The only people, then, who really understand how society works and are therefore in a position to make judgements on how we should organize it are scientists, 'men in white coats'. Ordinary people, it is further implied, are not qualified to make critical comments on the judgements of 'experts' who should therefore be left in sole charge of social management.

(b)   That history is about harmony rather than conflict. If each element of culture is functionally related to the next, it is difficult to see where conflict between groups might come from. In addition, if the moral of functionalism is that all parts of the system are adapted to one another and that there is a 'natural' tendency towards balance or homeostasis, then by definition we live in a well-adapted system. Rather than think in terms of class conflicts and contradictions between groups, we are encouraged to treat social discord as something that can be 'managed away' by the white-coated experts mentioned above. One person's systemic management problem is another's revolution.

This is an over-simplified version of an argument developed by Jürgen Habermas and others within the 'critical theory' school of social philosophy, namely that *systems theory is an ideology of control*. In this view, systems thinking is an authoritarian political statement masquerading as neutral science. It must be opposed, in this view, on basically political grounds.

(5)   Processual thinking is an attempt to understand society from the outside. Regardless of whether one is studying Neolithic Europe or Formative Oaxaca, systemic thinkers still seem to divide up their cultures into the same elements – subsistence, trade, social, ritual ... Right or wrong, these are general categories imposed by the archaeologist on to particular cultures. And, of course, they are (in this argument) specifically Western, bourgeois categories.

Now it may be that we should be trying to understand culture from the inside. To clarify, if we want to understand why cultures changed in the past in may be necessary to understand something of 'their' worldview, 'their' ideas of how the world works. Now their ideas may not have divided the world up into such neat little blocks, or they may have divided the world up into different blocks.

This distinction between 'outside' and 'inside' views of a culture is one that is made time and time again in different areas of the social sciences. The anthropologist Marvin Harris describes such a distinction in terms of *emic* (inside) and *etic* (outside); sociologists talk of a distinction between *behaviour* (what can be objectively observed) and *action* (what the behaviour means to the participants). The argument that it is necessary to look at 'their' view of 'their' world is one that is central to 'interpretive' and 'postprocessual' views of archaeology.

Processual Thinking Modified

The force of the criticisms raised above was felt greatly by most scholars, and has meant that more monolithic and hard-line forms of systemic and processual thought held less and less popularity in archaeology after the early 1980s. Most current versions of processual thinking are rather modified, and have developed partly in response to some of the issues raised above.

In practice, two responses can be taken:

1   Some archaeologists claim to reject all models of culture process and have tried to adopt entirely different ways of thinking about societies (most obviously within 'postprocessual' approaches; see chapter 7). In this attempt they have followed the lead of sociologists, most notably Anthony Giddens. They have managed to distance themselves from thinking in terms of cultural process with varying success.

2   Others have tried to separate modified, looser versions of processual thinking from much of the intellectual and historical 'baggage' of functionalism. Several propositions are involved here:

(a)   We can separate functional explanation from the sins of functionalism as described above.

(b)   Processual models of culture can incorporate conflict and contradiction within their parameters.

(c)   If (b) holds, then change from *within* the cultural system can be understood and fruitfully explored in processual terms. We don't need to rely on an external 'kick' as Flannery did in his early work; we might, for example, look for class or gender inequality within a culture, and view that as a source of tension that leads to transformation. Processual models can therefore, on this argument, develop understandings of very sudden transformations, and are correspondingly less dependent on ideas of adaptation to an external environment to explain where change comes from.

(d)   We can look at cognitive factors ('their' view of 'their' world) within a processual model, either by modelling 'cognition' as a separate subsystem or by some other means. 'Cognitive archaeology' will be further discussed in the next chapter.

As a result, processual thinking in archaeology, particularly in North America, has moved on from a view of cultural systems as purely or primarily adaptive to an external environment, and as monolithic entities that are characterized by harmony and homeostasis. Three more contemporary trends can be distinguished.

(1)   First, a move away from purely or primarily adaptive models, and an exploration of conflict. Elizabeth Brumfiel expressed this move in processual thinking well in the title of her review essay: 'Breaking and entering the ecosystem – gender, class and faction steal the show' (1992).

In this view, culture process remains central as a way of thinking about past cultural systems. However, there are many qualifications from earlier versions. In particular, we can look at conflict and competition between different elements within the cultural whole. The dimensions of such conflict and competition include political and social faction, class, gender, and other social groups. Conflict of this kind can lead not to homeostasis but to social transformation. So instead of seeing systems as monolithic, a stress on ideas such as heterarchy and factional competition leads us towards a much more dynamic idea of systemic change – and further, one that is much less dependent on ideas of adaptation.

I will consider this work further in chapter 9, as it can also be considered as a logical outgrowth of developments in thinking about cultural evolution and early state societies. It also owes a great deal to developments in Marxist thought, and particularly a Marxist view of political economy.

(2)   'World systems theory' claims to unite elements of systemic and Marxist thought. We shall discuss Marxism in the next chapter, but Marxist models clearly involve many of the factors that early systems thinking in archaeology had been criticized for ignoring: class conflict, contradiction, inequality, exploitation.

World systems theory had its origins in the analysis of the origins of modern capitalism; it is associated with the work of Emmanuel Wallerstein. Wallerstein pointed out that capitalist social formations involved more than the nation-states of Western Europe. Rather, if we wanted to understand how capitalism emerged in the fifteenth, sixteenth and seventeenth centuries, we had to look at the way different societies across the globe were brought together into a single *world system*. Such a system had a *core*, in this case of the nascent capitalist states of early modern Europe, and a *periphery*, the other ends of the developing trade routes with Africa, Asia and the Americas. Core and periphery were related through trading networks that had social implications at each end of the link: thus capitalist development in Europe was transformed through the arrival of increased quantities of gold and of traded commodities, while 'native' societies changed rapidly, often developing new élites and nascent states, partly in response to the influx of European goods. The entire globe, taken as a whole, could be modelled systemically, with stress on the interdependence between core and periphery, so that change in one could be seen to lead to change in the other, often many thousands of miles away. The social systems of both were understood by reference to functional linkages.

Archaeologists have suggested that we can use a world systems model to explain a variety of ancient social networks. In particular, they have looked at the interaction and networks of dependence between core state societies and peripheral pre-state societies in a variety of contexts (Bronze and Iron Age Europe, pre-Hispanic Central America, for example). Santley and Alexander, for example, develop a generalizing typology of units (the 'dendritic political economy', the 'hegemonic empire', the 'territorial empire') and then a set of processes involved in transformation (disenfranchisement, population redistribution, labour organization and power).

(3)   Simulation and mathematical modelling: from the late 1970s onwards Renfrew and others argued that systems could be simulated on computers, and that moreover we could build chance, historical contingency and human decision-making into these models. This led in turn to an interest in new models of the natural world being produced by natural scientists. For example, chaos theory looks at how apparently random and small-scale phenomena can trigger much larger patterns. By analogy, many systemic thinkers have explored *stochastic* models (that is, models with elements of chance or random variation built into them) and asked how systems might be set off on different trajectories by *contingent* or chance events.

These strands of thought are very different one from another, but what is certain is that over the last 30 years there has been a 'softening' of processual thinking. Cultural systems are no longer seen as monolithic structures, and contingency and historical accident is allowed for; room has been made for cognition (see next chapter); and heterarchy and conflict have become popular buzz-words.

However, I want to stress that an idea of process remains central and even foundational to much academic archaeology, particularly in North America; in later chapters, I shall argue that much of 'postprocessual' archaeology is much more dependent on concepts of culture process than many of its proponents care to admit.

Culture, Process and the Individual

Stop – you've finished before discussing the most important criticism of processual thinking of all. Human beings don't act like this. They're not just pawns in a system. They are irrational and unpredictable. Processual theory can never work because human actions are random. You can't fit human beings with all their idiosyncrasies and peculiarities into a model.

Ironically, the one criticism of processual thinking that is most popular is also the one that, in my view, is utterly misconceived.

Are human beings unpredictable? Almost certainly not, though we like to think so. Cupid is supposed to be blind, but the vast majority of us manage by some amazing coincidence to find partners of very similar ethnic and social origins to ourselves.

In any case, unless you are a methodological individualist (see Glossary), you cannot reduce the understanding of long-term social processes to what we do as individuals. This is a classic debate not just within archaeology, but within the human sciences as a whole.

Consider an example from the modern world, one examined by Emile Durkheim in a classic pioneering study in the social sciences: the suicide rate. The reasons why individuals commit suicide are as varied as they are tragic, but the overall rate of suicides within society as a whole rises and falls with other factors (such as the unemployment rate, whether the country is at peace or at war). A social scientist cannot predict individual suicides, but can, given sufficient data on contemporary social trends, predict rises and falls in the suicide rate, more often than not with a great deal of success. Consider also powerful individuals. Scholars may seek to explain events in terms of powerful or charismatic people – emperors or great leaders – but this always begs the question of where their power comes from, what makes their power possible.

If such a view works for the present, it is surely even stronger in prehistory, where archaeologists manifestly have to deal with trends and processes that span hundreds and even thousands of years, rhythms of time than are beyond the compass of any individual.

Western thought has an emotional attachment to the idea of 'the individual' that is simply not borne out by the reality of the world around us, and still less is a valid basis for thinking about the past. We can't say in advance whether individuals were or were not important in the past. Other cultures have had different ideas about individuality and the importance of the individual versus the community. Westerners may find some of these ideas strange, even disturbing or objectionable, but this is no excuse for taking the modern Western 'cult of the individual' as self-evident, or true for all times and all places.

There is a more sophisticated argument within much of contemporary archaeology, namely that we have to understand social *agency* and the individual subject. Pots are made by people, and I believe that the archaeological record is as much about the detritus of individual actions as it is about long-term aggregates or processes. There is also a moral or philosophical argument that 'freedom' is a meaningful term to use in historical analysis, but only in the presence of the absence of freedom, for example in discussions of slavery. But before we can consider such ideas, the Romantic notion of unqualified individual freedom has to be firmly squashed. It may sell Hollywood blockbusters (count the number of mentions the word 'freedom' gets in *Braveheart*) but it is no basis for a serious analysis of past societies.

6

Thoughts and Ideologies

The last chapter mentioned in passing the question of how we might understand or account for the thoughts of people in the past. Looking at thoughts in the minds of people long dead is obviously very difficult. Is it necessary?

The question 'do we have to look at thoughts in the past?' is deceptively simple. It is embedded in deeper questions, for example:

1   What are 'thoughts', anyway? Are these conscious or unconscious? The major influence of Carl Jung and Sigmund Freud on the human sciences was to show that our conscious thoughts were only the tip of the iceberg; human mental processes were much deeper, more complex and more difficult to understand than the 'rational' surface. Should we take a 'deep' view of thoughts or a 'shallow' view?
2   Are all human beings united by the same cognitive systems, or are these diverse? To use some common jargon, are we justified in making *essentialist* claims about the nature of cognition, or is human knowledge of the world *socially constructed* and therefore variable between different societies? If it is variable, how can we be justified in making assumptions about the individual or group psychology of prehistoric cultures on the basis of studies of modern populations?

These are all very deep questions that are not exclusive to archaeology. They are questions that all 'human sciences' have had to grapple with in different forms.

In this chapter, I want to expand on this theme and look at some of the ways theory in the human sciences at large has coped with this problem. These themes are, first, the influence of the structuralist and semiotic traditions of thought, second, the influence of Marxism, and third, the move towards cognitive approaches.

Looking at Thoughts

Do we really have to look at cognition, at thoughts? Many would say 'No'. A large number of positivists both within archaeology and within the human sciences in general argue that you can never test thoughts. They give two reasons:

1   You can never scientifically verify what is between someone's ears; in archaeology, we can never go back to talk to the long-dead people who created the monuments and artefacts that we study. Thoughts are therefore untestable. They are consequently beyond the domain of Science. This is a common view of some though not all positivists.
2   We don't study human actions, we study the archaeological record – a mute collection of stones and bones, matter arranged in time and space (back to figure 2.1). We can explain what we see in terms of past cultural systems; their dynamics of change, how they were adapted to their environment. We do not need to do this with direct reference to mental factors. Reference to mental factors would involve the error of mentalist explanation in any case (see chapter 5). Forms of this argument have been advanced by Binford and others.

Many traditional archaeologists also argue that it is difficult if not impossible to use the archaeological record to recover past beliefs. Archaeologists like Christopher Hawkes argued for seven levels of archaeological inference ranging from the relatively straightforward to the very difficult. Archaeological material, said Hawkes, could be used with reasonable security to tell us about technology in the past. Economic inferences were more difficult; inferences about cultural and religious life were almost impossible except in exceptional circumstances. This view of the limitations of archaeology was held with fanaticism by some:

> I was back in Devizes, along with a packed audience of several hundred people, to hear the principal living authority on Stonehenge, Professor Richard Atkinson, give a lecture... When this was done the chairman, the equally authoritative Professor Stuart Piggott, called for questions. There came some requests for various elucidations of technical points, which were given. Then a young man stood up at the back.
>
> 'Would Professor Atkinson care to say anything about the peoples who built the three main phases – their culture and religion?'
>
> He might as well have asked a synod of Methodist ministers whether they could consider publishing a new edition of De Sade's *120 Days of Sodom* ... All such speculation was futile, the wicked fellow was peremptorily told. Such information was strictly dependent on written records, the Stonehenge peoples

did not have writing, we knew nothing, we would never know anything; to speculate on such matters was not only totally unscientific, but far worse, it encouraged the lunatic fringe. In the slightly shocked silence that followed this icy douche ... Professor Piggott rose to announce that the lecture was at an end. No more questions. (Fowles 1980: 9–10)

Whatever orientation one takes, there are clearly immense difficulties in recovering thoughts. Behavioural psychologists argue that we can never 'know' what someone else is thinking in the present; we can only record their behaviour, which can be externally measured and observed. How much more difficult to recover the minds of women and men not just long dead, but members of an extinct culture, with an utterly different view of the world! Such a task is difficult enough for archaeologists of historic periods; prehistorians have to do so using material remains, with no documentary records to assist.

Why, then, should we be trying to get at past thoughts and beliefs? In my view, to argue about whether or not it is *difficult* to do so is to miss the point. It is simply *necessary*. I suggest there are three reasons for this.

(1) We all actually make assumptions about past thoughts whether we like it or not. Take, for example, a dry, straightforward typology of pots. When archaeologists classify decorations of a certain type together, they generally do so on the assumption that shared design must have something to do with shared meanings in the minds of the makers and the users of the pots, for example ideas of *zeitgeist* mentioned in Chapter 5.

What a lot of 'atheoretical' archaeologists do in practice is assert that we can never recover past thoughts, but do so in practice by slipping assumptions about mental attitudes back into their arguments as 'common sense'. Thus, for example, putting fireplaces and chimney-stacks in houses rather than rely on open hearths is common sense because it makes the house warmer, less full of smoke, more 'comfortable'. The problem with such arguments is that they depend on assumptions about what is 'natural' or 'normal' in human beings: in this example, a desire for domestic comfort is assumed as 'natural'. It is 'common sense', then, to satisfy those desires. These assumptions tend to fall apart when closely examined, since one can always point to the diversity of human practice; in particular, different ethnographic examples where the practice is not 'normal' or 'natural'.

The problem with common sense in this context is that what is 'common sense' to 'us' may not have been common sense to 'them'. Anthropologists study other cultures in the present that have very different cultural attitudes. For the Azande, when some unfortunate accident occurs, it is common sense to go to a witch-doctor or diviner to find out who was responsible for the magic behind it. It is logical to assume that other cultures in the past may have had other common senses.

Lurking in the wings behind the common-sense argument are implicit beliefs in *essentialism* and *ethnocentrism*. Essentialism is the belief that there are certain attitudes or emotions (such as the desire for privacy, for domestic comfort, or the sex drive) that are 'natural' or biologically endowed, either to humans in general or to a specific sex. Thus the statement 'in prehistory, men must have been more warlike than women as they lacked the mothering instinct' is an *essentialist* statement since it assumes that 'the mothering instinct' is endowed naturally or biologically to all women. Now there may or may not be certain 'human universals' of this kind; that is a matter for debate; I am sceptical about most of the possible candidates. Whatever the case, however, such essentialist statements need to be argued through rather than simply assumed.

Ethnocentrism is the belief that the values and attitudes of one's own culture are normal and universal. Thus an assumption that, for example, witchcraft belief is 'irrational' is ethnocentric, since it assumes that Western logic is the only form of rationality around. Belief in witchcraft must therefore be irrational since it fails to satisfy the criteria of Western logic. (Of course, Western logic fails to satisfy the criteria of Azande witch doctors.) Again, belief in the human desire for privacy is ethnocentric, since it assumes that the high stress on the individual and hence his or her right to privacy in Western society is universally normal and natural.

(2)　Any archaeologist working outside the deeper recesses of prehistory (that is, before ethnohistorically attested, protoliterate or literate societies) has to deal with evidence that is strictly 'historical' in nature; that is, with documentary or textual evidence in some form. But such documents are nothing if not statements of thoughts – however mundane or 'obvious' those thoughts are. If we are therefore going to relate archaeological to documentary evidence, then, some critical attention must be given to the mental attitudes and ideas that played their part in producing that evidence.

(3)　There is a philosophical point to do with the way we study human societies. As we explored in the last chapter, it is almost impossible to describe human behaviour without referring to mental concepts. Imagine trying to describe – to get a third person to 'understand' – the actions of a woman withdrawing money from a bank solely with reference to physical movements and actions. This is a point made most elegantly by one of my favourite and most entertaining writers, the sociologist Erving Goffman:

> Take … an act which is tolerably clear: a man driving through a red light. What is he doing? [Goffman lists 24 different reasons, including] 1. Where he comes from they have signs, not lights. 2. The daylight was bad and he couldn't see. 3. He's lately become colour-blind. 4. He was late for work.

5. His wife is giving birth in the back seat and he'd like to get to a hospital.
6. The bank robber in the front seat is holding a gun on him and has told him to
run the light ... 15. He's an inspector testing the vigilance of the cops on duty
... 22. He was drunk, high. 23. His mother has a lamentable occupation, and
he has a psychiatrically certifiable compulsivity with regard to red lights ...'
[He concludes]: So our man has passed through a red light. But at his hear-
ing when the judge asks him what he was doing running a red light, he will
provide an argument as to what was really happening. *Obviously, what makes
driving through a red light a discernible, isolable event is that a rule stipulated
in regard to the light was broken. The objective 'fact', then, must be as variable as is the individual's possible relation to the rule.* (Goffman 1971: 132;
italics mine. Note in passing that we understand the action by reference to its
context, a point developed in the next chapter.)

The belief that thoughts and ideas are more important than the material
world is called *idealism*. Historically, the idealist tradition of philosophy is
a long one, including the names of such philosophers as Plato, Vico, Berkeley,
Kant, Descartes and Hegel, through to the linguist Ferdinand de Saussure
and anthropologist Claude Lévi-Strauss. Paradoxically, although it stresses
the importance of thoughts and concepts, a belief in idealism can lead to a
very conservative theoretical position. Because thoughts in the idealist view
are very important but also very difficult to get at, all the archaeologist can
legitimately do is describe and classify:

> Do you wish to understand the true history of a Neolithic Ligurian or Sicilian?
> Try, if you can, to become a Neolithic Ligurian or Sicilian in your mind. If you
> cannot do that, or do not care to, content yourself with describing and arrang-
> ing in series the skulls, implements, and drawings which have been found
> belonging to these peoples. (Benedotto Croce, 1917, *Theory and History of
> Historiography*, trans. R.G. Collingwood 1921: 135)

The idealist philosophical tradition has been profoundly influential in continental Europe, particularly on traditions of French and Italian archaeology. Postprocessual archaeology was not claimed to be an idealist philosophy
by its advocates, but it was profoundly influenced by idealist notions.

The rest of this chapter will examine three bodies of thought that archaeologists have used to approach the question of thoughts: structuralism, Marxism,
and 'cognitive' approaches.

Structuralism

One of the key ways in which idealism has affected archaeological thought
is via the school of thought termed structuralism. Like both functionalism
and Marxism, this theoretical current has developed and changed as a

critical tradition over the years. It has few adherents in its original, classical form today, but (like systems theory) has had such a profound influence on archaeological thought that it cannot be ignored. Like Marxism also, structuralism is a term much misused and abused, referring more to a vague impression of pretentious Paris intellectuals sitting in cafes on the Rive Gauche than a given set of ideas. I am going to go back to the roots of structuralism so that its present influence can be more easily understood.

For functionalists, culture is like an organism, different parts of the body/ society performing different functions and the whole adapted to its environment. For structuralists, culture is *like language.*

Structuralism was originally a body of thought developed in linguistics by Ferdinand de Saussure. The most important point for our purposes is to observe that for Saussure, *language is composed of hidden rules* that we use but don't articulate. As I write and you read this sentence, I use a set of grammatical rules to compose my text. You know that set as well. Your knowledge of that set of rules enables you to decode, to 'read' what I write. You can do this even though each sentence that I produce is unique; each sentence is one that has never been composed before in the history of the English language. Indeed, I can generate a theoretically infinite set of different statements or sentences from a fairly simple set of grammatical rules.

Both of us, however, understands those rules at a deep, *implicit* rather than surface, *explicit* level. We both have a pretty hazy idea of what a gerund or a subjunctive clause is. Neither of us puts those rules 'into words' though we 'know' and use them constantly and habitually, and in general we both get them right. (Otherwise, if we did not get them right, we would not be able to decode each other's utterances and understand each other.)

In short, the rules that govern language are *hidden*, deep inside the human brain. If you want to explain the different forms of language, then, you need to refer to the hidden (cognitive) rules that generate sentences.

Archaeologists influenced by structuralism suggest that the same is true of the material things that we find in the archaeological record. They see artefacts as another expression of human culture in general. If you want to explain human culture, then, you need to uncover the hidden (cognitive) rules that generate cultural forms.

Structural models have been used to produce classifications of different kinds of archaeological material. Henry Glassie, for example, used the analogy of 'grammar' to examine the layout of ordinary houses in eighteenth-century Virginia. He proposed that ordinary people designed these houses by taking a series of basic spatial units and applying a system of grammatical rules to those units to produce different house plans. He called this scheme a *transformational grammar*: that is, it described the way in which units were transformed through a series of cognitive stages into houses. Similar exercises have been performed for other classes of material, for example Leroi-Gourhan's work on Palaeolithic cave art and schemes of pottery decoration.

But the implications of structuralism are deeper than simply offering tools for fresh classifications. So whereas a processual thinker's immediate instinct might be to ask 'How does this social practice function within the culture as a whole? And how does this help the cultural system to work, to be better adapted, within a wider environment?', the structuralist will ask 'What are the underlying rules governing this structure? And what do those rules tell us about the way this culture sees the world?' For functionalists, culture is fundamentally *adaptive*, a coping device; for structuralists, culture is fundamentally *expressive*, a system of (hidden, cognitive) meanings.

Marxism

It is impossible at the present time to write history without using a whole range of concepts directly or indirectly linked to Marx's thought and situating oneself within a horizon of thought which has been defined and described by Marx. One might even wonder what difference there could ultimately be between being an historian and being a Marxist. (Foucault 1980: 53)

A second school of thought that has had a profound effect on archaeological thought is that of Marxism. Like structuralism, Marxism has developed almost beyond recognition since its original formulation and development by Karl Marx in the nineteenth century. I want to highlight a very few aspects of Marxist thought that are of relevance to archaeological theory.

In its original form, Marxism is a *materialist* philosophy. That is, it proposes that material things are more important than ideas. If so, then human history is about the growth of human productive power, the growing human ability as history unfolds to produce material things: Gerry Cohen suggests that 'history is, fundamentally, the growth of human productive power, and forms of society rise and fall accordingly as they enable or impede that growth' (Cohen 1978: x). In Karl Marx's own phrase, humans are what they do rather than what they think: 'it is not the consciousness of men that determines their being, but on the contrary, their social being that determines their consciousness' (cited in McClellan 1977: 389).

At any time, Marxists argue, people produce things in a certain distinctive way, which Marx calls the mode of production. Marxists have spoken of 'tribal', Asiatic, Ancient, feudal and capitalist modes of production among others. The ancient mode of production, to take one example, is distinctive for Marx because it relies on slave labour at its base, whereas feudalism depends on the labour of unfree peasants or 'serfs' tied to the land. Each different mode of production results in a different kind of class antagonism: in ancient societies between slave and master, in feudalism between peasant and feudal landlord, in capitalism between proletarian and bourgeois.

The mode of production, Marx argues, can be split into the *forces of production*, that is the raw materials, apparatus, labour power, and the social *relations of production*. For example, the forces of production in capitalist society consist of the machines and hardware of the factories, while the relations comprise the factory system – the division into workforce and management.

For Marx, there will always be antagonism and conflict between these two elements: 'the forces of production, the state of society, and consciousness, can and must come into contradiction with one another, because the division of labour implies the ... fact that intellectual and moral activity – enjoyment and labour, production and consumption – devolve on different individuals, and the only possibility of their not coming into contradiction lies in the negation in its turn of the division of labour'. For this and other reasons, there will always be conflict at the heart of human societies. Contradictions and class antagonisms will tear at the heart of any social formation, developing slowly or quickly in different circumstances. Eventually, however, they will bring the whole structure crashing down, and a new social formation will rise on its ruins.

This 'classical' model has been much criticized; the road from classical to modern Marxism is too long to pursue here. I do want to pick out two key points that emerge from this account of classical Marxism, however, that have direct relevance to the development of archaeological thought:

(1) Marx's account, if it works, provides a *scientific basis to communism*, or more loosely, in this later time, *a scientific basis to political assertions about a more just society*. In this sense classical Marxism shares many parallels with the belief in a positivistic basis to Science that was discussed in chapter 3. Contrary to positivism, however, Marx argues forcefully that *intellectuals cannot divorce academic thought from political action*.

Archaeologists influenced by Marxism, then, have seen a close link between archaeology and politics. They have seen archaeological practice and interpretations as partly or wholly political in nature, and in turn have often seen their own archaeological work as in part a wider political exercise. And they argue that to try to deny this is to bury one's head in the sand.

(2) The process of historical change in the Marxist model is *dialectical*. A dialectical model is one that depends on the development of contradictions and conflict within an entire social formation or totality. These contradictions can only be understood within that total social formation. For example, the terms 'peasant' and 'landlord' do not have the same meaning regardless of time and place. We can only define and understand peasant

and landlord classes within a total understanding of the feudal social formation. When that formation breaks down, it leads to a completely new formation and the development in their turn of new conflicts.

A dialectical model of social process contrasts with other models of change. In culture history, and earlier forms of systems thinking, change is often presented as a smooth process of accretion and adaptation. In place of this, a dialectical model stresses contradiction and conflict – it was partly as a result of the influence of Marxist concepts that systems thinking came to be modified as we traced in the last chapter. The dialectical model also leads us to question social categories and definitions that claim to be true for all times and all places.

Marxism has thus led archaeologists to question either/or oppositions such as subjectivity and objectivity. They point out that such terms only oppose each other within a total framework, and it is that total framework that they seek to question and transform.

As a result, Marxism has had a wide and pervasive influence on different archaeological traditions around the world. 'Latin American social archae-ology' uses a Marxist analytical framework to understand social forma-tions, and insists on an engagement with social justice issues. It will be considered in chapter 9.

In the old Soviet Russia and other areas of eastern Europe, Marxism was an official orthodoxy until the break-up of the old Stalinist regimes at the end of the 1980s. In many cases, the influence of Marxism was shallow, being confined to ritualized acknowledgement in a Preface or introduction before a more orthodox descriptive or culture-historical approach being taken in the text. Ironically, since the fall of Communism in eastern Europe, there has been more fruitful and sustained examples of analyses informed by Marxist thought from these countries.

Marxism has also been a profound influence on Mediterranean archaeol-ogy, though its influence is not always explicitly laid out in the literature. For example, there is an ongoing debate over the origins of Rome and its transformation from a small protohistoric village into an Imperial city and the hub of the Roman Empire. A major figure in the archaeology of Roman Italy has been Andrea Carandini, who developed an interpretation of the rise of Rome that was directly influenced by Marxist ideas. Subsequent debate over this interpretation was, in part, an implicitly theoretical debate over the utility of these ideas and their alternatives.

Ideology

Later Marxists (or 'neo-Marxists'), particularly those from different tradi-tions in western Europe, have focused attention on the role of *ideology* in this model. For Marx, the forces and relations of production were the 'infrastructure', the heart of the system: the political and legal system sat on top of this, along with a set of ideological beliefs. In a simple view, while social foundations are creaking and society becomes increasingly unequal and unjust, people's beliefs act to 'paper over the cracks', to make the existing system appear legitimate.

'Vulgar' ideology is obvious: in our society, one might cite flag-waving, advertising, appeals to patriotism, motherhood and apple pie. But Marxists believe ideology also works on a far more subtle level than this. In particular, ideology:

1   naturalizes; that is, it makes the existing social order with all its inequalities appear timeless, God-given, 'just scientific fact', or without any conceivable alternative;
2   makes interests that are sectional (for example, the economic wellbeing of the upper classes) appear universal (of benefit to everyone); and
3   masks what is 'really going on', for example by denying that social or economic inequalities exist.

To take a straightforward (and therefore overly simplistic, 'vulgar' and easily decoded) example, a Marxist would argue that we only have to open the pages of most newspapers to see ideology at work ('competition and the rules of the free market are not arbitrary human constructions that can be changed, they are out there in nature; look at how cold, wet, miserable life was in the Middle Ages, in other words, before the benefits of capitalism'). Sectional interests are presented as universal (wage rises are presented as 'harming the nation' rather than just harming the profits accruing to the wealthy capitalists). An ideology of equality ('anyone can become President, everyone is equal under the law, I want to build a classless society') masks what Marxists see as very real divisions and inequalities in gender and wealth.

This interest in ideology has led to the detailed exploration of how ideology works, and a stress on the unmasking of the relations behind ideology. Paradoxically, then, Marxism started as a materialist model, but has ended up influencing Anglo-American archaeology through its analysis of ideological beliefs and practices. This move away from materialism is one of the key points behind the Frankfurt School of *critical theory*. The Frankfurt School, most famously in the work of Jürgen Habermas, sought to look behind the mask of ideology, to show how modern Western systems of belief were not neutral or objective, but actually ideological constructions that legitimated modern capitalism. It aimed to emancipate ordinary people and promote democractic values by heightening consciousness of the power and pervasiveness of ideology.

Of course, interest in ideology in archaeology has two aspects. One can look at ideology in the past, how for example a particular belief system legitimated the position of an élite in ancient societies. But one can also look at the present – how archaeological writing is itself ideological. For example, Bruce Trigger has written extensively on how different interpretations of North American prehistory served to ideologically portray Native American cultures as backward and unchanging.

Cognitive Archaeology

A third body of thought, developed largely by archaeologists themselves, has emerged in the last 20 years: that of 'cognitive archaeology'. Cognitive archaeology aims to 'develop a secure methodology by which we can hope to learn how the minds of the ancient communities in question worked and the manner in which that working shaped their actions' (Renfrew 2005: 41). Cognitive archaeologists often describe themselves as working within the general assumptions and framework of processualism. Consequently, much of this work describes itself as *cognitive-processualism* by its advocates.

These authors look at 'mind' in two ways. First, cognitive archaeologists are interested in human origins, and specifically the role of cognitive development in the evolutionary origins and development of hominids. For example, archaeologists have asked about possible correlates in the archaeological record for the development of language, such as the development of more complex *chaines operatoires* in the production of stone tools. This work has close links with the application of Darwinian models to archaeology, in that it deals with a process that is at least in part about the biological development of species, and uses insights and observations from evolutionary psychology (see chapter 10).

The second interest is in cognitive processes in human societies after the emergence of our own species, *Homo sapiens sapiens*. Renfrew and Zubrow have argued that, for example, we can identify religious or cult behaviour in the archaeological record. They have suggested that there is no contradiction between a broadly scientific view of archaeological theory and an insistence that we need to look at cognition. Kent Flannery and Joyce Marcus, for example, have looked at functional linkages between the 'ideological subsystem' and other areas of cultural subsystems, and stressed the compatibility of their work with subsistence and settlement analysis:

> Our own first effort [in cognitive archaeology: Flannery and Marcus 1976] was an attempt to understand the ancient Zapotec Indians more fully by combining their cosmological beliefs with a more traditional analysis of their subsistence and settlement. ... We simply tried to show that one could explain

a higher proportion of ancient Zapotec subsistence behaviour if, instead of restricting oneself to a study of agricultural plants and irrigation canals, one took into account what was known of Zapotec notions about the relationships of lightning, rain, blood sacrifice, and the 'satisfizing ethic'. We also stressed that we could only do so because the 16th-century Spanish eyewitness accounts of the Zapotec were so rich. (Flannery and Marcus 1993: 260)

Flannery and Marcus identify the study of cosmology, religion, ideology and iconography as legitimate areas of cognitive analysis, stressing that all such work must be empirically grounded. Again, Steven Mithen has talked of 'thoughtful foragers' – looking at how we might model the decision-making processes of hunters and gatherers within an adaptive framework, yielding a range of cognitive inferences (Mithen 1990: see also chapter 10, this volume).

The argument of all these authors is that we can look at thoughts while retaining the essential components of a processual approach: belief in scientific objectivity and 'testing'. But other archaeologists have claimed that the need to look at thoughts has led them to question the very basis of processual archaeology, as we will see in the next chapter.

> *All this is very interesting, but we've heard very little in this chapter about archaeology. How, precisely, do the different views lead to concretely different archaeological explanations?*

I'll be discussing some more practical examples in the next chapter, but here is an 'interim summary' for the time being.

For many in the processual tradition, the artefacts we find are evidence of different parts of a cultural system that existed in the past. For some, artefacts form a *fossil record* of human behaviour. Many processualists argue that as we cannot see thoughts scientifically, so we can't explain artefacts in terms of the ideas in the minds of the makers – though following Flannery and Marcus, we can include 'cognitive variables' in our analyses, if used with caution. Instead, we look at different parts of past cultural systems and the links between them. Processualists claim to have the ability to test between alternative hypotheses about the way those systems worked through the development of middle-range theory.

For structuralists, artefacts are evidence of systems of belief in the broadest sense, evidence of 'mind-sets' or 'worldviews'. Just as language is structured by rules that remain hidden, so is material culture. Structuralists look at oppositions in the particular form of artefacts, the placing of artefacts within graves, for ideas about the constitution of gender, oppositions between nature and culture, and so on. Since we can never prove the existence of hidden rules, this tradition suggests that we can never really 'test' any single interpretation of the past; there is a tendency towards developing multiple, complex interpretations rather than trying to reduce culture to one single pattern.

Marxists look for contradictions and inequalities in culture. For example, is burial practice legitimating or masking what happens in life? Marxists ask: how does the belief or worldview expressed by this piece of material culture relate to what is really going on? For example, does an egalitarian burial practice mask inequalities in society?

Conclusion

In the second part of this chapter, I have picked out developments within three schools of thought within social theory as a whole – Marxism, structuralism and cognitive archaeology. I could have looked at other profoundly influential movements treated elsewhere in this book (feminism, the reaction against unilinear social evolution). These three movements, however, give some flavour of the intellectual currents that came to influence archaeological theory in the 1980s.

Marxism gives us an interest in conflict and contradiction, a stress on ideology, an insistence that academic discourse is fundamentally also political discourse in the present, and a model of structure and agency. Structuralism gives us an interest in the hidden workings of language, an interest in cultural meanings and in culture as expressive. Cognitive archaeology, though fully developed as a body of theory more recently than the 1980s, originated in part as an insistence that looking at thoughts is not just an admissible scholarly activity, but a central part of the archaeological endeavour.

All these themes were taken up into a group of new theoretical strands in the 1980s, that came to be known collectively as 'postprocessual archaeology'.

7

Postprocessual and Interpretive Archaeologies

'Postprocessual archaeology' grew out of a very specific context that it is important to understand. Part of that context within the human sciences as a whole – developments in structuralism and Marxism – was presented in the last chapter. Now, I want to look briefly at developments *within* archaeology in the 1980s.

In the late 1970s and early 1980s, a number of archaeologists became increasingly dissatisfied with the direction archaeology was taking. In particular, they pointed to the need to address cognitive factors, the difficulties of positivist epistemology, and the problems with developing middle-range theory – issues dealt with in chapters 3 to 6.

One such archaeologist was Ian Hodder, and his intellectual development epitomizes this shift in many ways. Hodder's early work was very much within a processual mould. Hodder was heavily influenced by the 'New Geography' and the work of New Archaeologist David Clarke on spatial models in archaeology. Hodder used statistics and computer simulation to develop a series of spatial models, particularly relating to trade, markets and urbanization in Iron Age and Roman Britain. This period was seen very much as an evolving system, with trade and urbanism being linked as part of an overall process of 'Romanization'.

But as the research progressed Hodder became more and more doubtful that such models and simulations did really 'test' or 'prove' anything. The same pattern or trace in the archaeological record, for example a pottery distribution or network of urban centres, could be produced by a range of different simulated processes. Therefore, a given pattern in the archaeological record could be satisfactorily interpreted or explained in different ways, with reference to a number of different possible processes. Hodder felt that there was no way to test absolutely between these alternatives. This is often referred to in subsequent literature as a problem of *equifinality*.

A reading of Hodder and Orton's *Spatial Analysis in Archaeology*, published in 1976, shows this shift. In case after case – attempting to simulate trade patterns and settlement systems using computers – Hodder and Orton showed how difficult it was to 'prove' or 'test' anything conclusively.

A good example was the study of goods used in prehistoric trade. Goods such as obsidian flakes or polished greenstone axes were often found on sites thousands of kilometres from the original source of the raw material. Such finds clearly represented trade or contact in some form, but ambitious New Archaeologists wanted to go further than this. Renfrew and others had suggested that different forms of trade would leave different traces in the archaeological record. If, for example, 'down-the-line' exchange was occurring, with community A collecting the material at source before giving community B half, then community B keeping half and handing half on ... then different quantities of traded material would be present in site assemblages than if everyone was going back to source and making their own collation of material.

Hodder found that if 'down-the-line', directional or other modes of exchange were modelled by computer simulation, similar rather than different curves were produced. Different forms of process left the same archaeological trace: in other words, they were equifinal (figure 7.1).

Lessons also came out of Hodder's ethnoarchaeological work. Hodder realized that however many archaeological facts you collected on a computer, the only way to get a handle on what they meant in terms of past activities is to look at the relationship between pattern and process in the present. This, of course, was a similar and parallel observation to Binford's perception of the problems underlying the 'Mousterian debate' as discussed in chapter 4. Like Binford, Hodder decided to turn to studies of 'archaeology in the present' to try to establish correlations between behaviour in the present and archaeological patterning. So Hodder went out to East Africa to examine, among other themes, how real living 'cultures' could be mapped archaeologically, what factors affected refuse disposal, and so on.

What Hodder found, again in a variety of instances, was that to understand patterning on the ground it was necessary to refer to people's attitudes and beliefs. We looked at Hodder's work with the Nuba in chapter 4. This led him to:

1   a rejection of Binford's confidence in the ability of middle-range theory to act as a neutral arbiter between different explanations;
2   a belief in the importance of people's thoughts and symbolism, and with this a belief that cultures could not be viewed purely as adapting to an external environment: 'their' view of 'their' world was important;
3   a belief that material culture was actively manipulated by people; that is, that people used things in different ways as part of particular

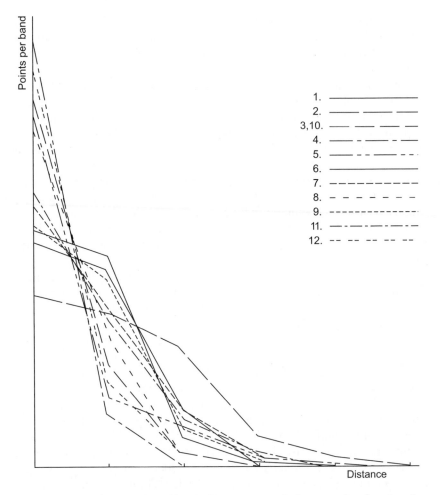

Figure 7.1 The results of Hodder and Orton's simulation exercise showing that 'different spatial processes can produce very similar fall-off curves', implying that 'this advises great caution in any attempt at interpretation' (Hodder and Orton 1976: figure 5.35 and p. 145

social strategies, rather than material things being a passive reflection of a set of rules.

How might we do archaeology in this way? Several theories dealing with 'thoughts', 'ideologies' or 'mind' were looked at in the previous chapter. In the early 1980s a new generation of students, many of whom were studying with Hodder at Cambridge, and others with Mark Leone as part of the

Archaeology in Annapolis project, turned to these theories. Many turned to structuralism as a way into understanding the mind. Others 'read around' Marxist and neo-Marxist texts and in particular critical theory. Others were influenced by feminist thinking, while others still looked at the writings of figures like Clifford Geertz in 'interpretative anthropology'. Together, these very diverse strands of thought coalesced into a very loose cluster of traditions that came to be known by both supporters and critics as 'postprocessual' or 'interpretive' archaeology.

Postprocessual Archaeology

There is no such thing as a 'postprocessual archaeologist'. Whenever I see the phrase 'the postprocessualists' used in the archaeological literature I expect some out-of-date and usually hostile over-generalization of theoretical attitudes to follow, and I am rarely disappointed. Just as New Archaeology was actually a very diverse set of concerns and ideas that coalesced around certain slogans, so the catch-all term 'postprocessual' conceals a great diversity of viewpoints and traditions. Indeed, 'postprocessualism' is better characterized as a historical term, referring, like New Archaeology, to a set of themes characteristic of a specific period that have evolved into a much broader and very diverse set of concerns and approaches.

So instead I shall try to characterize postprocessual thinking as a historical moment, a crystallization of concerns raised in the 1980s and 1990s, that has gone on to inform archaeological thought as a whole. I shall do so in the form of eight key statements that convey the *flavour* of postprocessual traditions, a way of looking at and thinking about the world. They should also indicate the debt owed to the intellectual movements described in the previous chapter.

(1)   *We reject a positivist view of science and the theory/data split. The data are always theory-laden.* Postprocessualists rejected the claims of Science as a unique form of knowledge, for the reasons advanced in chapter 3. Generally, they aligned themselves with other non-positivist conceptions of what science is or does, particularly *social constructivism* whether in its 'strong' or 'weak' forms.

Or to put it another way, postprocessualists did not argue that 'we should not test things'; rather, they suggested that in practice neither scientists nor archaeologists ever test things in ways that satisfy positivist criteria. They pointed out, for example, that Renfrew's 'testing' of his territorial model of megaliths in figure 2.7 was no such thing; the territories delineated are far from uniform, with many megaliths centred within totally unconvincing territories; archaeologists use a much looser set of criteria to agree (or disagree)

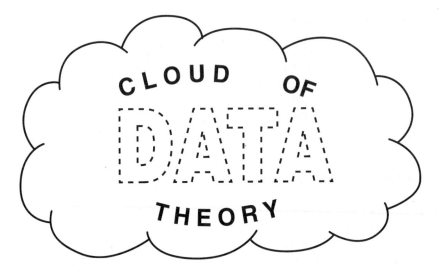

Figure 7.2   The relationship of theory and data in postprocessual archaeology; data exist, but are perceived fuzzily through a cloud of theory (contrast with figure 4.1)

that Renfrew's is a convincing argument. Postprocessualists suggested that archaeologists can never confront theory and data as two clearly independent and opposable categories; instead, we see data through a cloud of theory (figure 7.2; contrast with figure 4.1).

(2)   *Interpretation is always hermeneutic.* This is a variant on Proposition (1). Hermeneutics is the study of meanings. When archaeologists interpret things, it was argued, they do this by assigning meanings to them, meanings that it is assumed were also in the minds of the ancient peoples who made and used them.

   Postprocessualists argued that all archaeologists do this whether they overtly admit it or not. When the Italian philosopher Croce, cited in the last chapter, talks about simply describing and classifying and going no further, the response is that even these simple actions of description and classification are making assumptions about what was in the heads of Neolithic Sicilians. Postprocessualists deconstructed accounts of 'scientific' testing to show that even Binford and others implicitly assume meanings and values in the minds of ancient peoples. Hodder, for example, looked at the day-to-day process of reasoning during an archaeological excavation and argued that this is always a 'hermeneutic circle' regardless of whether or not the excavators consider themselves theorists, a proposition that he has developed and explored in the ongoing project at Çatal Höyük.

(3)   *We reject the opposition between material and ideal.* We have seen how normative and culture-historical approaches were rejected by processual archaeology as idealist, and how processual archaeology introduced a materialist emphasis. We have also looked at the idealist approach taken by structuralism, and at how Marxism moved away from a purely materialist base.

Postprocessualists claimed that we should reject the whole opposition between material and ideal in the first place. A good example is the idea of landscape. On the one hand, a materialist view of landscape tends to stress how it may be seen in terms of a set of resources, for example for hunter-gatherers or early farming groups. This leads one to turn, for example, to optimal foraging theory and other economic models for an understanding of how people exploited the landscape 'rationally'.

Postprocessualists suggested that landscapes are always viewed in different ways by different peoples. They rejected the 'rational' view of 'landscape-as-set-of-resources' as that of our own society and one that is ideologically loaded in its own way, loaded towards ideas of commodity and exploitation found in our own society. They suggested instead that ancient peoples would have had different views of what was 'real' in that landscape.

On the other hand, an exclusively idealist view of landscape does not work either. Postprocessualists stressed that such an understanding of landscape was not formed in the abstract, as an ethereal or detached set of preconceptions – that the way people moved around and used that landscape affected their understanding of it. They argued that ancient people's understanding of a landscape was not just a set of thoughts they happened to possess; everyday movements through the landscape, farming, domestic activities were all media through which understanding of the landscape was perpetuated and transformed.

Postprocessual archaeology therefore developed an interest in *practice* – for example the everyday rhythms of moving around a village or a landscape, the repetitive actions of daily rounds. It stressed that thoughts and ideas do not arise in the abstract, but through these practical activities and rounds.

(4)   *We need to look at thoughts and values in the past.* The most coherent example of this proposition was Hodder's advocacy of R. G. Collingwood's position of *historical idealism*. Collingwood was a philosopher by training, though he also practised history and archaeology. He argued that, in practice, historians always try to rethink the thoughts of the past. Take for example a classic historical question: why did the British naval leader Lord Nelson not change into plain dress before the naval battle of Trafalgar? (In the battle Nelson's medals and gaudy appearance made him a natural target for snipers, and he was fatally wounded.) Historians, says Collingwood, explain that it was considered dishonourable for a commanding officer to go below deck once battle had commenced; and that Nelson had no such

opportunity before the first shots were fired. So, argues Collingwood, when historians 'understand' or 'explain' Nelson's actions, they explore by definition the culture and assumptions of a British naval officer, they rethink his thoughts – in other words, they use *empathy*.

Hodder, following Collingwood, argued that archaeologists do this all the time no matter what theoretical pose they claim to adopt. When, for example, traditional archaeologists 'explained' the placement of Roman forts on the northern frontier of Britain, they did so in terms of an evolving military and political strategy – in other words, they ended up trying to rethink the past thoughts of Roman commanders and emperors. Again, the argument is that all archaeologists actually practise empathetic thinking whether they admit it or not.

(5)   *The individual is active*. Postprocessualists disliked the way they felt 'the individual' is lost in much archaeological theory. Individuals, they complained, were just pawns in some set of normative rules or adaptive systems or set of deep structures. They argued that all these different views of the world portrayed people as passive dupes who blindly follow social rules.

Instead, postprocessualists stressed *agency*. Agency is a term used to refer to the active strategies of individuals. In this view, women and men are not passively duped by the system around them. Some archaeologists borrowed the idea of a *recursive relationship between structure and agency* from the sociologist Anthony Giddens. Giddens suggested that there are social rules in the world around us, but that people understand these rules and manipulate them creatively rather than follow them passively. In so doing, they reinforce or alternatively transform the structure itself – the relationship is therefore recursive, or back-and-forth. Giddens's ideas on structure and agency are often referred to as *structuration theory*.

A different way of saying a similar thing was borrowed from the work of the French anthropologist Pierre Bourdieu. Bourdieu was reacting to the orthodox structuralist anthropology of his time, in which he felt humans were simply seen as passively acting out a set of structural rules. Bourdieu showed how in different ethnographic situations different actors had their own ideas about social rules and situations. He argued that we needed a theory of practice – a theory of how individual social actors actually practised living in, reproducing and transforming the culture around them.

In terms of interpreting the archaeological record, then, archaeologists need to look at rules that are not just followed, but are creatively manipulated by social actors. A good example of such manipulation comes from an unpublished anecdote from Hodder's work with the Nuba. In one area, there was a cultural belief that women were associated with the 'inside' of the domestic compound, and with the hearth; also, that women were 'polluting'. Women were therefore enjoined to dump the ash from the hearth inside the compound, rather than outside where it would pollute the male sphere. But Hodder once saw a woman self-consciously gathering up the hearth ash and dumping it outside, some way from the compound where all the men could see it. Now in so doing she was acknowledging that the rule existed, but deliberately breaking it. We cannot understand her action and the archaeological signature it produced without (a) understanding the cultural system of rules, but (b) understanding her position towards those rules.

(6)   *Material culture is like a text*. How do we understand the meanings of material culture? Think about the way you read any written text:

(a)   A text can mean different things to different people, and different people can read texts in different ways.

(b)   These meanings can be actively manipulated. Individuals do this with material culture in obvious and trivial ways, most obviously with clothes (we can define the formality of a meeting according to whether we put on a skirt or a jacket and tie, for example).

(c)   Such manipulation is often implicit and unspoken. Readers do not consciously think through grammatical rules as they read a text; similarly, we don't consciously think through rules governing material culture.

Consider for example the action of coming into a room without knocking; we might consider somebody doing this to be 'impolite'. At the same time we might deliberately break the rule, for example not knocking if we thought the room was 'our' space and we wanted to make that point to the person currently occupying it. Underlying this grammar of actions are assumptions and cultural values about the nature of space, rules of 'privacy', respect for the individual, and so on. We know what those rules are in our own society, and we manipulate them, though we do not consciously articulate them – we would not give a lecture on cultural anthropology to someone breaking that code, we would simply ask them to be more polite in future. Similar things go on with ancient material culture in general. Postprocessualists pointed to ethnoarchaeological studies in which the meanings of space in houses and compounds are rarely overtly discussed, for example, but which are manipulated by social actors with reference to certain rules.

(d)   If the meanings of material culture are really this complex, then its different meanings can never be definitively or finally tied down in some final 'conclusion', a single all-embracing analysis. Therefore there can be no 'final' reading of a text – each generation, and even each individual, brings fresh readings to a Shakespeare play, and each reading has its own validity. There can, in this view, also be no single 'right' or 'wrong' reading of a text in any absolute sense. A text can always be deconstructed and shown to contain hidden meanings opposite to those on the surface, as we have seen in the last chapter. Similarly, the meanings of a pottery design or a burial rite can never be finally tied down; there is no one 'right' or 'wrong' reading. Postprocessualists therefore encouraged experimentation with multiple interpretations, and denied the necessity of coming up with one final conclusion that explains 'everything'.

(e)   The meanings of a text are outside the control of its author – the well-known phrase coined by poststructuralists: the 'death of the author'. If a text is open to multiple interpretations, some of these may be quite at odds with the reading that the author might consciously prefer. We cannot therefore refer to the author's conscious intention in producing a text, whether literary or archaeological, as the only correct reading.

(7)   *We have to look at context.* How do archaeologists get at different meanings? Through, postprocessualists argued, looking at the context of the artefact or the practice being discussed. Let's return to our burial. We see that a particular grave good, say an axe, has a particular meaning through its context – where it is buried in the grave, the person it is buried with, the objects with which it is associated. We then widen that context and look at other axes in other graves from the same cemetery. We find that the axe is used differently in different contexts – it is associated with different assemblages, or is placed in a different position in the graves of women, men and children. We infer differences in meaning from these differences in context.

Archaeologists might then expand the argument contextually by looking at axes within our ancient culture generally – whether they are deposited in other contexts such as 'domestic' or 'refuse', or by looking at how they are used in domestic arenas. Gradually, a whole web of associations and placements for the axes is built up.

(8)   *The meanings we produce are always in the political present, and always have political resonance. Interpreting the past is always a political act.* If scientific neutrality is argued to be a myth, then statements about the past are never cool objective judgements detached from the real world. They are always made here, in the present, with all its heady and complicated, jumbled mixture of political and moral judgements.

Note that this does not mean that individual archaeologists are insincere in their attempts to be objective. If the meanings of a text are outside the control of its author, then readings of a text can proliferate in ways never consciously intended by its 'author'. It has been argued for example that some New Archaeologists working on Native American sites stressed that the value of their work lay in their ability to use this material to generate cross-cultural generalizations, that is statements that were true about all human populations in all places. By doing so, some argued, these archaeologists implicitly devalued the importance of looking at Native American tradition in its own right – the implicit message could be read as 'the only valid way to look at this archaeology is to stress its relevance to white people'. Such a 'reading' is not to argue that such archaeologists were being consciously racist; indeed, many such archaeologists were active campaigners for Native American rights.

Case Studies: Rock Art and Medieval Houses

In *Material Culture and Text: The Art of Ambiguity* Chris Tilley (1991) explored the interpretation of a group of rock carvings in Nämforsen in Sweden (figure 7.3). At this site, figures and motifs were pecked into the stones in the third millennium BC. This material was recorded by the Swedish archaeologist Hallström around the turn of the century; many of the carvings have now been destroyed. Tilley does not choose to organize his analysis in an orthodox way, with chapters on approach preceding those on material. He starts instead with a consideration of the material itself and of Hallström's recording of it, moves on to develop a grammar of design form, and then tries to understand that form through its 'structural logic'. Having developed such a logic and explored different ways in which that might relate to the communities that produced the figures, Tilley moves on to look at different ethnographic parallels, both of a direct historical nature with modern groups such as the Saami and of other traditions such as the Australian Aborigines.

Thus, two-thirds of the way in, we have reached the critical point of the book. Tilley has given us an interpretation of the meaning of the carvings. But in the final third of the book, he proceeds to deconstruct his own interpretation. Tilley refuses to give the reader one 'pat' answer to the meaning of the carvings: 'the point I am really trying to make is that these rock carvings invite a response from us. ... There is no fixed meaning and we must remember that images cannot in fact be reduced to words, "read"... I do not present a proper conclusion because this is an impossibility' (1991: 172). Tilley, then, has given us one final answer, but has then deconstructed that answer and shown that it is not final at all.

A second example comes from my own work: the interpretation of the rural house in the later medieval period in England (*c.* AD 1350–1530).

In southern and eastern England, thousands of ordinary houses built during this period still stand and are used as modern homes, albeit usually heavily modified. Their plan varies, but invariably has one central element: a large

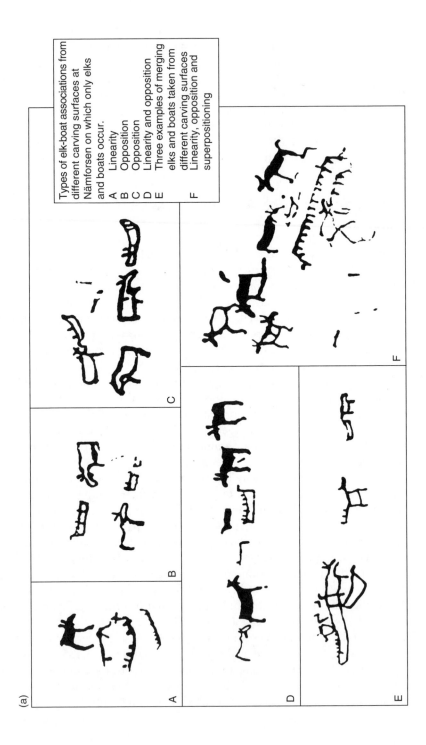

Types of elk-boat associations from different carving surfaces at Nämforsen on which only elks and boats occur.

A   Linearity
B   Opposition
C   Opposition
D   Linearity and opposition
E   Three examples of merging elks and boats taken from different carving surfaces
F   Linearity, opposition and superpositioning

(a)

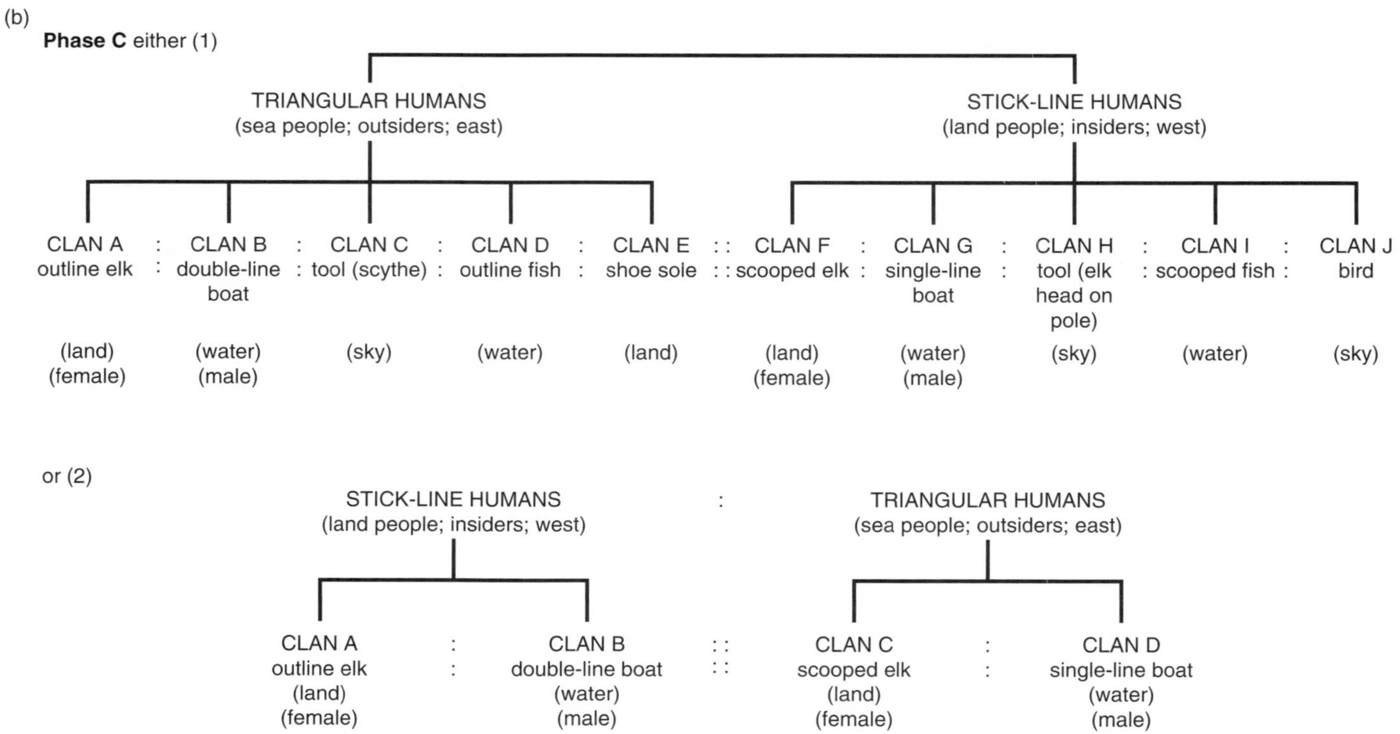

(b) **Phase C** either (1)

or (2)

Figure 7.3 (a) Carvings from Nämforsen, (b) part of Tilley's structural scheme for interpreting the carvings

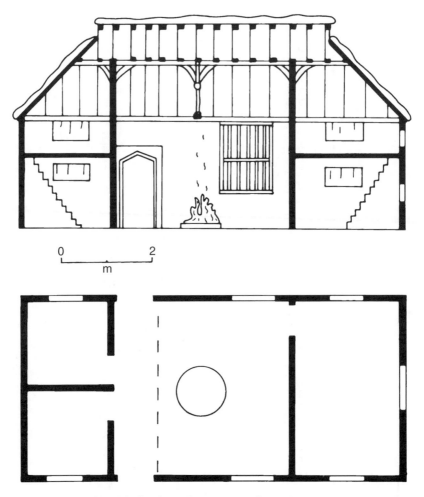

Figure 7.4   A medieval hall (after Johnson 1989: figure 2)

hall or central room, open to the roof. This room was usually heated by a central open hearth, the smoke rising to and dispersing in the rafters and thatched roof (figure 7.4).

Traditional archaeologists and historians had done much work identifying these buildings and assigning dates to them, often on the basis of technological, stylistic and typological features. We knew much also about who lived in them. Such houses had been built by socially middling groups – tenant farmers, often combining farming with rural industry, particularly cloth production. We had analysed the technology and building practices embodied in the houses – the carpentry and framing techniques. Much work had also been done on the economic background to these houses – how and why such non-élite groups could afford a substantial, permanent house for the first time.

These questions were interesting, but I wanted to ask: why was the hall the *form* that it was and what *meanings* did that form have for those that built and lived in it? Many previous writers had claimed that the hall was simply a matter of common sense: the openness to the roof space was needed to allow smoke from the open fire to disperse among the rafters. I felt this was not the whole story – chimneys had been known in this society and used at upper social levels in buildings like medieval castles and palaces for several centuries. The peasants occupying such houses were wealthy enough to afford chimney-stacks if they so desired; they simply chose not to have them.

The hall was an open space, but was divided into upper and lower ends by a series of architectural features. The doors were symmetrically placed at the colder, draughtier, 'lower' end, which also offered access to 'service' rooms. At the other, 'upper' end there were often fittings for a raised chair or bench to seat the master and wife; the area was lit by a large window. The bay in the upper end was often one rather longer than that in the lower; the bench at the upper end was fixed by pegs to the wall.

It was easy enough to see the hall, then, as a piece of ideology. Upper and lower ends reflected upper and lower social divisions. The hall presented the social divisions of the household as fixed and immutable through the architecture. The master and wife occupied the upper end and the chamber beyond; servants worked in and around the lower end. At mealtimes, the hall acted as a microcosm of the social order. Everyone ate in the same place, stressing the household as community, but at different ends, stressing differences in social status between different elements of that household.

But the interpretation of the hall could not be this simple. There were other divisions in the late medieval household that cut across the upper/lower divide and could not be fitted into a single pattern so easily. Women occupied important and powerful economic positions within the late medieval household: they controlled brewing and dairying activities, and were identified in idealized religious and political texts with the 'domestic' side of the house as opposed to the 'public' outside sphere of the roads and fields. There was tension and conflict, then, between the important economic position and everyday routine of women's lives and the formal ideology of patriarchy. So I tried to explore how other groups, women and servants in particular, may have had different 'readings' of the same space. These different 'readings' were rarely overtly articulated; they were, rather, implicit.

I also tried to look at the context of the open hall by looking at other kinds of use of space in the same period. First, I looked at fields, and argued that just as the open hall was open to all but in fact subdivided, so it was in the 'open field': medieval fields were often unbounded and farmed co-operatively, but divided into strips. Then I looked at churches, and suggested that ritual space was also divided, between the nave and chancel of the parish church. So I was arguing that a series of common spatial metaphors ran across ordinary people's experiences of the world around them, that ran between the domestic, the agrarian and the religious.

The whole debate between archaeologists over the meanings of the open hall could not be seen independently of its cultural and political context. The 'vernacular house' occupies a central place in images of rural England. In particular, these images implied continuity with an essential, unchanging rural past of 'old England' in which 'the English' are seen as a traditional, conservative organic community. In the same year that I published my work, Conservative Prime Minister John Major linked 'old England' to a vision of 'British' continuity when he exclaimed that:

> Fifty years from now Britain will still be the country of long shadows on county grounds, warm beer, invincible green suburbs, dog lovers and pools fillers and – as George Orwell said – 'old maids cycling to holy communion through the morning mist' and – if we get our way – Shakespeare still read even in school. Britain will survive unamendable in all essentials. (John Major, speech to Conservative Group for Europe, 22 April 1993)

In placing these houses within a context of profound rural crisis and change, and emphasizing their different meanings to different elements of the household, I was implicitly commenting negatively on that profoundly conservative image of the English countryside and 'Englishness' in general. This political comment was unavoidable; it was there whether I liked it or not. At the time, it wasn't my conscious intention to comment implicitly or explicitly on John Major's views, but a subsequent reading of 'my' work in such a light would nevertheless be a perfectly valid one – though it is one of several possible readings.

Phenomenology

Stop – I've lots of questions already! Can I drag you back to Point Six? Surely there are lots of problems with this analogy with text.

Yes, there are. I've emphasized text here because it is a good introduction to the underlying ideas. We all read texts, and can all grasp the analogy quickly. The analogy with text has a heuristic value – in other words, it helps us learn.

However, many archaeologists have argued within the postprocessual tradition that we should get away from this analogy, that it is fundamentally limited. In particular, it can be argued that material things convey meaning in fundamentally dissimilar ways to texts.

Material things are exactly that – physical objects. Their properties are, in many ways, very different from words. Material things can be functional in ways that words are not. Further, the sign is rarely arbitrary as it is in structuralism. The material world, then, is not reducible to language, and more broadly, the material world is a complex thing that is not easily understood in its own right. Perhaps, in that case, archaeologists should not talk about 'meanings', but rather more broadly about 'understanding' and 'experience'.

Thinking about the material world in this way has led to an interest in the last decade in questions of *materiality*, from both within and outside postprocessual traditions. How, precisely, do objects come to carry meanings, and how do the properties of the material world and of the social world interact? Should we even make this distinction in the first place? I will return to materiality, along with agency, in the concluding chapters of this book, as an area of common interest and concern from different theoretical viewpoints.

Perception that the textual analogy was limited in this regard led postprocessual archaeologists to explore other ways of thinking about how we might explore meaning through archaeological evidence. One such method or philosophy is that of phenomenology:

> Phenomenology involves the study and description of phenomena. A phenomenon is any entity (thing or event) which presents itself as a subject in the world. So the central concern is with the conceptualization of subject-object relations. It involves a description of things as they are experienced in the world by a human subject ... Processes of ordinary human description are of central significance: seeing, hearing, touching, smelling, tasting. Phenomenologists try to ground their descriptions of the social and material world in the manner in which people think and feel about it rather than in an abstract manner. (Tilley 2005, 201–2).

The philosophical origins of phenomenology go back to German Romanticism, but from that point branched out into a number of different traditions, including the 'phenomenological sociology' of Alfred Schutz. Archaeologists have borrowed particularly from the thinking of Husserl, as refracted through the work of Heidegger, Merleau-Ponty and Sartre. Instead of thinking about monuments as texts being read in different ways, archaeologists have talked about how people move through monuments, what they can or cannot see from different points, how the physical experience of the monument affects its perception.

Phenomenology has been applied particularly to the study of landscape and to monuments in the landscape. Classic case studies include studies of the megalithic monuments of Wales, the landscape settings of the great monuments of prehistoric Wessex such as Stonehenge and Avebury, and the Neolithic Dorset Cursus. In all these cases, phenomenologists direct attention away from the map and the plan view, which, it is claimed, offers only a top-down, scientific, Cartesian view divorced from everyday experience. Instead, phenomenologists try to describe what it is like in human terms to walk along, around, through these monuments, what one sees and hears at different points, how one's experience is affected by temporal rhythm (the order in which one sees things, the appearance of sudden 'surprises' over the horizon).

One of the advantages of phenomenology is that in its stress on the body and on bodily movement, it stresses the falsity of the opposition between material and ideal mentioned above. The body is undeniably real and physical – as Shakespeare said, 'there was never yet philosopher/That could endure the toothache patiently' – and yet at the same time undeniably constructed according to certain socially specific and variable ideas – different societies have different ideas of the individual, of gender, of how the body works.

A second advantage is that, for all its reputation as an obscure and esoteric philosophy, phenomenology directs the attention of archaeologists to aspects of experience which are (arguably) both accessible and observable. What objects and landscapes look like, the sensations of touch, taste and smell, are, on the face of it, things that can be talked about quite readily by archaeologists. Archaeologists do not dig up factional competition or differential access to resources or the rise of the Roman Empire; these processes are actually quite indirectly inferred from the evidence that we have. On the other hand, we do know how dark it is inside a Neolithic chambered tomb, we can experience how sound travels or fails to travel between different spaces, or how difficult it is to climb to the top of a castle wall.

Nevertheless, phenomenology is a particularly controversial as well as vibrant area of archaeological theory. Phenomenology started out as a philosophical questioning of how we might understand subjective human experience. In practice, however, practical applications of phenomenology to archaeology have to assume some kind of empathetic unity to human experience, an assumption that 'our' experience now has a direct link to 'their' experience in the past, in order to be convincing. In the examples given above, how do we know how 'darkness' was experienced in the Neolithic? How can we assume that sounds were experienced or given meaning in the same way? Doesn't the difficulty of climbing a castle wall depend on one's age and gender, or whether one has a disability? The human subjects described by phenomenologists often appear, when one thinks about it, to be quite culturally specific. The people depicted by some phenomenologists wandering around the landscape are often solitary; they are not carrying children; they are free from impairment or disability. In short, critics have rather cruelly but perhaps accurately suggested, they are curiously like some of the archaeologists doing the analysis.

A second development from a dissatisfaction with texts is to think more deeply about semiotics. If structuralist and poststructuralists models of the material world are limited or flawed, perhaps there are other theories to which archaeologists can turn.

Semiotics is the study of signs. It can be argued that the world around us is, fundamentally, made up of signs as part of a total signifying system. Recently, the work of the philosopher Charles Peirce has gained in popularity among archaeologists. Peirce saw the sign, the object, and the interpretant in a triangular relationship, and developed a complex typology of different kinds of signs. These included the the icon (where there is a formal relationship between sign and object), the index (where there is a relationship of contiguity), and the symbol (where the relationship is arbitrary, as Saussure argued for language).

A Peircean semiotics is highly complex. However, it has value as a way of thinking about the world in terms of signs. Semiotics, then, addresses the need to understand meanings without resorting to the disputed textual analogy of structuralism.

> *So postprocessualists denied the value of testing. Doesn't this mean they were open to the charge of relativism?*

Well, to repeat, they didn't 'deny its value'; they claimed that, in practice, no archaeologist whatever their theoretical stripe actually tests theory against 'raw data' in the way described by positivists. However, the identification of postprocessualism with relativism by its critics led to a quite bad-tempered debate in the 1990s which occasionally resurfaces today.

I will discuss this issue further in chapter 12; but as an interim statement, we can note a softening on all sides. On the one hand, we have noted how within processual traditions, a hard-line, positivist language of 'testing' has been softened over the decades, to an insistence that archaeologists' ideas about the past must be evaluated against the evidence, and that archaeologists should do this in a robust and rigorous manner. On the other hand, in part as a response to the repeated criticisms of the 1990s, most archaeologists associated with postprocessual ideas take pains to stress that interpretations of the past are at the very least constrained by reference to the evidence.

In my view, the critical question is not 'should interpretations be evaluated against the evidence?'; of course they should. Rather, the key question is, 'what, in practice, are the methods by which archaeologists do so? And how can those methods be strengthened?'. I have tried to address this question in my work on traditional landscape archaeology, arguing for a series of methods to bring theory and data more closely and rigorously together.

> *Well we certainly can't 'test' people's thoughts. How can we ever understand what people were really thinking? Not only are they now dead, but their culture and values were almost certainly very, very different to our own. It's striking that the two examples you chose (Nelson and Roman forts) were from military history.*

It is very difficult – but archaeology is very difficult. It's certainly true that to my mind many of the most exciting and fruitful 'postprocessual' case studies have been done in historical archaeology, where there is plenty of documentary and ethnohistoric data to bring to bear on questions of mentality (see chapter 11). This shows the importance of context – of having plenty of contextual information to work through. It is also true, as we have seen, that archaeologists influenced by phenomenology have preferred to talk about 'lived experience' and 'understanding' rather than specific cultural 'meaning'.

A more complex answer to your question is that we may never be able to grasp fully the content of ancient belief systems: we will never 'know' that this figurine was a depiction of that goddess, or 'know' the stories and myths told about the goddess using the figurine as a prop. But we can move towards an anthropological description of what a figurine or architectural space might have meant at a deeper level, for example by noting that 'female' figurines are found on the left side of a temple while male figurines are on the right. Anthropologists do this as standard practice, for example moving beyond the overt stories told by a community or folk tradition to inferences about the 'underlying meanings' of those stories – underlying meanings that might be overtly denied by the community in question.

So, to give an example, we might take the story of Little Red Riding Hood and interpret it in terms of ideas about gender and fears of adolescent sexuality in Western culture. With prehistoric or ancient cultures, we will never know the stories, but we can use the archaeological material and its contextual associations to get some sense of what such underlying ideas might be.

> *I've heard an awful lot about 'the postmodernists' lately. Is post-processual archaeology the same thing as postmodernism?*

Oh dear, I was hoping you wouldn't ask that. This is a thorny issue that had better wait till chapter 12.

8

Archaeology, Gender and Identity

In the first half of this book, I have tried to present some of the historical background and content of current debates within archaeology. I have tended to present this background as a series of distinct traditions, drawing on distinct strands of social and cultural theory in general and having distinct and sometimes contradictory notions of where archaeology is or should be going.

In the process, I have had to over-simplify. I have presented these different traditions as both unitary and irrevocably opposed to one another: that all culture historians, processualists or postprocessualists think or thought this or that. The reader could be forgiven for thinking that the bars at archaeological conferences have lines of empty tables running down the middle of them separating distinct huddles, one muttering into their beer about cultural evolution, taphonomy and middle-range theory, the other getting agitated about hermeneutics, structuration theory and political commitment, while the culture historians have not even seen the need to turn up.

To put it another way, I have taken a very diverse and multi-stranded picture of archaeological thought, and have *reified* elements into distinct traditions. In other words, quite diffuse currents of thought have been converted mentally into definite things. Theoretical tendencies or interests have been presented as unified schools with a definite existence and autonomy of their own. Such a reification is, I suggest, a necessary evil, to introduce different strands of theory to the reader.

When explored in more depth, however, theoretical practice is much more varied and diffuse than this – just as archaeological practice is also much more varied and diffuse than many practical textbooks might indicate. We can use the analogy of political parties. I could write a description of what the British Conservative Party stands for, the history, intellectual traditions of and influences on Conservatives, and list ten or twelve points of current policy. But this is not to say that all individual Conservatives have the same beliefs or agree on the same policies.

First, as I stated in the Introduction, this book is very much a portrayal of theory that is structured around debates in the English-speaking world. Other traditions thrive in other areas of the globe – for example Latin American social archaeology, other strands of Marxist theory, different traditions of culture history in central and eastern Europe.

Second, the depiction of radically different traditions engaging in battle, in particular the processual/postprocessual divide, is rather out of date for the theoretical scene after 2000 if not earlier. Two decades of work since 1990 have, in different ways, combined elements of different traditions. As we have seen, Colin Renfrew has asserted that a broadly 'scientific' framework can be combined with a recognition that cognition is important and scientifically accessible. Tim Earle, Elizabeth Brumfiel and others have combined elements of cultural evolution and a generalizing perspective with a stress on competition, conflict, gender, and so on, as I discussed in chapter 5 and will return to in the next chapter. This 'softening' of processual thinking may be in response to postprocessual criticisms, or it may have happened anyway as part of a more general move within the human sciences. Or it may have happened as a result of practical necessities – even the most hardline positivist now has to deal with the legal and ethical requirements of dealing with Indigenous peoples or different elements of the community as part of the research process, particularly in contexts like the United States and Australia. However it happened, whatever route was taken, the destination is the same.

Some have talked of a consensus in theory, or of traditions at two extreme ends of a spectrum within which there is a comfortable middle position. I feel that 'consensus' is often asserted as an oversimplification, borne of an impatience, a desire to take a theoretical short-cut, to seek out a middle ground without necessarily putting in the hard theoretical labour needed to understand and critically evaluate different sides of the debate in the first place. There is also the point that a 'spectrum' between different positions is necessarily one-dimensional; there may be other dimensions or tensions which are glossed over or ignored. Nevertheless comments like the following are now commonplace to the point of orthodoxy within Anglo-American circles, that combine generalizing, 'processual' comments with explicit attention to meaning and context:

> Goods and ideas moving among societies had variable significance in the groups to which they were introduced ... what may have been a utilitarian item near its source could serve as a badge of office within a more distant locale. ... In reconstructing interregional networks, we must be able to place the objects and styles which define them within their original behavioural

contexts. Treating them as the undifferentiated products of monolithic, homo-geneous cultures will only obscure the socio-political significance of ancient transactions. ... Determining the behavioural significance of objects and styles invariably depends on careful analyses of their contexts of recovery. (Schortman and Urban 1992: 237)

Third, there are contemporary movements and interests that cut across the battle lines of previous traditions. Recent work, for example, in feminist archaeology and the archaeology of gender, has been done from a variety of theoretical frameworks. And interests common to many archaeologists in theoretical issues such as 'space', 'agency', and 'trade and exchange' cut across the divisions presented here. In the Conclusion, I will look at how some of these themes bring archaeologists of different theoretical orienta-tions together in sometimes surprising ways. In this sense, the current state of 'archaeological theory' might be better characterized as a complex mosaic or changing kaleidoscope of themes and interests rather than as a titanic clash of different schools.

Fourth, the view taken in previous chapters presents different traditions as competing with one another. This was often the way that New and post-processual archaeologies presented themselves in the past. But different tra-ditions may be as much complementary as contradictory. For Robert Preucel (personal communication) 'theory is best understood not as a succession of different theories, with each new theory superseding the previously favoured theory, but rather as a web of interrelated theories and approaches, with each constraining and enabling the others.'

Preucel is right: but there are, I feel, major contradictions between differ-ent theoretical views of the way the world works which are not easily resolved. It is very tempting to gloss over these differences, since we all like to feel that our own view occupies the 'middle ground', combines the best elements of all traditions, and that it is everybody else who is being 'extreme'. Archaeologists, like politicians, like to be seen to be occupying the middle ground whatever the reality is. It is equally difficult to oppose the seductive argument that each theory has its own legitimate place within the grand scheme of things, with its overtones of tolerance, moderation and 'fair play'. Ironically, the search for such a 'middle ground' carries the risk of its own disabling relativism – a superficially tolerant view in which no theory is better or worse than any other.

To get across some of the variety (and intellectual vitality) of this activity I want to use the next few chapters to look at different theoretical approaches to a number of current themes. All these issues cut across the theoretical schema laid out before; I could have written a book with politics, gender, history, evolution as the core themes, and added chapters to these defining different overall traditions.

Gender

One of the most popular themes in archaeological theory is that of an archaeology of gender. This interest has become widespread and overt since the early 1980s. As with other interests, this rise of an explicit concern has been paralleled by a growing interest in gender issues in virtually every other discipline in the humanities and human sciences, particularly sociology, literature, anthropology and history. It has also gone hand-in-hand with the growth of the feminist movement and feminist theory generally, though archaeological thought has lagged behind these other areas somewhat.

The archaeology of gender encompasses several different themes. These include: correction of male bias in archaeology; a critique of existing structures of archaeological practice; a reassessment of the history of archaeology; an examination of gender in the archaeological record; and a critique of what is seen as the male-biased nature of academic knowledge and the academic world in general. These different interests have, to an extent, succeeded and supplemented one another chronologically since the early 1980s. I have also listed them in a very rough order, from less to more controversial.

Bias Correction

Interest in the archaeology of gender started, in part, with a critique of *androcentric* assumptions. Androcentrism is the belief that men are at the centre of things, either making up society exclusively or with women on the margins.

The most obvious example is what feminists see as the sexist use of language – the use of 'Man' for human, or of 'he' when 'she or he' is meant. Consider the following quotes, collated by Fiona Burtt (1987) from a study of children's books:

> The favourite subjects of prehistoric artists seem to have been animals and women. This is quite logical as both were indispensable to prehistoric man (just as they are both indispensable to 20th century man). Animals guaranteed that he survived from day to day and women that he survived from generation to generation. (Mitchell 1981: 31)

> Early man made a home in a cave. ... He made scrapers and bones. ... His wife used the scraper to clean the underside of animal skins. (Unstead 1953: 7; see also figure 8.1)

Or consider the following example, more 'academic', rather less obvious and as a result more difficult to disentangle, given as an explanation of the

Figure 8.1   Prehistoric life according to children's books. From Unstead (1953: 20)

shift from the medieval castle to the Renaissance country house in England, made yet again by an avowedly atheoretical writer:

> In the late Middle Ages ... the individual was left by default to establish his own position and maintain his own security by means of a personal affinity of retainers and a public display of strength. From the late 15th century onwards, however ... states that were rapidly growing in authority were increasingly able to circumscribe the power of the individual at the same time better able to guarantee his freedom within strictly defined boundaries ... the individual is left to make good his claims to status and authority not only through the exercise of powers bestowed on him by the state but by the cultivation of more personal distinctions. (Cooper 1997: 120)

What is missing from this passage? Is 'the individual' here exclusively male, or does it include women as well? (Note the 'as well' that the reader is seamlessly drawn into). The author might reasonably expect his reader to 'know' (or simply to assume) that this society was largely patriarchal, and therefore he is referring largely to men when he talks of the individual. But then again, a minority of housebuilders of the period were women; the reader of the passage either mentally defines such women out of existence, treats them as surrogate men with exactly the same ideas and attitudes, or assumes they were 'exceptions' in some sense. What were women's views on this 'freedom' in a period when many of them were regularly beaten with the sanction of the state and in which they were considered in law, politics and religion to be inferior to men? The passage does not tell us. Read the passage again, and form a picture of the individual in your mind, and I predict that you will find that it is a man.

By leaving women out of such discourses, any attempt to 'put them back' has to involve a lot of work: a complete rewriting of established common-sense terms and turns of phrase such as 'public display', 'power', 'authority'. These terms which at first reading seemed obvious now appear rather opaque. It therefore becomes very difficult to place women 'back into the picture'; subconsciously, we are disinclined to make the effort, particularly as the passage is written so apparently lucidly and smoothly. (It also becomes difficult to put men below the level of the elite, or children, back into the picture: a point we will return to towards the end of this chapter.) Women therefore become a 'problem'; the literature is full of discussions of the methodological difficulties of interpreting women's thoughts and activities during this period. But the 'problem' has in fact been created at least in part by a pre-existing discourse that is taken for granted. (It has also been created by reliance on a particular mode of historical narrative, a point discussed in chapter 11.)

Feminists argue that it is important to isolate these androcentric assumptions because when someone tells you that, for example, male dominance is normal or natural to the human species, they refer implicitly to the way males have always been – in the distant past, or in the primate and animal world. But this argument, they suggest, is circular. When we look at 'empirical' archaeological studies of the past, or ethnographic studies of other cultures, or anthropological studies of primates, we find that they have been studied from a viewpoint biased in favour of the male of the species. This bias is all the more pervasive because it is often unconscious.

Ethnographic studies are a good example. Various cross-cultural studies have suggested that 'male dominance' is universal. But consider for a moment the nature of this information. Much of it was collected in the nineteenth century by predominantly male ethnographers with literally Victorian attitudes towards such issues. Ethnographers would 'naturally' choose to ask the men of the tribe about the nature of its political system rather than the women, and tend to interpret the varying and ambiguous replies that they got back in terms of their own Victorian expectations and preconceptions. Therefore, feminist anthropologists argue that such information derived from ethnography needs to be questioned and theorized rather than accepted blindly and uncritically. The same point goes for what we 'know' from other disciplines.

Another example of androcentrism is the history of archaeology itself. Read many traditional textbooks and you will find that archaeology developed via the discoveries and intellectual insights of, in the main, 'great men'. Many have argued, however, that the contribution of women to archaeological thought has been systematically minimized by historians of archaeology. Figures such as Dorothy Garrod or Jacquetta Hawkes tend to be left out of many such narratives, or treated as somehow less important. An important recent strand of feminist archaeology has consisted of the rediscovery and rewriting of the history of archaeology to reflect the achievements of these women. The motivations for this rewriting may include a simple desire to 'tell the past as it really was', or to provide an inspiration for young women archaeologists in the present. It is striking that in response to this critique, successive editions of standard textbooks have been heavily modified (compare, for example, successive editions of Willey and Sabloff's *A History of American Archaeology*, or the first and most recent editions of Renfrew and Bahn (2008)).

Critique of Archaeological Practice

Feminist archaeologists question the position of women within the archaeological profession. Overt and implicit sexism in recruitment policies, academic funding and promotion have all been interrogated, very much in line with the general questioning of discriminatory practices in Britain and North America generally.

For example, Joan Gero analysed the granting of research funds to different people. She found that men were statistically more successful at getting grants for excavation and 'fieldwork' in general, whereas women were statistically less likely to be awarded financial help, and more likely to be awarded grants for what Gero termed 'archaeological housework' – pottery and small finds analysis, environmental material. Was it then any surprise, she asked, when the interpretations produced by this fieldwork emphasized stereotypical images?

It is important to note that many of what Alison Wylie calls these 'chilly-making activities' are not dependent on overt bias, openly chauvinist attitudes or political discrimination as such, but are dependent on deeper and less obvious practices such as the use of language, hidden assumptions about career trajectories, even patterns of writing and conversation. This observation has two implications. First, it can be argued that scholars all participate in sexist practices however consciously they oppose sexism in principle, particularly if they are hostile or resistant to open reflection on their conduct ('it's just manners, it's just a joke, it shouldn't be taken seriously, it's political correctness gone mad'). Second, the minutiae of everyday behaviour (how he is spoken of as assertive but she is spoken of as aggressive in the coffee room, the way we choose to dress for work) links in to wider practices – 'the personal is political'.

Much of these first two points is fairly uncontroversial – few dispute the fact that past interpretations have reflected the conscious and unconscious sexism of their time, or that women continue to be discriminated against in contemporary society in a variety of ways, and that career development in archaeology reflects this. The next two points move on to more disputed territory.

Archaeologies of Gender

The third point is a desire to look at different constructions of gender in the past, as revealed in the archaeological record. If archaeologists think it is legitimate to take societies long extinct and look at 'social ranking', at trade and exchange, even at cognitive factors, why can't we also look at different gender roles in the past?

These gender roles, it is argued, vary from culture to culture. A theoretical distinction is made between *sex* and *gender*. Sex is, it is argued, biological – most of us are born men or women, and our biological makeup does not vary (though even this can be questioned; see below).

There is a difference, however, between being born a biological male or female, and the experience of being 'gendered', of the experience and cultural practices of being a woman or a man in a given society. It can be argued that there is nothing 'normal' or 'natural' about acting like a man or a woman. For example, it was considered manly in the Middle Ages for élite men to weep and swoon on a regular basis; by the nineteenth century, the women were doing the weeping and swooning while the men were keeping a stiff upper lip. In some cultures women are considered sexually assertive and men are expected to be passive; and so on.

Gender, then, is culturally constructed, even if we accept the argument that gender is usually assigned on a biological basis. Gender varies from culture to culture. There is much debate about the extent of this variation (is it completely variable? are there some cross-cultural universals, for example to do with 'domestic' and childcare activities?) and how closely gender and sex are linked.

It follows that if archaeologists are interested in the past, we cannot assume that women and men behaved in the same way in all societies. For example, we cannot assume distinctions that we often take for granted existed in the past. These include 'common-sense' distinctions between domestic and public, between hunting and gathering, between the household and the wider world.

Instead, archaeologists need to ask questions about the different roles and experiences of women and men in a given period. These roles and experiences may have been similar or different; but the question needs to be asked rather than particular kinds of division assumed. Indeed, we need to question the assumption often made that a rigid binary division of labour ('the men did this and the women did that') existed at all.

Many argue that in practice all archaeology is 'gendered'. They point out that many archaeologists make assumptions about gender in their work, as we pointed out above, and that there is no such thing as a 'gender-neutral' account of the past. Think of the quotes given above, or the way, for example, different human activities are valued. There are countless descriptions of craft specialization in the literature, but few of changing methods of food preparation. There is, feminists argue, an implicit assumption in much of the traditional literature that specialized craft activity was done by men and is therefore important, and food preparation was done by women and is less so. Food preparation may or may not have been performed by men, women or both; whoever prepared the food, it is certainly important in the constitution of culture.

An archaeology of gender, then, has led in practice to a re-examination of the small scale such as the archaeology of the household, and the reinterpretation of the domestic as an important part of social and political life in the past rather than simply a 'domestic retreat'.

Men, Women and Knowledge

The *phallocentric nature of knowledge* is a difficult point to grasp, since it involves questioning the very basis of academic enquiry, or indeed what it is to be a student or a teacher.

Think about the way academics praise an argument, or denigrate it. We praise 'strong', 'robust', 'well organized', 'powerful' arguments; conversely, we denigrate arguments that are perceived as weak, woolly, tentative, inconclusive. The language of archaeological theory itself can often be the language of battle – theories conflict and clash, different schools muster allies to strengthen their arguments. Debate is adversarial and confrontational: one side gets the better or the worse of the 'argument'. Students are taught to be impersonal in their essays – to separate emotions and feelings from academic argument, to omit personal experience from their writing.

Many feminists argue that the academic structuring of knowledge in this way is *phallocentric*. That is, the academic establishment treats stereotypically 'male' ways of thinking and acting as legitimate, and stereotypically 'female' ways as illegitimate, 'out of court'. Phallocentric discourse claims to be fair and neutral, to offer a 'level playing field'; the professor will tell you that anyone can write a first class paper if they follow the correct academic rules and have the necessary commitment and intellectual ability. In practice, however, the rules of this game are discriminatory, since (among other reasons) it requires women to think and write 'like men', at least stereotypically, if they are to succeed. If men have been socialized into this way of thinking from birth, the argument continues, is it any surprise that they are 'better' at this academic game than women?

What is needed, feminists suggest, are different rules for the game. Why can't we be 'emotional' when writing? What is wrong with multivocality – telling stories with different voices, different conclusions? Why can't we write stories about people's personal experiences? What's wrong with ending one's presentation with a question rather than a final, firm conclusive statement?

In this way, much feminist critique ends up at a very similar position to that of many postprocessual archaeologists; indeed, many of the postprocessual arguments rehearsed in chapter 5 owe a profound debt to feminist thinking on this and other points (see below).

Case Study: What This Awl Means

Janet Spector's book *What This Awl Means: Feminist Archaeology at a Wahpeton Dakota Village* is a study of a nineteenth-century Native American settlement, Little Rapids, in what is now Minnesota in the Midwestern USA. Rather than attempt to write a neutral, distanced, objective site report, however, Spector consciously and explicitly sets out to explore her original, emotive reasons for wanting to be an archaeologist: 'these motives are empathetic – a longing to discover essences, images, and feelings of the past – not detached, distanced, objective' (Spector 1993: 1).

Spector breaks three rules of academic discourse in the opening chapters. First, she goes into her own past life history and explores her personal reasons for doing archaeology and coming to the Little Rapids site. Second, rather than looking at 'big questions' such as social complexity or the pattern of trade between Native and white Americans, she focuses initially on one very tiny artefact, apparently insignificant in itself – 'a small antler awl handle' (figure 8.2). Third, Spector writes a story about this handle – how it was lost, what the young woman who owned it was doing at the time, what the experience of life at Little Rapids was like. The story is backed up by Spector's extensive knowledge and understanding of the archaeological and historic data, but is self-consciously written as a story nevertheless, intended to evoke the emotions and spirit of the inhabitants of the site.

Spector contrasts the story she has told with previous archaeological work on awls. Previous typologies of awl handles present themselves as neutral

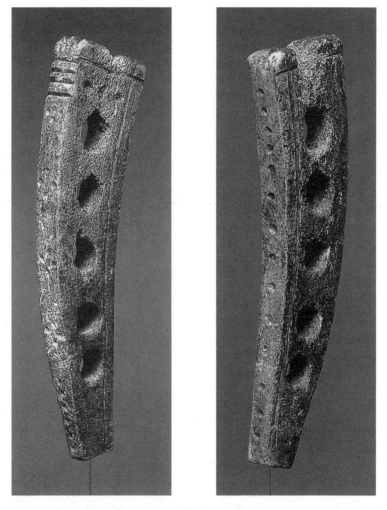

Figure 8.2   The awl handle excavated by Spector's crew. Spector's narrative links it to the young girl Mazaokeyiwin who lived at Little Rapids and may have lost the awl in the 1840s (Spector 1993)

classifications, Spector argues, but they are in fact biased in respect both to ethnicity and gender. Conventional typologies treat awls first and foremost as trade goods brought in by Europeans, rather than as artefacts related to Native American ('Indian') women's activities:

> An important but hidden assumption … is that European-produced metal awl tips are more important than Indian-produced awl handles. Built into [these]

Figure 8.3 The elderly Mazaokeyiwin working a hide (Spector 1993)

classifications and table titles, this theme leads to emphasis on metal awl tips as markers of European influence on Indians and implies the disintegration of native culture. This would have been insulting, annoying, or simply wrong to Indians who used awls, particularly to women who inscribed their bone or antler handles to display publicly their accomplishments. (Spector 1993: 31–2)

Spector tells stories also about the progress of the dig, the discovery of the awl, the experiences of different dig members, and frankly explores tensions and cooperation with Native Americans in the course of the research project. She is helped in her task by the extensive historical and ethnographic documentation of the Dakota people and of the site, that allows her to give names and personalities to many of the nineteenth-century inhabitants of Little Rapids (figure 8.3).

It is striking that Spector's openly feminist perspective leads her to accentuate the small scale and personal (what the awl handle meant to its owner, not the awl's position within wider trade networks). It is laid out in a personal and engaged way (the personalities and excitement of the research project) rather than attempting to be rhetorically dispassionate. It leads very quickly to other dimensions of social and cultural identity (the transition from being a girl to being an adult woman in Dakota society). It is also striking how Spector's feminist account is also immediately and unavoidably engaged in other questions of politics and identity, most obviously that of relations between Native Americans and whites.

> *This all sounds fine, but I'm getting a little confused over terminology here. Is gender archaeology the same thing as feminist archaeology?*

Not necessarily. It is without question that interest in gender issues in archaeology grew out of the rise in feminist concerns since the 1960s. But remember that it is pretty undeniable to assert that all archaeology makes assumptions about gender, unless it forswears any attempt at social reconstruction. If we need to look at gender in the past, there is no *a priori* reason why a specifically feminist perspective needs to be used.

Conkey and Gero (1997) argue that the archaeology of gender is increasingly diverse in the theoretical positions it has taken. They show that sociobiology, social constructivism, cultural and biological evolution, political economy, and agency and performance theory have all been used to structure enquiry into gender in the archaeological record. They point to the very deep differences in theoretical assumptions behind many of these schools, and assert that many studies of gender do not draw extensively or even at all on feminist critiques within the human sciences in general.

Of course, it all depends on definitions of feminism, which vary. 'I myself have never been able to find out precisely what feminism is: I only know that people call me a feminist whenever I express sentiments that differentiate me from a doormat or a prostitute' (Rebecca West 1913; cited in Humm 1992: 34). More specifically, Conkey and Gero draw on feminist critiques of science and point to four areas that they feel distinguish specifically feminist enquiry in archaeology:

1 The recognition that 'politics and the substantive products of knowledge are essentially inseparable';
2 The recognition that rationality is a 'mythical conflation that never exists in actual scientific practice';
3 'Association with a cognitive style that favours "intimate" knowledge and nuanced understandings of data over categorical thinking';

4   A challenge to 'basic disciplinary arrangements' and the fostering of alternative views. (Conkey and Gero 1997: 427–8)

Conkey and Gero argue that feminist archaeology is, or should be, a dangerous and transforming exercise. They distance themselves from considerations 'of gender in prehistoric studies without reconfiguring archaeology in any way' and assert that

> An archaeology that takes feminist theory seriously is self-transformational and communal. Radical reappraisals – rigorous, scholarly, informed, and purposive – emerge from feminist theory precisely because traditional assumptions and values really do look profoundly different when viewed from a woman-centred perspective. Some have wanted to call this 'seeing gender everywhere', with the derogatory term 'genderlirium'. But 'genderlirium' is an equally apt term with which to critique Western androcentrism, with its hard-headed rules for a single way of knowing and its single vision. (Conkey and Gero 1997: 424, 430)

For Conkey and Gero, then, archaeological studies of gender come from a variety of theoretical viewpoints, but a specifically feminist standpoint is one that questions existing archaeological practice at a very basic level.

OK, so we can't assume men and women did this or that in the past. But in that case how can we ever begin to talk about gender?

This impinges on the question of *essentialism*. In the view of some feminists, there is nothing essential to 'feminine nature'. Some attack 'biological essentialism', that is, the attempt to define cross-culturally gender roles based on biological 'facts' such as men's greater upper-body strength or women's role in childbirth and infant care. They argue that such 'facts' are socially constructed. For example, they question the way gender differences are always presented in a binary fashion, rather than as a continuum, in biological studies.

The problem you raise is that if we cannot say with certainty which activities were undertaken by which gender, or even that activities were or were not gendered, then we cannot say anything positive about the construction of gender in a given society, particularly a prehistoric one.

One way out of this that is frequently taken is to construct a contextual argument. For example, one can look at which artefacts are associated with which gender in burials, and then extend this argument outwards, to look at the same classes of artefacts in domestic contexts. Another way out is to rely on a limited essentialism: for example, that the necessities of child-rearing do involve an association of women with domestic and household contexts.

> *You've said that an interest in gender cuts across previous theoretical categories. But it seems to me that it's closely related to postprocessual archaeology. Both movements relate archaeology to politics, both try to look at conflict and inequality, both try to write different narratives that include the personal...*

Historically, the archaeology of gender and postprocessual archaeology have close links both with each other and with feminist thought in the human sciences. Many of the younger archaeologists in the 1980s and 1990s were closely involved with both movements, particularly in Britain. Specifically, we can point to: (a) the widening of the definition of 'political'; (b) stress on small-scale, local and household contexts as important; (c) stress on multivocality; (d) stress on meaning and lived experience; and (e) stress on conflict as being played out through everyday practice. Indeed, I suspect that when the history of postprocessual thought in the 1980s comes to be written it will be found that the role of individual feminists has been under-acknowledged.

But many would argue that bias correction (point 1 above) is a legitimate and indeed essential part of any scientific archaeology. Within science as a whole, much work has been done to correct what are seen as specific biases; for example, critiques of Charles Darwin's terminology when he attributes 'passive' and 'active' roles to female and male apes respectively.

Similarly, there is no necessary conflict between a positivist view of science and stress on recruitment and equal rights issues within archaeology. It is perfectly possible to argue for 'scientific method' in archaeological reasoning, while acknowledging that the archaeological profession needs to address issues of discrimination. But in accordance with positivist method, one's stance on 'political' issues such as equality should be kept separate from one's academic judgements.

Some feminists, particularly in the human sciences as a whole, argue strongly against what they see as the slippery nature of the way some arguments under the postprocessual banner see everything in a very multifaceted, deliberately ambiguous way, in which the very real powerlessness and exploitation felt by many women seems to them to be glossed over. Isn't it ironic, they point out, that just as women are beginning to get a small slice of the cake, making a real difference at work and so on, that it's revealed that such bread-and-butter issues are only a 'language game' anyway? Alison Wylie writes that:

> strong constructivist and relativist positions embody what seem to be patently an ideology of the powerful. Only the most powerful, the most successful in achieving control over the world, could be constructed as they choose. ... Any who lack such power, or who lack an investment in believing they have such power, are painfully aware that they negotiate an intransigent reality that impinges on their lives at every turn. (Wylie 1992b: 25)

A related argument is that of inclusiveness. Feminists often feel that their arguments are 'hijacked', made part of some 'wider argument' such as that of Marxism or of postprocessual archaeology and in the process subsumed and ultimately ignored. It is striking that Spector prefers her argument to stand on its own two feet. Her bibliography refers to very little of the 'postprocessual' literature. In practical terms, just as the majority of New Archaeologists were pushy young men, so some feminists argue that postprocessualism was a distinctly male phenomenon in its early years, with an aggressive and uncompromising tone to its rhetoric; many men initially associated with postprocessual ideas have now slid seamlessly into senior academic positions.

Archaeologies of Identity

We noted above how Spector's argument about gender led very quickly into other issues of social identity – for example, of age, of ethnicity. They also led very quickly into an attempt to write in a different way about the past, a way that was engaged and emotive rather than detached and 'purely objective'. What this demonstrates is that an archaeology of gender leads inevitably into a number of other areas and dimensions of social identity.

'Archaeologies of identity' take their lead from gender and feminist archaeology, in that they all take an interest in how social identities are constructed, how those identities might be explored in the archaeological record, and how identity formation itself is always 'socially constituted' – in other words, it is variable, unstable, fluid and changing, rather than being fixed or essential. Archaeologists have explored, among other areas, archaeologies of masculinity, of childhood, of race, of sexuality, and of disability.

The first and most obvious of these constructions is masculinity. If the roles and identities of women were variable in the past, then it follows that men's were too. An archaeology of masculinity and of men's changing identities is therefore a necessary part of any full understanding of gender.

For example, in my own work, discussed in chapter 11, I have looked at how medieval castles, and their transformation into Renaissance palaces, was tied up with changing notions of élite masculinity – what it meant to be a knight or a gent. In the later middle ages, to be a man was closely associated with the ability and training to fight. Masculinity was associated with values like honour and chivalry. Chivalry and martial values were given material expression in the towers and battlements of castles, in the labour invested in suits of armour, and in the ability to ride a specially bred war-horse and to use a lance and shield while on horseback, for example in the ritualized violence of jousting and the tournament. The 'decline of the castle' and the shift to an unfortified Renaissance architecture gave expression to new values of what it meant to be a man, a new 'self-fashioning', in which ideas of civility, of literacy and familiarity with the works of Classical literature, and of 'courtly' behaviour became much more important. I tried to draw out two points from this discussion: first, 'what it meant to be a man' was not the same in all times and in all places; second, these meanings were materially expressed in the appearance, layout and decorative schemes of buildings.

Again, Laurie Wilkie has looked at the architecture and material culture associated with men's fraternity houses at the University of California at Berkeley at the beginning of the twentieth century. Wilkie looks at the ceramics and other evidence for dining practices, and the changing layout and locations of the fraternity houses. These young men, she argues, had their identities shaped around contemporary ideas of a 'primal masculinity' that was in part a reaction to changing women's identities of the period.

If men's identities were variable, so also 'childhood' has to be treated as a constructed category. Just as theorists made a distinction between sex and gender, so it can be argued that the physical process of growth and ageing can be separated analytically from the socially constructed experience of 'childhood'. Ideas, for example, of when a child becomes an adult vary from culture to culture, as they do for old age. In pre-industrial England, many children were sent away from home to be servants in other's households from an early age, giving a socially defined intermediate period that corresponded very roughly with adolescence. Jo Sofaer has explored different constructions of childhood, both through the treatment of children in burial practices and through analysis of aspects of the lives of children, such as nutrition and different activities, through human skeletal evidence.

Archaeologists have also rethought other dimensions of social identity such as race and ethnicity. It has long been accepted, since the work of Franz Boas and the rejection of racist theories of culture a century ago, that race is a socially constructed category, rather than a simple matter of DNA or skin colour. Since the time of Boas, social scientists have preferred to talk of 'ethnicity' on the basis of social and cultural rather than biological distinction.

I have argued in earlier chapters that essentialist statements like 'the Celtic spirit' have the potential to be used in problematic ways that often seem to suggest or imply some kind of inner racial essence. In historical archaeology, changing constructions of African-American identity have been explored, looking, for example at an 'archaeology of resistance', how elements of African identities were maintained and transformed by enslaved peoples in the most oppressive of contexts. I will look in chapter 12 at the archaeology of the African Burial Ground in New York.

If ideas about gender are variable, the same also goes, it is argued, for ideas about sexuality. I wrote above that 'sex' can be argued to be biological, whereas gender is socially constructed. Inevitably, things are not as simple as this. Sexual identities were also variable in the past, and cannot be assumed in the archaeological record. It may be that there were other sexual identities in the past. An archaeology of sexuality, like the archaeology of gender, spans empirical enquiry (for example, drawing attention to depictions of same-sex relations in Swedish rock art or on Classical vases) to a theoretical reformulation of archaeology.

The project of 'queer theory' in the human sciences has led to the advocacy of 'queer archaeologies'. Queer theory is a drawing-together of insights from gay and lesbian studies. If traditional scholars in the human sciences often make androcentric assumptions (assuming the male experience is normal and/or central in the past), they also make heterosexist assumptions (assuming heterosexual orientations or relationships were normal and/or central in the past). Queer archaeologies move from an identification of evidence for other forms of sexuality to a wider project of 'queering the past', just as feminist archaeologists move from identifying changing constructions of gender to an attempt to change archaeological practice.

Just as ideas in feminist archaeology mirrored discussions in other social sciences, so too have discussions of disability. Traditional accounts have either not considered disability, or have seen disabled people in the archaeological record as dependent on the able-bodied, and 'care' for disability as an index of civilized behaviour. The classic example is the famous interpretation of the Neanderthal individual 'Shanidar I'. Summarizing Ralph Solecki's arguments, Trinkaus and Shipman state that:

> Careful study of his bones revealed a plethora of serious but healed fractures ... someone so devastatingly injured could not possibly have survived without care and sustenance ... a one-armed, partially blind, crippled man could have made no pretence of hunting or gathering his own food. That he survived for years after his trauma was a testament to Neandertal compassion and humanity. (Trinkaus and Shipman 1992, 340–1)

The point here is not that the interpretation of Shanidar I is 'wrong', but that it is one-sided. It follows older models of disability in seeing the individual exclusively in terms of what he could not do, as opposed to what he could do or might have been able to do, and in terms of the need for 'compassion and humanity' from (it is implied) able-bodied others. This individual's survival might be a testament not simply or solely to 'compassion', but to this person's many other skills and qualities that he brought to the social group. Ironically, it fell to the author Jean Auel in her novel *Clan of the Cave Bear* to use the evidence of Shanidar I to imagine Shanidar I as a shaman, a powerful figure, a person defined socially not simply in terms of his impairment but in terms of his magical power over the social and natural world.

In the human sciences generally, and in parallel with the distinction between sex and gender, scholars have drawn a distinction between 'impairment' and 'disability'. Disability is, in this view, a social category or experience rather than the 'objective' medical condition of impairment. To take a classic example, wheelchair users have an impairment, but the social experience of disability is conditioned by, for example, the choice to use steps instead of ramps, the layout and design of buildings and pathways, all of which are commonly designed with the needs of the 'able-bodied' in mind – and by the unconscious and unconscious biases and assumptions of others ('she can't possibly do this', 'given his handicap, doesn't he manage well').

An archaeology of disability, then, spans a number of related themes: issues of access to archaeology as a profession, and workplace issues of disability, to an empirical investigation of the relation between impairment and social identities in the past.

Performativity

In line with discussions of gender, theorists in the social sciences have insisted that all these categories (gender, race, age, sexual identity, disability) are *performative*. 'Performativity' is a centrally important idea in understanding identities; it is particularly associated with the theorist Judith Butler. For example, what it means to be a man or a woman is only partly determined by biology, as discussed above. It is also determined, at least in part, by the daily performances men and women put on – their manner of speech, choice of dress, behaviour in social situations. These performances can be thought of as little pieces of theatre, even if the audience is one (the self).

There are four important implications for archaeological practice that arise from an appreciation of performativity. First, performance leads to a stress on the importance of material culture. Performances occur in material settings (the open halls of houses; structured stages like Roman parade grounds or Maya temples or Greek stoa). They frequently occur in relation to material objects and are defined through material use (dress, make-up). So performativity gives an important dimension to archaeologists' appreciation of materiality and the nature of the material world.

Second, performances structure and define 'who you are'. Further, they are manipulated by people. Gay and lesbian subcultures use dress and behaviour to redefine 'what it means' to be gay and lesbian. 'What it means' to be African, or British, or a citizen of the USA can change or be manipulated by performance – the choice of 'traditional' or Western clothes, the choice to celebrate chicken tikka masala rather than fish and chips as the nation's favourite dish, to wear a Barack Obama T-shirt or a Stetson. Therefore, for archaeologists, material culture cannot be interpreted as the manifestation of some pre-existing essence – for example we cannot assert 'who the Slavs were', or talk of 'middle-class identity' or ways of life, and then look for their archaeological 'expression', or lack of expression, in the archaeological record. I will return to this point in discussing materiality in the Conclusion.

Third, performances often take place through the body. 'The body' emerged as a key theme in current thinking when I discussed the 'lived experience' explored by phenomenologists. Here, the body is important because it too is a piece of material culture that can be manipulated. Much of the archaeological record is about different constructions of the body – most obviously with grave goods, but also 'personal' items like jewellery, grooming items such as combs and tweezers, and more broadly dress and other personal items. People's bodies, then, become a key, even central, element of their performance.

Fourth, performativity applies just as much to contemporary practice as it does to interpretations of the past. Performances occur in the lecture theatre or classroom, or indeed on the archaeological excavation. The roles of professor and student, site director and finds assistant are just as open to a performative analysis as roles in the past. Therefore, as with feminism and Marxism, there is an important *reflexive* component to archaeologists' thinking about performativity. *Reflexivity* refers to the back-and-forth, double-edged nature of academic enquiry, in which what we learn about the past is always and immediately bound up with practices in the present (for example, where critique of past ideologies immediately reflects back on ideology in the present, or where critical thinking about past gender roles requires us to reflect on sexist assumptions in the workplace and in our own heads).

Conclusion

What all these approaches and themes share in common is:

- a stress on identities as socially constructed;
- a scepticism towards the idea that identity is somehow 'given' by some core or essential feature, for example through biological sex or DNA;
- a stress on agency and performativity in the active creation of identities;

- a belief that while these themes were initially explored in other disciplines, archaeologists need to engage with them;
- a continuum or tension between 'orthodox' empirical studies of a particular theme and a wholesale recasting of the rules of academic enquiry;
- a stress on the connections between study of identities in the past and identity politics in the present;
- a stress on the reflexive relationship between both the study of the past and the present, and between academic study and the everyday politics of the 'real world'.

As we have seen, there is a tendency with each of these interests to style itself as a different sub-field or species or method of archaeology: thus 'queer archaeologies', 'archaeology of sexuality', 'archaeology of disability'.

This proliferation of archaeologies of identity can be highly fruitful and enabling. It has the potential to make archaeology not just more sensitive to different aspects of identity in the past, but open and relevant to different elements of the community in the present. However, it can also be problematic for several reasons.

In the first place, it is possible to argue that a particular structuring principle is not just another -ism or another archaeology, but is in some sense primary. Most obviously, many feminists continue to assert gender as a primary structuring principle to human societies in the past, to place a feminist agenda as primary in the present, and to resist assimilation to a 'wider project' or classification as just one of a series of themes. Many such feminists would be sceptical of the presentation of an 'archaeology of gender' alongside other archaeologies of identity, as I have done here. Again, it is possible to argue that race is a fundamental structuring category, not just another dimension of identity to be set against others.

Second, some archaeologists are wary of what they fear will be an endless proliferation of 'archaeologies'. If many different kinds of identity can be explored, and each has its own distinctive archaeology, it can lead paradoxically to the trivialization of all of them. Social theorists have criticized an unrestrained identity politics as leading to a position where people can just pick-and-mix different identities, like products off a supermarket shelf. Paradoxically, then, a proliferation of identities can be argued to be a feature of what Marxists call 'late capitalism'. (It has to be said in reply, however, that archaeologists with such worries turn out, all too often, to be able-bodied white men.)

For me, the critical point is that current thinking in feminist and gender archaeology, and in archaeologies of identity, express some of the key tensions in current archaeological theory. They embody some of the difficulties, and potentials, of doing archaeology in a complex modern world. I will return to these difficulties and potentials in chapter 12.

9

Archaeology and Cultural Evolution

In this chapter I want to look at the way different theoretical approaches treat the question of cultural evolution. As with the archaeology of gender, we shall find that different attitudes to evolution tend to betray different attitudes to archaeological theory and practice as a whole. Again, we shall also find that different theoretical attitudes within archaeology are paralleled by a similar range of attitudes within the human sciences as a whole.

As with other terms, the word 'evolution' is not easily defined. Evolution has come to have an array of different meanings, some at odds with or even completely contradicting others. The best way to explain what these different meanings are is to look at the history of archaeology and of evolution. The origins of evolutionary ideas can be traced back to the Renaissance of the fifteenth and sixteenth centuries, and in particular to the first encounters between Europeans and other peoples around the world. If we consider these origins, we find that early evolutionary ideas were closely bound up with the development of archaeology as a discipline, to the extent that it is difficult to conceive of one without the other.

Before the fifteenth century in Europe, there was a consciousness of a historical past. Texts, most obviously the Bible, gave a range of dates for events and occurrences that stretched back to the creation of the world (famously glossed by Archbishop Ussher as the night preceding 23 October 4004 BC). There was also an emphasis in the medieval world on the importance of custom and tradition, ideas which served to articulate past and present and to provide a justification for practices and community identities in a world where most ordinary folk were illiterate. However, it is possible to argue that there was little or no conception of the past as fundamentally different from the present. People in the past were considered to be 'just like us'; look at any portrayal of St George, a Roman soldier, in a medieval stained glass window, where he is given medieval armour and weaponry (figure 9.1). Roman emperors were described in terms that made them

Figure 9.1 St George and the Dragon, as depicted on St George's Altarpiece, National Gallery, Prague, *c.*1470. from *Bohemian Art of the Gothic and Early Renaissance Periods*, Press Foto, Praha, http://commons.wikimedia.org/wiki/File: St_George_and_the_Dragon-altar_wing-NG-Praha.jpg

sound like medieval princes. The idea that past peoples practised different ways of life, had different cultures and beliefs, and that these needed to be studied on their own terms was, therefore, problematic before the Renaissance.

Fifteenth- and sixteenth-century European explorers and colonists faced an intellectual paradox when they encountered peoples in other areas of the globe, in particular Native Americans. Native peoples were clearly *different*. This difference posed a very basic intellectual challenge to Renaissance intellectuals, a challenge articulated for example by Shakespeare's play *The Tempest*, in which the encounter and struggle for power between the Milanese magician and book-lover Prospero and the native 'monster' Caliban is placed literally at centre stage. In the view of many European thinkers, here in the forests of what the poet John Donne called the 'new-found land' of America were human beings who practised none of the civilized arts – they went naked, had no formal code of law, no state, and above all, no (Christian) religion. *And yet such 'savages' could act in noble and civilized ways.* This was difficult to explain within the sixteenth-century European scheme of things to say the least.

One way out of the intellectual conundrum was to suggest a powerful idea: *perhaps 'we', the civilized peoples of Europe, were like this in the past.* Perhaps, in other words, such 'savages' represented some sort of earlier or lower order of human existence from which Renaissance 'Man' had evolved. Hence, for example, the portrayals by early antiquarians of 'early Britons' were often closely modelled on those of Native Americans (figures 9.2 and 9.3).

At the same time as Europeans were exploring other parts of the globe, early antiquarians were exploring historic and prehistoric monuments in the landscape around them in Europe. As a result of the colonial encounter and the intellectual challenge it posed to European thinkers, early antiquarians began to think about a distant prehistoric past while simultaneously they began to explore its antiquities through barrow-digging and surveying of ancient monuments. From reflection on these discoveries emerged the idea that is central to many versions of cultural or social evolution, namely that *different peoples in different areas of the world went through similar sorts of social changes and processes.* At its most simple, these social changes and processes were conceived of as a single, fundamental transition that all societies went through, between 'savagery' and 'civilization', 'them' and 'us'.

In its earlier forms, evolutionary thought was presented as an abstract story. The seventeenth-century English philosopher Thomas Hobbes for example talked about how, before the emergence of a central power, the life of humans was 'nasty, brutish and short', there being no rule of law to ameliorate a general anarchy, with every man for himself. Hobbes related how, therefore, men's independence was given up to a 'commonwealth' or a State power over everyone. Hobbes' story was never intended as a factual

Figure 9.2 A Native American chief, drawn by John White in the 1580s

Figure 9.3   An 'Ancient Briton', drawn by John White in the 1580s

account of the past; its intended focus and message was largely about the political events of Hobbes' times. Hobbes sought to justify and legitimate political obedience and the rule of law in a very turbulent seventeenth-century world, in which a divinely-appointed King Charles had just been executed in the name of the Commonwealth, and in which therefore divine legitimation for obedience to the state had been abruptly and violently removed.

It is possible to trace Hobbes' abstracted account of evolution through later thinkers, for example Rousseau's social contract, and more generally the rise of the idea of progress in human affairs; however, for the purposes of this chapter, we will move to a critical moment in the middle of the nineteenth century.

Darwin, Marx and Spencer

A number of intellectual strands came together in the middle of the nineteenth century. First, the colonial expansion of Europe across the globe went along with an ethos of 'discovery'. For the natural world, scholars mapped and classified different species (though it is worth noting that both prior to and including Darwin, observation of the local landscape such as that of southern England was equally important to their findings). Intellectuals also mapped the different human cultures to be found across the world, and needed a ordered and coherent system in order to classify what they had found.

One such scheme was that of Lewis Henry Morgan, published in 1877 as *Ancient Society*. Morgan drew on the earlier work of Tylor, and classified different social forms and institutions such as subsistence practices, family and kinship forms, language and religion. His ordering scheme was in terms of human progress, with 'savagery' being followed by 'barbarism' and then 'civilization'.

Morgan's work was drawn on heavily by Karl Marx and Friedrich Engels. We saw in chapter 7 how Marx's scheme of human history could be classified as evolutionary, in its delineation of a succession of ever more complex social forms from 'primitive communism' upwards to capitalism. In *The Origins of the Family, Private Property and the State*, Engels argued that the modern institutions of marriage and properly relations were not 'normal', but rather were specific historical creations, which came into being alongside State society. The evidence for Marx and Engels' arguments, and before them those of Morgan, was arguably flawed, but the implications of their arguments that, for example household and gender relations were intimately tied to the State went on to be highly influential on feminist thinking. This body of work also influenced Gordon Childe, who in *Man Makes Himself* and *What Happened in History* adopted Maine's savagery-barbarism-civilization scheme and attempted to link it to the three-age system of Stone, Bronze and Iron Ages.

Though he did not deal primarily with archaeology, Herbert Spencer's work was especially important in that he elaborated and popularized the idea that all human societies move from a less to a more complex state of organization. He further linked this idea to notions of morality and human 'progress', and set the tone for a generation of self-confident Victorian intellectuals. In Spencer's thought, 'civilized' society was not only a historical development: it was more moral than 'savagery'. It is partly as a consequence of Spencer's thought and its impact on later nineteenth-century intellectual life that terms like savagery, barbarism and civilization remain loaded, ambiguous terms, even today.

Spencer went further. He suggested that the idea of Progress was more than just a moral belief or value judgment. The new positivist Science of Spencer's time, building on eighteenth-century Enlightenment philosophy and observation of the natural world, had given Western society the ability to objectively measure and confirm its belief in progress. Spencer therefore gave this belief in progress a scientific mandate – the visible, scientific proof of Progress lay in observation of the world.

Further, Spencer claimed to build on the evolutionary concepts of Charles Darwin – the famous phrase 'survival of the fittest', often popularly attributed to Darwin, was actually coined by Spencer in his 1864 *Principles of Biology*. Spencer interpreted Darwin to give a mandate to ideas of cultural evolution and particularly of progress. There were undoubtedly close intellectual and cultural links in the nineteenth century between the versions of evolutionary ideas developed by Spencer and Darwin. However, later generations, particularly current proponents of versions of Darwinist evolution as applied to archaeology, draw a very sharp distinction between the two versions as we shall see.

Spencer's ideas were popular in an age of Victorian imperialism. The thought of Spencer and others contributed to a view of the world where Europeans perceived themselves as being admirably fitted to govern subject peoples. Not only did Europeans have Christian religion and the moral order on their side, but they also believed that they were confirmed in their right to rule by the objective findings of the natural sciences. Any objective observer of the world, in this view, could see irrefutable evidence that different societies could be ranked on a ladder of progress, and further that European societies were at the top of this ladder. Native peoples such as the subjects of the British Empire might in this view aspire to progress to civilized states, but their upward progress might well be very slow, so slow as to be imperceptible to the contemporary observer, just as upward progress had been slow in the origins of civilization in the first place.

Spencer's ideas were also popular among North American and European political élites in an age of class divisions, inequality and the growing consciousness and political confidence of an urban working class. Spencer argued that legislation to foster social reforms and to ameliorate inequalities was misguided, since it interfered with the natural workings of the 'survival of the fittest'. Augustus Lane Fox Pitt-Rivers, often seen as the father of British field archaeology, argued strongly that if evolutionary principles were properly understood by ordinary people, they would desist from pursuing deluded notions of reform and revolution. Pitt-Rivers, then, organized the display of artefacts in his museum along evolutionary lines to educate the public in these principles.

It is worth elaborating upon this point. It has been suggested that evolutionary ideas that treat human history in terms of a 'league table' of progress have always been popular when the intellectual basis of a culture is feeling self-confident. Thus, ideas of progress were popular in Victorian Britain, but waned in the twentieth century with two world wars and the end of the British Empire; whereas in the United States, they were especially popular during the 1960s, but lost popularity after the military and political disaster of Vietnam.

Cultural Evolution

It is difficult to over-estimate the impact of cultural evolutionary ideas on the development of archaeological thought. Many different schema of social development are 'evolutionary' even if they do not necessarily spell this out explicitly.

Ideas of cultural evolution were formative in the development of archaeology as a discipline in the later nineteenth century. Lubbock's great book *Prehistoric Times*, for example, published in 1865, was sub-titled *As Illustrated by Ancient Remains, and the Manners and Customs of Modern Savages*. In other words, Lubbock brought order and system to prehistory by making the assumption that societies moved from simple to complex, and therefore that 'the manners and customs of modern savages' could illustrate earlier periods of British and European prehistory.

But if one stands back from this nineteenth-century context and considers evolutionary principles in abstract terms, there is no *a priori* theoretical reason why the direction of cultural evolution should be from simple to complex. Most schemes of cultural evolution tend to classify societies in this way, on the grounds that this, empirically, is the story of human development: from 'simple' hunter-gatherer forms many thousands of years ago to the 'complex' modern states of today. For Leslie White, this move from simple to complex was explained as a tendency to harness ever more vast quantities of energy, as cultural systems became more entropic or tightly integrated. Durkheim's and Spencer's views of evolution also specified a definite direction from simple to complex. In many versions of evolutionary theory, however, there is no reason why social forms cannot move in the other direction in certain circumstances, that is from complex to simple, just as organic forms can do in biology. This is what is proposed with the collapse of cultural systems and their 'return' to 'simpler' forms of society, like the Ancient Maya after the 'Classic Maya Collapse' or the ancestral pueblos of Chaco Canyon.

There is also no *a priori* theoretical reason why more complex forms of society are better adapted to the natural environment than less complex forms. If modern capitalist society is wiped out in, say, excesses of industrial pollution, or in global warming, it may well be the case that 'simpler' forms of human society based on subsistence agriculture or on gathering and hunting will be proven to be more adaptive in the long run to this planet's environment than 'complex' industrial forms.

Third, there is no *a priori* reason why change should not be very sudden rather than gradual. The Victorian view of cultural evolution was ideologically saturated with the notion of change as gradual as it was inevitable. This equation of evolution with gradual change continues to be very strong in popular circles (one reads of modern institutions and companies proposing periods of 'evolutionary change', by which they mean that change is to be gradual and incremental rather than sudden). However, there is no reason why change should not be very sudden and transformative – as it was, arguably, in cases of the formation of early states or of systems collapse.

Finally, to state the obvious, there is no reason why we should accept Spencer's and Durkheim's insistence that cultural evolution leads to a more moral, just or civilized society. It is perfectly possible to take the view that while in practice, human societies have moved from less complex to more complex forms, this tells us nothing about the moral worth of those societies – most advocates of cultural evolution today would insist on this qualification. Indeed, Romantic thinkers often posit the reverse – a moral decline attendant upon social complexity and specifically industrial society, the loss of a more authentic and less alienated way of life that is in some way supposed to be 'closer to Nature'.

It is important to stress that different evolutionary schema can be very different from one another, both in their classifications and in the suggested mechanisms for social transition. Some evolutionary schemes are *unilinear*; that is, they suggest that there is one broad pattern or trend to cultural evolution. Others are *multilinear*, suggesting a number of divergent evolutionary paths a particular cultural sequence can follow. These multilinear schemes can diverge or converge (figure 9.4).

Fig 28a The tree of organic phylogeny with its characteristic forking branch pattern.
Source: Kroeber 1948, p 260.

Fig 28b The tree of cultural phylogeny with *its* characteristic reticulated branch pattern.
Source: Kroeber 1948, p 260.

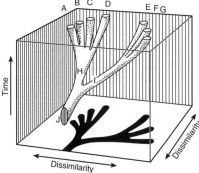

Fig 28c A section of an organic phylogenetic tree in three dimensions, one of time and two of phenetic dissimilarity. The 'shadow' of the tree on the base indicates the purely phenetic relationships of the branches.
Source: Sokal and Sneath 1963, p 234.

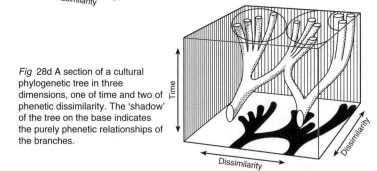

Fig 28d A section of a cultural phylogenetic tree in three dimensions, one of time and two of phenetic dissimilarity. The 'shadow' of the tree on the base indicates the purely phenetic relationships of the branches.

Figure 9.4 Clarke's contrast (drawn from Kroeber 1948) between organic and cultural evolution

We might contrast for example the two unilinear schemes of the cultural anthropologists Elman Service and Morton Fried. Both were compiled by assembling many examples of different human societies from ethnographic research, and both have been particularly influential on archaeologists. Service gives us a fourfold typology ranging along the scale of simple to complex of band, tribe, chiefdom and state. Fried offers an alternative scheme of egalitarian, ranked, stratified and state. Note that while they differ in their terminology, the descriptions of Service and Fried share a great deal of common ground. Both start and stop at the same point (they start with 'simple' gatherer-hunter societies, though their definitions of such societies differ, and end with the modern state). They both also share a similar methodology; in other words, the methods that have been used to draw them up are very much the same: Service and Fried collated many different ethnographic examples of different social systems, and then ranked or classified them according to perceived criteria of complexity.

Note that this is another example of archaeology being influenced by thinking developed in other disciplines. In practice, much earlier archaeology within the tradition of cultural evolution has followed the method of ascertaining what the archaeological correlates of each stage might be, and then looking for them in the archaeological record. For example, Service suggests that chiefdoms will include the following features among others: a settlement hierarchy; redistributive trade networks; religious complexity involving monumental construction and so on. Much archaeological effort has been spent in refining these criteria and seeking out relevant evidence in the archaeological record in a wide variety of contexts, from Renfrew's work on Neolithic and Early Bronze Age Wessex to Tim Earle's work on chiefdoms in Southern America and Polynesia.

In a more recent example, Raymond Kelly studied a range of different 'pre-state' societies. He was interested in the relationship between war on the one hand, and social segmentation on the other. By comparing different segmented and unsegmented societies, Kelly concluded that segmentation of societies was related to the development of a group mentality, which in turn enabled and facilitated inter-village raiding. Kelly's general scheme was then applied to archaeological data from ancient Mexico by Flannery and Marcus (2003).

One of the great strengths of cultural evolutionary theory, from the point of view of North American archaeology, is that it strongly integrates archaeology within the discipline of anthropology as a whole. It suggests and facilitates cultural anthropologists and 'anthropological archaeologists' working together in a strong collaborative programme into what are perceived as important, concrete, empirical questions. These questions are generalizing and comparative in nature and are of relevance to the modern world (ranking, warfare, the origins of the State). Within this project, archaeologists are an important and central part of the wider thrust of a generalizing anthropological theory.

Criticisms of Cultural Evolution

Many of the criticisms of cultural evolution echo postprocessual critiques of archaeology as a whole. Shanks and Tilley, for example, write: 'The concepts of function, adaptation, and evolution have no explanatory role in a consideration of the social and need to be either completely abandoned or reduced to a simple descriptive vocabulary' (1987: 210). Mark Pluciennik's 2005 *Social Evolution* comes very close to a complete rejection of any form of evolutionary thinking. Why do they suggest this?

First, it is argued that evolutionary schema apply criteria from 'outside'. Polynesia, Wessex, Iron Age Denmark, the 'Anasazi' are all treated as belonging to the same stage of evolution, and the same factors and mechanisms for change are examined in each context – class conflict, environmental stress, development of a managerial élite, and so on. Cultural evolutionary models, it is therefore argued, 'flatten out' past societies. Past people's own views of themselves are, it is argued, seen as unimportant, and the unique qualities of particular cultures – for example, their artistic or cultural achievements – are not seen as important or capable of producing generalizations. In short, critics of cultural evolution suggest that such schema find it difficult to encompass the *particularity* of historical sequences.

There is a moral and political dimension to this point. Indigenous peoples, the 'subjects' of comparative ethnography, often feel that the unique and particular qualities of their ancestral traditions and modes of life are ignored or suppressed in this flattening-out. Further, their mode of life is presented not as vibrant and meaningful, worthy of study in its own right. Rather, it is treated as some relic of a past and outmoded way of living; the only way forward for them, in such a scheme, is to move forward in the evolutionary scheme by embracing 'modern' Western ways of living.

Second, earlier cultural evolutionary models often seem to leave little room for *contingency* or historical accident. Societies seem to be on a smooth, high, inexorable road to state formation. Critics argue that history could have happened otherwise, purely by chance. A favourite variant of this claim is that all such models are implicitly *teleological*. A teleological view of history is one in which there is a strong sense of direction, of humanity moving inexorably towards a predefined and predetermined goal (*telos*).

Third, in their simpler forms, cultural evolutionary models tend to ignore diffusion and cultural contact. If each society goes through a fundamentally similar set of stages, what account is given of contact between societies? How might such contact alter or deflect social change?

Fourth, it is argued that the individual is also ignored. Human beings are presented as pawns, locked into an inexorable evolutionary process over which they have no control. Again, in parallel with systems thinking, evolutionary models are open to the attack of critical theorists like Habermas and others discussed in chapter 5.

As a result of these criticisms and responses to them, simple models of cultural evolution, particularly unilinear ones, have been all but abandoned. Archaeologists using evolutionary theory have taken one of two courses: they have either made the attempt to abandon evolutionary theory entirely (such as many postprocessualists), or alternatively have attempted to develop cultural evolutionary ideas to take account of these criticisms. As I discuss this latter attempt below, the student will observe that some of these developed forms, particularly different strands of multilinear evolution, link up with the modifications to systems thinking discussed in chapter 5.

Multilinear Evolution

All the evolutionary schemes discussed above suggest that there is one basic scale, simple to complex, and societies move up and down that scale. However, as indicated in figure 9.4, one can propose that there can be more than one scale or pathway. Trajectories of social change can miss out particular stages, particularly as the result of contact or diffusion between societies. Or there might be a much looser typology of different social practices.

These points were developed in the earlier part of the twentieth century, particularly in a backlash in North America against the schema of classical sociocultural evolution discussed above. In particular, the anthropologist Franz Boas led criticism of unilinear evolution as ethnocentric, dependent on flawed ethnography, and harnessed to an unacceptable idea of Progress. As a result of Boas' and others' criticisms, for much of the twentieth century, cultural evolution was at best a minority pursuit among North American anthropologists, though we have seen how this minority, particularly Leslie White, had a profound effect on New Archaeology.

As a result, later forms of cultural evolution were often 'multilinear' rather than 'unilinear' in character. What does this mean? First, and most obviously, multinear evolution proposes that societies can take different paths or trajectories. These trajectories may or may not lead to a common end-point, for example State societies. Or they may lead in quite different directions.

More subtly, proponents of multilinear approaches pursue alternative ways of thinking to the grand evolutionary stages of classic sociocultural evolution. For example, early discussion of 'chiefdoms' took chiefdom society as an intermediate stage in unlinear evolution, between earlier and state societies. However, chiefdoms might be seen equally well in the interstices of social formations – the networks of contemporary drug barons, pirates, warlords and gang leaders, for example, fit many of the criteria of 'chiefdom societies', but clearly exist within the wider social networks of modern states.

It is also possible to attempt to decouple the question of social complexity from the more specific features of hierarchy and stratification. Carole Crumley has argued that social complexity need not imply a rigid hierarchy or order. Rather, complex societies are characterized by 'heterarchy': 'structures are heterarchical when each element is either unranked relative to other elements or possesses the potential for being ranked in a number of different ways' (Crumley 1987, 158). In this view, hierarchy is only one possible form of heterarchy, and in practice, most societies exhibit a range of different ranked and unranked forms.

As a result of the criticisms raised above, and as a result of development in evolutionary thought as a whole, most of those working in cultural evolution have abandoned any simple idea of stages. Much work within evolutionary traditions has looked at diverse trends or trajectories of development. It has also looked at evolution not as a monolithic process or as a simple ladder of classification. It has attempted to include accounts of agency, practice theory, factional competition, and conflict in its models, and located the source of generalizing inferences not in formal comparisons or rankings of societies on a notional scale, but rather in thinking carefully about process. It is interested in corporate entities and the role of individual identity and factional politics. It has attempted to link up state formation on the one hand and rhythms of daily life on the other.

Cultural Evolution and Marxism

As we have seen with the constellation of Darwin, Marx and Spencer, there is a great deal of common ground between much of evolutionary thought and classical Marxism. Marxism can be seen as one form of cultural evolutionary theory, and conversely, much cultural evolutionary theory can be seen as a form of Marxist thought, though often the Marxist content is implicit or coded. Indeed, Leslie White was attacked in the McCarthyite paranoia of his time for his political beliefs, though conversely he was accused of watering down his Marxism by others such as Maurice Bloch. Several of the autobiographical accounts of New Archaeologists make it clear that cultural evolutionary ideas of the 1960s were discussed and advocated within a North American intellectual and cultural environment in which Marxism played a very significant role, even if this was not overtly acknowledged at the time.

Classical Marxism, as discussed in earlier chapters, proposes that all societies go through the same set of stages: primitive communist, ancient, feudal, capitalist. Marx and Engels, indeed, read and were profoundly influenced by the thought of several nineteenth-century evolutionary thinkers, most notably Maine and Morgan. Marx wanted to dedicate *Das Kapital* to Charles Darwin, though Darwin declined the honour.

Cultural evolution also shares many of the problems of classical Marxism. One of these is that in its 'classical', unilinear form, Marxism allows little or no room for contact between societies. If societies evolve from one state to another, what role is there for cultural contact and diffusion? Others have argued that to propose one single scheme of evolution is simplistic. Societies might develop along different paths.

One particular form of Marxism which engages with evolutionary questions is 'Latin American social archaeology'. Latin American social archaeology had its origins in the 1970s and 1980s as an application of Marxist, and implicitly evolutionary, ideas to the archaeological record, particularly via Gordon Childe's discussion of social evolution. Latin American social archaeologists make an analytical division between socio-economic formation, mode of life or *modo de vida*, and culture.

The first of these three categories, socio-economic formation, refers to the general historical stage of a society; the last, 'culture', refers to its particular properties. The intermediate category, *modo de vida*, refers to the range of different modes of existence that can occur within a general socio-economic formation. For example, within the general socio-economic formation of hunter-gatherer societies, one might have different forms of *modo de vida* according to different relative stresses on hunting and gathering, and still more different particular examples of different 'cultures', each with particular features. Latin American social archaeology, by dividing social analysis in this way, makes the claim that it can combine forms of unilinear and multilinear evolution within a single framework of analysis.

A second form of thinking relevant in this context is political economy. Political economy, as a general term, refers to the relations between political and economic practices and systems. It was developed as a body of thought by Karl Marx, who drew on earlier 'classical economists' such as David Ricardo and Adam Smith. Key themes developed by nineteenth-century political economists included: the importance and nature of property rights, for example over land; the way value is created within different economic systems; the division of labour, and its relationship to issues of alienation. Marx's particular interest was in modern capitalist societies, but political economy has been developed within archaeology with reference to pre-State and early State societies.

Archaeologists taking an approach derived from political economy are interested in different economic practices (the provision of labour services, subsistence agriculture, household economy, gift exchange, circulation of prestige goods). They explore how these practices intersect with issues and processes of political power (ranking, the rise and collapse of chiefdoms, state formation). Archaeological studies of political economy take a broadly evolutionary approach, in that they engage with, for example, the economic processes that structure social ranking, and especially the processes and structures that are involved in state formation (see below). They are also part of the broader body of approaches that developed out of earlier systems thinking discussed in chapter 5.

Origins of the State

An important, even central, strand of thinking in cultural evolution has been the development of generalizing and comparative theories of the origin of the State. It can be argued that 'state origins', or more broadly the origins of social complexity, is one of the Big Questions in archaeology, alongside the origins of *homo sapiens sapiens* and the origins of agriculture. States are generally defined in terms of their use of force and their legitimation of political inequality. In the archaeological record, it is argued by evolutionary theorists, states can be seen as having bureacracies, settlement hierarchies, palaces and temples, and as seeking to build up territory and Empire. Many archaeologists working on state origins insist that most or all of these features can be seen cross-culturally, in contexts of 'primary state formation' ranging from Mesoamerica to Mesopotamia to China.

For example, a relatively traditional study is Spencer and Redmond's review of the evidence for state formation in Mesoamerica. Spencer takes as given the unilinear scale of progress between chiefdom and state, and he is working within an established tradition that maintains that distinct archaeological correlates can be seen for each. They review archaeological work in different areas, organizing it 'according to three diagnostic criteria: a) the emergence of a four-tier regional settlement-size hierarchy; b) the appearance of royal palaces and specialised temples; and c) the conquest/subjugation of distant territories'. They conclude, for example, that:

> for the La Venta region, surveyors have reported a three-tier settlement hierarchy for the Middle Preclassic period. No convincing plans of palaces or standardized, multiroom temples have resulted from excavations … There is no compelling evidence that the Olmecs of the Southern Gulf Coast carried out an aggressive takeover of any distant region. We conclude that the Formative period Olmecs are appropriately interpreted as chiefdoms, not states. (Spencer and Redmond 2004: 175, 187).

In a classic example of how cultural evolution has attempted to move beyond unilinear models, Baines and Yoffee have stressed how early state societies were not all the same as one another. They shift emphasis away from comparing specific societies in terms of ticking off a check-list of different features such as bureaucracies and temples, and towards developing generalizing comments about processes 'through an investigation of the instrumental principles of hierarchisation, of the restriction and display of certain kinds of wealth and the devaluation of other kinds of symbols, and of constitutive institutions of legitimation that emphasise the dispersive ties between rulers and ruled' (Baines and Yoffee 2000: 13).

Again, Adam T. Smith has discussed the relationship between the constitution of landscape and political authority in early states. He rightly criticizes earlier evolutionary models for treating space as unimportant – that is, comparing Mesopotamia with Mesoamerica with China, without thinking with sufficient care about the landscape differences between these very different locales. However, Smith does not forsake a generalizing approach, and ends up with a general stress on the importance of landscape and the centrality of political authority rather than 'environment' as generalizing comments on what he calls 'early complex polities' – though it is striking that Smith ends up being equivocal about the utility of this general term (Smith 2003: 278).

Case Study: Cahokia

Cahokia is a complex of around 120 earthen mounds and other features in the midwestern United States, near Collinsville, Illinois in the American Bottom floodplain, across the Mississippi River from St Louis, Missouri; the site was occupied between AD 650 and 1400. Cahokia dominates the surrounding landscape, being the largest site of its kind by far; at its peak, the site was the largest settlement north of Mexico. The central monument, Monk's Mound, is the largest humanly constructed earthen mound in the Americas, big enough to be termed by some a pyramid (figure 9.5); it is one of around 120 mounds. The whole site may have had a population of up to 20,000 people.

The interpretation of Cahokia, and the 'Mississippian culture' of the surrounding region, has become a classic example of the development and application of theoretical ideas. Early studies concentrated on description, chronology and 'culture history'. The development of cultural evolutionary models led archaeologists to debate whether Cahokia could be classified as a chiefdom or as an early state, and if so, how complex it was, whether it could be described as a 'city'. Thus studies of the site tended to maximize or minimize its size and complexity, while studies of the surrounding region either stressed how dominant and far-reaching Cahokia's power and influence was,

Figure 9.5 Artist's impression of the site of Cahokia at its peak, by William R. Iseminger

or conversely, tended to minimize this dominance and argue that the site was the centre of no more than a 'complex chiefdom' (Milner 1998: 3).

Cobb comments on the study of the Mississippian culture in terms that could be extended to the study of other areas and periods:

> If there is a historical trend in studies of Mississippian complexity it is one that first emphasized hierarchy. This was followed by a consideration of the horizontal power links, the heterarchical structure, between segments of society. Finally, some researchers have moved to a practice-based approach that emphasizes agency and relations more than system or structure. Yet these changes in perspective represent more of a Doppler shift than a complete reorientation – scholars may represent different areas on the spectrum, but they do not seem to have lost sight of the importance of the spectrum itself (Cobb 2003: 79).

The most recent assessment of Cahokia exemplifies this trend: Julie Zimmerman Holt's characterization of a 'theatre state' (2009: 231). Holt is struck by the similarity of the monuments and associated practices at Cahokia to the description by the cultural anthropologist Clifford Geertz of the Balinese 'theatre state'. Holt hinges her argument on specific cross-cultural comparisons in her use of Geertz's Balinese material, and she draws attention to both archaeological and historic evidence for sacrificial and other rituals, including human sacrifice, and games such as chunkey.

In so doing, Holt brings together many of the recent developments in thinking about cultural evolution and state origins. She asserts: a) a questioning of simplistic models and accepted categories of cultural evolution, for example a cut-and-dried distinction between 'chiefdom' and 'state'; b) a rejection of the distinction between power and ritual as a false choice; c) a rethinking of stress on the importance of theatre from Geertzian anthropology; and d) an implied stress on the importance of practice – including strategies used by leaders and commoners to such as 'group-building' or 'group-distincting'. In this way, an interpretive stress on agency and practice has been built into a wider, generalizing and comparative framework.

Cultural Evolution Strikes Back

My response to the debate over the utility of cultural evolutionary models is to observe that, however much they have been overtly abandoned by some scholars, archaeologists resort to underlying ideas of cultural evolution far more frequently than they sometimes care to admit. Those underlying ideas are often unacknowledged, and are often of the most simple and basic kind, tending back, implicitly, to unilinear models.

The key tension in current thinking, then, is not between archaeologists who affirm cultural evolutionary principles and those who disavow them, but rather between different elements of what all archaeologists do and what they claim that they do – a tension that is part of a broader tension in contemporary archaeology that I will return to in the concluding chapter.

Most obviously, the terminology used to describe and classify different cultural stages and phases remains that coined by an earlier, evolutionary age. Terms like archaic, formative, classic, and post-classic still abound. An excellent reason for the survival of these terms is simple inertia, or a dependence on a common terminology or set of reference points. For an archaeologist who has grown up with classifications of the material framed in this way, it is arguably a waste of intellectual time and effort to attempt to get academic consensus for a renaming. Whether archaeologists like it or not, the classification and terminology of Stone, Bronze and Iron Ages will still be with us in the decades and centuries to come; Classical civilization will still be Classical civilization and the Dark Ages will still be the Dark Ages; the Palaeolithic will still be divided into Lower, Middle and Upper.

Some archaeologists would claim that these terms are no more than simple descriptive usages. However, one very compelling point of the critiques outlined in chapters 7 and 8 is that language is more important than this. It is naïve to see terms as 'unimportant' or 'just descriptive', just as it is naïve to attempt to dismiss the sexist use of language as unimportant. However if it is accepted that the terminology persists, it follows that the older schemes of unlinear evolution are not simply passé; they continue to structure archaeological thought in often unacknowledged ways.

However, I suggest that what is at stake here is much more than the problems of terminology. Let us take as an example phenomenological interpretations of Neolithic and Bronze Age Wessex, of the sort discussed at the end of chapter 7. Such accounts are often laid out with implicit reference to a strong position of overt rejection of evolutionary theory and generalizing models of archaeological process. However, interpretations of people moving across the landscape, what they see and experience at different points, and what meanings and understandings those experiences related to, have been set out against a backdrop of an implicit, shared understanding of what Neolithic and Bronze Age society and culture was like – what sort of social forms operated, how society worked at that time.

For example, visual references to tombs of different kinds are interpreted as references to the 'ancestors'. These arguments are only convincing if one thinks it plausible or compelling to propose that links to the ancestors conferred territorial rights, or were pertinent to territorial claims; or more loosely that kin ties and rights over land were intimately related. Such a general understanding of Wessex society is clearly derived from, at the very least, a general awareness of comparative ethnography, of groups around the world, even if that general awareness is not overtly referenced. But for such examples to be relevant, and for the reasoning to convince an archaeological audience, it must be assumed that there is some general comparability between this prehistoric past and the ethnographic present. It is difficult to see how this implicit assumption is justified, unless some model of cultural evolution, however vague and unstated, is being deployed.

It can be argued, moreover, that some kind of engagement with the issues raised by cultural evolution, however critical and qualified that engagement is, necessarily starts the moment one asks 'why?' questions. Take, for example, my account of the medieval open hall, which was presented in chapter 7 as an example of interpretive archaeology. The obvious next question, which is frequently asked of me by colleagues raised in evolutionary traditions, is: why was the open hall abandoned when it was, in the sixteenth century? To answer this question properly, one has to refer outwards – to, for example, a change in underlying sentiment and mentality, for example a 'rise in privacy'. But why a rise in privacy? Well, a greater sense of the individual, related in turn to Renaissance ideas and the rise of market relations. Why the rise of the market? And so one goes on: ultimately it is very difficult to avoid being drawn into some kind of generalizing account of feudalism-to-capitalism that is at the very least influenced by Marxist and other evolutionary accounts of general social change.

At a more basic and general level, it is possible to identify the assumptions of cultural evolution at an implicit level within much of archaeological discourse, particularly when that discourse claims not to be theoretical. Many such discussions of the 'rise of civilization', for example, in treating it as a narrative rather than questioning its causes, see the rise of civilization as a natural and inevitable process: traditional accounts of the rise of the Roman Empire are a case in point. Again, many 'common-sense' discussions of technology make the assumption that technology simply gets better and better through 'natural qualities' of human ingenuity and problem-solving. Ironically, then, ideas of cultural evolution are most tenacious, and evolutionary ideas are expressed in their most simplistic and questionable form, in areas of the discipline that consider themselves to be free from 'theory'.

In my view, then, claims of the death of cultural evolutionary theory have been over-stated. It is very difficult to specify an interpretation of the past which is broadly social and processual which does not, at some level, rest its foundations on assumptions about cultural evolution. It is arguable that there has been a relative decline in the quantity of archaeological literature that deals explicitly with questions of cultural evolution, whether of unilinear or multilinear strands. There is certainly a major difference in the profile of evolutionary ideas between North America, where cultural evolution remains an important and even dominant tradition, and much of the rest of the world, especially Britain and the rest of Europe. However, I would argue that cultural evolutionary ideas continue to underpin a very large part of what archaeologists actually do, whether we like it or not. I will come back to how this tension might be negotiated in the concluding chapter.

10

Archaeology and Darwinian Evolution

> If you think you understand [evolution], you don't know nearly enough about it ... evolution must be the best-known yet worst-understood of all scientific theories (LePage 2008: 24).

I traced in the last chapter how evolutionary ideas were a central element of the intellectual origins and basis of archaeology as a discipline. Further, I tried to show those ideas were given a decisive cast during the decades of the mid to late nineteenth century, an intellectual framework that created the intellectual foundations of archaeology as a discipline. The chapter then diverged, choosing to follow Spencer's cultural evolution rather than self-styled 'Darwinian strands' of evolutionary archaeology.

In this chapter, I will start by describing a few elements of Darwin's thought. Without Darwin, archaeology would not be the discipline it is today. We noted in the last chapter how ideas of cultural evolution continue to structure much archaeological enquiry whether overtly or implicitly. Much the same can be said of Darwinian ideas. These are often described as controversial in archaeology and in their application to human culture generally, and indeed many of them are. However, it is equally true to say that the intellectual framework encompassed by the thought of Darwin remains absolutely foundational to much of the discipline of archaeology, and foundational to intellectual life in general. With apologies to Harold Macmillan, we are all Darwinians now; Darwin's thought established a cultural horizon without which archaeology, and the human sciences, would not exist in the form they take today.

The long-term impact of Darwinian ideas has been sharpened in the last 20 years. In this period, a number of explicitly 'Darwinian' archaeologies have flourished, in tandem with the heightened profile of Darwinist evolutionary approaches to the human sciences as a whole. Theoretical writing styling itself Darwinian has ranged from general outlooks on the human sciences as an intellectual project, to specifically archaeological theories and approaches, to particular methods and research strategies, to particular explanations of elements of the archaeological record or episodes in the past.

In their many forms, different Darwinian 'archaeologies' often look very different from one another. Their starting assumptions and methods often seem to be very varied to the outside observer, and their style, tone and rhetoric often differ very markedly. It is therefore impossible to summarize a single Darwinian or evolutionary archaeology, perhaps even more so than the difficulties in generalizing about other schools such as cultural evolutionary thought or postprocessual archaeology. However, all these theories share one thing in common: a claim to be descended from the thought of Charles Darwin and his theory of evolution.

Darwin's Dangerous Idea

Darwin published *The Origin of Species* in 1859. It is difficult to over-state the excitement and impact of this book, in both scientific and cultural terms. *The Origin of Species* was a central element in the constellation of ideas discussed in the last chapter. It was the outspoken manifesto of a view of the world that was explicitly and unashamedly scientific and evolutionary. Its arguments, and those of Darwin's later *The Descent of Man*, resonated not just through the sciences, but across society as a whole, provoking responses from the shocked to the vituperative to the satirical (figure 10.1). Spencer, Marx and others applied evolutionary ideas to the study of human society.

Darwin's ideas filtered through into the arts and humanities also. The poet Tennyson wrote of 'Nature red in tooth and claw' ten years before *Origin* was published, but Tennyson was influenced by proto-Darwinist ideas, and the phrase spread rapidly, like a virus or what some Darwinists would call a meme. Many of the artist and critic John Ruskin's ideas about aesthetics were framed in bitter opposition to Darwin, while Spencer's phrase 'survival of the fittest' resonated through thinking on philosophy and human culture. It is arguable who influenced whom within this maelstrom of ideas; what is clear is that all these ideas formed an intellectual horizon in nineteenth-century thinking whose importance cannot be overemphasized. In all this rapid take-up of evolutionary ideas across a range of disciplines, it is easy to lose sight of the core elements of evolution as laid out by Darwin himself.

Evolution has been defined as 'descent with modification' (Mace, Holden and Shennan 2005: 2). Darwin proposed that plants and animals pass on their characteristics to their offspring. Different offspring, however, vary from one another. (Darwin was unsure of why this happened, and it is interesting to note this gap in nineteenth-century evolutionary thinking; it fell to later generations of scientists to discover and explore the cause of biological variation, namely the operation of genes and genetic mutation.)

Figure 10.1   Charles Darwin, from a cartoon in 1871

The resulting variations between different plants and animals mean that, by chance, some are better suited to their environment than others. The ones that are better suited to their environment stand a better chance of growing and surviving, and a better chance, critically, of reproducing, and thus passing on that variation to succeeding generations. Those plants and animals that are more successful in reproducing will, in time, expand in numbers, and come to drive out their 'competitors'.

Darwin's theory was quite simple in its essentials, but exceptionally powerful, and exceptionally dangerous in terms of its implications for understanding the natural and human world. It provided a basis for the scientific explanation of observed variation in the natural world; no serious scholar now disputes its basic principles. However, I want to focus here on the cultural impact of Darwin's ideas, since (as evolutionary thinkers frequently complain), while they remain as an accepted basis for biological evolution, their implications are often under-appreciated in the human sciences.

First, and perhaps most fundamentally, Darwin's theory demystified the natural world. For nineteenth-century readers of evolution, the natural world was no longer simply or only God's work, a mysterious source of eternal wonder to be understood through divine revelation. Rather, the natural world was to be understood with reference to Science. In my view, all the current debates over the implications of Darwin's findings for belief in God miss the more important point. Whatever one's religious beliefs might be, as a scientist or scholar, the world was now much more open and amenable to rational and empirical enquiry than it was before Darwin's theory. Different readers of this book will disagree about whether or not the world is ultimately to be understood as God's creation, but it is a matter of scientific agreement that the natural world has within it abundant evidence for a series of processes that explain its tremendous variation in evolutionary terms.

When viewed with hindsight, Darwinian thought can be held to represent the logical end-point of a process of opening up the world to scientific enquiry that can trace its origins back to early modern science and natural philosophy. In the sixteenth century, Copernicus demonstrated that the earth moved round the sun and not the other way around. By doing so, he destroyed the traditional conception of an earth-centred universe. More broadly, the great empiricist philosophers such as Bacon, Hobbes and Locke insisted that the world was to be understood not through abstract thought, but through empirical observation and rational method. In so doing, their work tended, in terms of the unfolding of intellectual history, to decouple scientific enquiry and natural philosophy on the one hand from religion and theology on the other. A Darwinian view of the world, then, is fundamentally opposed to for example a Romantic view, in which emotional affinity and revelation of the nature or essence of things through mystical experience are often placed at centre stage.

Second, Darwin's theory was able to explain tremendous variety and complexity in the natural world around him with reference to the operation and interaction of a few simple processes. The end result – the biological variety we see around us, the thousands of species of plants and animals and their interactions – was infinitely complex, and required careful and complex scientific study to elucidate. But crucially it could be explained, in its essentials, in a relatively simple way. He expressed this point in a famous passage, a tableau drawn not from his more famous voyage around the world on the *Beagle*, but rather from his daily walks across the green fields and hills of the English landscape around his home at Down House in Kent, south-eastern England (figure 10.2):

> It is interesting to contemplate an entangled bank, clothed with many plants of various kinds, with birds singing on the bushes, with various insects flitting about, and with worms crawling through the damp earth, and to reflect that these elaborately constructed forms, so different from each other, and dependent on each other in so complex a manner, have all been produced by laws acting around us (Darwin 1859 [Wilson ed. 2006, 760]).

Figure 10.2   An entangled bank, close to Down House, Darwin's home

Darwin's thought, then, was reductionist. Reductionism is a term often used in a pejorative way, but I do not mean it in a pejorative sense here. Darwin made the great intellectual achievement of reducing the study of tremendous complexity and variety to the interaction of a few key laws and variables. In this sense, ideas of cultural process as discussed in chapter 5, in their stress on cutting through their 'noise' of surface variability to the underlying cultural processes, owe a great intellectual debt to Darwin.

Reductionism of this kind is also evident in the development of nineteenth-century geology. The early date of the Industrial Revolution in Britain, and its consequent demand for raw materials such as coal, meant that the British Isles was the first part of the globe to have the details of its geology mapped out through surface observation and through examination of the sections through the earth's crust revealed in mine shafts. The result was a beautiful, but apparently complex and confusing, mass of different rocks to be found on the surface (figure 10.3). However, this complex surface pattern was the result of an underlying stratification that is in essence very simple. The strata of the British Isles are tilted up toward the north and west, so that younger and softer rocks are exposed in the south and east. The 'elaborately constructed forms' of the geology and physical geography of the British Isles, then, and

Figure 10.3   William 'Strata' Smith's map of the geology of the British Isles

the world beyond, had been produced by processes which at their heart were very simple however complex the final pattern that they produced.

Reductionism, then, is often criticized as an intellectual process, particularly by humanists who accuse some Darwinists of simplistically reducing social and cultural variability to a biological 'core'. However, it can be argued that properly executed, the development of reductive explanations is a necessary and unavoidable part of modern science.

Third, Darwin's thought had radical implications for the study of humanity. It implied that *homo sapiens sapiens* was an animal like any other. Humans were no more 'unique', in principle, than any other species. The methods of study that were appropriate for the natural world, then, were logically applicable to the human world also. One of the reasons for Darwin's impact was that he wrote in a clear and accessible style, and as a result, no reasonably intelligent reader could escape or evade the appalling implications of *The Origin of Species* for human descent. Indeed, in his later book *The Descent of Man*, Darwin went out of his way to rhetorically emphasize the point. In a passage which shocked a European world accustomed to thinking of Man as made in God's image, he described human ancestors as fanged, hairy, even Satanic with their pointed ears and tails:

> The early progenitors of man were no doubt once covered with hair, both sexes having beards: their ears were pointed and capable of movement; and their bodies were provided with a tail ... our progenitors, no doubt, were arboreal in their habits, frequenting some warm, forest-clad land. The males were provided with great canine teeth, which served them as formidable weapons (Darwin 1871 [Wilson ed. 2006: 894])

Writing like this challenged claims made by scholars in other disciplines. For example assertions in the humanities that humans were in some way 'special' or 'different' from 'mere animals' were given a severe jolt. In this way, Darwinism can often be described as a highly positivist philosophy, in the sense of the positivist belief that the human sciences could or should follow the principles of the natural sciences.

Darwinism leads one, then, to a highly sceptical view of the idea of human essence. Claims can often be found in philosophical, theological or humanist literature about what makes us 'distinctively human'. Darwinists are often dismissive of these claims. For Darwinists, the key question is not a meditative, philosophical or abstract one ('what makes us human, deep down?') but a scientific question: what combination of traits, for example large brain size, a larynx enabling complex sounds and therefore language, opposable thumbs, or primate social organization, made early hominids adaptively successful? Darwinist thought is in this sense profoundly and aggressively *anti-essentialist*. In earlier chapters we saw how much culture-historical or traditional archaeology is implicated in notions of what makes us 'essentially human', notions that again can trace an intellectual ancestry to philosophies of Romanticism and/or idealism. Darwinism encourages the view that such notions lack intellectual credibility or at best are unscientific.

Humans are, arguably, an extremely successful species, but the reasons for that success are not to be found by reference to divine will, or to particular civilized or 'cultured' attributes, or to some kind of human 'essence'.

Rather 'culture' itself can be redefined radically. For succeeding generations of Darwinists, culture was the means by which humans adapted to their environment. Great art and architecture, literature, music, systems of morality, and all the other professed attributes of 'civilized' life might be fine and pleasurable things to contemplate, but could be explained scientifically in terms of their attributes as part of a functioning cultural system. Victorian notions of morality were undercut by such a theory, emphasizing as it did that emotional or sentimental phenomena as 'innocent' as a maiden's blush were sexual in origin.

Darwinism also leads to a highly sceptical view of any purpose, mission or teleology to human history. Such a view might sound strange, because in the nineteenth century Darwinism was harnessed to Herbert Spencer's and Karl Marx's philosophies of a definite human progress. It also sounds strange because the term 'evolution' is often associated in popular discourse with just such a teleology. However, a powerful implication of Darwin's theory is that chance – random variation, the contingent combination of different inherited characteristics – plays a very large part in the world. In cultural evolution, and in humanistic study generally, the world has a purpose. In Darwinian evolution, by contrast, 'the nature of genes is to make copies of themselves not with any grand plan or purpose in mind but simply because that is what they do' (Cartwright 2000: 53).

All these points may sound quite obvious to a twenty-first-century generation for whom Darwinist ideas are apparently very familiar. However, I invite the student to think about them very carefully. One of the characteristics of Darwinist principles, as Michael LePage hints, is that people profess to accept them, but their implications are not always thought through in practice: 'today, more than a century after Darwin's death, we still have not come to terms with its mind-boggling implications' (Dennett 1995: 19). This perceived failure to roll-out the implications of Darwin's dangerous idea is especially apparent when the student turns away from the 'natural world' towards the study of human beings. Darwinists in the human sciences often complain that their colleagues and students continue to think of the human world in humanistic and Romantic ways long after these notions have, in their view, been utterly discredited.

Cultural Ecology

Darwinist ideas were based around a small group of key concepts, including variation, drift, adaptation, and natural selection. The central argument of Darwinist applications to the human sciences is very simple. Each of these ideas can be argued to apply not simply to the natural world, but to human and cultural life also. In this view, human and cultural life is part of that natural world.

Darwinist archaeology, then, is part of a wider movement in the human sciences, a movement which makes the claim that Darwinist principles are applicable not merely to biology, but to human culture also. If this claim is correct, then all or part of the archaeological record can be explained with reference to evolutionary ideas such as variation, adaptation and natural selection.

What is the evidence for this claim? First, variation can be seen in culture as well as in the natural world. Variation can be seen on many different levels and in different ways, from the zigging and zagging on pottery decoration, to variation between individuals and small groups, to variation between whole cultural groups however defined.

In biology, variation is argued to be random: it proceeds through genetic mutation, though as we have observed, the operation of genes was not understood in Darwin's time. To take a classic and over-simplified example, why do giraffes have long necks? When giraffes reproduce and the result is variation in neck length between offspring, there is no intentionality behind this. Giraffes do not get longer and longer necks because they desire or want longer necks. Nor do giraffes act in a conscious or purposive way, for example by stretching and stretching in an attempt to get them. Rather, the variation is random. What happens is that natural selection acts upon the variation between offspring of giraffes. Giraffes who happen to have inherited longer necks from their parents find it easier to reach the leaves in higher branches of trees. They are better nourished, and stand a better chance of reproducing and passing on their genes to their offspring. Over time, then, giraffes with longer necks will come to numerically predominate.

In human culture, the causes of variation are more complex. They might be argued to be 'random' in some cases. For example, what has been termed 'stylistic drift' has been argued to occur when decorative features such as zigging versus zagging on pottery has no obvious or direct adaptive benefit. (It may well have an indirect adaptive consequence, however, for example by its function as a stylistic expression of group cohesion). However, much human behaviour is undeniably purposive or intentional. People in the past chose to build houses of a certain form, chose to plant particular crops, or chose to dress in a certain way. It is very difficult to see the patterns these choices produced as the result of 'random mutation'. Rather, the choices were in part purposive – choice of what crops to plant or form of houses to build was informed by an appreciation of what strategy was likely to be successful (thus people do not choose to build igloos in central Africa or to attempt to grow yams in the Arctic).

Darwinists argue, however, that evolutionary principles can act on any variation regardless of whether it is 'random'. Indeed, human intention and the cultural choices that humans make can mean that many evolutionary 'dead ends' are avoided. A giraffe with a short neck is the simple recipient of sheer bad luck, and there is nothing the poor animal can do about it. A human individual or group, however, can choose this subsistence strategy over that one; can discover and utilize new sources of food; can make the choice to move to a different area with a different or more abundant set of natural resources. In practice, very few human individuals or groups consciously choose a strategy that they believe or know to be a poor one – though examples can be argued. For example, one explanation for the failure of the Scandinavian settlement of Newfoundland in the early Middle Ages is that they attempted to persist with subsistence strategies more appropriate to their homeland, rather than follow the more 'rational' choice of adopting the strategies of their Inuit neighbours.

The study of human adaptation to the environment has been termed *cultural ecology* or *human behavioural ecology*. Cultural ecology is the belief that societies will be more or less adapted to their material environment, and therefore that the characteristics of those societies can be explained in terms of such adaptation. A powerful argument in much of 'cultural ecology' is the observation derived from ethnography that humans usually have a deep and sophisticated understanding of their environment, and will modify their behaviour to adapt to changes in that environment.

It may be the case that much human behaviour has unintended consequences for survival and reproduction. The reasons why human groups change their behaviour might be complex, and ostensibly governed by intentions unrelated to adaptation and reproduction – building temples to please the gods, or burying their dead with elaborate grave-goods for the afterlife. Nevertheless, cultural ecologists argue that much behaviour that has no obvious or immediate significance in facilitating reproductive success nevertheless does have consequences when looked at in detail and depth.

Much cultural ecology and cultural materialist anthropology concerns itself with taking cultural practices that appear 'odd' to Western eyes, or at least not obviously adaptive or utilitarian, and showing how such behaviour does have adaptive consequences and/or can be explained using an adaptive model. Many of its adherents are anthropologists working with modern societies. Examples of ideas from cultural ecology that have been taken up and used by archaeologists are site catchment analysis, optimal foraging theory, risk and seasonality.

Site catchment analysis is a body of techniques based on the mapping of resources around a site. It is assumed that people will exploit the landscape 'rationally', and they will utilize resources in such a way as to maximize returns. The technique, then, consists of drawing a line around a site's location and looking at the resources within two, three, four hours' walk of the site.

What constitutes the most adaptive strategy in the long term, however, is not simply a question of how to exploit the most resources; it also involves issues of risk and seasonality. Interest in 'risk' is based on the observation that it is not so much the overall productivity of an environment that is important for understanding human adaptations, but the degree of risk within it. Neolithic farming communities, for example, may be worried not so much about producing more food as such, but about what might happen during the odd 'bad year' of disaster and famine. It is no use a village producing enough food to support 500 people nine years out of ten if there is only food to support 100 people in the tenth, famine year.

Many economic, social and even religious strategies, then, can be understood as risk minimization. Extended networks of kin, trading contacts, food storage: all these phenomena have been interpreted by anthropologists and archaeologists as ways to mitigate the risk of subsistence crisis. If food is short one year, one can call on one's distant cousins; or on trade partners who owe you obligations; or on the tribe to whom you gave marriage partners. Thus, elaborate social networks such as those of Australian Aborigines or Inuit Native Americans can be explained as adaptive responses to 'high-risk' environments such as the Australian desert or the Arctic tundra.

'Seasonality' refers to an interest in how human groups survive through the year. There may be plenty of resources in an environment for most of the year, but this is of no use if people will starve 2 months out of 12. Peter Rowley-Conwy looked at the Ertebølle culture of Denmark and suggested that the collection of oysters, though not important in terms of overall caloric intake, was absolutely critical at a certain time of year when few other resources were available. This observation in turn helped Rowley-Conwy explain site location and other aspects of Ertebølle behaviour.

Cultural ecology, then, explores the ways in which human culture is 'adaptive' at the level of the cultural group. There is, however, a second set of approaches, which examine selection, variation and adaptation at different levels – of genetic transmission between individuals.

Genes and Memes

One application of Darwinism to human culture is to argue that much human behaviour is not determined by 'culture' at all, but rather is genetically programmed or determined. Sociobiology is a form of theory that attempts to explain features of human behaviour as being the result of genetic/biological rather than social, non-genetic causes. It suggests that certain behaviours are the result of genetic propensities that were adaptive at some point in the past. Sociobiology is an exceptionally controversial theory of culture, since the stress on particular propensities for behaviour (aggression, group loyalty, altruism) being rooted in genes is often interpreted by its opponents as being racist or sexist. For example, some sociobiologists argue that it makes adaptive sense for males to spread their genes around widely and reproduce as much as possible; female primates, by contrast, can only have a limited number of children, and need a stable partner for protection against predators and other environmental dangers. Therefore, it is argued, women in modern Western society are genetically predisposed to stable relationships, whereas men are genetically predisposed to sleep with as many sexual partners as possible. Opponents of sociobiology see this as a thinly-disguised attempt at an ideological justification for male infidelity – 'I couldn't help it, dear, it's in my genes'. Sociobiology is seen by many, including many Darwinists, as excessively simplistic in its approach; it is very difficult to point to convincing or sustained case studies that apply sociobiology to the archaeological record.

A more subtle way to think about the genetic basis of human behaviour is proposed by evolutionary psychology. Evolutionary psychologists develop explanations of human cognitive traits as the products of past processes of adaptation and natural selection. We saw in chapter 6 that evolutionary psychology was an important part of cognitive archaeology, in that is proposes evolutionary explanations for the development of language, of symbolic thought, and so on. Much of this work was prefigured by Darwin himself, who in his later years looked at the expression of emotion in humans, relating it to patterns of behaviour that he hypothesized had been adaptive in the past. Evolutionary psychology tends to have a more complex view of the relationship between genetic make-up and human culture, a view taken up by co-evolutionary theory (see below).

A subtle way to avoid some of the conceptual issues raised by sociobiology and evolutionary psychology is to think more carefully about the unit of selection. In biology, the unit of selection can either be the gene, or the individual organism; there is a complex and ongoing debate in biology over which of these is the appropriate unit of analysis. Richard Dawkins' famous book 'The Selfish Gene' was arguably mistitled; genes are not selfish, they are just genes; they do what they do, that is, replicate themselves. However, his point was that it is genes which replicate and which are or are not successful in doing so, not individual organisms.

Darwinists studying human culture have explored the implications of Dawkins' observation. Dawkins proposed that while biological transmission occurs genetically, human culture consists of memes. A meme can be defined as any cultural unit that is passed from one person to another by non-genetic means. A meme can be an idea, a particular behaviour, or a cultural value; and it can be passed from one individual to another by imitation, teaching or other forms of cultural transmission. Memes are in this view like genes, in that they carry code. However, the mode of transmission of behaviour here is memetic, rather than genetic. Memetic transmission can be analogous to genes, or it can be very different: thus, while genetic variability is the result of 'copying errors', cultural behaviour may change not just through 'drift' but also through intentional behaviour, for example innovation or adoption of different cultural practices. As a result, many of the problems of sociobiology, both conceptual and ethical, are avoided.

The idea of memes is attractive to Darwinian archaeologists because it gets around a key problem. Sociobiology asserts the primacy of genetic transmission of behaviour; but clearly, in human history, there have been cultural practices that have been very successful and have flourished, though they have not necessarily facilitated the reproduction of particular individuals.

Co-Evolutionary Theory

A particular form of Darwinist thought that has proven popular among archaeologists is 'co-evolutionary' or 'dual inheritance' theory. Co-evolutionary theory does not claim to reduce 'culture' to biology or vice versa. For Richerson and Boyd, culture is part of biology, but not reducible to it:

> Much evidence suggests that we have an evolved psychology that shapes what we learn and how we think, and that this in turn influences the kind of beliefs and attitudes that spread and persist. Theories that ignore these connections cannot adequately account for much of human behavior. At the same time, culture and cultural change cannot be understood solely in terms of innate psychology. Culture affects the success and survival of individuals and groups; as a result, some cultural variants spread and others diminish, leading to evolutionary processes that are every bit as real and important as those that shape genetic variation. These culturally evolved environments then affect which genes are favored by natural selection. Over the evolutionary long haul, culture has shaped our innate psychology as much as the other way around (Richerson and Boyd 2005: 4)

One of the strengths of this argument is that it moves beyond rather sterile 'nature' versus 'nurture' arguments, which Richerson and Boyd regard as misguided. On the one hand, humanists and others have often taken a 'superorganic' view of culture, insisting that the mind is a 'blank slate' upon which different cultural systems are more or less free to write what they like. On the other, some Darwinists have tended towards a naïve sociobiological position in which everything that we think and do is genetically determined. Richerson and Boyd reject this opposition; culture for them, is obviously implicated in biology, but genes act as a recipe, not a determining code.

One of the powerful implications of this argument is that Richerson and Boyd do not divorce or oppose culture to biology, but they do affirm that culture changes evolutionary processes qualitatively: 'Culture is interesting and important because its evolutionary behavior is distinctly different from that of genes.' Part of culture can be seen as memetic, that is operating in a manner analogous to genes, but memetic processes are not the only cultural processes at work.

Richerson and Boyd's views are controversial, but they do open up an intellectual space which moves beyond sterile nature/nurture debates, and enables one to explore the interaction of culture and biology without having to sign up to a reductionist position. It is striking that recent Darwinist archaeologies of a more eclectic and theoretically flexible brand such as those emanating from the UCL Centre for the Evolution of Cultural Diversity have drawn heavily on Richerson and Boyd's work.

Selectionist Archaeology

A stronger and more fundamental position of is that of the 'selectionist archaeology' of Robert Dunnell and his students. Selectionist archaeology starts from a very strong assertion of archaeology as a science, and a dogmatic rejection of other forms of archaeological enquiry as basically misconceived. For example, the entire project of cultural evolution is dismissed as 'unscientific' and having nothing to do with biological models. Dunnell separates two very different strands of nineteenth-century thought: Spencer's stress on social totalities leading to cultural evolution; and the adaptationist arguments of Darwin. Only the latter, he claims, is 'scientific'. Cultural evolution is unscientific because it substitutes cause/intention for a scientific framework: 'it employs different notions of cause, lacks theory in the usual sense of the word, and employs an entirely different research strategy' (Dunnell 1989: 38). Dunnell also rejects sociobiology, on the grounds that most transmission of traits is cultural rather than genetic.

Instead of positing the individual as the unit of selection, selectionist archaeology focuses on the 'phenotype'. Phenotypes are defined as the physical and behavioural elements of organisms; 'artefacts are the hard parts of the behavioural segment of phenotypes', like shells or nests for other species. Selectionist archaeology, then, focuses on the success or failure of phenotypes in replicating. Much of selectionist archaeology has focused on a very sharp distinction between style and function. It is proposed that functionally advantageous traits will be selected for. However, stylistic traits will be subject to 'drift'.

Selectionist archaeology makes two interesting intellectual alliances. First, in its stress on understanding the archaeological record rather than on the human actions and processes, and also in its rejection of cultural evolutionary models, it ends up in a similar position to much traditional culture history. Second, as Dunnell has pointed out, it reverts to a version of evolutionary theory earlier than that of Darwin. Recall the example of the giraffe's long neck discussed above. An earlier generation of biologists, particularly the eighteenth-century thinker Lamarck, had posited that giraffes get their longer necks through some kind of conscious or unconscious striving on their part. Selectionist archaeology claims to revert to this Lamarckian rather than Darwinian model, in that artefacts or phenotypes are the 'hard' or 'fossil' part of human culture. The programme of selectionist archaeology has been especially popular in North America. Conversely, in other parts of the world, scholars have tended to see it as resting on a misunderstanding of Darwinist principles; it is striking, for example, that Shennan's work makes very little reference to it.

Selectionist archaeology has few case studies worked through in detail to back it up, in part, I think, because its challenge to established modes of archaeological enquiry is so fundamental and far-reaching. If Dunnell is correct, then we must abandon much of traditional archaeology, including what he terms 'model descriptions' of phases, cultures and periods, as well as 'behavioural reconstruction'. Bettinger and Eerkens note 'an unfortunate parallel between evolutionary archaeology and the weather: everyone talks about it but no one does anything about it' (1997: 177). Nevertheless, models such as these have attracted a committed following in the last few decades, particularly in North American archaeology.

Case Study: Art, Handaxes, Population and Innovation in the Palaeolithic

A range of examples of how Darwinist ideas have affected archaeological interpretations can be taken from human origins research. The first is Steven Mithen's explanation of the archaeological record of the Palaeolithic, including cave art and handaxes. Mithen suggests that the creativity of cave art is an adaptive response to an environment full of risk and fluctuation, in which there was often plenty of game around but in which sharp fluctuations could occur. He draws attention to the content of the art – images of animals that he interprets as encoding valuable information for hunters – and its distribution – in an area rich in game and possibly dense in population at this period.

Mithen suggests that the art relates to critical moments in changing hunting strategies when changes in the environment forced hunters to adapt by turning from group activities to solitary hunting. The art, then, helped prepare hunters for such changes. Mithen suggests that hunters were aware that troughs in reindeer/red deer populations would occur, but were unsure when.

What is striking about Mithen's approach is its use of different ideas. He uses ideas of adaptation to a changing environment to explain a phenomenon – art – not normally regarded as amenable to an adaptive approach. Mithen insists that 'creativity' and 'adaptation' are not mutually exclusive; indeed, he comments:

I am left wondering about a possible connection between the creative act of producing images and the creative thoughts about hunting behaviour that such images helped create. I feel that these must have fed off each other in a spiral of creativity leaving us today with the splendours of Palaeolithic art and enabling the Palaeolithic hunters to adapt to their uncertain world. (Mithen 1990: 13)

Mithen's explanation here is loosely inspired by cultural ecology, but his more recent interpretations of handaxes as 'products of sexual selection' (Kohn and Mithen 1999, 518), in collaboration with Kohn, is more directly and fundamentally derived from Darwinian ideas. Handaxes are one of the most common, and classic, artefacts of the Acheulian (figure 10.4); one of their most striking features is that their form remains extremely stable over a million years. Kohn and Mithen observe that many of these handaxes are very carefully produced, in a way that goes beyond what is needed for utilitarian purposes. In particular, forms of handaxe are carefully designed to be as symmetrical as possible. Kohn and Mithen draw on Darwinian models of sexual selection theory, which stress how reproduction is the outcome in part of female sexual selection, and which explores why females choose certain traits in the male over others. Sexual selection theorists have

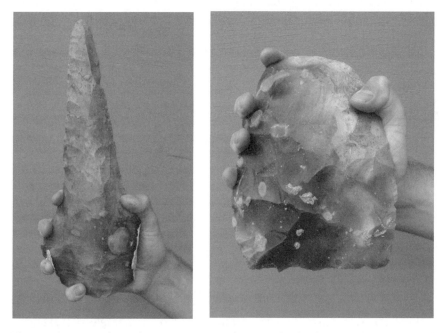

Figure 10.4   Handaxes from Cuxton, southern England. Photographs courtesy of Francis Wenban-smith

pointed out that symmetry, in biology, is an indicator of good genes, and is one criterion of 'mate selection'. They are arguing for a bias on the part of females towards symmetry, and that symmetrical handaxes would be read at some level as an indicator of good genes, or more broadly in terms of the male's success at acquiring resources, health, and social and cognitive awareness. Males, then, learnt to produce particularly impressive and symmetrical handaxes for the purpose of attracting mates.

This theory is a classic example of Darwinist ideas in archaeology, even down to the way like so many Darwinian arguments it has been popularized (and viewed with humour, by both proponents and detractors) as 'sexy handaxe theory'). It can be criticized from both within and without a Darwinian perspective, for example on evidential grounds: right or wrong, there are quite a number of very wide and bold inferential leaps between observed patterns in the archaeological record (symmetry in handaxes) and explanatory theories (female sexual selection). For example, there is no hard evidence that males rather than females were producing handaxes, or that there was competition between males for females as mates; both these features may be suggested by comparative studies of primates, but remain unproven.

A third example is Stephen Shennan's study of cultural innovation and the emergence of modern human culture after 60,000 BP. Shennan is interested in the relationship between population size on the one hand and cultural innovation on the other. He takes a co-evolutionary approach to understanding cultural transmission and innovation, and discusses the means of transmission and change in craft traditions, most obviously stone tool production. Shennan develops a complex mathematical simulation which demonstrates that the larger the population size, the more successful innovation is likely to be:

> When cultural innovation processes take place and the results are passed on by a combination of vertical and oblique transmission, larger populations have a very major advantage over smaller ones. Quite simply, members of larger populations are on average both biologically fitter and more attractive as models for imitation, by virtue of the fact that the deleterious sampling effects present in small populations decline as population sizes increase. When populations are small, innovations which are less beneficial reproductively and less attractive to imitate are more likely to be maintained within them. (Shennan 2001: 12).

Shennan concludes, therefore, that a key to understanding the increased rate of change in human culture after 60,000 BP is the relatively rapid increase in population size after this date, compared with very low population levels before that date: 'demographic fluctuations may be the single most important factor in explaining how and why the emergence of modern human culture occurred when it did' (Shennan 2001: 15) – and conversely, Shennan adds, low population levels may explain why earlier handaxes changed so very little over time.

Darwinian Archaeologies: Criticisms

Criticisms of Darwinist archaeologies and their inspirations in Darwinian applications to the human sciences are difficult to list in a straightforward fashion. As we have seen, the school of thought itself is a varied and complex beast. Criticisms directed, for example, at cultural ecology are quite misdirected at certain forms of biological evolution or other programmes such as optimal foraging theory. As Darwinian models of evolution vary in what they consider to be the appropriate unit of analysis (individual, culture, phenotype), and as proponents are quite insistent that these variations are fundamental scientific differences rather than changes in nuance or relative emphasis, critique of one model is not necessarily applicable to others.

Shanks and Tilley come closest to a complete rejection of such models. They reject any kind of evolutionary or ecological theory on grounds that are basically similar to their rejection of systems thinking. Concepts such as time budgeting, risk and cost-benefit analysis are, Shanks and Tilley argue, ideas that are derived from modern economics: that is, the study of modern capitalist societies. If, as Shanks and Tilley suggest, people in the past had systems of cultural values that were other than those of modern capitalists, it follows that such concepts are inapplicable to them. In fact, we can go further: if cultural ecologists claim that such analyses hold any truth, then they are in fact claiming that capitalist values are true in all times and all places. Cultural ecology is therefore, for Shanks and Tilley, ideological – as we discussed in chapter 6, an ideology is a system of beliefs that makes certain values appear universal, normal and natural.

Cultural ecologists counter that, as we look at other cultures, their beliefs are indeed more or less 'rational'. Modern ethnographic studies, they claim, show that all or most cultures do in fact have a 'rational' view of their environment, and that therefore we can apply modern 'rational' concepts such as time-budgeting and risk.

This is an unresolved argument, but it is worth pointing out its roots in economic anthropology. In the 1960s and 1970s, many anthropologists working on the economics of modern non-Western societies claimed that all such societies made 'rational' economic choices that could be understood using the ideas and vocabulary of Western economists – marginal cost, energy flows, risk, etc. This was called the *formalist* school of economic anthropology. Formalists were opposed by *substantivists*, who argued that Western ideas were inappropriate for the study of the economic choices of other cultures. The 'formalist versus substantivist debate' has lost its heat more recently, but it continues to surface from time to time in debates over the claims of cultural ecology.

A related attack on evolution and ecology has come via social constructivism, the social critique of science that we discussed in chapter 3. If a culture is indeed adapted to an external environment, it is argued, what was that environment? The resources and risks in that environment are delineated by the techniques of Western Science. But if those techniques are themselves socially constructed, they cannot claim to be a 'neutral' or 'objective' mapping of the resources in that environment. A different way of making the same objection is via an attack on *essentialism*: that is, if one deconstructs the idea that the body has certain 'natural' or 'biologically endowed' needs and desires, then the landscape cannot be interpreted as a set of resources that may fulfil those needs and desires.

Constructivists tend to make very strong critiques on the basis that Darwinism is an unacceptably reductionist view of human behaviour, a crude take-over attempt by biologists of the human sciences. Darwinists respond that constructivism is an anti-science agenda, a crude take-over attempt by the human sciences of biology and the natural sciences. Who is right? Read the literature, and then make up your own mind.

Conclusion

The application of ideas of Darwinian evolution to archaeology today continues to be one of the most controversial topics in archaeological theory. No serious scholar doubts the theory of natural selection, any more than they doubt the theory of gravity. However, there remains a major underlying tension in the way archaeologists think about human culture, and specifically the question of whether and how far Darwinist models of descent with modification and natural selection are useful or productive ways of understanding human behaviour generally, or the archaeological record in particular.

Like many theories, there is a great deal of bad Darwinism around, most frequently to be found in the popular press. Studies such as the following are of dubious origin and methodology, and are frequently quoted by opponents as exemplars of bad science:

> Shoppers are using instincts they learnt from their Neanderthal ancestors, researchers have found.

> Dr David Holmes, of Manchester Metropolitan University, said skills that were learnt as cavemen and women were now being used in shops. He said: 'Gatherers sifted the useful from things that offered them no sustenance, warmth or comfort with a skill that would eventually lead to comfortable shopping malls and credit cards. In our evolutionary past, we gathered in caves with fires at the entrance. We repeat this in warm shopping centres where we can flit from store to store without braving the icy winds.'

> The study was commissioned by Manchester Arndale shopping centre ... (Ben Leach, *Daily Telegraph*, 25.02.2009)

In my view, there is a major underlying tension in the way that archaeologists approach the study of the past. As with cultural evolution, supporters, and critics, of such ideas, do not always do what they say they do. Darwinian archaeology is often (though not always) associated with a strong belief in Science, and a resistance to what are perceived as social or political agendas to deconstruct or to devalue Science. However, as we saw with the sexy handaxe theory, there are arguably as many evidential gaps in Darwinist explanations of the archaeological record as there are in parallel and competing interpretive theories. This is not to say that Darwinist applications are necessarily wrong, but it is to make a plea that it give up the strong rhetorical statements it makes to be a superior, or indeed the only, way of constructing scholarly knowledge of the past.

Darwinism is often presented as a single way of knowing, a theory that is very simple in its essentials and provides a powerful key to explaining human behaviour. Its proponents characteristically make the claim that theirs is not just another way of thinking about the past, but a better, even the only, scientific way of understanding the archaeological record. Darwinism promises to deliver a methodologically complex and difficult, but theoretically simple and unitary, way of thinking about the archaeological record. Its language and rhetoric is often uncompromising, even fundamentalist. For more dogmatic Darwinists, their way is the only way, both much more difficult and at the same time much more valuable than the fluffy humanism of lesser colleagues: 'to gain an appreciation of just how different Darwinism is from other theories about the natural world, one cannot simply read a few books or articles and come away with the requisite understanding. Rather one needs to wade through myriad epistemological issues' (O'Brien and Lyman 2000: 72).

However, what Darwinian applications to the human sciences actually deliver, when their results are examined critically and in detail, is a series of themes that are just as slippery and multifaceted as the most 'nuanced' set of interpretive archaeologies. What is different is the rhetorical style taken, of confrontation rather than accommodation; the interpretive 'difference in emphasis' or 'chosen interpretive turn' is the Darwinist's 'fundamental misunderstanding' or just being 'wrong'.

The student seeking to understand Darwinian thought, and to apply it to the archaeological record, is rapidly disillusioned by the promise of a definite method or theory. He or she is presented with difficult choices after his or her first introductory readings. Darwinist archaeology is not, in practice, a single way of knowing, but rather a series of divergent routes, the choice of which will lead to ritual denunciation from the spurned parties. What is the unit of selection – the social/cultural group, the population, the individual, the gene or the meme? How is the 'environment' defined? Is a strictly Darwinian model appropriate, or a Lamarckian model, à la Dunnell? Within this forest of arguments and choice, a path can be traced that is not necessarily incommensurate or incompatible with interpretive models. Darwin, after all, 'is sometimes said to have biologized human culture, but he is more accurately accused of culturizing biology' (Richerson and Boyd 2005: 16).

An important and exciting body of work that I have alluded to briefly in this chapter is that of placing Darwin in his nineteenth-century context, and his cultural impact and role as an intellectual in his time. The supreme irony is that the man whose work initiated a scientific dismantling of much of the essentialism of the study of 'human culture', and has led to such unabashed claims of the superiority of 'science' over other forms of knowledge, has become a cultural icon, in ways that (in my view) are very difficult to explain using a Darwinist framework. Darwin is now a megastar. He is one of the very few scientists (along with Albert Einstein) whose face is instantly recognizable (figure 10.1); he appears on the British ten pound note, on artefacts such as mugs and bumper stickers, and was voted the Fourth Greatest Briton in a BBC TV poll (behind Winston Churchill, Isambard Kingdom Brunel and Lady Diana, but beating William Shakespeare into an ignominious fifth place).

What is needed, then, is a renunciation of loud position statements proclaiming the inherent superiority of the Darwinist project, or conversely blanket condemnations of its moral or political iniquity. Rather, future decades should see a very difficult project demanding hard theoretical work on both sides, namely an understanding of the evolution of human culture and society that does not seek to reduce culture to biology, but which does seek to grasp the very subtle and complex relationship of different elements of human behaviour. In my view, it is striking that the most impressive and convincing applications of Darwinist ideas have done exactly this. For example, in *Origins and Revolutions* (2007), Clive Gamble has used ideas derived from the history of brain evolution alongside interpretive ideas of landscape, personhood and materiality.

This is a massive and very difficult undertaking, spanning as it does the concerns of the humanities and human sciences as much as it is a project internal to archaeology. Indeed, its difficulty is such that simple name-calling of other schools as 'unscientific', or conversely as 'reductionist', is often preferred to engaging in such a project. But however difficult it is, I would argue that such a project is not 'good' or 'bad' – it is simply necessary.

11

Archaeology and History

For many in North America, archaeology is seen as a subfield of anthropology, or at the very least the two disciplines are seen as closely linked. In Europe, a straw poll of the views of most archaeologists would suggest that the sister discipline of archaeology is history.

In part, this difference reflects the different subject matter in North America and Europe. The archaeology of North America is largely pre-historic until the first colonies of the fifteenth, sixteenth and seventeenth centuries AD. There is a flourishing and vibrant 'historical archaeology' of the period of the American colonies and of eighteenth- and nineteenth-century North America, but numerically it is very much a minority pursuit within Americanist archaeology. The archaeologists based in North American Classics departments are sometimes at the forefront of theoretical debates, but not always. In contrast, the 'historical horizon' is much earlier in Europe. Europeanists have historical texts that bear on the pre-Roman Iron Age; archaeologists specializing in this or later periods form over half the teaching staff in most British universities, and at a rough estimate over half the excavations in Europe take place on Classical or post-Roman sites. All these archaeologists deal with historical texts, and therefore with university colleagues in Classics or History departments, in some form. The full story of this divergence between Britain and North America in terms of disciplinary allies, however, goes a little deeper than this. As we saw in chapter 2, this different disciplinary configuration led to the differential impact of the New Archaeology in Britain and America, and between prehistoric and Classical archaeology. It also led to the continuing flourishing and variety of 'traditional', culture-historical approaches in Britain and especially continental Europe.

In this chapter, I want to look at some of the different theoretical views taken on the relationship between archaeology and history. Before I can do this, however, we must look at different views of historical theory and practice. The theoretical positions of historians are as varied as those of archaeologists. To an extent, debates within historical theory run in parallel to those within archaeology.

Traditional History

Historians often like to trace their roots as a discipline back to the nineteenth century with figures such as the German historian Ranke. Ranke espoused what today would be seen as a narrow empiricism: his aim was to tell history *wie es eigentlich gewesen*, 'as it really was'. He criticized grand theoretical schemes of human history and attempts to draw moral and political judgments from historical material. The task of the late nineteenth-century historian was simply to amass piles of facts, which, it was held, would speak for themselves.

Coupled with an empiricist and inductivist approach to the material went a stress on history as a narrative of political events. Traditional historians told a story. Traditional history books often have a beginning, a middle and an end to their plots. Indeed, it can be argued that while traditional historians protested (and protest) that they have no theory, in fact they follow literary rules of narrative and emplotment that have been ably characterized by the historical theorist Hayden White.

Traditional political history of this kind continues to be written to the present day. However, there has been a widening of historical thinking in several directions too wide-ranging to even detail here. One example of this widening of approach is the Annales school of French historians (named after their journal, *Annales: Economies, Societies, Civilisations*) such as Marc Bloch, Fernand Braudel, Emmanuel Le Roy Ladurie and Jacques Le Goff. The Annales school has been much cited by archaeologists as a useful inspiration for archaeological thought, so it is worth reviewing its theories briefly.

The Annales School

First, Annales historians broadened their interests to include all aspects of past societies. They looked not just at the political machinations of the élite, but also at economy, society and cognition. In this sense the Annales school helped history become more anthropological and processual – that is, to understand total cultural systems rather than just tell stories about its political events.

Second, the Annales school broadened historical interest in the nature of time. Traditional historians tended to see time as no more than just a series of events such as battles, political treaties, births, coronations and deaths of monarchs. The task of the historian in this view was simply to describe these events as they happened one after another. The Annales school wanted to look at longer-term processes that underlay particular events. Underneath the 'surface froth' of battles and treaties, they saw economic, environmental and demographic trends and cycles. As discussed by Fernand Braudel, history moved at three scales or rhythms:

1   that of events, *l'histoire evenementielle*;
2   medium-term cycles such as economic boom and bust; and
3   the very long term, 'enduring structures' or *longue dureé* (climatic changes, physical geography).

Note the similarity between the Annales notion of the long term and the archaeological concept of process as a trend underlying specific variability (discussed in chapter 2). Note also two areas of debate prompted by Annales thinking that have parallels within archaeological theory:

1   Which (if any) of the three levels or scales of time is dominant? Each timescale might have its own logic; they might intersect at specific conjunctures. At times Braudel implied that the *longue dureé* dominated the other two levels; other Annales historians implied that the three levels interacted and that no one level was dominant.
2   Are people's thoughts important, or does the environment dominate? Some writers suggested that what they called 'mentalité' or mentalities could be just as much part of the *longue dureé* as climate or physical geography. For example, Jacques Le Goff talked of 'the medieval mind' as a mentality spanning five centuries that structured medieval people's attitudes towards economic life and the natural world. So while Braudel tended to equate environment with the long term and to treat environment as a base-line, no such equation is logically necessary.

For example, in his book *The Peasants of Languedoc* Emmanuel Le Roy Ladurie looked at the lives of peasants in southern France. He used quantitative evidence, for example on the nutrition of peasants and of daily wage-rates; he used a loosely systemic model to understand why populations grew, stabilized and contracted at certain points; he emphasized the importance of 'environmental' variables such as climate. At the same time, his book *Montaillou* is one of the most famous reconstructions of peasant mentalities in historical literature. Le Roy Ladurie's work, and Annales thinking in general, therefore incorporates many of the tensions between environment and society, short and long term, seen in archaeology and the human sciences in general.

The Linguistic Turn

In the decades after 1980, however, there has been a move taking historians still further away from traditional forms of historical discourse: this has been called the 'linguistic turn'.

A good way to explain this shift is to look at the story of English 'social history'. In the 1960s, very much in parallel with New Archaeology and New Geography, and influenced also by the Annales school, historians working within the Cambridge Group for the Study of Population and Social Structure turned to new areas outside traditional history. Some writers even termed this the 'New Social History'. The New Social History sought answers to the dynamics of past societies through the use of statistics and looked at processes such as demographic cycles and fertility rates, using systemic jargon to understand the links between these. Cross-cultural analogies were used, for example between Europe before and during the Industrial Revolution and modern 'developing' societies.

But the New Social History rapidly found that key elements of the answers to the questions it was asking lay in 'sentiment' and 'mentality' – that is, in the realm of thoughts and ideologies. A good example is the New Social History's attempt to understand changing patterns of marriage. Historians could not understand statistics of changing age of marriage, for example, without looking at changing attitudes and sentiments (for example, changing attitudes towards illegitimacy, attitudes towards patriarchy, or the rise of the modern notion of romantic love).

As a result, historians turned to other forms of evidence to explore people's attitudes. These included such 'non-statistical' sources as conduct books prescribing manners and behaviour, court accounts of popular sentiments expressed at church, even literary and poetic descriptions of feeling and behaviour.

At the same time, historians became responsive to the argument that there was no one objective historical truth or 'social reality'. If the sentiments underlying 'marriage' had to be explored, these sentiments obviously varied. There was no one correct answer to the question 'What was marriage really like in seventeenth-century England?'; there were many different experiences of marriage, many possible interpretations of what people 'really thought' about marriage – different views of women, of men, of the élite, of the working classes. And these interpretations were unavoidably subjective – any historical account of marriage was written and was read within a contemporary society in which the idea of marriage seemed to be under grave threat or at the very least to be changing.

As a result, social historians saw the dissolution of objective facts to the extent that some historical theorists proclaimed the 'end of social history'. Many argued that we could not have 'social reality' because 'what was really going on' in any given historical situation was open to multiple interpretations; people's social lives were constructed within cultural understandings and beliefs. These beliefs, of course, were variable and could be 'read' in different ways, just as in chapter 7 we discussed different 'readings' of archaeological material. Instead of an objective society with a concrete existence, we had a more amorphous set of cultural beliefs. Behind 'social reality' lay cultural perception. So out of the New Social History was born ... the New Cultural History. This move was paralleled within the Annales School itself; where an earlier generation had studied '*mentalité*' as a fixed and invariant deep structure, a later generation headed by Roger Chartier preferred to write more nuanced histories of particular cultural practices.

This excursion into historical theory is brief, potted and incomplete in the extreme. I want to make two points with it, however:

1   *The history of archaeological thinking runs in parallel with that in history in particular and the human sciences as a whole*, though the jargon used is often different. I could have given similar potted histories of thought in sociology, economics, politics, etc.
2   There are many different forms of historical thinking, many different theories of historical method. It is not sufficient, therefore, to say 'we should reject history' or indeed conversely 'we should adopt tried and tested historical methods' without specifying what those methods are and examining those methods within their own disciplinary context. While the theories of other disciplines can be a source of useful new ideas, there is therefore *no salvation for archaeological thought in turning to the methods of another discipline*, since *the unity of methods professed by that discipline is invariably illusory* whether we are discussing the methods of the natural sciences or those of history or of literary criticism.

Unsurprisingly, we find that different schools of archaeological theory have turned to different elements of current historical practice as allies.

Jacquetta Hawkes famously wrote of archaeology: 'however scientific the methods employed, the final aims of the discipline remain historical: the description of individual events in time' (Hawkes 1968: 258). Even when she wrote, this was a description of only one form of historical practice, and a narrowly traditional form at that. It was a form that Gordon Childe modelled his early culture-historical work on also. Childe in his later life came to question the theoretical assumptions of his earlier work and wrote critically of it in his 'Retrospect' (1958).

Recently, some archaeologists have turned to the ideas and methods of the Annales school for inspiration. In particular, they have stressed Annales interest in different timescales and its interplay of the material and the world of 'mentalities' in which no one feature is dominant. Finally, many postprocessualists derived inspiration from the methods and theories of historians involved in the New Cultural History.

Historical Archaeology

In the first part of this chapter, I looked at the relationship between history and archaeology in the abstract. I now want to look at how the two disciplines interact in practice, in different approaches to the archaeology of historic periods. My definition of 'historical archaeology' differs from that of many North American archaeologists, for whom this refers exclusively to the post-1500 period; I shall be discussing examples from Classical and medieval archaeology also.

Much traditional archaeology has found itself in alliance with traditional forms of history mentioned above. An earlier generation of archaeologists working in Classical periods or early medieval Europe deal with areas of historical discourse that, with exceptions, are still largely traditional in scope. In many cases, the archaeologists concerned took their first degree in Classics, History or a related discipline, and came to archaeology through a desire to attack questions defined in advance through (traditional) historical methods: Who was the king buried at Sutton Hoo? What was the appearance of the Forum in Rome? When was this medieval village deserted?

Subservience to historical accounts has meant subservience to traditional models of culture history and a normative view of culture. The classic example is the story of the Anglo-Saxon settlement of England. The eighth-century historian Bede tells us that three groups of settlers came to Britain in the fifth century AD: the Angles, the Saxons and the Jutes. Bede tells us where they settled and which kingdoms they founded. A generation of traditional archaeologists looked at the grave-goods from cemeteries in these areas and interpreted them by looking to north Germany and southern Denmark for parallels. Thus, because Bede tells us the county of Kent was settled by Jutes, material from Kent were labelled 'Jutish' and stylistic parallels sought – and found – with material from Jutland in Denmark of similar or slightly earlier date.

Though this is culture history based on theories of migration rather than diffusion, the parallels with prehistoric culture history are obvious. More recent work has criticized this model, either seeking to minimize the impact and numbers involved in fifth-century migrations, to be more critical about the historical record, or to stress social change at the level of small-scale structures rather than large-scale migrations.

Historical Archaeology and the Text

In North America in the 1960s and 1970s, a group of historical archaeologists worked to adapt the tenets of New Archaeology to the archaeological study of historic periods, following Binford's insistence that 'specialists in this field should provide the most informative tests or evaluations of ideas set forth by archaeologists in general' (1977: 169). We saw one example of such an approach in Hodges's systemic analysis of Dark Age trade in chapter 5.

This work attempted to generalize and be anthropological in the sense of getting away from traditional historical descriptions of colonial and later history. It attempts to look for pattern – to define diagnostic patterns of artefacts; and tries to generalize about the societies under examination. For example, the work of Kathleen Deagan and others in St Augustine, Florida, a town populated in the seventeenth and eighteenth centuries by a number of different ethnic groups, has tried to look for different archaeological patterns associated with these groups. The aim here was in part to elaborate a more rigorous approach to the definition of ethnicity based on the definition of quantitative measures.

One way in which historical archaeology has taken up such concerns is to try to treat documents as a form of middle-range documentation. Remember that Binford argued that we could look to independent sources of information to build 'robust' arguments (chapter 4). In the Palaeolithic, he looked to animal and plant behaviour. Many have argued that in historic periods, documents can play a similar role. Account books at ports, for example, can tell us exactly what was being imported and exported and at what price, a pattern we can then match or fail to match against those goods or their containers when we find them in rubbish pits.

Conversely, many have turned to elements of postprocessual and interpretative thought for an alternative model of the integration of archaeology and history. Remember the importance of context in postprocessual thought. Documents read from this view can provide a special form of contextual information, for example on the individual or on different views of gender. We have already seen one example of this work: my discussion of the late medieval hall in England in chapter 7.

As a result, many explorations of recent theoretical trends have come in historical archaeology, particularly in colonial contexts – South Africa and North America especially. Two themes can be picked out in particular: first, the historical archaeology of capitalism; and second, identity in historical archaeology.

A historical archaeology of capitalism focuses on the interpretation of the period after 1500, and the way in which archaeology can address the most fundamental transition between medieval and modern worlds. This can be termed the 'origins of capitalism', the 'feudal/capitalist transition', 'industrialization' or the 'origins of modernity'; each of these terms having different theoretical affiliations, and rather different nuances. A leading figure in the field is Mark Leone, who over the last 30 years has developed an account of the archaeology of capitalism in eighteenth- and nineteenth-century Annapolis and the Chesapeake, on the east coast of the United States. Leone and his students developed the idea of the 'Georgian Order', a material pattern first delineated by Henry Glassie and James Deetz. They saw principles of order, symmetry and segregation running through different classes of material culture – eighteenth-century architecture, gardens, pottery, landscape. The Georgian Order was interpreted by Leone and his students as linked to the emergence of merchant capitalism in the Chesapeake and beyond. Order, symmetry and segregation related to an ideology of the individual and of liberty, however much that ideology was contradicted by the realities of a class-divided and slave-owning eighteenth-century society.

Archaeologies of identity, discussed in chapter 8, have some of their most powerful case studies in historical archaeology, where different identities can be seen to emerge and be re-negotiated in both the archaeological and documentary records. Barbara Voss, for example, has shown how a distinctive 'Californio' identity of nineteenth-century Californians of Hispanic origin emerged as part of a whole complex of rapid cultural changes following the annexation of the area by the United States. 'Archaeologies of resistance' have looked for material evidence of identity formation, for example in institutional contexts such as prisons.

Historical archaeology as a whole, however, refuses to fit into the neat theoretical boxes that have very often been defined by prehistoric archaeologists. A good example of how historical archaeology simply does not 'follow the rules' is provided from the archaeology of castles.

Case Study: Bodiam Castle

There is a long-standing debate about castles in medieval England. Castles are high-status buildings, and combine accommodation for a great lord and his household with 'defensive' features – towers, ramparts, battlements, gatehouses, moats and ditches.

Interpretation of castles has traditionally been dominated by scholars with a military background. Developments in castle architecture have been interpreted in terms of changing techniques of attack and defence. This narrative often claims to be factual and atheoretical, but can easily be shown to be an evolutionary and progressive one: attack and defence become more technologically sophisticated over time. Both the evidence of archaeology (the changing form of walls, towers, gatehouses) and documents (narratives of sieges) have been used to tell a story about castles, quite literally: most traditional books on castles consist of a narrative history of the 'rise and fall' of the castle, with individual castles being cited as illustrative anecdotes.

In this story the documents take centre stage. By the very use of the word 'castle', rather than the more neutral and anthropological 'high-status dwelling', scholars use a word that is derived from the documents, and whose meanings are to some extent defined before archaeological analysis starts. Similar categories defined by the documents can be found across most of Classical and historical archaeology – 'Roman villas' (a 'villa' being defined with reference to Classical texts), 'temples', 'churches', the study of 'enclosure'. Most narratives start with definitions of 'castles' based on the (usually Latin) texts within which words like 'castrum' and 'castellum' are defined. Next come the obviously military features. Residential features within the walls receive less attention, and the landscape context of castles – the villages and towns outside their walls – even less attention.

To over-simplify, these élite sites have generally been approached by archaeologists in 'culture-historical' ways, stressing influence, contact, diffusion of new architectural ideas. This document-based narrative is rarely questioned, let alone tested. Nothing like a 'processual' approach to castle studies has ever been proposed let alone pursued.

In recent years, some historians and archaeologists have asked other questions: what of the social dimensions of these buildings? Are not their lordly functions (judicial centres, lordly residences) at least as important as their supposed military/strategic role? Some have gone further still: what of the symbolic dimensions of these structures? Are the battlements and towers not in fact to do with military requirements, but rather the self-image of a masculine military élite basing its ideology on images of knighthood?

Bodiam Castle, near the Kent/Sussex border in south-east England (figures 11.1 and 11.2), was built in the 1380s by Sir Edward Dalyngrygge, an old soldier from the Hundred Year's War in France. The interpretation of this castle has centred on the question: is this a seriously defensively strong castle, as the military theorists would have it? Or are its features better interpreted in a more complex symbolic and cultural way, as more recent scholars have argued?

Military theorists have drawn attention to the proliferation of military features: gunloops commanding the approach ways, twin towers flanking the gate and other towers dominating the tops of the walls. Most particularly, Bodiam is situated within a small rectangular lake that has been artificially created. The lake is a complex piece of hydraulic engineering, and is held back on two sides by an earthern dam. It apparently forms a formidable obstacle to any would-be attacker. The main entrance to Bodiam runs at an angle across this lake, exposing attackers to fire from the battlements.

Not only is Bodiam clearly militarily very strong on this analysis: the final 'proof' of the military thesis comes from a historical document, a 'licence

Figure 11.1 Bodiam Castle: photograph of the north front and gatehouse across the lake

to crenellate [fortify]'. Translated from the Latin, it states apparently quite unequivocally that Sir Edward Dalyngrygge sought and duly obtained licence in October 1385 'to fortify with a wall of stone and lime the dwelling-place of the manor of Bodiam next to the sea ... and to construct and make thereof a castle for the defence of the adjacent countryside and for the resisting of [the king's] enemies'. Here is a clear, irrefutable documentary statement of the military purpose of the castle. Or is it?

Disbelief in the exclusively military view of the castle has been relatively recent, and comes from three sources:

1 A reassessment of the architecture of the castle. Charles Coulson has shown convincingly that many of the apparently 'military' features of the castle do not appear to 'work'. Gunports are not placed effectively; guns placed in them do not command an effective field of fire. Other openings are almost impossible to use by longbow or crossbowmen; the fighting parapet is not easily accessible; the list could go on.

2 A detailed survey, carried out independently, of the landscape context of the castle (figure 11.2). First, the earthwork dam is utterly undefended; in several estimations it could be cut through by a dozen workers in one night. The lake itself is not as deep as it could be; it is more a sheet of water like those of eighteenth-century ornamental gardens than a serious obstacle. Outside the lake are the earthworks of a large formal landscape, around which the movement of people and their views of the castle were carefully structured.

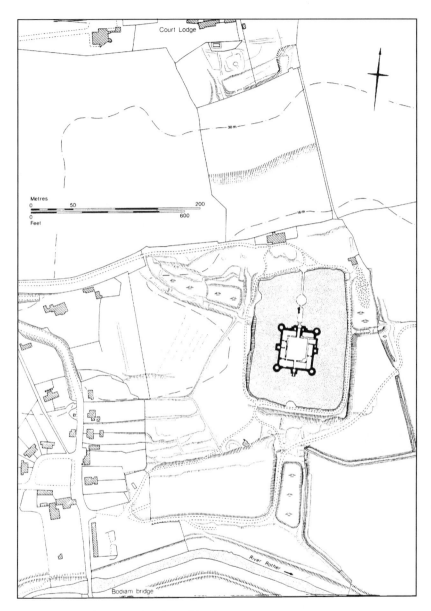

Figure 11.2 Bodiam Castle: plan of landscape context

3   A reassessment of the meaning of the licence to crenellate. Bodiam is not 'next to the sea'; it is 14 kilometres north of the coast, at the end of a winding tidal estuary. Documents of this kind cannot be taken at face value as prehistorians might suppose. Coulson suggests that the production of such documents was largely part of a system of chivalric honour, and the references to defensive intent should not be read as an historical record, but rather as part of a knightly code of chivalrous values. He writes suggestively:

> Reasoning from illusive defensive effects mechanistically back to imagined military causes has, in the case of Bodiam, led to the famous licence of October 1385 being taken at its face value. ... Because no study has been done of licences to crenellate as a whole ... *many misjudgments have arisen partly from lack of contextual awareness.* (Coulson 1992; emphasis mine)

Coulson's detailed knowledge and experience of late medieval documents, inductively acquired as part of his practice as a documentary historian, leads him to have a better 'feel' for the quality of the evidence than other writers on the subject.

But this reinterpretation is not simply a statement that 'symbolic is more important than military'. Coulson writes:

> The wisest course is to resist the temptation to write off any feature as 'sham', or to take any element as purely 'functional' (by which 'defensive' is intended normally). It is an artful combination which expresses ... all the complex seignorial associations of the medieval castle-image, which included the deterring (and, if necessary, the defeating) of attack at whatever level was appropriate ... the bravado of double portal chambers, 'murder holes' and three portcullises is mere rodomontade when the lateral doors are so weak. There is no 'military' logic in trebling the main closures while leaving a short and direct approach to a weak back door (Postern) which entirely lacks elaboration. But there is a powerful psychological sense nonetheless: it is closer to Jean Froissart (and perhaps also to Franz Kafka) than it is to Vegetius or to the Sieur de Vauban. The fairy-tale element is here, allusive and romantic. ... 'Fortification' was surely metaphysical as well as material; a matter of imagery and symbolism, not just of technology. (Coulson 1992: 66, 83)

What theoretical lessons can be drawn from the Bodiam story? First, the arguments are over formal rather than quantitative analysis. In other words, scholars argue not over the numbers of things, as they did over the relative proportions of different tool types in a given Mousterian assemblage as discussed in chapter 3, but over their form, whether that is of the form of the lake or of the gunloops. Such a way of debating derives in part from an existing archaeological tradition hitherto little discussed in this book. The so-called 'English landscape tradition' is a school of thought looking to the local historian W. G. Hoskins as its founder. The landscape tradition stresses close empirical analysis of pieces of landscape, a view of landscapes as both very old and as complex documents on which many phases of settlement are 'written', of the integration of history, archaeology and geography using an inductive model, and of hostility to 'grand theory'. Such an approach has both strengths and weaknesses: it stresses interdisciplinarity and close attention to detail, but is essentially anecdotal in its approach. That is, it uses closely worked-through case studies but gives little consideration to how typical the case study or 'anecdote' is of the wider context. More seriously, it is almost never consciously theorized.

This debate, and the wider landscape tradition of which it is a part, does not follow the established rules of archaeological theory. While some approaches are more or less 'culture-historical' in nature, there is no established 'processual' view of Bodiam. No one has tried formally to characterize Bodiam in terms of a settlement hierarchy. No approach to the landscape around Bodiam that might approximate to a processual analysis has been taken. Archaeologists have not explicitly discussed English medieval society in terms of factional competition, religious legitimation, or access to resources, though the material for such an analysis is readily available and would make a compelling account. Conversely, Coulson's discussion does not fit easily into theoretical categories: his discussion is peppered with aesthetic value judgements appropriate to the discourse of traditional architectural history but reading quite oddly to someone trained as a prehistoric archaeologist (Bodiam is 'charmingly proportioned', 'elegant', 'nicely moulded'). Indeed, in my view Coulson's arguments could be strengthened by reference to such theory, considering for example which social groups and/or genders would have 'read aright' the symbolism of Bodiam, and considering in more depth the peasant–landlord antagonism of the period.

Conclusion

Archaeological theory has tended to be played out over certain classic 'case studies' (I almost flippantly wrote 'playgrounds') such as megaliths, cave art, the Mousterian question. These have tended to be prehistoric, for several reasons. First, prehistory is perceived as 'pure' archaeology. Second, most histories of archaeology have seen historic periods as secondary to the main story of the development of prehistoric chronology. In passing, it is worth noting that such histories themselves need rewriting; for example, nineteenth-century European medievalists were well aware of stratigraphy in buildings archaeology, and documented such stratigraphy carefully, independently of more well-known prehistoric studies of excavated stratigraphy. Third, the stress on very long-term processes within New Archaeology tended to make the shorter-term perspectives of historical archaeologists marginal to the discipline.

The story of historic archaeology shows that we do not need to stick to the notion of prehistory as 'pure' archaeology, and that the archaeology of historic periods throws up equally relevant and complex problems of interpretation. In addition, the cross-cutting influence of different disciplines (archaeology, history, literature, etc.) throws up a series of unexpected theoretical debates that enrich archaeological discourse as a whole. If you want to find the most informed and up-to-date studies of gender and other aspects of identity, to examine the cultural and political engagement of archaeology, or to explore themes like agency and materiality, then it is increasingly the case that the most exciting and compelling studies come from historical archaeology. In the last 20 years, historical archaeology has moved from the margins of the discipline to centre stage.

12

Archaeology, Politics and Culture

> *I'm puzzled. We've almost reached the end of the book, but the most popular buzzword in theory has hardly been raised yet – 'postmodernism'. I've heard lots about postmodernism recently, most of it negative, though no one ever tells me what this means, let alone why it might be relevant to archaeology.*

Well, the question of postmodernism is in many ways a red herring. But I guess I'd better try to deal with it as briefly as possible, though it may take a whole chapter to do justice to it and all its implications. Again, I'll go through the theory before discussing its application to archaeology.

The 'postmodern condition' has been defined by the French philosopher François Lyotard as *incredulity toward metanarratives*. Lyotard suggests that the postmodern condition is the condition of knowledge in Western capitalist societies.

A metanarrative is a big story, or a grand claim of absolute truth. Examples of metanarratives are:

1   A belief in scientific progress, that our ideas of the world are getting better and better through the use of rational method. In this sense post-modernists see belief in Science as a metanarrative.
2   Any total scheme of cultural evolution in which societies move from one stage to another. For example, a belief in a scientific Marxism – that through an objective science of society we can see grand, successive stages in human history leading inexorably towards communism. Or again, a classification of societies into band, tribe, chiefdom and state.

3 A belief in any absolute system of morality true in all times and in all places, whether that morality is derived from religious, nationalist or ethnic claims.

4 Any scheme of 'progress' in human history. Such progress may be aesthetic or artistic: for example, much traditional art history assumes that artists get better and better at representing Nature. It may be technological: that humans have more and more 'complex' or 'efficient' technology through time. Postmodernists argue that assumptions of 'progress' implicitly underline many apparently atheoretical typologies (for example, pre-Classical to Classical or Gothic to Renaissance in the history of art and architecture, or most 'progressive' archaeological accounts of ancient technology in which advance succeeds technical advance).

For postmodernists, such beliefs can be traced back to the basic assumptions of the Enlightenment of the eighteenth century. Enlightenment philosophers claimed that with the use of Reason, we could study human affairs in a rational and objective manner. Enlightenment philosophy therefore implied:

(1) Belief in some kind of *Utopia*. If Reason can be applied to the study of human affairs, it follows that it can be applied to its organization. Therefore, we can reach some kind of perfectly organized state, or we can at least aim for that goal even if it is unattainable within our lifetime. It can even be a goal that we know we shall never attain but nevertheless wish to aim for as an ideal, such as perfect 'scientific' knowledge of the natural world. Examples are for Marx, communism; for Fukuyama, bourgeois capitalism; for some physical scientists, a final, unifying post-Einsteinian theory of the physical universe.

(2) A notion of *teleology* in human affairs. A teleology is an assumption of an underlying grand process with a definite start point and end point; for example, within Marxism, the drive towards ever greater inequality and alienation, culminating in its ultimate overthrow and dissolution under communism. Cultural evolution tends to be more or less teleological, though we saw in chapter 9 how recent work in this area has tended to minimize or deny this teleological element. For the Enlightenment, a teleological account could be the steady unfolding of Reason as human history progressed, or variants thereof.

(3) A belief in essential properties of a 'real world' out there, separate from language, that we can study independent of the text, independent of what we write about it. If there is such a real world, then meanings can be fixed. But for critics of modernity, there is no such fixity. For Jacques Derrida, '*il n'y a pas de hors-texte*'. The translation of this phrase can be debated but is generally

rendered as 'there is nothing outside the text'; there are, instead, a proliferation of other texts.

In other words, the text apparently refers to a 'real world', but when we look at that real world, we find that it too consists of a set of signifiers that refer to something else. The word 'pot' refers to a definite thing made of clay with handles, but the thing made of clay with handles itself refers to other things. Any self-evident factual statement can be pulled apart by its own internal logic, since it cannot refer to a stable external world beyond the text – the signifiers just go on and on. Derrida demonstrates this through the technique of *deconstruction*, in which he shows that however self-evident and factual a text appears to be, its meanings can be turned against itself.

As a result, it is argued that the postmodern condition is of a world with fluid, unstable meanings with no final reference point. Instead of looking for deep, underlying, 'core' or 'essential' features of a phenomenon, there is simply endless fluidity and play across surface meanings.

(4)   A questioning of *disciplinarity*. In the eighteenth century, the study of the 'real world' was divided into different disciplines dealing with different kinds of phenomena. Thus, physics and chemistry deal with physical processes, whereas biology deals with organisms. But if all texts refer outwards, if the chain of signifiers just goes on and on rather than stopping, there is no certainty, no final reference point, in language – everything just refers to everything else; there is no final meaning or interpretation. So there can be no distinct 'disciplines' dealing with distinct fields of study. Divides between disciplines are in this view arbitrary, depending on historical accident or contingency – how the history of systems of thought happened to unfold during the Enlightenment.

Some postmodern thinkers, for example, have deconstructed the barrier between history and literature. Since all historical documents are also literary texts and all historians write narratives, and all literature exists within a certain historical context, it is argued that there can be no *a priori* distinction between history and fiction. Reliance on factual content, postmodernists argue, is problematic at best: it is rare to read a novel in which Paris is not the capital of France, or human beings do not have two arms and two legs. In practice, it is argued, 'disciplines' such as history or literature are constituted and their boundaries maintained not through 'real differences' in their subject matter, as traditional scholars would claim. Such claimed differences would owe their reality to an outside world that does not have any fixed or stable boundaries at all (the 'logocentric fallacy').

At the end of the twentieth century, the postmodern argument continues, Western thought entered 'the postmodern condition'. Historically, all these grand narratives, certain distinctions and disciplinary boundaries have fallen away; we don't have any large stories or certainties left that we can rely on. The most obvious example given is that of Marxism. In 1900 Marxists could be confident that world history was on the high road to revolution and communism. They had a system for explaining the world which seemed to work and which gave definitive pointers to the way they should think and act in the present. Now, after the fall of the Berlin Wall in 1989, things are not so certain, to say the least.

Postmodernists spread the attack more widely, however: they also point to the erosion of confidence in a single 'scientific method' discussed in chapter 3 and also in the decline of Victorian ideas of evolutionary progress (chapter 9).

Postmodernism is a way of thinking that has affected much of Western thought within and beyond the human sciences. Within architecture, for example, modernists believed that creation of functional buildings along 'rational' principles (for example, the use of tower blocks) could contribute to the solution of social problems such as inner-city crowding and deprivation. The failure of these beliefs, postmodernists allege, reflects the intellectual failure of underlying modernist philosophies.

To an extent, then, we should talk not so much of postmodernism but of *the postmodern condition*: it is alleged that the decline of confidence in the Enlightenment, in human perfectibility, or to a final and intrinsic Truth, is not really a proposition to be debated back and forth. Rather, it is a general state, the way the world is in the twenty-first century.

Postmodern thought often refers to two 'heroes'. The nineteenth-century thinker Nietzsche stood against the Enlightenment, arguing against the sway of Reason. For the twentieth century, they cite the philosopher Ludwig Wittgenstein. Wittgenstein started his intellectual career as a logical-positivist philosopher (see chapter 3). He attempted to create a philosophical language that was perfectly neutral, a language that described the outside world in completely objective terms. When this attempt collapsed, Wittgenstein 'saw the light' and spent the rest of his career arguing that communication was simply an endless 'language game' in which the rules were arbitrary but by which we nevertheless agree to play.

I want to pick out one contemporary thinker in particular as important in the development of postmodern thought, as he is cited more frequently than anyone else by contemporary archaeologists: Michel Foucault.

Foucault looked at many of the concrete institutions of the Enlightenment, places where Enlightenment values of Reason held sway. These included the reform of prisons, the replacement of 'barbaric' methods of punishment with 'rational', 'enlightened' penal systems; the development of modern scientific medicine and clinical practice; the treatment of madness and the development of the 'enlightened' idea that madness was an illness that could be treated medically. He tried to show that far from representing 'progress' or the rise of more rational or humane ways of treating human beings, all these institutions were bound up with new forms of oppression in what he called 'the disciplinary society'.

Foucault's second theme was an attack on *essentialism*. Human beings in the Enlightenment were assumed to have a set of 'natural' or 'normal' faculties: the possession of Reason, a certain form of sexuality, desire for privacy and for individual freedom. In each case Foucault showed how each historical epoch had its own ideas about what was 'normal' and 'natural' for the body to desire or feel. There cannot, therefore, be reference to a biological base-line for scientists such as 'the sex drive' because there can be no cross-cultural definition of such a base-line.

Postmodernism, perhaps more than any other buzz-word or idea in contemporary theory, acts as a locus of very strong emotional or visceral responses, both for and against. Most frequently, 'postmodernism' is used as a term of abuse. Many thinkers identify postmodernism with a denial or deconstruction of any kind of rational method or empirical enquiry into the past. It is claimed that postmodernism lays the way open to a disabling relativism, in which if there is no final truth in the world, all views of the world, or of past history, are equally valid.

It is further alleged that postmodernism leads to a kind of nihilism. If there is 'nothing beyond the text', then the implication, according to opponents, is that postmodernists view the whole world as 'just a text'. Note the inserted 'just' or 'merely' here, carrying the implication that words are not important. You will remember that empiricism is, in part, based on a radical division between 'words' and the real world, and the prioritization of the latter. For many scientists and other empiricists, postmodernism threatens to become a denial of what they see as the real world, and of the possibility of rational enquiry.

This allegation of nihilism can take a moral turn. If there is 'nothing beyond the text', then there can be no one overarching system of morality that is true in all times and all places. Postmodernism, then, is equated with a moral as well as intellectual relativism.

For Marxists, some feminists, and other committed to ideas of social justice, postmodernism is interpreted as holding an additional danger. It appears to reduce very real issues of equality, deprivation, and even violence against powerless individuals and groups to the status of a 'language game'. Much criticism of postmodernism, then, comes from the political Left, many of whom see its stress on surface play and irony as the ideological froth of late capitalism, the last, wildest, most decadent party before the inevitable collapse back into grim reality. As I write these words, and the 'credit crunch' unfolds and widens into what is generally agreed to be a profound crisis of global capitalism, such an analysis seems to gain in strength day by day.

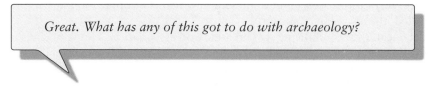

Great. What has any of this got to do with archaeology?

First, much postprocessual thought clearly shares ground with postmodern thinking: the loss of confidence in Science, the attack on essentialism, the stress on a diversity of readings and a lack of fixity of meaning.

I would argue against an easy equation with postmodernism, however. The postprocessual turn in archaeology *parallels* the postmodern turn in the human sciences rather than being derived from it. In other words, the changes that archaeological thought went through in the 1980s and 1990s were one small example of a wider set of changes across the human sciences as a whole. This is why I suggested at the start of this chapter that postmodernism is in some ways a 'red herring'.

Second, the postmodern questioning of disciplinarity has led to interest in breaking down disciplinary boundaries. At the same time, it also implies a fragmentation of method. If there is no one Truth 'out there' waiting to be discovered any more, it is difficult to see how there can be one 'right' or 'wrong' way of doing archaeology.

The implication for archaeology is therefore (a) can we really talk about a single 'archaeological method' distinctive from that of other disciplines? and (b) is there such a thing as a unified method in archaeology anyway?

Third, postmodernism does suggest that archaeologists need to engage with other forms of knowledge outside the traditionally conceived purview of 'archaeology' or of 'science'. At the very least, scholars have to think carefully and seriously about the world outside the academic and professional practice of archaeology, rather than simply dismissing other views of the past as a 'lunatic fringe'. Postmodernism suggests that if there can be no one neutral method, then other views of the past can have validity, and not simply be ruled out of court because they do not conform to established procedures of archaeological method.

For example, archaeologists may not agree with the ley line hunters, Native Americans, other Indigenous peoples, or others who have come to their version of what the past was like by rules that are not strictly those of archaeology as an academic discipline – but archaeologists do have to take them seriously. We cannot simply continue to write about the past 'as [we think] it really was' independently of the present. In short, we have to look at the social, political and cultural context of archaeology.

Archaeology is Not in a Vacuum

Whatever their theoretical differences, most would agree that archaeological interpretation does not exist in a vacuum, isolated from the outside world. Before the practising archaeologist goes to work, he or she reads the morning papers, worries about all the wars in the world and imminent economic recession. At work, relations of status between teacher and student are constantly invoked; out on site, decisions about what to dig and how to dig it are orders from the site director, arrived at after debate between (usually senior) members of the team or crew. In short, decisions are taken and archaeology practised within a definite set of social and political relations whether we like it or not.

How, if at all, does this political environment affect archaeological interpretation? If it does, it does not necessarily do so consciously. Take, for example, the study of the rise of the Roman Empire. Most traditional historians of the Roman Empire would angrily, and sincerely, protest that their accounts of 'Romanization' were simply descriptions of 'what really happened', free of any conscious bias. More recent writers point out that these writers are certainly not consciously biased, but never see the need to ask the question: why did natives so rapidly and readily assimilate themselves into an imperial system? This is at least partly due to the fact that for the previous generation the benefits of Empire were obvious and self-evident; conversely, for our generation they need explaining at the very least.

So for some, even as archaeology proclaims its neutrality it is deeply committed:

> At heart, archaeology is a colonialist endeavour. It is based on, and generally perpetrates, the values of Western cultures. Privileging the material over the spiritual and the scientific over the religious, archaeological practice is solidly grounded in Western ways of knowing the world. (Smith and Wobst 2005a: 5)

> Archaeology, as cultural practice, is always a politics, always a morality. (Shanks and Tilley 1987: 212)

Politics as seen by these thinkers is more than 'party politics'. It is about power in the broadest sense, from the policies and practices of the State down to the smallest human interaction. In this view, everything that we say and do is political in some sense. When a site director gives instructions to his or her team, when we write that an argument is 'strong' or 'weak', when we choose which site projects to fund and which to ignore, when a self-confident student cuts across a more diffident and nervous student in debate – these are all political decisions and actions.

This point is an emotive and controversial one. Many students have told me that they dislike politics, and specifically chose the study of archaeology to get away from it. The Classical author Livy wrote his *History* with this aim in mind also. But we have seen many times in this book how we always return to the present in the end, whatever philosophical viewpoint we take. In chapter 2 we noted that the data are mute, that the past does not exist; rather, statements about it are made in the here and now. In chapter 6 we discussed the concept of ideology, and earlier in chapter 5 we saw early versions of systems theory condemned by critical theorists as just such an ideology. Chapter 8 saw feminists criticizing archaeology and academic discourse in general for its phallocentrism.

The common point of all these critiques is very simple: when an archaeologist claims that their position is neutral and apolitical, what are they trying to hide?

Case Study: African Burial Ground

During the eighteenth century, between 10,000 and 20,000 people of African descent were buried in an area of New York City that came to be known as the African Burial Ground. In one estimate, 'at least half of the present African-descent population in the United States probably has at least one ancestor buried in this area'. The area fell out of use after 1795, and the land was filled in and overbuilt. The role of slaves of African descent in eighteenth-century New York was gradually forgotten. According to Michael Blakey:

> The very existence of an African Burial Ground in colonial New York raised the issue of false historical representation. The vast majority of educated Americans had learned that there was little if any African presence in New York during the colonial period, and that the northern American colonies had not engaged in the practice of slavery. The Burial Ground helped show that these notions comprised a kind of national myth. (Blakey 1995: 546)

In 1991 the burial ground was 'rediscovered' and partly excavated by archaeologists in advance of redevelopment. Over 400 burials were excavated before public concern led to legislation to suspend excavation and to protect and display the site.

This concern had come from members of the African-American community in New York. The nature of this concern and the way it affected archaeological practice is revealing. In the first place, formal lawsuits arguing that the site should be preserved found little comfort in existing legislation, which had been framed around a narrow view of 'archaeological significance' rather than the cultural associations a site might have for specific ethnic groups. Such lawsuits were however backed up by the support of black activist groups, Mayor Dinkins and the Congressional Black Caucus. At one point, a one-day blockade of the site halted redevelopment work.

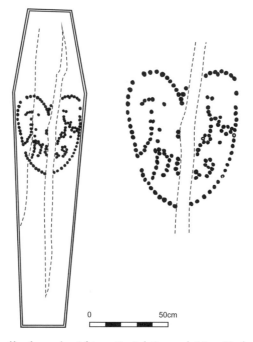

Figure 12.1   A coffin from the African Burial Ground, New York. The heart shape is made of tacks; it has been interpreted as a west African symbol

Second, the archaeological research was transformed. Initial work on the bones was done by the Metropolitan Forensic Anthropology Team (MFAT), but public pressure ensured that in late 1993 the bones were transferred to the Cobb Biological Anthropology Laboratory at Howard University.

The analysis of the bones was not simply done by a different team: it had a different research design that linked together political concerns (who controls these remains?) with new intellectual ideas about ethnicity, of the sort discussed in chapter 8, and new techniques of archaeological practice.

Not only was the research design changed; the Howard University team publicized the research design and offered it up to criticism and modification from the descendant black community. Even the name of the place and the project became a contested topic. The site had been referred to as 'The Negro's Burial Ground' before objections coupled with academic arguments led to it being renamed the 'African Burial Ground'. In 1993 the burial ground was designated a National Historic Landmark and plans for redevelopment were scrapped. In 2006, the site was designated a National Monument, and a memorial and grounds have been laid out on the site (figure 12.1).

The results of archaeological analysis paint a compelling portrait of the exploitation and violence suffered by enslaved Africans, and equally to the active resistance of people of African descent to this exploitation and violence. Most of the dead were buried in coffins and shrouds, and oriented east-west, like white New Yorkers; but the presence of beads and shells point towards continuing African traditions.

The major implication for the practice of archaeology is that while what we do is unavoidably political, changing the way we do it is far from straightforward. In this case, it was not simply a matter of rewriting a research design, but of opening up that design to scrutiny from non-archaeologists – people who themselves occupy a problematic position within their own communities. There was no one 'right' or 'wrong' way to handle the African Burial Ground controversy, though there were better and worse ways. To a great extent, sympathetic and sensitive handling of the archaeological interpretation depends on the acknowledgement that there is a multiplicity of different views.

Indigenous Archaeologies

> Many archaeologists have come to recognize that archaeology is based on, and generally reflects, the values of Western cultures. In privileging the material, scientific, observable world over the spiritual, experiential, and unquantifiable aspects of archaeological sites, ancient peoples, and artifacts, archaeological practice demonstrates that it is solidly grounded in Western ways of categorising, knowing, and interpreting the world (Atalay 2006: 280).

One of the key developments in the development of archaeology in the last 20 years has been the growing engagement with archaeology by Indigenous peoples. 'Indigenous' is a difficult term to define, and is often spelt with a capital I to denote its complexity, but generally refers to 'native' peoples who have been dispossessed in colonial contexts, such as Native Americans or the Indigenous peoples of Australia.

A specific locus of disagreement has been the collections and storing of cultural artefacts and human remains. Huge quantities of archaeological and ethnographic material were collected in the nineteenth and twentieth centuries by Western scholars from around the world, as any wander round the store-rooms of many museums will indicate. The motivation for this collection varied, but was often done within a framework of unilineal cultural evolution, that saw the collection and classification of this cultural material as a cornerstone of evolutionary and scientific study. For many 'native' peoples, however, these actions are more accurately seen as acts of plunder, the cultural counterpart to the processes of colonialism and in many contexts cultural and physical genocide that accompanied the colonial process.

For many Indigenous peoples, cultural tradition unites present and past, and the Western dichotomy between present and past (as visualized for example in figure 2.1) is rejected. Within such a world-view, cultural objects are more than simply 'artefacts' belonging to some distant past, and are certainly not commodities that can be alienated. Objects are sacred and have spiritual power. The attribution of a profound cultural value is especially true of human remains.

Archaeology has engaged with these issues in different ways. First, the importance of genuinely collaborative research and engagement with 'user communities' has been stressed. In the past, archaeology was often justified exclusively in terms of 'science' or 'pure research' – knowledge about the past for its own sake. Increasingly such a justification is seen as not good enough, on the grounds argued above, namely that knowledge is never pure and disinterested in nature, and when such a claim is made ('I'm not interested in politics, I just want to collect and study old artefacts in peace') it usually masks the real power relations at work. As with the African Burial Ground, it is argued that archaeologists need to take seriously the views of Indigenous and other local communities, and to collaborate in the framing of research, rather than merely treating those outside the archaeological community as an 'audience'.

Second, an increasing (though still small) number of Indigenous people are now trained and work as archaeologists. Many of these scholars are working actively to construct new kinds of archaeology – 'Indigenous archaeologies' – that move beyond what are seen as colonial practices. Indigenous archaeologies are by their very nature a varied and developing set of practices. They draw, in part, on postprocessual critiques, on many of the issues of identity and interpretation discussed in chapter 8, and on postcolonial thinking in the human sciences. Indigenous scholars acknowledge the irony in this situation: 'we must sometimes use the master's tools … to create a counter-discourse to Western approaches that have consistently worked to destroy or silence our Indigenous ways of knowing' (Atalay 2006: 296).

Third, political legislation has changed the relationship between archaeologists and Indigenous peoples in different countries. As the rights of Indigenous peoples have been increasingly asserted, their claims over cultural material and human remains have been legislated for in different ways. The most notable example is NAGPRA (North American Graves Protection and Repatriation Act), passed in 1990. NAGPRA specified that most federally-funded institutions such as museums and universities draw up inventories of their collections and send summaries of all Native American human remains, sacred and ceremonial objects, and other objects deemed to be of 'cultural patrimony' to tribes likely to be associated with such material. What NAGPRA meant, then, was that much of North American archaeological practice changed radically after this date, with issues of 'Indigenous knowledge' and relations with Indigenous groups gaining a much higher profile than before, and the notion of the archaeologist as detached scientist being seriously eroded.

A classic example of the conflict between 'Western' and Indigenous cultural values is the dispute over 'Kennewick Man'. In 1996, human skeletal remains were found on the bank of the Columbia River at Kennewick, in Washington State in the northwestern USA. These remains were carbon-14 dated to over 8000 years old. According to some academics, the remains showed 'Caucasoid' traits, and Kennewick Man became a controversial pawn in the context of a debate over the single or multiple nature of prehistoric migration to the Americas.

For local Umatilla and other Native American groups seeking owner-ship of the remains, the scientifically determined date of the skeleton was irrelevant, since their religious beliefs told them that their people had been present since the dawn of time. They requested custody of the remains, with the intention of reburying them. The Native American claim was rejected in a 2004 court judgment, as the court determined that 'kinship' between the modern Umatilla and Kennewick Man could not be 'proven'. The remains have been extensively studied by scientists, and are now at the Burke Museum in Washington.

The conclusion of the Kennewick Man case points up a key issue in the future development of Indigenous archaeologies: the definition of the 'descendant community'. It is easy to assert Indigenous rights, but in prac-tice, the question of who are the descendants of the Indigenous community is not always an easy one. In the past, archaeologists often tended to ignore or write out of their interpretations any reference to descendant groups. For example, the use of the term 'Anasazi' (meaning 'the vanished ones') to refer to the builders and inhabitants of Chaco Canyon and the adjacent region in the American Southwest tended to downplay links between these sites and descendant Hopi groups. Conversely, the replacement of the term Anasazi with Ancestral Pueblo acknowledges and affirms these links.

However, different cultural groups often have competing claims to terri-tory and to cultural resources. If archaeology is not a neutral science, then it follows that the role of archaeology in adjudicating these claims cannot be a simple or straightforward one. The classic case of such competing claims is the site of Ayodha, in northern India, held by Hindus to be the birthplace of the god Rama. Until 1992 the alleged site of Rama's birth was occupied by a Muslim mosque, itself five centuries old. This mosque was destroyed by Hindu nationalists in 1992; over 2000 people were killed in associated riots. After the destruction, archaeological excavations claimed to 'prove' that, stratified below the mosque, were the remains of an earlier Hindu temple. Many, if not most, archaeologists would wish to distance themselves from one-sided claims of exclusive ownership of the Ayodha site, and to be very wary of being drawn into uncritical sup-port for a single set of claims; in this case, then, a simple assertion of the rights of a single cultural group, or indeed an assertion that archaeologists should simply describe and record objectively what was found, is simply not enough on its own.

Multiculturalism, Diversity and Inclusion

Three theoretical buzz-words have come to dominate much of the cultural and political context of archaeological work: multiculturalism, diversity, and inclusion. All are strongly related to the theoretical agendas laid out in Chapter 8, and all are theoretical concepts whose impact on archaeology has occurred in part through their application through legislation – they are probably familiar to the student from contemporary cultural discourse. I will define each in turn and explain something of their relevance to archaeology.

Multiculturalism stresses the importance of different cultures, races and ethnicities within a single population or nation-state. It tends to celebrate different cultural practices, to see this difference as enriching rather than threatening within a society, and to resist the idea that nations or populations can or should attempt to 'assimilate' different groups to a single culture. Diversity refers not simply to cultural difference, but to other dimensions of difference also – to gender, class, family circumstance, and disability. Archaeological and other organizations are required to acknowledge and respect diversity, for example in the workforce. Inclusion is about making diversity work in practice – of taking the necessary steps to ensure that people of different backgrounds are given the same opportunities, and that employers and institutions do not simply assume that all their staff or participants are of a particular cultural background (for example, ensuring that working hours can respect a variety of religious practices, or proactively ensuring and extending access for people with disabilities).

Archaeologists have engaged with all these themes in a variety of ways – as with NAGPRA, legislation has compelled institutions to comply whether their senior staff were personally in sympathy with such agendas or not. We have already seen how it was not good enough for archaeologists to sit back and 'objectively' study the remains from the African Burial Ground – it was crucial to explore ways of actively engaging with descendant and other communities. Government legislation to promote agendas of diversity, multiculturalism and inclusion have been rolled out, particularly in Britain and the European Community. Consequently, the key priorities of heritage bodies and museums have been transformed.

Most crucially, in many contexts it is now necessary for archaeologists to engage actively with these issues rather than simply sit back and take an intellectual pose. In Britain, for example, there has been a welcome shift in the last decade away from what I have termed a national 'culture of complacency':

> No longer could universities shrug their shoulders and claim that they would admit more students from underprivileged backgrounds if they made the effort

to apply; it was now incumbent upon them to show that they had an active policy of encouraging recruitment and were monitoring its effectiveness. No longer could established heritage bodies like museums, English Heritage, and the National Trust shrug their shoulders and say that they would welcome more ethnic minority visitors if they only came through the doors; relevant policies to attract such visitors and make monuments and displays relevant to them had to be shown to exist. (Johnson 2006: 166)

Ironically, then, the values of an engaged and committed archaeology have been promoted in many countries not simply through the activities of some archaeologists, but also through the necessities of complying with Government legislation. They have also, in many cases, been thought out and promoted through museums and 'heritage' agencies more widely, deeply and effectively than they have through Universities. Consequently, much of the most current, original and radical thinking on the engagement of archaeology with social justice issues has come not from academics, but from those working in 'heritage management', 'community' or 'public' archaeology however defined.

The Relativism Question

> *Well, it seems to me we've reached an impasse. There is no future in ideas of academic objectivity. We've seen that all versions of the past are political in some sense. So it seems we just make up whatever stories suit us, are convenient in the political present.*

No, that will not do. There are better and worse interpretations of the past. I do not know of a single archaeologist of whatever theoretical stripe who would disagree. Even Jacques Derrida writes that '[the relativist] definition of deconstruction is false (that's right: false, not true) and feeble; it supposes a bad (that's right: bad, not good) and feeble reading of numerous texts, first of all mine' (1988: 136–7).

The criticisms of an unrestrained relativism are many, various and irrefutable. It is demonstrably wrong: archaeology has 'progressed', we no longer believe in the Creation of 4004 BC. Relativism involves a logical fallacy: 'all views are of equal value – including this one'. Relativism undercuts the value of archaeology as a form of knowledge about the past, and if pursued to its logical implication would do archaeologists out of a job. For many, the most fundamental and damning criticism of relativism is that it destroys our ability to speak out against politically undesirable and even obnoxious views of the past, the classic example being Holocaust denial groups. Archaeologists might wish to engage with Indigenous groups at a variety of levels, and acknowledge the validity of different views at the African Burial Ground – but who would suggest that this means we have to acknowledge racist views as of equal value?

Modern theorists take several roads out of this impasse. Many continue to insist that most archaeological facts and interpretations are mundane, beyond politics. Politics does play a part in this view, but at a level of theory that happens 'after' primary interpretation – we can collect our pottery sherds, and worry about the politics when it comes to interpreting them. This is a position implicitly taken by many traditional or culture-historical archaeologists.

Alternatively, one can stress a positivist view of scientific method as a way to avoid the relativist trap. Remember that positivists stress the importance of separating the context of discovering or suggesting an idea from the context of its testing and evaluation. A processualist might well write: 'Of course we are influenced by contemporary ideas. It couldn't be any other way – our hypotheses about the past processes, by definition, are framed in the present. But the essence of science is to use rigorous procedures of testing to move beyond this, through observation of the archaeological record. This is why the development of middle-range theory is so important. Only by developing robust ways of testing our ideas against archaeological material can we move beyond simply telling stories about the past.

'For a scientist, you can get an idea about how atoms might work, or about physical processes, from the newspaper, from a conversation, or from a drug-crazed hallucination. It doesn't matter where the idea comes from. What does matter is that you then test that idea. That is, you set up that idea as a rigorous hypothesis and then test it against material that you observe. That is the way science works, and it is the way it has been proven to work.'

Thus, for example, Jerry Sabloff is quite happy to note Wilk's work relating different explanations of the Classic Maya collapse to contemporary political events, but takes care to suggest how this can help us do better science:

> While Wilk's correlations are interesting, they do not prove that current intellectual trends determine which views of the collapse became popular, nor is there anything necessarily 'wrong' about archaeologists letting political trends influence their thinking. However, if his correlations are valid, they indicate how careful scholars must be to ensure that current biases are not blinding them to alternative hypotheses or limiting the kinds of data they collect. (Sabloff 1990: 166–7)

In other words, such a view will grant that everything we say is in some sense political, but by using science we can and should move away from just telling stories.

There has been a series of discussions attempting to steer a middle course between positivism and relativism. Bruce Trigger has suggested that the course of archaeology is driven both by political context and by a progressively better understanding of the data. He advocates a modified version of middle-range theory to grasp the interplay of different kinds of influence. Alison Wylie suggests that the way we relate theory to data will vary according to the context or locality we are working in:

> The question of what epistemic stance is appropriate ... should be settled locally, in the light of what we have come to know about specific subject matters and about the resources we have for their investigation. We should resist the pressure to adopt a general epistemic stance appropriate to all knowledge claims. (Wylie 1992b: 35)

In my view, the definitive discussion of this problem is Elizabeth Brumfiel's analysis of the quality of textiles in Aztec Mexico. In this period, women under Aztec rule had to produce tribute cloth; Brumfiel's feminist perspective made her sceptical that the women were ideologically 'duped' and led her to expect that through time 'the quality of tribute cloth was deteriorating ... because Indian women were engaged in resistance. Indian women were deliberately turning out undersized, loosely woven cloth with thick, loosely spun thread as a form of opposition to tribute extraction'.

However, the archaeological evidence suggested that quality did not decline. 'Rejecting the hypothesis', however, 'did not lead [Brumfiel] to reject the entire framework of theoretical propositions from which it was derived'; rather she created an *ad hoc* modification of her theory: 'resistance to exploitation does not occur when activities ... are vulnerable to supervision and control by the dominant class. This enabled me to continue to affirm that proponents of ideological domination have underestimated the frequency of resistance and the importance of coercion in maintaining dominance' (Brumfiel 1996: 454, 458).

Brumfiel concludes that:

> Long before the choice between coercion and ideological domination is decided by appeals to data, the need to choose will be eliminated by a theoretical insight that clarifies the complementary relationship between the two phenomena. Even so, data will have an important role to play. ... For example, these observations on the quality of tribute cloth production ... have opened a new line of enquiry for me concerning how the vulnerability of men and women to state coercion may differ because of differences in the location of their work or in the kind of goods that they produce for the state. The knowledge I have gained from this enquiry will affect the way I regard ideological domination and resistance in future studies. (Brumfiel 1996: 459)

My own view is largely in agreement with Brumfiel; indeed, I know of no archaeologist who would, either openly or implicitly, declare themselves to be an unqualified relativist. In fact, peace has broken out in the realm of epistemology. With the notable exceptions of hard-line positivists and behavioural archaeologists, few would disagree that archaeologists are unavoidably influenced by our social and political circumstances, and that 'raw data' do not exist in any unproblematic or unbiased way. Conversely, few would disagree that the data are important, and that at the very least they form a network of resistance to the interpretations we wish to put on them. Most of us would say this network of resistance is very strong, and that our methods should try to strengthen it.

Discussions over the perils of relativism are, I suspect, far more to do with the perceptions, fears and uncertainties of the contemporary world, in particular the uncertain place of academic and intellectual practice in its wider context. Rather than replies to or refutations of a postmodernist philosophy, they are symptomatic of the difficulties of working within a very challenging set of cultural circumstances within which archaeology is unavoidably engaged. All the contributors to this debate have seen through the naïve certainties of positivist rhetoric with its definite and simplistic divide between data and theory to the realities of a world that is uncertain and difficult to live and work in.

13

Conclusion: The Future of Theory

> *Now just hold on a minute. There's one huge omission from the entirety of the preceding text that can't be permitted to go on any longer. What exactly is theory? You can't get away with not defining theory for the entire book.*

Well, we saw in chapter 1 that there were different definitions of what theory is. I provisionally defined theory as 'the order we put facts in', and also made reference to why we do archaeology, and to 'issues of interpretation'. As we have seen in the course of this book, however, there are different theoretical views of what facts are and how they relate to theory, different rationales or ideologies behind archaeological practice, and very different views of what constitutes 'interpretation'.

Remember figure 4.1. For many positivists, theory is a definable set of propositions that can be set up and tested against data. For advocates of middle-range theory, archaeologists have been developing a set of methods over the last 30 years that enable us to test theory against data.

In this view, theory is defined quite narrowly and precisely. It is simply a set of general propositions. These can be either generalizations about the archaeological record ('the rise of early states correlates with the emergence of redistributive trade networks') or about how we should do archaeology ('we must make testability the central criterion of our epistemology'). The data that archaeologists manipulate cannot be changed in this view: data just exist independently of the theory we are using. Many of the things we do as archaeologists (site catchment analysis, random sampling, retrieval of surface scatters of pottery) are in this view simply techniques. The questions the techniques are designed to answer may be theoretical, but the techniques and the data are outside the purview of theory.

At the other extreme, all archaeology is theoretical; theory is defined very broadly. As we have seen, postprocessualists have argued that both techniques and data are 'theory-laden', and that we must theorize 'interpretation at the trowel's edge'. Many would go further and, following critical theory, argue that site catchment analysis and other techniques masquerade as neutral but are actually deeply theoretical. Remember that for poststructuralists even a banal factual statement like 'there are 23 pig molars from Layer 346' is a statement within a text that can be deconstructed. Or they might take a different angle: 'Of course the number of pig molars is a factual statement – but why does it appear where it does in this text? Why did the site director decide to put so much emphasis on economic reconstruction at this site to the exclusion of all others? In short, the question may be 'factual', but we want to question the question.'

So, just as feminists argue that inequality penetrates deeply into everyday life, and just as many would draw a broad and deep view of the political engagement of archaeology, so in the interpretive view all or almost all of archaeological practice is drawn within the remit of theory. Indeed, one of the key developments in the last decade has been the theoretical questioning and exploration of field practice (see below).

How one defines theory, then, depends on one's own theoretical viewpoint. It would be wrong for a book written as an introduction to different theoretical views, that claims to be sympathetic or at least fair to a diversity of views, to nevertheless insist on one definition of theory to the exclusion of others. My preferred definition is 'the order you put facts in', in part because this is a short and accessible definition, in part because this seems to me to be vague in the right places – it allows different theoretical viewpoints to coexist within such a definition (though not all, admittedly). More importantly and fundamentally, it draws attention to the way that data and theory are dialectically related. In other words, 'data' and 'theory' have to be understood as part of a larger whole in which the nature of one cannot be understood without the other.

Where We Are Now

In 2009, what is the current state of archaeological theory? Such a superficially simple question is very difficult to answer. One of the striking things about the responses to the first, 1999 edition of this book was that they differed very sharply, not just in their evaluation of which strands or movements in archaeology were or were not productive, but more fundamentally – in their descriptive assessment of what was or was not 'central' or 'marginal', 'serious' or 'frivolous' in archaeological theory. 'I don't know why you waste time in your book discussing position X; no serious scholar believes that now', was a frequent comment from a fervent believer in position Y; one week later, at another institution, the comment would be 'I don't know why you waste time discussing position Y; everyone settled on position X a long time ago'. The mental alarm bells of any scholar should ring loudly every time a different view is not engaged with, but rather summarily dismissed on an *a priori* basis, rejected as a 'basic misunderstanding', or ruled 'out of court' in this way.

One critical difference in the perception of where we are now remains the different institutional position of academic archaeology in different countries. I have commented in earlier chapters on the position of much North American academic archaeology within Anthropology departments, versus the European tradition either of separate departments or of closer alliances with Classics and History. In the last decade, this contrast has had two important consequences.

The first is a difference in the impact of postmodernism and what has been held to be its implications. In North America from the 1990s onwards, postmodernism had a huge impact on cultural anthropology in particular. At the same time, there was a wider cultural context of a 'war on science' in which, culturally and politically, it seemed that science was both being politicized and its integrity attacked by Creationists and others. It seemed, then, to many North American archaeologists that the themes they held dear as essential to a responsible and rigorous archaeology were being seriously eroded. In retrospect, it seems to me that many of the more extreme and negative reactions to the early polemics of British postprocessual archaeology were in part displaced reactions to what was going on closer to home, across the corridor in Anthropology departments, and across the road in City Halls and in the White House.

The second consequence is a differently constructed relationship with Indigenous peoples. In North America, and also in other contexts around the world such as Australia, there has been in the past a very sharp dividing line between how 'archaeologists' construct the past, and beliefs in the past held by Indigenous peoples. For many, there is a binary opposition between these two world-views, which often appear at first sight to be quite incommensurate. Kennewick Man, discussed in the last chapter, is a case in point.

For Europeans, the relationship between archaeology and Indigenous peoples is constructed in a different way. First, with arguable exceptions such as the Saami, there are few clearly Indigenous goups, and no obvious or straightforward definition of what an Indigenous people is. For example, British people of Anglo-Saxon descent can be accused by the Welsh of having driven out the 'native British' from much of England in the centuries after AD 400. Second, cultural claims of descent and ownership of territory do not always reflect the aspects of a struggle of the dispossessed, but rather take on a nationalist and politically unpleasant tinge, for example in arguments over who has rights to what land in the former Yugoslavia.

Making a judgment on what is important in theory today is rendered especially difficult by the great diversity of contexts in which 'theory' operates. I have argued that all archaeology is theoretical, but overt discussions of theory are constructed or inflected in different ways between and within communities of archaeologists – for example, between different regional or national traditions, between different area/period specialisms, or between archaeologists working in different contexts (academic versus 'professional').

The Fall and Rise of Empiricism

One way to look at the question of where we are now is to put it the question in very crude terms – to ask: what, in practice, is the theoretical attitude adopted by most archaeologists, 'professional' as well as academic, around the whole world? I suspect that the answer would have to be that it remains a crude and unreflective empiricism, in the sense that the data are held to speak for themselves, without the need for intervening theory. Empiricism in this sense can to some extent be seen as lurking behind a number of varied positions and statements about theory that often sound quite obvious and inoffensive in themselves until their implications are teased out, for example:

- that only academics have the time for theory, and 'professional' archaeologists, or those working in museums or cultural resource management, have 'no time' to do it;
- that as an archaeologist one can choose between taking or not taking a theoretical approach; and/or that some approaches are 'very theoretical' while others are 'very empirical';
- that the moment for 'doing theory' occurs after 'a basic grasp of the data' (a moment that never seems to be 'now');
- a rhetoric which implies that 'theory' is somehow less empirically grounded than archaeology without explicit theory; this rhetoric usually comes with an implicit reliance on 'common sense';
- an implication that 'plain speaking' is superior to a theoretical 'rhetoric' (an assertion which, paradoxically, is itself a classic piece of rhetoric);
- the notion that 'more empirical' studies will be of more 'enduring value', whereas theories are merely 'passing fads';
- the definition, on criteria that are taken as commonsensical and not in need of explication, of questions which are more knowable or legitimate than others; for example, that 'subsistence' or 'lordship' is a legitimate explanation for patterns in the landscape whereas exploration of memory or gender is 'wild' or 'fanciful'; and

- at the most basic level, the notion that the accumulation of more data, in and of itself, will automatically lead to a better knowledge of the past.

All these positions make a false assumption. They imply that while theory may or may not be a 'legitimate' part of what archaeologists do, somehow *there is a position from outside theory* from which arguments can be evaluated and more broadly archaeology can be practiced. I have insisted over and over again in this book that all archaeologists are theorists, whether we like it or not. There are many different possible positions to take – but they are all theoretical ones.

More profoundly, all these positions imply an assertion of community. What I mean by this is that they assert theoretical criteria that 'we all know'. We all know what we read in a site report; we all know a 'plausible' explanation when we see one. But who are 'we' in this analysis? When the great seventeenth-century empiricists Bacon, Hobbes and Locke used simple, direct, 'plain English' phrases like 'we can see that …' they were actually writing for and to a very narrow circle of their friends and contemporaries – male members of the English gentry classes. The most important lesson of multiculturalism, of diversity issues, and of engagement with Indigenous perspectives, has been that who 'we' are cannot be taken for granted. Indeed, 'we' can be argued to be the most theory-laden word in the English language. It is certainly one of the most ambiguous.

If a naïve empiricism is so obviously flawed, why does it endure? I suggest that its endurance is partly due to the fact that deep down, at a discursive and even emotional level, *we are all empiricists*. Two of the distinctive features of archaeology are its nature as a field-based discipline, and its engagement with material objects. Put very crudely, 'we', archaeologists, love the physical activity of digging, love handling old objects, love the feel, touch and smell of the past. However much archaeologists tell themselves that objects in themselves tell us nothing about the past (as discussed in chapter 2), they still love working with things, and 'deep down', at a visceral level, archaeologists can hear the artefacts speaking to them, without the need for intervening theory.

Part of the enduring strength, then, of the empiricist tradition is that however easy it is to condemn intellectually, empiricism remains present in a large part of the archaeological practice of everybody.

Processual and Postprocessual Archaeologies

A second way of approaching the question of where we are now is to ask what has changed since the turn of the century. It is possible to assert that the so-called 'processual/postprocessual wars' that characterized much of theoretical debate in the English-speaking world have ended (see figures 13.1 and 13.2). In the opinion of many, including myself, the term 'postprocessual

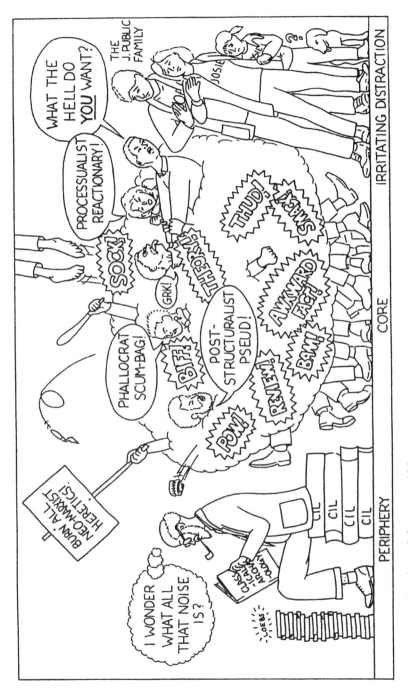

Figure 13.1 Archaeological theory in 1988

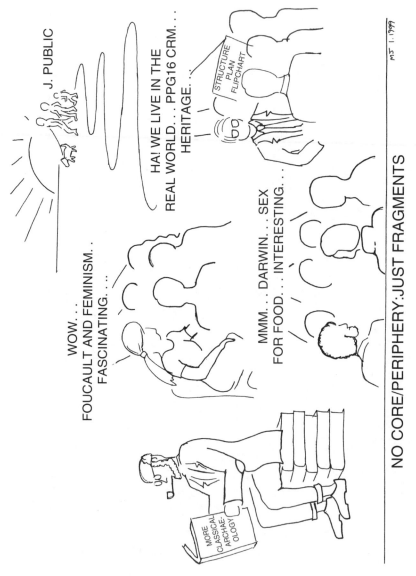

Figure 13.2 Archaeological theory in 1998

archaeology' ceased to have much meaning after about 2000. The term still crops up, usually in critical comments by self-proclaimed opponents of 'postprocessualism' that are to my mind rather out-of-date.

There has been a growing articulation of a shared terrain or a shared set of concerns in much of archaeological theory. In the late 1990s I was suspicious of this move, for two reasons. First, I was not convinced by some of the case studies that claimed to back up this asserted middle ground. It seemed to me to be a wishful assertion, a piece of rhetoric even, rather than a seriously argued and substantive position. Second, I was unduly influenced by the depressing experience of reading countless student essays, and quite a few academic papers, that substituted phrases like 'there is something to be said for both sides' for any kind of intelligent and informed evaluation of the arguments. Ten years later, I have modified my views in this respect.

We saw in chapter 5 how thinking in terms of cultural process had shifted, away from ecosystem models, and towards a much more nuanced understanding, taking on concerns about agency, conflict, and gender. At the same time, much of the early programmatic polemic of postprocessualism had faded away by 2000. Angry claims and counter-claims about relativism and its dangers had largely subsided.

One version of this articulation has been termed 'processual plus' by Michelle Hegmon in relation to North American archaeological theory. Hegmon argued that much of North American archaeology had taken on the themes and issues of gender, agency, symbolism, and materiality, and had engaged with the political and cultural context of archaeology. She drew attention to the way processual themes and language had shifted: away from the evolution of culture to diverse trajectories of change, from social organization to social strategies, from humans in the environment to humans as part of the environment. (I would add to her list a shift from a language of 'testing' to a language of 'evaluation'.)

Hegmon's views drew a quick response from others. While Hegmon insisted that 'I am not suggesting that there is a theoretical rapprochement ... nor do I think that this kind of homogeneity would be a good thing' (Hegmon 2003: 233), others felt that it left important and dissonant elements out, in particular those elements of theory that engage with social justice issues, including Indigenous, Marxist, feminist and postcolonial archaeologies; it could be added that Hegmon was also open about leaving behavioural and Darwinian archaeologies out of her synthesis.

I think that Hegmon's assessment is important in two respects. First, she is looking for a way to move theoretical debate forward constructively. Conflicts are not necessarily bad; in many respects, a discipline can be defined not through its common ground but through its disagreements – for example the Obeyesekere/Sahlins debate in cultural anthropology, or the origins of the English Revolution or the feudal/capitalist transition in history. However, an inclusive and diverse discipline, and above all a mature discipline, should be able to move its theoretical debates beyond a clash of schools or what she calls 'egos' in which the winner takes all and the loser is crushed. Second, she is correct in her assertion that a series of common themes can be seen to emerge across theoretical battle-lines in the early twenty-first century. I will discuss three as examples: agency, materiality, and field practice.

Agency

The first common theme that can be said to have emerged is an interest in human agency and the individual human subject. This interest spans theoretical divides. Darwinists are interested in the individual organism, and in the role of chance and contingency in evolution. Co-evolutionary explanations examine the interactions of individual variation and cultural innovation, and the population as a whole. Faction, gender and other agencies have come to the fore in processual thought about the origin of social complexity and states. Giddens' structuration theory has been deployed in different theoretical traditions, while phenomenology rests at some level on an exploration of human subjectivity.

Agency is a classic example of theory being counterintuitive, of pointing out insights that run counter to orthodoxy, but which appear simple when thought about in a different way. One of the most frequent clichés heard is that we cannot 'see' the individual in the archaeological record. However, pots are made by people: in a very large part, the archaeological record contains very direct evidence of individual actions and human intentions – the digging of a rubbish pit, the construction of house foundations, the manufacture of objects, the deposition of grave goods.

Stated in this way, an interest in agency sounds quite obvious and undeniable. However, over and over again in this book, we have seen different theoretical attitudes leading us away from agency. Basic archaeological classification into phases, assemblages and cultures leads us away from seeing the very simple human actions that lay behind the production, use and loss of, for example, Mazaokeyiwin's awl handle, and towards their aggregation and assimilation into broader categories and processes.

Materiality

The second common theme is an engagement with materiality. Put very broadly and simplistically, a concern with materiality is a stress on the material world as important and in some sense active. Interest in materiality comes from a wide range of theoretical sources. Political economists are interested in property and expressions of value; Marxism is a materialist philosophy; phenomenological approaches stress the physical experience of the world and the intransigence of artefacts; behavioural archaeology examines the relationships between people and things in all times and places. All these approaches share common ground. They insist that the relationship between people and things is important, that it is complex, and that things (objects, buildings, monuments, landscapes) are not simply passive reflections of other aspects of culture.

Archaeology has struggled in the past to free itself from a series of approaches that saw the material world and material objects as somehow secondary or less important. In chapter 6 we saw how the idealist philosophy of Croce, in which ideas were more important than things, implied that archaeologists should content themselves with description and classification. In culture history, we saw how for the normative approach artefacts are (imperfect) reflections of 'cultural norms' which exists inside people's heads. In many processual views, artefacts are the fossil record of past 'processes' which do not necessarily have a direct physical existence, and which again are defined either in 'adaptive' or in 'social' terms. Within an interpretive framework, artefacts are often held to 'represent', 'reflect' or 'express' social values or meanings, values or meanings which are implicitly held to have a prior existence.

All these views share common ground, in that they tend to view the archaeological record as somehow a by-product of what archaeologists are really interested in (human history, cultural process). Arguably, then, they all implicitly treat the subject-matter of archaeology, old things, as less important or somehow inferior or secondary to other disciplines. In a more popular sense, traditional archaeologists of Classical and historical periods often look in the material record for evidence of a process that is pre-defined through the documents – thus an 'archaeology of lordship' concerns itself with castles and village layout, an 'archaeology of the Roman Empire' with forts, villas and cities. These approaches appear to be an advance on traditional models, in that they are 'social' or 'anthropological' in nature, referring to social structures and processes rather than simply historical narratives. But they still treat the world as epiphenomenal, or in other words a secondary by-product of what is really important.

A concern with materiality proposes, first, that the material world is important, and second that it cannot be comprehended using previous models such as 'text' or 'norms'. In this view, objects mediate social relationships, or 'materialize' them. It flows, in part, out of the concerns with phenomenology and subjective experience, and the role that material objects and landscape play in constituting and mediating that experience, discussed in chapter 7. A key preoccupation is with *ontology*, that is, the study of the being or essence of things, or of being in the abstract. Objects are seen as active, and as having agency. Objects are also seen as changing the human subject – a man with a gun is a very different being from an unarmed man.

One particularly strong tendency within the concern with materiality has been the recent emergence of a school of 'symmetrical archaeology'. Symmetrical archaeology 'begins with the proposition: humans and non-humans should not be regarded as ontologically distinct, as detached and separated entities ... neither our analyses nor our explanations nor our inter-pretations should ever begin with such asymmetric dualisms. Thought and action, ideas and materials, past and present are thoroughly mixed ontologi-cally. ... Any radical separation, opposition and contradiction between peo-ple and the material world within which they live is regarded as the outcome of a specifically modern way of distributing entities and segmenting the world' (Whitmore 2006: 546). The 'actor-network theory' of Bruno Latour has been influential on this point. Latour proposes that social scientists have been too ready to ascribe the causes of surface phenomena to an underlying 'reality' they call 'the social'. However, he points out that 'the social' doesn't exist in these terms: you and I have never touched, felt or smelt 'the social'. Chris Witmore lists six characteristics of a symmetrical archaeology: that archaeology begins with mixtures, not bifurcations; there is always a variety of human and non-human agencies; there is more to understanding than 'meaning'; change arises from fluctuating relations between entities; the past is not exclusively past; humanity begins with things (Witmore 2006: 549).

Symmetrical archaeology represents, for better or worse, a fundamental challenge to the way most archaeologists operate and to the theoretical underpinnings of much of the discipline, just as one of its key inspirations, 'actor-network theory', challenges the underpinnings of the human sciences. For example, this book has insisted, over and over again, that archaeology is fundamentally about human beings (it is nothing if not anthropological), and about 'why?' questions (we can do more than just describe and classify); it posited a radical separation between present and past (figure 2.1). All these assumptions are questioned by this perspective. I am profoundly scep-tical of the claim that symmetrical archaeology can achieve a fundamental reordering of the discipline, but it does represent a hardening and unifying of different strands of theory into a coherent manifesto.

Theorizing The Field

The third common thread that can be said to have emerged is a widen-ing and deepening of the purview of theory to include reflexive approaches to the everyday activities of fieldwork and artefact analysis. Two distinc-tive features of archaeology are its nature as a field-based activity, and its materiality, as discussed above. Archaeology derives much of its emotional appeal from these features. One of the most exciting and encouraging developments in theory, then, has been the opening-up of field practice.

The classic example of reflexive fieldwork is Ian Hodder's work at the Neolithic site at Çatalhöyük in Turkey. Hodder has attempted to develop a 'reflexive excavation methodology', in several senses. First, the way of working is claimed to be 'always momentary, fluid and flexible' (Hodder 1997: 691); day-to-day working methods include the keeping of site diaries, discussion and questioning of appropriate strategies. Second, there is an attempt to be open and inclusive to different interests at the site, from Californian Goddess-worshippers to the different local groups and authorities. Third, the site archive has been developed through relational databases and web-based material in such a way as to make it open and accessible, and to make clear the subjective elements behind the objective record or data-set. Çatalhöyük is a 'flagship' site and a well-funded project of the highest profile; but theorizing 'the field' has taken place in a wide range of other contexts. Gavin Lucas, for example, has considered the development of the theory of stratigraphy, while my own work has looked at the methods of English landscape archaeology as a form of field practice inspired by Romanticism.

More broadly, there has been much theoretical reflection on concepts such as 'heritage', 'landscape', 'diversity' and related issues in recent years. This reflection has emerged as much from professional institutions such as English Heritage or the US National Parks Service as it has from the universities. It has been prompted in part by changing legislation. In Britain, for example, there is now a statutory requirement on public bodies such as heritage organizations, museums and universities to explicitly reflect on issues of diversity and inclusion and to develop specific policies and programmes of action to promote these values. We saw in the last chapter how in the USA, the NAGPRA legislation has compelled archaeological practice to engage with these issues.

Where Theory Is Going

I have not selected the three strands of agency, materiality and field practice at random. It can be argued that they represent three different elements of moving-on rather than synthesis: 'what is needed is not a merging or a fusion of processual or post-processual archaeology, but a moving on from a debate caught in a tired opposition between subject and object' (Hodder 2006: 23).

My response to Hodder is very simple: he is right, but moving on from tired oppositions is a bit like trying to change the weather: easy to state as a goal, but a lot more difficult to do in practice. If I am correct and empiricism is enduring because, deep down, there is part of us all that remains empiricist

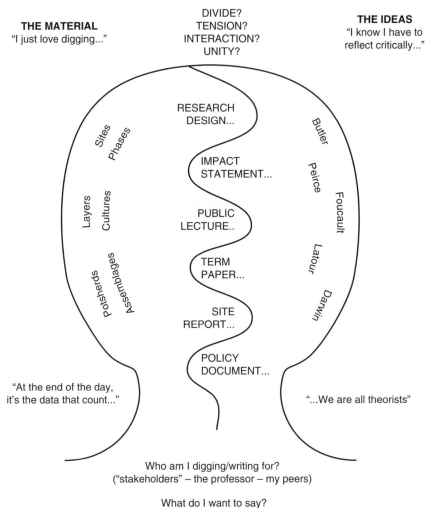

THE MATERIAL
"I just love digging..."

DIVIDE?
TENSION?
INTERACTION?
UNITY?

THE IDEAS
"I know I have to
reflect critically..."

RESEARCH
DESIGN...

Sites
Phases

Butler

Peirce

IMPACT
STATEMENT...

Foucault

Layers   Cultures

PUBLIC
LECTURE..

Latour

Potsherds   Assemblages

TERM
PAPER...

Darwin

SITE
REPORT...

POLICY
DOCUMENT...

"At the end of the day,
it's the data that count..."

"...We are all theorists"

Who am I digging/writing for?
("stakeholders" – the professor – my peers)

What do I want to say?
(the truth – whatever gets a good mark – something new – something "relevant")

Figure 13.3   Archaeological theory in 2008: the struggle between different elements of thought and activity, in the mind of every archaeologist

(figure 13.3), then it makes such a moving-on all the more difficult. How might we undertake this highly desirable, but very difficult and laborious, theoretical task in the future?

In the contemporary world, theorists have not had a good track record of influencing the future. Twentieth-century theorists had a very mixed record at making prescient observations about historical developments such as the rise of fascism and its attendant horrors, the continuing resilience of capitalism, the development of new technologies. I am, therefore, very reluctant to make predictions of my own as to where theory is going. All too often, such predictions sounds like wish-fulfilment – one reads over and over again of the imminent death of evolutionary approaches, of cultural materialism, of postmodernism, or even of theory itself. These predictions invariably come from opponents of the theoretical movement in question who clearly desperately wish that their baleful diagnosis is going to be an accurate one. But a few years later, the patient in question seems to be wandering around the landscape looking perkier than ever.

I would like to predict the continued implosion of avowedly 'atheoretical' approaches in archaeology. I would like to see a world in which no serious scholar can get away with simply dismissing 'theory' as irrelevant, or bypassing or trivializing the need to make his or her theoretical views explicit. Unfortunately, I don't see such a happy situation emerging any time soon. In many areas, theory has been 'accepted' and there is a lively theoretical scene, but in others, theory remains an either/or alternative or an optional extra. Far too frequently, one reads comments like 'X's approach is very theoretical; an alternative is the more empirical approach of Y'. If theory is the order we put facts in, theory is not an either/or option. I am tempted to make the rather harsh comment that as a discipline, archaeologists cannot and should not tolerate colleagues who do not choose to engage with theory in some sense, any more or less than they could tolerate colleagues who denied the theory of stratigraphy or of evolution.

There is a simple step that advocates of theory could take to advance this situation: instead of sitting with gritted teeth through yet another exposition of Hallstatt typologies, we could ask two simple, courteous questions in every seminar we go to, without exception: What is your preferred theoretical framework, and what are your criteria for selecting it over possible alternatives? Why do you choose to put the facts in that particular order?

I am not being entirely serious here. There are good reasons why most academic papers do not begin with a general theoretical excursus, among them that they work within an accepted discourse or paradigm. This discourse or paradigm is accepted by the audience they are addressing and the networks they are familiar with. There is also an important argument to be made that theoretical traditions in some areas of the world are vibrant and important, but do not identify themselves as distinct, explicitly defined bodies of specifically *archaeological* knowledge or practice with a corpus of literature of their own. It can be argued that much of central and Eastern European archaeology, for example, does work within a sophisticated theoretical framework, but that explicit reflection upon that framework in such a manner as to enable the identification of a specific body of literature on 'archaeological theory' is problematic.

Progress and Impact

Does archaeological theory progress? 'Progress' is a loaded word, as the chapter on cultural evolution discussed, and perhaps carries too much cultural baggage and is best avoided. I do think that, as a discipline, archaeology has a record of developing better, more accurate, more robust, deeper, understandings of the past. And I think that archaeological theory has played a critical role in this process.

It may help to turn the question upside down. Can we claim that theory does *not* progress? I don't think we can. Archaeological theory does not just ramble around in an endless and inconclusive 'debate' in which all views are possible and equal. Looked at historically, theory has moved in particular directions at particular times. This movement has been complex, and the moves made were very difficult to predict beforehand, but particular patterns, trends or processes can be discerned. These patterns or trends have been responses to major cultural and political questions of the time, but they are also in part responses to what archaeologists perceive as major empirical issues of the time, and they are also both constrained and enabled by the data.

One demonstrated way that theory has 'progressed' is in a broadening and deepening of its concerns. I am particularly interested in the vernacular practice of archaeological theory, as opposed to complex ontological questions of the essence of things. What I mean by this is that archaeology could do with more reflection on the everyday judgements and assumptions that are made by practicing archaeologists, and the way these reflect underlying theoretical categories.

Many of the conceptual categories that archaeologists use remain quite ill-defined. Indeed, the more basic and foundational they are, the more implicit and ill-defined they seem to be. This observation will not surprise cultural anthropologists, who are used to the idea that the more basic a cultural idea is, the less explicitly it is articulated; and archaeologists are nothing if not a rather peculiar culture or tribe. A classic example is the definition of 'process', first introduced in chapter 2, and returned to in chapter 5, which involves a cluster of related meanings. It is difficult to think of a more important term, at least in North American archaeology, and yet it is very rare to find an explicit and tight definition of it. Similar comments could be made about words like 'type', 'phase', 'structure', 'change'. Ironically, the less overtly contentious an idea is, the less sharply it is defined.

Does archaeological theory have an impact on the 'real world', however defined? Of course, but the way in which it has an impact needs careful reflection. Part of the problem with assessing the impact of theory is its very complex relationship to practice on the one hand, and to the context of what we do on the other.

For example, one can ask: what active role did 'theory' play in the changes in North American archaeology seen in the last decade as a result of NAGPRA, changes discussed in the last chapter? One could argue that NAGPRA played a far more important role than the postprocessual critique in opening North American archaeology up to Indigenous and alternative knowledges. On the other hand, one could argue that 'the postmodern condition' was one part of the cultural and political climate that led to the passing of NAGPRA under a Republican President, George H.W. Bush.

One could deploy the deeper and more subtle argument that 'theory' is not necessarily a guide or a recipe-book, but rather an attempt at *description* rather than prescription. In other words, theory is an attempt to classify and comprehend the difficulties and contradictions of working within a particular context. In the case of NAGPRA, the legislation concentrated archaeologists' minds – it made the intellectual necessity of engaging with Indigenous knowledge a priority. NAGPRA, the cultural and political context, 'theory' and archaeological practice moved together. Further, it did so in such a way that makes it difficult to specify cause and effect, but also in such a way as to demonstrate their close relationship – and to demonstrate the relevance and impact of theory, archaeological practice, and cultural and political context upon each other.

Diversity and Pluralism

In the first edition of this book, I stressed the importance of a diversity and multiplicity of viewpoints, and the importance of students thinking for themselves rather than accepting the approaches or positions that professors and other senior figures would like to hand down to them. I still believe in these points just as strongly. There is a necessary complement to be made. Theoretical views have to be argued through with reference to the literature, just as rigorously and with just as much careful thought as with any other academic endeavour. Theory should be democratic, but I do not believe it should be anarchic. It is not a place where one is free to pick whatever version one cares to choose – there is always a price to be paid, in terms of the time and effort required to gain deep knowledge and understanding.

Empiricism, the reader will recall, is (among other things) a division between the world of data and of words or concepts, and a rhetoric of prioritizing the former. In some ways, one of the most pernicious, pervasive and hidden aspects of empiricism in archaeology is the underlying proposition that while archaeologists have to work hard with the data – read the site reports, tramp across the landscape, handle the pottery and artefactual material, 'master' the stuff – we do not have to make a corresponding effort with our theory. We need to know our typologies and our chronologies, but archaeologists are allowed to get away with position statements and theoretical judgements that are not informed by the literature.

In the first edition I wrote that 'Papers that end with the depressingly banal conclusion that 'there is something to be said for both sides' or that 'we should look for a middle ground' should be banned – not because a middle ground is in itself a bad thing, but because the search for such a middle ground all too often becomes an easy replacement for the hard work of serious yet sympathetic critique of one's own and others' theoretical positions'. This passage was selectively quoted by at least one author to imply that I was advocating a rejection of any kind of consensus or middle ground; I was not. What I should have added, as a necessary and equal complement, is that the other phrase that should be banned from papers is 'I just think that ...'.

If one believes that theory is a part of archaeology that is as difficult and subtle as any other, archaeologists need to do the work, be familiar with the literature, and argue from a well-read and informed perspective. Archaeologists slip too easily from statements like 'at the end of the day, it's the facts that count' to the position that archaeologists can make a judgment about theory that is not informed by the literature. In short, as Conkey and Gero stated for feminist research:

> If we want to explore a configuring of contemporary archaeology, it is simply 'poor research' to ignore a large and diverse body of theoretical, analytical and conceptual possibilities that pertain to and substantively inform the questions at hand ... 'Do I have to do the readings?' We would say the answer is, 'yes'. (Conkey and Gero 1997: 426)

Archaeologists, then, can assert any theoretical position they like – as long as they are prepared for an immediate and rigorous interrogation into the basis of that position and the degree to which it has been informed by a detailed knowledge of the material. Theory is hard work, and it should also, if it is done properly, be uncomfortable work. Good theory should cause archaeologists to reflect on what they do, both as scholars and human beings. This reflection should not leave basic assumptions unarticulated or undisturbed: a response a theorist should aim for is: 'You know, that's really helpful, I never thought about it like that ...' In this sense, good theory should cause people to feel challenged about their everyday working practices as archaeologists, but also enabled and to think and act in new ways.

Archaeology is a broad church. A diversity of viewpoints is to be encouraged. On the other hand, there comes a point at which 'diversity' becomes 'fragmentation'. An excessive pluralism can appear to be tolerant, but in fact act as a cloak for suppression of debates – why should two views bother to engage critically with the other if both are 'valid'? The most obvious example of a position that is simply unsustainable is the rejection of theory itself – I have repeatedly stressed how there is no choice to be made between 'theoretical' and 'atheoretical' archaeology.

There is also a balance to be struck between an insistence on doing the reading and a theoretical Calvinism. The sixteenth-century theologian Calvin argued for a form of Protestant belief in which only a very few people, the 'elect', could be saved. Theoretical Calvinists are as tiresome a breed as theoretical know-nothings. All archaeologists have to make choices about what and how much they read, just as they have to make choices about what to sample from the archaeological record. There is a regrettable attitude among a few theorists that if you have not read Lévi-Strauss in the original French, you have no right to comment on the broad thrust of theory. The literary critic Jonathan Culler writes that:

> One of the most dismaying features of theory today is that it is endless … It is an unbounded corpus of writings which is always being augmented … Theory is thus a source of intimidation, a resource for constant upstagings: 'What? You haven't read Lacan! How can you talk about the lyric without addressing the specular constitution of the speaking subject?'… the completion of one task will bring not respite but further difficult assignments. ('Spivak? Yes, but have you read Benita Parry's critique of Spivak and her response?'). (Culler 1997: 15)

Given the necessary open-endedness and indeterminacy of theory, and the need that Culler identifies for the theorist to be constantly placing him or herself in a vulnerable position, aggressive denunciations which treat differing views not with respect but as 'basic misunderstandings' are unhelpful. They can only be seen as a barely coded attempt at what Culler calls constant upstaging, leading to intellectual exclusion and a negation and closing-down of diversity.

It is important that these tensions between plurality and dogmatism, and over what and how one should read theory, be understood in pragmatic and pedagogical terms. In other words, the question is not just 'what do we, as archaeologists, want to do?' or 'what is the essence of archaeological theory?' but also 'how should academic archaeology encourage students to be questioning – what practical strategies can we adopt to open up the discipline to dialogue?'

Conclusion

I came to archaeology as Roger Beefy, the bluff 'dirt archaeologist' character who has been questioning things in this volume. Most of the practising archaeologists I had worked with before university were openly contemptuous of theory; in late 1970s Britain, 'rescue archaeology' was at its peak, and there seemed to be too much digging to do to worry about linear movement zones and mutual causal deviation amplifying processes. Of course, those familiar with the subsequent history of British rescue archaeology will be well aware of how mistaken this anti-theory view proved to be: how much of the material excavated and recorded was never adequately published and failed to contribute to better accounts of the past, in part because the lack of a broader theoretical framework within which to set research priorities and guide the writing-up and interpretation.

The first year of my undergraduate course, which was strongly oriented towards a narrow view of cultural evolution and the New Archaeology, tended to confirm suspicions that theory was just a waste of time. Grand evolutionary schema seemed boring and irrelevant to the particularities of archaeological practice. I'd read around history and historical sociology, and as Bruce Trigger also noted in his *Time and Traditions*, which I read around that time, the rejection of history seemed especially naïve. In retrospect, this was a biased and partial reading of the literature; but it was the one I made at the time.

This view was reinforced through experiences of theory outside mainstream archaeology. My work on the 'English school' of landscape history, which I first engaged with before university, and experience of historical theory drew me to an appreciation of how different disciplines really did have very different theoretical criteria and methodologies. In this sense, the insight that arguments are never evaluated in conditions of pure objectivity, but are always formulated and considered within a certain social milieu, was not a theoretical lesson that I learnt but a practical one derived from talking and working with archaeologists, historians, architectural historians and geographers. Again, practical experience rather than theoretical demonstration has led me to see a fragmentation of method within the discipline as a whole; I see very little in common between the method and theory of, say, the archaeology of the American Southwest and that of the medieval European church. Both would consider the methods of the other as utterly unproductive; if a 'theorist' has any role in archaeology, it must surely be to translate – to show how both schools have their own validity, their own intellectual credentials, and why both should respect the other's traditions and take the time to talk to the other.

In the last decade, I have not changed my outlook on archaeology fundamentally, but I have shifted emphasis in my views in three areas. During this time, I published two books, one on the archaeology of castles, and one on the study of landscape. The critical reaction to these two books impressed two lessons upon me. The first was about epistemology: that rhetorical statements about the importance of the data, or conversely one-sided deconstructions of understandings of the past that exposed their political basis, were not enough. Getting one's boots muddy and one's trowel worn down told you nothing in and of itself about the past. The critical point was to develop better, more accurate understandings of the past. The way to do this (as any New Archaeologist would rightly have insisted 40 years ago) was not to follow one's instincts, that is to simply excavate another village or survey another field and wait for the data thus gathered to speak for itself. It was to think clearly and critically about rigorously addressing how *this* body of data led to *that* explanation, and how the links between data and explanation might be strengthened.

The second was that the basis for any understanding of the past had to be, in part, through an informed, anthropological understanding of structure and process. The archaeology of castles and of the English landscape remain areas dominated by culture-historical approaches, and by methods that implicitly assume the primacy of documents as discussed in chapter 11. In attempting to articulate an intellectually coherent way forward for these fields of study, I found myself arguing in terms that stressed system, structure and process as a necessary backdrop to explorations of identity and practice.

The third lesson I have learnt is that the real theoretical struggle is not between different -isms, but rather, between a gut attachment to a naïve empiricism, and a cerebral insistence that we are all theorists. This struggle is all the sharper and more profound because it exists not simply between different advocates or schools, but rather *within all of us* – within the heads of all archaeologists (figure 13.3). There is no clear 'enemy' – there is, however, a constant and unceasing struggle between the comfort of what archaeologists take for granted and the ceaseless questioning of any responsible and mature discipline.

My main aim in writing this book was to persuade the reader of the excitement, importance and relevance of theory, and to encourage him or her to adopt a consciously critical attitude to the things she or he is taught by senior figures – 'experts' – about the theory and practice of the discipline. The rather naïve hope behind this was that a diversity of approaches to the archaeological record is a good thing, as the interaction of different approaches tends to produce interesting and fruitful results, a more truthful and more stimulating account of the past; and more broadly, that the intrinsic value of liberal academic study lies in its development of a positive critical attitude to the self and to society and culture as a whole. I don't much care which 'ism' future generations of archaeologists find most appealing, except in so far as it enhances and fosters such critical attitudes. The moment an archaeological theory begins to sound like a recipe-book to be followed blindly is probably the moment at which it has outlived its usefulness.

What I do care about is debunking the enduring notion that somehow theory is an optional extra, or that it is an addition to or easily separable from the 'core' activities of archaeology. Theory is not the only important element of modern archaeology, but it is one of the essential ones. Or to put it another way, theory is a little like a visit to the dentist – to argue about whether it is enjoyable or not is to miss the point.

Though unlike a visit to the dentist, it can also be enjoyable.

Selective Glossary

> Sir, I have found you an argument; but I am not obliged to find you an under-
> standing. (Dr Johnson, to a tedious interrogator; Boswell, June 1784)

Many of the terms discussed below have led to confusion since they mean different things to different people. Terms like 'class', 'culture', 'evolution', 'process', 'type' and 'power' can appear quite simple but very often tend to mystify since they are used by the author in one sense and read in quite another. A good example is the term 'theory' itself (see below). Part of the problem with such terms is that they vary their meaning according to context or disciplinary background. For example, 'cultural materialism' has entirely different, almost diametrically opposed meanings in the respective fields of cultural anthropology and literary theory.

I have only listed terms here that appear in the text but that deserve further amplification. I started out with the aim of compiling a full glossary of all the specialized terms I have seen used in archaeological theory, but it became rapidly apparent that such an exercise would require a further book. A number of terms (for example, materiality, perfomativity and reflexivity) are, I feel, better understood through reading the relevant chapter than through a glossary entry. Renfrew and Bahn's *Archaeology: The Key Concepts* (2005) is extremely useful. Hodder. Shanks, Alexandri et al. (1995) has a good glossary. Further help with the human sciences generally may be sought in Johnson (1995), while Humm (1992) has a glossary on feminist thought. Lechte (1994) has brief discussions of contemporary thinkers. Raymond Williams's *Keywords* (2nd edn, 1988) should be part of the reference library of every scholar – read his entries on 'culture', 'nature', 'experience' and your view of the world will never be the same again. The appendix in Culler (1997) offers concise views of the main schools in literary theory.

If many terms are not here, those that are have considerably over-simplified definitions. The best way to appreciate the full meaning and context of many of the words examined here is to read the relevant chapter(s) – terms can only be understood within the context of the intellectual movement(s) of which they form a part. Terms also change their meaning. Between my writing of these words and your reading of them, many of these terms will have subtly changed.

Agency   The issue of how we think about intentional action and the resources needed to act, as in 'structuralism lacks a theory of agency' (in other words, structuralism can't explain why individuals act in a diversity of ways rather than blindly executing a preconceived pattern). Often paired with STRUCTURE.

Annales school   A French school of historical thought, part of which stresses the interrelationship of different timescales (the *longue dureé* or long-term, the medium-term, and short-term events of *l'histoire evenementielle*). Annales historians also focus on the study of mentalities. See chapter 10.

Antiquarianism   In this book, mere collection of ancient artefacts without relating these to past processes. The antiquarianism of sixteenth- to eighteenth-century Europe and America was more sophisticated than this and demands more complex treatment, however.

Behaviourism   The proposition that we should focus exclusively on observable behaviours and refrain from referring to people's thoughts in our explanations of that behaviour.

Cognitive archaeology   'The study of past ways of thought as inferred from the suriviving material remains' (Renfrew 2005: 41). Cognitive archaeology claims to be more modest than the postprocessual search for 'meaning'. It focuses on two areas: the evolutionary development of cognition in early hominds, and the subsequent cultural development of cognitive capacities, for example the development of writing.

Contradiction   A term with Marxist connotations: see DIALECTIC.

Critical theory   See chapter 6. A school of thought derived in part from Marxism, associated with Adorno, Habermas and Marcuse, and often referred to as the 'Frankfurt School'. Critical theorists aim to unmask the inner workings of a society which they suggest lie concealed from view by the mystifications of ideology.

Culture   An archaeological culture is a repeatedly recurring assemblage of traits – pottery and house forms, burial practices – seen over a discrete time and space. It may or may not relate to a human culture. In the broader sense, a culture can be many things, including:

1   a body of shared ideas and beliefs (the normative view);
2   an 'extra-somatic' (outside the body) system adapted to the external environment (systemic view);

3 a structure or code analogous to language; and
4 an attribute of civilized behaviour, as in 'every cultured person should have some knowledge of archaeology'.

Culture history   A term usually used in North America to refer to a traditional approach to the mapping of cultures and cultural influence.

Cybernetics   The science of energy flow, often associated with systems theory.

Decentring   Humanists see individuals as autonomous, coherent and authors of their own meaning: the poststructuralist 'decentring of the subject' deconstructs all these ideas.

Deconstruction   A weapon from the armoury of poststructuralism. By showing that any word or sentence has many meanings and that those meanings themselves refer to a multiplicity of other meanings within language, any text, however apparently obvious or banal, can be 'deconstructed' or shown to have many meanings other than its apparent one. Deconstruction can be used in politically radical ways (to show for example how the word 'masculine' is both unstable and privileged) though it has also been held to lead to a disabling and politically neutral relativism.

Diachronic   Through time (as opposed to SYNCHRONIC).

Dialectic   A complex term from Hegelian and Marxist thought. It refers to the contradiction or conflict of ideas or of groups within a wider framework. That framework collapses from within, resulting in the rise of new social or intellectual forms that in turn develop new contradictions. Thus, for example, Marx's account of feudalism is dialectical since it suggests that there were contradictions within the feudal system that brought the whole system crashing down, to be replaced by nascent capitalism and its own contradictions. A dialectical view of social change or of intellectual development can be contrasted with an evolutionary or progressive view.

Diffusion   The spread of ideas between cultural groups.

Direct historical approach   A North American term, referring to the project of delineating culture groups in prehistory by working from 'known' groups in ethnography and ethnohistory back into the protohistoric and prehistoric past.

Discourse   A set of rules of how to write and think that is specific to particular disciplines or institutions: thus 'all the apparatus of empiricist discourse are mobilized in this article?...'. A buzzword among archaeologists influenced by Foucault.

Diversity   Taken to refer to the acceptance and respect of differences between people, for example of gender, ethnicity, sexual orientation or religion. Often paired with inclusion, with reference to changing the cultures of institutions.

Empiricism   Popularly, the belief that the data will 'speak for themselves' without the need for intervening theories. Often used loosely as a term of abuse to indicate theoretical naiveté in general: 'Oh well, you'll call me an old empiricist I know, but I think we should just dig and not bother about theory'. In its more sophisticated form, as developed in seventeenth-century philosophy, empiricism rests on a conceptual division between 'things' or 'the real world' on the one hand, 'words' or 'concepts' on the other, and the prioritization of the former. Also used loosely, interchangeably and confusingly with POSITIVISM.

Epistemology   How we know what we know, or the validity of knowledge claims. For example, the question 'can we ever really know what people were thinking in the Formative Period?' is an *epistemological* question.

Essentialism   The belief that there are certain attitudes or emotions that are 'natural' or biologically endowed, either to humans in general or to a specific sex; much debated by feminists and others. Thus the statement 'in prehistory, men must have been more warlike as they lacked the mothering instinct' is an *essentialist* statement. Essentialist claims are often supported with reference to biological arguments (for example, that men's and women's brains are structured differently); essentialist statements therefore often have a basis in sociobiology, evolutionary psychology or related schools of thought. Alternatively, they are derived from humanism.

Ethnocentrism   Two meanings: the belief that one's own values and attitudes have held true in all times and places; and/or the belief that one's own culture is morally superior to others, not simply different.

Evolution   'Descent with modification' (Mace, Holden and Shennan 2005: 2). A term historically derived from Darwin and Spencer. When used in archaeological writing, its meaning varies. It can involve some or all of:

1   the application of Darwinian principles to humans in the past; and
2   the idea that human societies can be ranked on a scale of complexity, and that through time there has been a move from simple to complex. This can be linked with ideas of progress in human life.

Falsificationism   The belief that while we can never 'prove' anything, science advances by coming up with hypotheses that it is possible to disprove or falsify.

Feminist archaeology   The belief that gender roles are partially or completely socially constructed rather than endowed by biology, and that women in particular have suffered from oppression in Western society. This has the implication that: (a) archaeologists need to examine gender roles and inequalities within the profession; (b) archaeologists need to be more critical about biases and assumptions made about ancient societies;

and (c) archaeologists need to question the way academic knowledge has been constructed in, it is argued, a 'phallocentric' or male-dominated manner. Not all archaeologists interested in 'an archaeology of gender' call themselves feminists, and not all feminists would necessarily fully agree with point (c) above.

Formalism   A school of economic theory that suggests we can extend Western ideas of economic rationality to non-Western societies.

Frankfurt School See CRITICAL THEORY.

Functionalism   The belief that the different institutions and practices of a human group are interrelated in a manner analogous to that of a body, so that the form of one can be explained by its functional relationship to other elements.

Hermeneutics   The study of how we give meanings to cultural products, or how we interpret human actions and their products (for example, written texts, social actions, works of art, or artefacts).

Heuristic   To find out, to learn or to throw up fresh ideas, as in 'we didn't gain any grand theory from this simulation, we just did it for heuristic purposes – it threw up some new ideas and possible interpretations that we need to test out in the next research stage'.

Historicism   Various meanings. Often used as a code-word for Marxism; alternatively, New Historicist literary theory is 'a critical movement insisting on the prime importance of historical context to the interpretation of texts of all kinds' (Hamilton 1996: 2).

Historiography   Various meanings, including historical theory and the history of historical thought.

Humanism   Broadly, the study of human culture; often associated with the belief that there is an essential 'human condition' regardless of historical circumstance.

Hypothesis   A prediction about the relationship between variables, as in 'My hypothesis is that marginal environments and risk are positively correlated.'

Idealism   Theoretical usage differs from commonplace usage. An idealist believes that thoughts are prior to actions, in other words that the mental world is more important than the material. In Collingwood's historical idealism, the central method of historical and archaeological interpretation is to rethink the thoughts of past peoples empathetically.

Ideology   See chapter 6. A set of overt or implicit beliefs or views of the world. According to Marxists, ideology serves to legitimate or mask the 'real' state of social relations.

Indigenous   Of a people inhabiting a region with which they have the earliest known historical connection, often with a history of dispossession by later immigrants; a term whose definition is much debated, and therefore often used with a capital I.

Inductivism The belief that archaeological research starts with observations from the data, building general statements from them (in contrast with the HDN model, in which data collection is hypothesis-driven).

Legitimation See IDEOLOGY.

Logicism A school of archaeological theory associated with the *Ecole Pratiques des Hautes Etudes* in Paris. Logicists focus attention on the structure of publications and interpretations rather than the archaeological remains themselves (see Gardin 1980).

Logocentrism For poststructuralists, logocentrism is the illusion fostered by positivist science that there is a concrete world beyond 'the text', to which the text refers, and that meanings can therefore be fixed in some final 'reality'. Poststructuralists argue that meanings are never fixed in this way and deny what they call 'the logocentric fallacy'.

Materialism Various meanings. Literally, a materialist believes that the material, physical world should be given more significance than the ideal or mental world. Some Marxists use the terms 'Marxism' and 'materialism' interchangeably. It is also used as a code-word by some North American archaeologists to indicate Marxism without its political connotations. For literary theorists, cultural materialism is the idea that culture and history are linked dialectically; it is sometimes seen as 'the British version of New Historicism', though it tends to be more openly committed to left-wing politics. Finally, materialism is used to describe an acquisitive mind-set that many archaeologists feel is bound up with the origins of capitalism, as in 'the increased comfort of homes in the sixteenth century reflects a new spirit of materialism'.

Materialschlacht a term referring to detailed presentation of material, on the (empiricist) principle of letting the facts speak for themselves; increasingly used in German archaeology in pejorative reference to largely descriptive dissertation theses which catalogue copious archaeological material with very little interpretation.

Methodological individualism The belief that societies are nothing more than collections of individuals, and that therefore we can only explain 'social' phenomomena through individual psychology.

Methodology The techniques and methods used to collect and interpret archaeological data. Some feel methodology is part of theory; others insist that it be kept separate.

Modernism Used loosely to refer to belief in Science, Truth and Progress.

Multiculturalism The celebration of diverse ethnic backgrounds.

Multilinear Of a model that suggests more than one possible course, for example of social evolution.

Nomothetic (also nomological) Generalizing, as in 'The New Archaeology had nomothetic aims'.

Normative   The assumption that artefacts are expressions of cultural ideas or norms.

Ontology   The study of the being or essence of things, or of being in the abstract.

Paradigm   A set of beliefs or assumptions that underpin the whole way of doing 'normal science'. The term was invented by Kuhn, who suggested that science was characterized by long periods of stability punctuated by revolutionary 'paradigm shifts', for example between Newtonian and Einsteinian physics. There is much debate about whether Kuhn's assessment is accurate, and if so whether the New Archaeology (or for that matter postprocessual archaeology) marked a true 'paradigm shift'.

Particularize   To explain or understand something in terms of its peculiar qualities.

Phenomenology   The study of human experience and consciousness in everyday life.

Polythetic   With many features or criteria.

Postcolonial   Postcolonial theory deals with the effects of colonization on cultures and societies, from a critical standpoint, and the issues these raise for academic and cultural enquiry.

Postmodernism   According to Lyotard, 'incredulity towards metanarratives'.

Practice   A term closely linked to agency, associated with Bourdieu rather than Giddens, referring to everyday actions and their relationship to structure.

Pragmatism   A philosophy originally developed by Charles Peirce and others proposing that the meaning of an idea or a proposition lies in its observable practical consequences.

Processual   A school of archaeological thought that stresses the idea of process, tends to generalize and adopts a broadly positivist approach. Processualism can be seen as a developed, more mature form of the New Archaeology.

Realism   A philosophical position which accords to known or perceived things an existence or nature which is independent of whether anyone is thinking about or perceiving them. In archaeology, realism tends to be adopted as a position between the extremes of positivism and social constructivism.

Reductionism   The belief that complex phenomena can be explained by reducing them to a set of often very simple variables: often linked to Darwinist, essentialist or sociobiological arguments. Often used as a term of abuse by its opponents. Thus, 'To suggest that we can explain the presence of weapons in these graves simply by reference to Man's aggressive instinct is both reductionist and essentialist'.

Reification   Taking an idea or cluster of ideas and treating it as a definite thing. Thus, 'the Neolithic', 'the Formative Period' and 'postprocessual archaeology' are all reifications. Usually used pejoratively.

Relativism   The belief that all possible accounts of the past are equally valid in their own terms, there being no neutral or objective way to judge between them. Also used in anthropology as the view that other cultures are simply different from our own, not 'better' or 'worse'.

Semiotics   The study of signs.

Social constructivism   Also known as social constructionism. The proposition that scientific knowledge is not a neutral body of data independent of cultural practices and values, but is actually created within society. In this view scientific data and practices are wholly social constructs (strong constructivism) or partly (weak constructivism). In practice, social constructivists are interested in laboratory practices and publication of information as processes to be studied sociologically rather than as purely 'scientific' debates in the narrow sense of the term.

Sociobiology   The idea that cultural practices are biologically rather than socially constructed, based on the drive to reproduce genes.

Structuralism   The belief that culture is governed by rules analogous to those of language.

Structuration theory   A term associated with Giddens to describe how social agents or individuals relate to social structures. Giddens suggests that actors are constrained by their social environments, but pursue active strategies; the clash of agency then produces, often as an unintended consequence, change in social structures.

Structure   Enduring cultural or social relations. Sometimes used interchangeably with 'system' by functionalists, though for Marxists and structuralists the structure underlies the social system.

Substantivism   A school of economic theory that holds that our ideas of economic 'rationality' are not applicable to other cultures.

Synchronic   At one particular moment in time (as opposed to DIACHRONIC).

Systems   Can be used in a variety of senses from the very general ('the social system that was the Roman Empire came under stress in the third century AD') to very particular. In its particular forms, systems theory is close to functionalist beliefs that cultures can be seen as bodies – themselves systems – composed of various subsystems. Change in one subsystem will thus react against other subsystems and either be 'dampened down' (negative feedback leading to homeostasis) or produce wider change (positive feedback leading to transformation such as systems collapse).

Teleology   A narrative with a definite development towards a point; for example, a traditional Marxist account of history is *teleological* in that it suggests an inexorable progress towards communism.

Theorifeindlichkeit   Used pejoratively in German archaeology to denote distance from or hostility to theory

Theory   General definition at the start of chapter 12. It has also been used specifically to refer to a particular kind of structural-Marxism formulated by Althusser and others; thus, E.P. Thompson's essay 'The poverty of theory' was actually an attack on Althusserian Marxism rather than on theory as such

Totalizing   A scheme of thought is totalizing if it attempts to place a set of diverse experiences within one large scheme applicable to all times and places. For example, social evolutionary models can be argued to be totalizing in so far as they place all human societies within one stage or another of a grand evolutionary scheme. Usually used pejoratively by opponents of such thinking.

Unilinear   Following one course, as in cultural evolution.

Zeitgeist   A very complex term from German Romantic philosophy. It refers to an essential or defining spirit, whether of an historical period, a 'people', or other cultural group or formation.

Further Reading

How To Read This Book

As stated in the Preface, this book is an introduction to archaeological theory. In this sense, the most important element within its pages is the Further Reading section below.

The main changes a reader will find in this second edition are as follows:

- *A slight change in style and tone.* Theory is invariably a very personal thing, and as Culler (1997) points out in relation to literary theory, it involves placing oneself deliberately in a vulnerable position. There is a very fine line between critique and personalized criticism, and I have tried to take care in this second edition to err on the side of caution in this regard. I have also steered away from the emotive and ambiguous term 'we', preferring the more neutral 'archaeologists' whenever possible.
- *Emendation and updating of the first four chapters.* To understand where 'theory' is today, I remain convinced that one still has to go back to New Archaeology; ideas of empirical enquiry and cultural process that emerged from this remain, I think rightly, foundational to much of archaeology. I've tried however to make the account of the development of these ideas more tied to the present – hence for example the renaming of 'Culture as a System' as 'Culture and Process'. Because much of the account in the first edition was written in the past tense, it was easy for the reader to assume that the ideas contained therein were somehow passé or superseded by later (postprocessual) trends. This was never my intention – ideas of science, variability, pattern, process, remain central to much of archaeology now and in my view have to be understood as a foundation to other areas. Conversely, postprocessualism has, ten years on, to be seen more historically, as a movement of the 1980s and 1990s, rather than as a term that is particularly meaningful today.
- *More extended discussion of 'traditional' or culture-historical archaeology.* Although often describing itself in terms that often makes little or no explicit reference to a specific body of archaeological 'theory', culture history remains an

important approach, particularly in Roman and later archaeology and in much of continental Europe.

- *Division of the 'evolution' chapter into two, one on cultural evolution, one on approaches variously labeled as Darwinist or selectionist.* This reflects a growth in applications of different forms of Darwinian theory to archaeology since the mid-late 1990s.
- *More coverage of theory outside the English-speaking world.* The first edition was a victim of its own success. My intention had been to write a book that chose to deal principally with traditions in Britain and North America, and to be open and explicit about this (see the repeated references to this on ps. xiii, 116, and 210). If I had known how successful and influential the book was going to be, and how it has taken on (despite my best intentions) the status of a key text, I would not have made this decision. This second edition includes much more reference to work from around the world, particularly in the Further Reading section. I have chosen to retain an overall structure that, some will find, continues to reflect an Anglophone bias; this seemed a lesser evil than attempting to write a separate chapter(s) on 'non-Anglo theory'. Inevitably the book, like any book, still bears the marks of the author's biases, preoccupations and language limitations.

I encourage readers to take a critical approach to this book as much as any other. See thoughtful and critical reviews of the first edition by Trigger (2000) and Holtorf (2000), and responses to my views by a variety of scholars in *Archaeological Dialogues*: Johnson (2007) and responses.

General Points

When reading any scholarly book in archaeology, theory included, it's a good idea to take a look at its reviews in major journals. These often tell you more about the prejudices of the reviewers than they do about the book, but are a good way of isolating areas of contentious debate. Articles in *Current Anthropology* and *Archaeological Dialogues* are especially instructive in this regard, since the article is followed by responses and responses-to-responses. *Norwegian Archaeological Review* also includes useful responses in succeeding issues.

　　American Antiquity, Antiquity, European Journal of Archaeology, Journal of Anthropological Archaeology, Current Anthropology, and *American Anthropologist* all have good theory articles. The *Journal of Archaeological Method and Theory, Journal of Social Archaeology, Norwegian Archaeological Review*, and *Journal of Material Culture* are of consistent quality. With the spread of theory in the last 20 years, other, more 'empirical' journals have ever higher numbers of articles that are explicitly informed by theory. Reviews of the literature on a given theoretical topic in the *Annual Review of Anthropology* are often a good place to start.

　　You can complement reading with attendance at conferences. The main British theory 'talking-shop' is the Theoretical Archaeology Group conference (TAG), which is held every December at a different university each year (the 'archive' is at (www.antiquity.ac.uk/tag/index.html). Many go to TAG simply to see old friends and drink some warm beer, but it is also a 'barometer' of what's the latest trend in theory today, at least in Britain. The majority of papers are given by research students or younger staff and organization is supposed to be 'bottom-up'. The fee is currently £50 or less, there is usually free floor-space for students and the unwaged, and everybody regardless of status pays their own way to come. Andrew Fleming and I explored the history of TAG and some of the tensions between its egalitarian ethic and the reality in Fleming and Johnson (1990).

There is also a Theoretical Roman Archaeology Conference held every second year in Britain, and a 'Nordic TAG' (Tusa and Kirkinen 1992; Anderson et al. 1997). The German 'Theorie-Arbeitgemeinschaft' ('T-AG': www.theorie-ag.de) has a newsletter, regular seminars and also organizes sessions in many of the larger German conferences (see Härke and Wolfram 1993). RATS (Radical Archaeologists Talk Shop) is 'an informal group of left-leaning archaeologists' (James Delle, personal communication) rather than a theory group as such. It brings together archaeologists from the northeastern USA and beyond and meets on an irregular basis somewhere in New England or New York.

Otherwise you have to pick and choose between sessions and papers at major conferences. In North America, the Society for American Archaeology and the American Anthropological Association (SAA and AAA) hold symposia with theoretical content; the European Association of Archaeology does also.

There is a proliferation of blogs, wikis, and email lists dealing with archaeological and social theory, though these change and develop so rapidly that it is difficult to be authoritative about them. Sites that are likely to be enduring include: http:// traumwerk.stanford.edu/archaeolog/; http://proteus.brown.edu/joukowskyinstitute/ home; and the arch-theory email list. Fora of the World Archaeological Congress http://www.worldarchaeologicalcongress.org/site/home.php are an important arena. www.area-archives.org links to discussions of the history of archaeology, with theoretical content. The Archaeology part of the UK History, Classics and Archaeology subject centre has useful materials for both learning and teaching in archaeological theory: http://www.heacademy.ac.uk/hca/home. www.theory.org.uk hosts some useful – and hilarious – material on social theory and cultural studies; http:// plato.stanford.edu/contents.html hosts a collection of articles on philosophical issues.

The reading list that follows is partial, and will be out of date between the time I write these words and you read them. It is largely confined to English-language publications, and there is a bias towards publications that will be readily accessible in a range of locations. I have first listed some introductory readings, and then given suggestions for further reading on a chapter-by-chapter basis. The aim of these references is not to provide a complete bibliography on a particular theme; rather, they indicate the background to the arguments laid out in the text, and contain suggestions for further reading which all students should take up.

Introductory Texts

Praetzellis (2000) is tremendous fun. I wish I had written it. The best place to start for a historical perspective is Trigger (2006). I do not agree with Trigger's assessment of where we are now (see Hodder 2006 and Wylie 2006, and others in Williamson and Bisson 2006, for friendly but critical comments), but his writings are consistently thoughtful and serious, and he has a good sense of the balance between academic and wider influences in the development of archaeology.

Renfrew and Bahn (fifth edition 2008) and Thomas and Kelly (2006) are excellent general introductions to archaeology with the merit of recognizing that theoretical concerns are integral to what we do. See also Renfrew and Bahn (2005). Gamble (2008) is accessible and gives a good sense of archaeology as an intellectually demanding discipline.

Binford, L. R. (2002) *In Pursuit of The Past*. This is well written, easy to read and gives a powerful, convincing account of his view of archaeology. Note that it was actually written by John Cherry and Robin Torrence from transcripts from Binford's lecture series in Britain and the Netherlands – Binford is a brilliant, charismatic lecturer.

Preucel, R. and Hodder, I. (eds) (1996) *Contemporary Archaeology in Theory: A Reader*. A collection of 26 articles on most key aspects of archaeological theory. Very good for browsing. Second edition edited by Preucel and Mrozowski forthcoming. See also Hodder (ed.) (2001), *Archaeological Theory Today*.

For the overall thrust of Americanist archaeological theory at present, with its tensions and debates delineated as much as common ground, read Hegmon (2003), the articles by Watkins (2003) and Moss (2005), and Hegmon's response in turn. It's worth comparing this exchange with Kristiansen's view of theory in Europe and the responses (Kristiansen 2008).

Meskell, L. and Preucel, R. (eds) (2004) *A Companion to Social Archaeology*. Oxford, Blackwell.

Preface: The Contradictions of Theory

Popular suspicion of 'intellectuals' is of course a precise inversion of intellectual fear and suspicion of the masses: see Carey (1992). Easthope (1999) is a witty exploration of the anti-theory bias in Anglo-Saxon cultural life. Sommer (2000) makes the important point that the definition of 'theory' as a distinct domain is itself a product of a particular cultural tradition.

Chapter 1   Common Sense is Not Enough

One of the most succinct and devastating demolitions of 'common sense' can be found in Kluckhohn (1939). The discussion of ley lines is drawn from Williamson and Bellamy (1983). See also Stout (2008).

Because most feel such debates are irrelevant, few 'atheoretical' writers have been moved to put defences of their position in print. Fieldwork as a masculine discourse: Joyce et al. 2002: 18–26), and Moser (2007). Conversely, Conkey (2007) has explored the way the practice of theory itself is gendered.

An account of the difficulties of theory in another discipline, with which I find myself in general agreement, is Culler (1997) chapter 1. See also Eagleton (2003), with the slightly misleading title *After Theory* – really a critique of the move from Marxist to postmodern forms of literary theory. Bentley (2006) is a provocative comment on jargon in archaeology (see comments in later issues of *Antiquity*).

Chapter 2   The 'New Archaeology'

I explore the links between Romanticism, empiricism (in the sense that the data are held to link directly to the past without the need for intervening theory) and historic landscape archaeology in Johnson (2007). Of Peter Ackroyd's novels, *Hawksmoor* and *The House of Doctor Dee* are cult reading among archaeologists. Sir Thomas Browne's essay can be found in Robbins (1972) and is discussed by Schwyzer (2007). Indigenous views of past and present: Watkins (2000, 2003) and Atalay (2006).

Further reading on archaeology before the New Archaeology: the often-repeated phrase 'long sleep' comes from Renfrew (1982: 6). Lyman et al. (1997a, 1997b) are introductions to Americanist 'culture history' and reprints of selected papers respectively. O'Brien et al. (2005) discusses the development of North American archaeology from 1960 onwards. I have avoided going in to the historical development of New Archaeology in any depth; such a project would involve looking at the anthropological/North American influences of White, Steward, Seltzer, Willey and Phillips on the one hand, and economic and geographical/British influences of Childe, Higgs and Jarman, Grahame Clark and David Clarke on the other. My thanks to Bob Preucel for clarifying this point.

Childe's view of culture is summarized in McNairn (1980: 46–74). It should be noted that Childe's thought changed markedly through his life – see his 1958 Retrospect. Grahame Clark's thought developed over time from a stress on the economic (for example, Clark 1952) to a celebration of a politically conservative humanism (for example, Clark 1982).

Meltzer (1979) and Patterson (1986) are good introductions to the New Archaeology. Leone (1972) is a reader that includes most of the key early papers and gets across the diversity and excitement of early New Archaeology well. Binford's early papers reprinted in his *An Archaeological Perspective* (1972) are essential reading for anyone who wants to understand the underlying mood and origins of the New Archaeology. His introduction and connecting passages are also entertaining and lucid, in contrast to his more formal academic writing style; see also Schiffer (1995: 1–24), for a rather different account of that time.

Flannery's edited volume *The Early Mesoamerican Village* (1976) is an edited volume of case studies that over 35 years later should be read by specialists in all areas and periods. The case studies show New Archaeology in action, warts and all; see also Flannery (2006). Lyman et al. (2005) examine archaeological publication in *Science* and *Scientific American*, showing that New Archaeology had little direct impact on publication.

Read some of the texts, particularly in anthropology, the New Archaeologists turned to. White's *The Science of Culture* (1949) is clearly written, and prefigures the processual stress on science and systems. The chapter on Akenaton is a brilliant demolition of the idea that individuals' actions are random, unpredictable or important in history. Much New Archaeology was anticipated by Walter Taylor in *A Study of Archaeology* (1948); his emphasis on a 'conjunctive' approach is a forerunner of functional emphases.

Clarke's *Analytical Archaeology* (1978: the second edition revised by Bob Chapman) is a difficult but essential read. It is hard to overestimate the influence of this book. Clarke's 1973 article also had wide impact and sets the theoretical basis of New Archaeology alongside parallel developments in method and technique.

Archaeology as anthropology: there is an important recent debate on the position of North American archaeology within what is called the 'fourfield approach' – a configuration of archaeology and linguistic, cultural and physical anthropology. See papers in Gillespie and Nicholls (2003) and Segal and Yanagisako (2005). Brumfiel (2003) makes the case for a renewed link with anthropology and also identitifies some of the tensions from an Americanist perspective; see also Borofsky (2002). Williamson and Bisson (2006: 8–12), comment on the differences between Canadian and US archaeology. For the history of the relationship of archaeology and anthropology, see Gosden (1999).

Megaliths: Renfrew (1973a) is a popular account. It's worth comparing Renfrew with more recent interpretations of megaliths – see, for example, Bender et al. (2007), Thomas (1999a), Bradley (1993) and Tilley (2004).

Hawkes (1968) is a short and in my view misconceived but influential and often-quoted critique of New Archaeology from the perspective of British traditional archaeology. Klejn (1977) gives a more balanced view of the state of play in the 1970s.

Chapter 3   Archaeology as a Science

Frankenstein: Mary Shelley's novel has been interpreted as a feminist critique of the moral limits of (masculine) scientific rationality: see Gilbert and Gubar (1979: 213–47) and Mellor (1988). A major caveat has to be added to comments on the disciplinary success of science from recent policy-making: the ongoing struggle over creationism and the political 'war on science' in the United States: see Mooney (2005) and Coleman and Carlin (2004).

On theory in Classical archaeology, see Morris (2004) and Shanks (1996); also Alcock (2002). Humanist distrust of science is often based on the implicit premise that what makes 'us' distinctively human (culture, art, religion) is precisely that which is ignored by science; therefore, uncritical use of science will move archaeology away from 'the proper study of mankind', that is 'man'. See C. Hawkes (1954) and J. Hawkes (1968).

Positivism in the human sciences: Roscoe (1995) is a useful commentary on parallel issues in cultural anthropology. Bell (1994) takes a 'refutationist' approach though he is still positivist in the broad sense used here.

Kuhn's philosophy of science is explored in a classic but long and difficult text (Kuhn 1962). For an introduction to the issues and a clearly written exploration of Kuhn's significance in the human sciences as a whole, see Fuller (1992). For Feyerabend, see (1988 and 1995). I could have led the reader away from positivism via the work of Hansen, Quine and Putnam also.

Alison Wylie's writings on epistemology (most collected in 2002) are absolutely central. They make dense reading, but this is because they deal with difficult issues and refuse to descend into platitudes. Gibbon (1989) is a comprehensive archaeological critique of positivism and a lucid view of a 'realist' position. Courbin (1988) argues, in detail, that there is no example of 'testing' in archaeology that can be shown to work in practice.

The literature on the 'science wars' is voluminous; for opposite ends of the spectrum see Gross and Levitt (1994), Wolpert (1992), and Latour (1987). Delanty (1997) steers a middle course. A summary can be found in Parsons (2003); it is striking there has been much less discussion of this topic since around 2000. Pickering (1984) is a brilliant case study but difficult to follow if you don't have a scientific background. Feminist critiques of science include feminist standpoint theory, for which see Harding (2004) and Wylie (2006).

Recent archaeological work bringing together interpretive theory and scientific practice: Jones (2001); Sofaer (2007); Boivin and Owoc (2004); Jones and Macgregor (2002); Wheatley et al. (eds) (2002). Pollard and Bray (2007) reviews this recent literature. Davies et al. (2005) combine scientific evidence for woodland clearance with a phenomenological approach.

Chapter 4   Middle-range Theory, Ethnoarchaeology and Material Culture Studies

The discussion on analogy here is necessarily brief. It owes much, first, to Orme's (1981) work stressing the large contribution ethnographic analogy has played in all archaeology however 'traditional' and, second, to Wylie's (1985) discussion, which demonstrates that there is no clear alternative to analogical thinking in interpretation. The new journal *Ethnoarchaeology* (first issue 2009) promises to be important.

The best place to start with Binford is his *In Pursuit of the Past* (2002, with a new Afterword, first published in 1983) before moving on to his more difficult writings, particularly *Bones* (1981b) and *Constructing Frames of Reference* (2001). Binford's first essay on analogy was1967; his Nunamiut work is discussed in 1980, 2002 and more extensively in 1978. For the Mousterian debate, see Binford (1983b), chapters 4 and 5.

Experimental archaeology: Ethnoarchaeological studies of crop processing include studies by Hillman and Jones in Zeist and Casparie (1984); also Hastorf (1988), Miksicek (1987). For taphonomy, see Huntley and Stallibrass (eds) (2000).

Behavioural archaeology: Skibo and Schiffer (2008) is a good place to start. Schiffer (1976, 1987, 1995), Skibo et al. (1995) and Gould and Schiffer (1981). For the Tucson Garbage Project, see Rathje et al. (1992) and references therein. Skibo and Schiffer (2008) set out a complete manifesto for behavioural archaeology.

Hodder's early work is in Hodder (1982a), though a more readable start to ethnoarchaeology is Hodder (1982b). He criticizes Binford's use of analogy in (1982b: 20–4). Moore (1987) is important not just in its implications for ethnoarchaeology but in its use of feminist and textual theory in the interpretation of space.

There has been much recent interest in interdisciplinary studies of modern material culture: start with Tilley et al. (eds) (2006) and Miller (ed.) (2005); see also Miller (1987, 1995). Good introductions are Woodward (2007) and Tilley et al. (eds) (2006). Mauss and Schlanger (2006), Faure-Rouesnel (2001) and Warnier (1999, 2001) are good places to start on the French anthropological tradition of material culture. Olivier (2000) discusses memory. There are a host of excellent case studies in the *Journal of Material Culture*; there is a useful review of that journal from an archaeological standpoint by van Dommelen (2000). See also further reading on materiality, below.

Chapter 5   Culture and Process

Metaphors of culture: Toynbee's twelve-volume *A Study of History* was fashionable in his day for his delineation of organic rhythms of civilizations, though he is almost forgotten now. The view of societies as embodiments of Big Ideas goes back to the nineteenth-century philosopher Hegel and beyond (Hegel 1956). Furholt (2008) is an effective case study critiquing the equation of archaeological 'culture' with cultural group; see also special issue of *Archaeologia Polona* 34 (1996).

Theoretical discussion in Central and Eastern Europe: Härke (ed.) (2000) and Gramsch and Sommer (eds) are good places to start. There is a themed section on *Central European Archaeology in Transition* in *Antiquity* 67. Kobyliński (2001); Biehl, Gramsch and Marciniak (2002), particularly article by Neustupný; Hensel, Tabaczyñski and Urbañck (1998); Kuna and Venclova (1995); Neustupný (1993). Klejn (1993c) is a comment on German archaeology. Hänsell and Harding (1998) is an English translation of a selection of Georg Kossack's essays. Gramsch (2000) is an especially thoughtful article. Klejn (1993b) comments on Soviet archaeology. Gheorghiu (2003) is a short but powerful plea for post-communist eastern Europe to resist the dominance of Western theory. Poland: Lech (1996); Tabaczyñski (2006, 2007).

For the intellectual sources of culture as a system, see the New Archaeology reading cited above, particularly Flannery, Renfrew and Clarke. Johnson (2004) demonstrates the continuing importance of the processual tradition. Early systems thinking: Earle and Erickson (1977) is a good collection of systemic approaches to exchange. Compare with Earle and Erickson (1982). Hodges (1982) is a processual approach to early medieval Europe.

Collapse: Tainter (2006) and McAnaney and Yoffee (2009) are both responses to Jared Diamond's influential *Collapse* (2005). Schwartz and Nichols (2006) look at regeneration after collapse. Yoffee and Cowgill (1988). For the Classic Maya collapse in particular, see Sabloff (1990) as an introduction; Neiman (1997) takes a self-styled Darwinian evolutionary perspective; his arguments convince though I am not entirely clear what is specifically Darwinian about his theory. For a review of Maya literature see Fash (1994). See also Wilks (1985) for an interesting perspective on how archaeologists' changing explanations of the collapse reflect contemporary political and environmental concerns. For Chaco Canyon, Sebastian (1996) advances a 'sociopolitically based' model in opposition to the environmental explanations. Nelson et al. (2006) make the point from the prespective of cultural ecology that 'reorganization' is a more common response than collapse.

Habermas's critique is much broader than is indicated here, extending to the nature of ideology in late capitalist society (see Habermas 1970, 1975; Bernstein 1985) and the nature of postmodernity. Giddens (1984) is another useful critique.

Revised processual thinking: the key paper is Brumfiel (1992). Crumley (1979, 1987); Brumfiel and Fox (1994); Brumfiel and Earle (1987); Renfrew (1986); Ehrenreich et al. (1995). See also broader collections of papers that balance generalizing approaches with emphasis on historical uniqueness: Scarry (1996); Flannery and Marcus (1983). Political economy: Earle (1997, 2002), Brumfiel and Earle (1987). Muller (1997) is a good case study. Bayman (2002) combines contextual analysis of the meanings of artefacts within a wider model of a prestige goods economy.

World systems theory: the general inspiration is Wallerstein (1974). Applications to archaeology include Kohl (1987), Kristiansen (1998), and Kristiansen and Larsen (1987). Kristiansen and Larsson (2005) is particularly interesting – many of the reviews of this book are coded evaluations of whether an 'archaeology of Europe' at a WST scale is intellectually admissible. World systems theory in Mesoamerica: Schortman and Urban (1994).

Chaos and complexity theory: Kohler (1993); Reisch (1991); Gerding and Ingemark (1997).

On 'freedom' and slavery, see Patterson (1982). I am grateful to Bob Preucel for drawing my attention to this point.

Chapter 6   Thoughts and Ideologies

Hawkes (1954) for his seven 'levels of inference' and the difficulty of looking at thoughts. Binford's views on the inadmissibility of cognition as a factor in archaeological explanation are best expressed in his paper in *Man* (1987) and his brief Commentary in Renfrew and Shennan (1982). Fogelin (2007) is a useful review of different approaches to ritual and religion.

Terrenato (ed.) (2000) brings out the importance of Croce and the idealist tradition (and the consequent reaction against idealism by materialist scholars) in Italian archaeology, particularly papers by Sestieri, Cuozzo, Guidi and Terrenato. There are useful papers also by Maischberger and Tabaczinsky on German and Polish archaeology respectively. See also Guidi 1996.

Structuralism: Bradbury (1987) is a brilliant parody. Conkey (1989) is a good summary of structuralist concerns, tied to the example of cave art. Other examples of structural analysis are discussed in other chapters, but examples include Glassie (1975), Deetz (1977), Washburn (1983). Bapty and Yates (1990) explore the implications of poststructuralism. French archaeological theory has not been as influenced by French structural traditions as one might expect: Demoule (1999), Fleury-Ilett

(1993), Coudart (1999); see also special issue of *Antiquity* vol. 73 (1999). Logicism: J-C Gardin (1980, 2002).

Marxism: Giddens (1979) is still a clear summary of the key points of classical Marxism; it is best to get a grasp of classical Marxism, and better still to read Marx himself (McLellan (ed.) 1977), before moving on to more recent strands of thought and to archaeological applications. Bloch (1983) discusses parallel debates in anthropology. McGuire (1992) is a sophisticated discussion. Childe is the most famous Marxist archaeologist – he combined a materialist model close to traditional Marxism with a diffusionary element. See Childe (1958, 1979), his 'popular' books (1936, 1942) and discussions in McNairn (1980) and Trigger (1980). For Roman Italy and the West, see papers in Keay and Terrenato (eds) 2001.

Ideology: Eagleton (1991) reviews the concept in general terms in an accessible and entertaining way. The writings of Mark Leone and the work of the Archaeology in Annapolis Project are the best examinations of ideology in archaeology. Start with Leone (2005) and move on to 1984, 1988 and 1995, and Potter (1994). See also McGuire (1992, 2008), Miller and Tilley (1984) and references for chapter 11.

'Cognitive archaeology': the best place to start is Renfrew (2007). Renfrew and Zubrow (1994) styles itself a collection of papers addressing cognition from a processual viewpoint, though in my view the intellectual affiliations of the various contributors are more diverse. Flannery and Marcus (1993, 1976) are important studies. Davidson and Noble (1996); Brown (1997) is a review of a variety of approaches as applied to the Eastern Woodlands of North America. Cognitive archaeology and human evolution: an important general book, written by a historian, is Smail (2008). Gamble (2007) is an important study that every educated person should read; see also Mithen (1997, 2005). Many of the key papers for both 'cognitive' and 'postprocessual' approaches are collated in Whitley (1998). De Beaune, Coolidge and Wynn (eds) (2009), and Renfrew, Frith and Malafouris (eds) (2009), are up-to-date collections of papers; see also Coimbra and Dimitriadis (eds) (2008) and Mellars and Gibson (1997).

Chapter 7   Postprocessual and Interpretive Archaeologies

The place to start is Hodder and Hutson (2003). Origins: the interview with Ian Hodder in Hodder, Karlsson and Olsen (2008) explains something of the origins of postprocessual archaeology. For problems of testing and simulation, see Hodder and Orton (1976); Hodder's ethnoarchaeological work can be found in Hodder (1982b). Watson's (1991) article pointed out to me the striking parallels between Binford and Hodder in their intellectual development.

Shanks and Tilley (1987 and 1992, first published 1988) had a huge impact on publication. They are both difficult, but absolutely central to any understanding of postprocessual archaeology. *Social Theory* has a summary at the back. It is worth asking as you read: most of this was hugely controversial when it was published: how much is controversial now? McGuire (1993) is not just an article about Marxism, but offers a useful survey of the relationship between different strands of postprocessual thought and their academic and social context.

Hodder et al. (1995) is an excellent overview. Many of the key early papers are reprinted in Whitley (1998). Hodder (1999) is good not just on how to do interpretive archaeology, but on theorized descriptions of what all archaeologists do in practice and how all those practices are underpinned by theory, 'interpretation at the trowel's edge'.

Historical idealism: Collingwood's *Idea of History* (1946) is his definitive statement of historical idealism; his *Autobiography* (1939) is shorter, more readable, and makes the context of his thinking much clearer – and also offers a cogent example of the political dangers of relativism.

Agency: the current interest in agency is not confined to postprocessualism; just as cognition is attracting attention from processual thinking, so is 'the individual' however defined. The origins of concerns with agency are usually traced to Bourdieu (1977) and Giddens (1979, 1984; see Held and Thompson 1989 for useful critique and bibliography). I have always found the work of Erving Goffman (1959, 1971) far more useful and lucid and recommend it as an introduction to the issues surrounding structure and action. A different approach to agency and structure is taken from within the postprocessual tradition through the idea of practice (Barrett 1994).

Dobres and Robb (eds) (2000) offer case studies from a variety of theoretical perspectives, while a double issue of *Journal of Archaeological Method and Theory* 12:3 and 12:4 discusses methods for 'doing' agency; the papers by Pauketat, Tomášková and Owoc are particularly useful. Dornan (2002) offers conceptual clarification. Dobres (2000) is an important study of agency and technology. Object agency: Gosden (2005), drawing on Gell (1998); see also references to materiality. For criticism of the limitations of agency as a model, see Kristiansen (2004) and succeeding discussion.

Critics of postprocessualism: many early critiques were responses to Hodder and Shanks and Tilley rather than to postprocessualism as such. These included Earle and Preucel (1987); Kristiansen (1988); Patterson (1990); Wylie (1992a); Binford (1987); Knapp (1996); Preucel (1995); and papers in Yoffee and Sherratt (1993). R.A. Watson (1990, 1991) criticizes Shanks and Tilley from the angle of positivism. Klejn (1993a, b) gives a reactionary view; see the thoughtful response to Klejn by Murray (1995). The debate between Thomas and Mithen is revealing (Thomas 1988 and 1991; Mithen 1991). Englestad (1991) and Smith (1994) are critiques of postprocessualism from a feminist perspective.

For an idea of the variance between different postprocessual traditions, compare Bapty and Yates (1990) and Baker, Taylor and Thomas (1990), two contrasting volumes that arose from the same conference.

Case studies: Johnson (1996, 2002) are my attempts to apply a postprocessual perspective to the archaeology of late medieval and early modern England, areas still dominated by culture-historical rather than processual approaches. Tilley (1991, 1994) apply textual and phenomenological approaches respectively to data from prehistoric Europe. McGuire and Saitta (1996) approach the traditional question 'were 14th century Southwestern pueblos egalitarian or hierarchical?' and show how an approach stressing 'lived experience' can move beyond such either/or thinking (though they would not give their approach a specifically postprocessual label).

See also the succeeding debate in *American Antiquity* 63: 2. Duke and Wilson (1995) looks at North American Plains archaeology.

Phenomenology: Much of the phenomenological literature is quite dense. The best place to start is the essay 'Building, dwelling, thinking' in Ingold (2000), though Ingold's thought is too diverse to be classified simply as a phenomenologist. Thomas (2004) and Tilley (2004) have been, rightly, profoundly influential; see Ingold (2005) on the latter, and also Tilley (2008) and Bender et al. (2007). See also Gosden (1994); Tilley (1994, 2008); Thomas (1999b). Ingold and Vergunst (eds) (2008) is also engaging and profound. Method: Hamilton and Whitehouse (2006). Criado Boado and Villock Vásquez (2000) explore the building of a method through an 'archaeology of perception'. Snead (2008) is a case study of ancestral Pueblo landscapes.

There is also an extensive literature on the subjective experience and construction of place, in tune with but not necessarily formally derived from phenomenological concerns, for example Bradley (2000); Sturt (2006); papers in special issue of *Journal of Archaeological Method and Theory*, 11:1 and 11:2.

Criticism of phenomenology: Fleming (2006) is a generalized denigration; Brück (2005) and Barrett and Ko (2009) are more sophisticated evaluations. Ingold (2007) is a thoughtful discussion of issues of 'materiality'; Whitley (2002) critiques the over-generalized use of 'ancestors'; Insoll (2007) critiques the human/natural opposition. In Johnson (2006), I explore the intellectual and practical context of phenomenology.

Semiotics: Preucel (2006) is an exploration and archaeological application of the ideas of Peirce.

Chapter 8   Archaeology, Gender and Identity

There is a plethora of books on feminism in general. Humm (1992) is an anthology that gets across the variety of perspectives; Harding's paper in that volume points to debates between different feminist philosophies of science. McNay (1992) is a powerful anti-essentialist account of feminist concerns. I've avoided going through the topic of sexist language; for the basic arguments see Spender (1980). Moore (1988) explores the background issues in anthropology with clarity and is a useful synthesis of anthropological thought.

Studies specific to archaeology: the most up-to-date assessment is Conkey (2007), which also lays down important challenges for the practice of theory in general; it could be read in conjunction with Nelson (ed.) (2007). Gero and Conkey (1991) is a definitive collection of papers with a lucid introduction to the issues. Among the best papers are Hastorf, Gero, Wylie and Handsman. Conkey and Gero (1997) is a useful review of the literature. Hays-Gilpin and Whitley (1998) is an excellent collection of significant reprinted articles. Wright (1996), Claassen (1992), Walde and Willows (1991), duCros and Smith (1993) and Balme and Beck (1995) are other edited collections. Franklin (2001) on a Black feminist-inspired archaeology. Karlisch (ed.) (1997) and Merterns (1993) on feminist approaches in German archaeology.

Issues of gendered archaeological practice: Gero (1985, 1991); Wylie (1993b); Hutson (2002) on citation practices; Moser (1996). Tomášková (2007) argues for greater feminist reflection on and transformation of field practice, with specific reference to mapping. History of women in archaeology: Diaz-Andreu and Sørensen (1998); Joyce (1994), Claassen (1994). Career issues: various articles in Reyman (1992) and du Cros and Smith (1995); Nelson et al. (1994); Wylie (1993); Gero (1985, 1988). Two websites provide a focus for British and North American women archaeologists: http://britishwomenarchaeologists.org.uk/index.html and http://www.saa.org/ForMembers/InterestGroups/tabid/129/Default.aspx.

Archaeology of 'women': Ehrenberg (1989) weds a traditional archaeological format to a search for 'women'. A famous study is Gimbutas (1989, 1991); most feminists would distance themselves from Gimbutas's arguments; see Russell (1993) for a discussion of the underlying issues.

'Processual' approaches to gender: Brumbach and Jarvenpa (1997) use 'a gender-resource mapping approach' in which gender is seen as a variable within a more general 'subsistence settlement model'. Again, Mobley-Tanaka (1997) develops a gendered view of pueblo architecture within a framework of 'social stress'. Evolutionary approaches: Hager (1997); McClure (2007) combines cultural inheritance theory with a gendered analysis. Pyburn (2003) looks at gender issues in the 'rise of civilization'.

Case studies (many of these could be put under the 'postprocessual' subheading): Gilchrist (1993); Hodge McCoid and McDermott (1996). Gender in historical archaeology: Wall (1994); Gilchrist (1993); Spector (1993); Yentsch (1991). Seifert (1991) is an excellent edited collection. Tomášková (2006) and Robin (2006) are important case studies that show how gender permeates other historical categories of analysis.

Sørensen (2000) argues for a clear distinction between 'gender archaeology' and feminist concerns. Anthony (1995) criticizes 'eco-feminist' approaches though most feminists would disavow these approaches in any case. Nicholas (1994) makes pertinent comments on the Goddess myth. Gero and Conkey (1997), writing from a feminist standpoint, make some critical comments, implying that much gender archaeology has failed to take the feminist critique sufficiently seriously. Greater 'feminist theorizing and engagement' is also urged by Englestad (2007), a theme that is also taken up by a special issue of the *Journal of Archaeologcial Method and Theory* 14.

Archaeology and identity: Insoll (ed.) (2007); Casella and Fowler (2005); Immonen (2005) for the case study of the Hanse. Hinton (2005), though it does not wear its theory on its sleeve, is a nuanced study of material culture and identity in the Middle Ages. Revell (2009) explores 'Roman' cultural identities. A special double issue of the *Journal of Material Culture* examines isues of identity as they relate to space and place: 11:1 and 11:2.

Masculinity: Johnson (2002); Wilkie (2010). Nottveit (2006) is a good case study on medieval daggers and masculine identity. Childhood: Sofaer (ed.) (2000); see also the new *Journal of Childhood in the Past*. Race: Orser (2004); Franklin (2001). Sexuality: Meskell (1999) argues that even 'sex' is culturally constructed. Voss (2008a) is a useful review of archaeological studies of sexuality, while Meskell (2002) is an important case study. Queer archaeologies: Dowson (ed.) (2000). Theoretical approaches to the body: Sofaer (2006). Crossland (2009) is a fascinating case study. For an archaeology of disability, see Hubert (ed.) (2000). An important critique of the social model of disability, and a readable introduction to disability studies, is Shakespeare (2006).

Performativity: Judith Butler is the key thinker, though her writing style is not easy. Butler (1990) and (1993) are classics that underpin much of the recent work on identity.

Chapter 9   Archaeology and Cultural Evolution

Pluciennik (2005) is an excellent, highly critical general introduction to social evolution. Chapman 2003 is the most authoritative recent book on social complexity. Yoffee (2005) is a robust 'apology' for cultural evolution, building in diversity to state studies. Peregrine (2001) is a stout defence of a unilinear and cross-cultural approach to social evolution. Trigger (1997) reviews the history of social evolutionary ideas. For a sample of current 'state of the art' approaches see Kohring and Wynne-Jones (eds) (2007).

Recent reviews of the literature include Stanish (2001) for state societies in south America and Cobb (2003) for Mississsippian chiefdoms. Smith (2004) discusses ancient state economies.

Earle (2000): cross-cultural survey of analyses of property within a political-economic framework. Beck et al. (2007) is a good example of a combination of structural and agent-centred analysis. Rousseau (2006) also combines human agency and evolutionary theory. Again, Ensor (2000) stresses the importance of daily life or *modo de vida*. Segmentation and war: Kelly (2000b), Flannery and Marcus (2003). Colonies: Hurst and Owen (2005).

Evolution of social complexity: a good overview of Americanist work is provided by Baines and Yoffee (2000), Crumley (1995), Wason (1994), Fash (1994), Kowalewski (1990), Kolb (1994) and Spencer (1997). Smith (2003), one of my favourite books, is a model study of how a different range of concerns from political economy can be integrated within a generalizing understanding of the 'political landscapes' of state societies. Criticisms of social evolution and a refined approach attempting to define and measure 'inequality' and 'heterogeneity' in societies is outlined by McGuire (1983). The studies in Part IV of Preucel and Hodder (1996) give a good flavour of the diversity of approaches to sociopolitical complexity.

Latin American social archaeology: Lumbreras (2005) and Bate (1998). English discussions can be found in Patterson (1994); see also the response to Patterson (Oyuela-Caycedo et al. 1997) and Patterson's response in turn, and McGuire (1993). Drawing on its terminology, Ensor (2000) stresses the importance of *modo de vida*. See also Oyuela-Caycedo (1994).

Cahokia: Pauketat (2001) uses the Mississippian as a case study in proposing a 'new paradigm' of 'historical processualism'. Holt (2009) on Cahokia as a 'theatre state'; also Brown (2006) and comments in Beck et al. (2007).

Criticisms of cultural evolution in archaeology: Yoffee (1979); Trigger (1984, 1997); Shanks and Tilley (1987); Patterson (1995); McGuire (1992). Problems with chiefdoms: Pauketat (2007).

My concluding comments on phenomenology and cultural evolution share ground with some elements of Whitley (2002), particularly his identification of 'ancestors' with processual and Marxist models.

Chapter 10   Archaeology and Darwinian Evolution

As I also feel with strands of theory such as Marxism, it is advisable for the student to grasp something of the structure of Darwinian thought before asking how to apply it to archaeology. For an introduction to Darwin and discussion of recent Darwinian thought, the two major thinkers are Steven Jay Gould (1989, 1997, 2002) and Richard Dawkins (1989). Both write accessibly and have been extremely influential; Gould in particular has stressed the role of contingency and historical accident in evolution, and has played an indirect role in the 'softening' of many evolutionary models in archaeology. I would add Richerson and Boyd (2005) as an accessible and compelling account of coevolutionary theory. The subtitle 'Darwin's dangerous idea' is taken from Dennett (1995).

Shennan 2008 is a good bibliographic review of the archaeological literature, complemented for North America by Clark (2003). Shennan (2002) is an important statement of a different approach to evolution – note that there is almost no reference to the 'Dunnell school' in this book. See also the critique of Shennan in Kristiansen (2004).

The style-function dichotomy: Brantingham (2007). Bentley and Shennan (2003) is a good case study in Darwinian approaches to cultural transmission. Costly signalling theory: McGuire and Hildebrandt (2005). See also subsequent exchanges in *American Antiquity* 72:2.

Selectionist archaeology: O'Brien (ed.) (1996) is a good place to start, and includes much of Dunnell's writings. See also Dunnell (1980, 1989); Rindos (1989). Teltser (1995) is a collection of papers dealing with methodological issues raised by selectionist approaches. Barton and Clark (1997) contains some good papers. In particular, Fraser Neiman is a lucid and enthusiastic proponent of such models (1997). Other recent collections include Maschner (1996), O'Brien (1996), Arnold (1996). For the argument that culture history came close to a Darwinian approach, see Lyman and O'Brien (1997a, 2006).

Case studies: Falk (1997) on the brain. Arnold et al. (1997) versus Raab and Larson (1997): two contrasting views of the interpretation of the same set of environmental data. Larson et al. (1996): compare with McGuire and Saitta (1996), both parties working on similar material.

Fabian (1998) is an edited volume of accessible articles that gives a good idea of the very wide variation in contemporary evolutionary thought. Ridley (1997) is a good introductory 'reader'. For a critical approach see Midgley (1985) and Giddens (1984).

Optimal foraging theory: see Mithen for an individual-based approach to cultural ecology; also the debate between Mithen and Thomas (Thomas 1988, 1991; Mithen 1991). Mithen (1989) on ecological approaches to art; compare with other studies in the same volume. Risk: Halstead and O'Shea (1989).

Case studies: Gamble (2007) is to my mind the best in its field. Larson and Michaelsen (1990) and Larson et al. (1996) see Anasazi cultural development as a response to population growth and climatic deterioration; see reply by Allison (1996) focusing on whether their chronology works. Contrast also with McGuire and Saitta in the same volume. A variety of work balances 'social' and 'ecological' approaches in a consideration of environment; for example, Hastorf and Johanessen (1991) and Schortman and Urban (1992). See also studies in Crumley (1994). 'Sexy handaxe theory': Kohn and Mithen (1999); Machin (2008); Mithen (2008). Neiman (2008) is a fascinating study from historical archaeology.

For the nineteenth-century cultural context of Darwin, see Beer (1996) and Smith (2009).

Schiffer (1996) argues for a *rapprochement* between behavioural and evolutionary archaeology.

Chapter 11　Archaeology and History

Current approaches to Classical archaeology: Morris (2004), Alcock and Osborne (2007). Hingley (2005) looks at Roman archaeology.

Moreland (2006) is an authoritative summary of current thinking on the relationship between archaeology and texts; see also Moreland (2001) and Tabaczyñski (1993). O'Keeffe (2007) discusses the relationship between archaeology and art history; in Johnson 2007, I discuss the relationship between archaeology and landscape history. Special Issues of *Archaeologia Polona* 44 (2006) has a series of papers on the relationship between archaeology, anthropology and history. Malina and Vasicek (1990) is a powerful statement of archaeology as a historical discipline, and a useful summary in English of many of the concerns of central and eastern European archaeology.

Early medieval Europe: Hills (2003), Halsall (1997), Staecker (2005) and comments in the next issue, Hedeagar (2006) and responses in succeeding issue.

Annales school: Le Goff and Nora (1985) is a collection of varied papers, ranging from (early) work on climate, demography and quantitative methods to (later) studies of ideologies and mental structures. Braudel (1980) is a collection of his papers; see also Le Roy Ladurie (1974, 1978). Annales archaeology: Knapp (1992) is the best collection of Annales-influenced papers, the best of which is Duke (1992), though Moreland's paper in this volume argues convincingly against the utility of Annales thinking for archaeology. Chartier (1994) is the best example of his work.

The 'linguistic turn': Joyce (1995); Easthope (1993). The work of Hayden White (1987) and Dominic LaCapra (1987) has been central in the critique of history as a narrative: see Jenkins (1995, 1997). Hunt (1989) is a useful introduction to the New Cultural History. For a critique, Evans (2nd edn 2000) is a passionately written, influential, lucid condemnation of postmodern forms of 'theory' in history. The responses of Evans's critics, and his response in turn, have been gathered together by the Institute of Historical Research (http://www.history.ac.uk/discourse/index.html, accessed 10.10.2008).

'Processual' approaches to historical archaeology include South (1977a,b), Binford (1977). Brumfiel (2003) explores the interfaces between history, archaeology and anthropology within North American traditions; see also Deagan (1991). Deagan (1983) for the St Augustine project: an excellent case study is Voss' (2008b) reformulation of gender, race and labour.

Deetz's work, particularly his application of structuralism to historical archaeology, has had a huge influence. His simply written yet theoretically sophisticated application of structuralism to historical archaeology, *In Small Things Forgotten* (1977), remains my favourite archaeology book. See also Deetz (1988) and Yentsch and Beaudry (1992).

The historical archaeology of capitalism is a huge field. A few introductory references are Leone (2005); Orser (1996); Johnson (1996); Delle (1998).

'Contact period' studies embody a wide range of approaches: compare Leonard (1993) with Turnbaugh (1993) in the same volume. Contrasts between colonial and Indigenous interpretations are discussed in Anawalt (1996) and Crowell (1997). Oral traditions and ethnohistory: Damm (2005) and comments in succeeding issues. Case studies: Bergman (2006) relates archaeology to Saami ethnohistory; see response by Knutson (2007). Hrobat (2007) looks at oral tradition, memory and landscape. David et al. (2002) is a model case study.

Case studies of historical archaeology: Little (2007) is a good place to start. Then Leone (2005) and Voss (2008c). McGuire and Paynter (1991), especially the paper by Yentsch; Kepecs and Kolb (1997); and Tarlow and West (1998). Yentsch (1994) is a classic study of historical archaeology. Lightfoot et al. (1998) is a fascinating study of practices and identities. Gilchrist (1993) is a study of medieval nunneries. See also Wall (1994), Spector (1993).

African historical archaeology: Schmidt and Walz (2007); Hall (2000). Schrire (1995) is a powerful and moving account of historical archaeology in South Africa, for which see also Lucas and Hall (2006).

Bodiam Castle: Coulson (1992), Johnson (2002). Ronnes (1999), Hansson (2006) and Virágos discuss comparable issues for other areas of Europe. Platt (2007) is a restatement of traditional views; make your own mind up.

Chapter 12   Archaeology, Politics and Culture

The postmodern condition: Lyotard (1984). Lyotard, rarely among postmodern thinkers, writes in an accessible and elegant way. Rorty (1989) also writes accessibly. Harvey (1989) is a classic review and critique of postmodernism from a Marxist perspective. See also Rorty and Engel (2007), and Hollinger (1994). Postmodernism in other disciplines: Jencks (1977: architecture), Gregory (1994: geography), Jenkins (1995, 1997), White (1987) and Hunt (1989: history; Evans (2000) for critique). No discussion of postmodernism would be complete without a discussion of the 'Sokal hoax': see Sokal and Bricmont (1998), and Sokal (2008). Ashman and Baringer (2000) contains a variety of responses to the hoax.

Foucault has an undeserved reputation as a difficult writer. It's best to take him on his own terms; he frequently writes in a rhetorical rather than analytical style, and frequently uses extended metaphors (most famously that of archaeology itself). Again, Foucault refuses to be pinned down to a set of concrete causes or a cut-and-dried 'model'. Read some of his books on tangible issues such as *Madness and Civilisation* and *Discipline and Punish* before moving on to his more methodological works such as *An Archaeology of Knowledge* and *The Order of Things*.

Archaeology and politics: parts VII and VII of Preucel and Hodder (1996), especially Gero and Root and Trigger. Fawcett et al. (eds) (2008) contains a range of recent work. See also Hinsley (1989). Eller (1997) is a concise and lucid general introduction to the issues around 'multiculturalism'. Bender (1998) is a passionate account of the politics of Stonehenge. Jones (1997) is a fascinating account of past interpretations of Chichen Itza. McGuire (2008) is a restatement of a Marxist view and a fascinating case study.

Archaeology and Indigenous knowledge: start with Atalay (2006) and Lippert (2006). Wilcox (2010) is an important discussion of NAGPRA which has influenced my presentation of the issues here. Tuhiwai Smith (1999) explores background issues. Watkins (2000) concentrates on ethical/legislative issues; see also Watkins (2003). Ferguson (1996) is a review of the literature on Native Americans and archaeology, now a little out of date. Kennewick Man: Thomas (2000), Burke et al. (eds) (2008). Lippert (2005) is an important move beyond simplistic and polarized issues of 'ownership'. López Austin and López Luján (2001) is a powerful account of Mexico's Indigenous past. Conkey (2005) discusses the intersection between feminist and Indigenous archaeologies: see also ensuing discussion. Indigenous archaeology in Australia: McNiven and Russell (2005), who recommend 'partnership research' beyond community archaeology, and the archaeology of oral tradition, as the way forward. McGhee (2008) is a controversial rebuttal of 'Indigenous archaeology'; as I write responses in future issues of *American Antiquity* are forthcoming. Blain and Wallis (2004, 2007) on modern Pagans.

Nationalism, for obvious reasons, is a major preoccupation with European archaeologists: Hamilakis and Yalouri (1996); Atkinson et al. (1996). Diaz-Andreu and Champion (1996) and Kohl and Fawcett (1996) are good collections of case studies, though see Hamilakis (1996) and Lampeter Archaeology Workshop (1997) for an effective critique of the latter. Cooper et al. (1995) and Walsh (1992) discuss the theoretical basis of 'heritage management' and cultural identity in Britain. Curta (2001) and Piontek (2006) discuss archaeology and Slavic identity; Piotrowska (1997–8) is an important discussion of Biskupin. Hamilakis (2007) is an important study, moving beyond an exclusive concern with nationalism. Nationalism and archaeology in Iran: Abdi (2001). Zimbabwe: Fontein (2006). Abu El-Haj (2001) is a scholarly and important study of Israeli archaeology.

Archaeology under the Nazis: Arnold (1990) and Arnold and Hassmann (1995); Härke and Wolfram (1993); Jones et al. (1996); Schulke (2000); Legendre et al. (2007). Diaz-Andreu (1993) on archaeology under Franco.

Community archaeology: Marshall (ed.) (2002) is an important collection of papers, especially Moser et al. (2002). The Annapolis Project is an excellent case study in building a critical public awareness. See Leone (2005); also Potter (1994). See also Sabloff (2008). Schmidt (2001) discusses theoretical issues in museums interpretation and compares the Anglo scene with Germany

Postcolonial issues: Gosden (2001); Chakrabarti (1998) on India; Andah (1995), Hall (2000) and Shepherd (2002) on Africa. Cultural hybridity: Falck (2003). Wilson (1999) is a fascinating series of studies of cultural contact. Hingley (2005) is a postcolonial view of Roman archaeology. Silliman (2005) discusses native North American archaeology and argues for seeing it the period as 'colonial' rather than one of 'contact'. Harrison (2003) explores mimesis in knapped bottle glass artefacts. India: Chakrabarti (2003), Pratap (2009). The Americas: Bernal (1980); Lumbreras (2005); Politis (2001, 2002); Politis and Alberti (1999); various in Funari et al. (eds) (2005). Scheinsohn (2003) argues that the dominance of North American scholarship has obscured South American diversity with regard to the archaeological record for hunter-gathers.

African burial ground: the National Parks Service website has a brief account and links to the final reports (http://www.nps.gov/afbg/historyculture/index.htm). On wider issues of African-American archaeology, see Ferguson (1992), Blakey (1995) and Singleton (1985, 1995, and references therein). On wider issues of the misuse of genetics, see Pluciennik (1996); Mirza and Dungworth (1995).

Relativism: Trigger (1989); Wylie (1992b); Brumfiel (1996). Fotiadis (1994) is a restatement that this claimed objectivity is illusory. Davis (1992), Gosden (1992) and Saitta (1992) offer thoughtful discussion of related aspects of this debate. Lampeter Archaeology Workshop (1997) offers a critical response.

World Archaeological Congress and social justice issues: Smith and Ward (2000) discuss the social background. Ucko (1989) is entertaining, but should be read with critical caution.

Issues of representation and performativity: Shanks (1992); Shanks and Pearson (2001). Moser (1996) discusses issues of visual representation.

Chapter 13   Conclusion: The Future of Theory

It is worth comparing consensual 'position statements' on aims and priorities for archaeology, for example that of Nordic TAG (http://www.aal.au.dk/nt/enkeltesessions/priorities, accessed 10.10.2008), the Archaeology Benchmarking Statement laying out a 'benchmark' for undergraduate teaching in the UK (http://www.qaa.ac.uk/academicinfrastructure/benchmark/statements/Archaeology.asp, accessed 10.10.2008), and its Australian counterpart (www.australianarchaeologicalassociation.com.au/files/by_degrees.pdf, accessed 23.08.2009). Critical comment on an earlier version of the UK Benchmarking statement can be found in Rainbird and Hamilakis (2001). Patrik's (1985) influential article argues for the coexistence of different schools of thought centred around different definitions of what constitutes the archaeological record.

The current state: an extremely useful volume is Holtorf and Karlsson (2000), which in its use of commentaries and replies by the author gives a good flavour of diversity across the globe. Funari et al. (eds) (2005) and Kobyliñski (ed.) (2001) are also useful in this context. 'World theory': Schmidt and Patterson (1995); Ucko (1995); issues of *Archaeologies*, published by the World Archaeological Congress.

Reflexive approaches to fieldwork: Berggrren and Hodder (2003); Chadwick (2003); Lucas (2001); Yarrow (2003); Holtorf (2002); Moser (2007). Much of this literature also contributes to the study of materiality and artfeact biography. See also the extensive literature on the Çatalhöyük project, including Hodder (1999) and http://www.catalhoyuk.com/. Tomáskóva (2007) explores field practices, particularly mapmaking, from a feminist standpoint.

Materiality: the proposition that things create people as much as people create things is set out most clearly by Gosden (2005). For a range of approaches, see Skibo and Schiffer (2008), DeMarrais et al. (eds) (2004), Brumfiel (2003), Knappett (2005), Meskell (2004), Meskell (ed.) (2005), Olsen (2003). Herva and Ikäheimo (2002) on rock art and materiality.

Symmetrical archaeology: Latour has been especially influential; I find his case studies (for example the Berliner Key essay in Graves-Brown (ed.) 2000 and the first part of Latour 1987) more compelling than his more general arguments, for example Latour (2005). Webmoor and Witmore (2008) set out the case for a critique of 'the social', drawing on Gell (1992, 1998) and Latour (2005). Witmore (2006); Webmoor (2007); Gonzáles-Ruibal (2006) and responses in succeeding issues; papers in Gonzáles-Ruibal (ed.) (2007); papers in World Archaeology 39:4.

Memory: Jan Assman's work (2006) is especially important. Van Dyke and Alcock (eds) (2003), Jones (2007), Campbell (2006) for a Polynesian case study. Temporality: Lucas (2005), Harding (2005).

Bibliography

Abdi, K. 2001. Nationalism, politics and the development of archaeology in Iran. *American Journal of Archaeology* 105: 51–76.

Abu El-Haj, N. 2001. *Facts on the Ground: Archaeological Practice and Territorial Self-Fashioning in Israeli Society*. Chicago, University of Chicago Press.

Alcock, L. 1976. *Arthur's Britain: History and Archaeology*, AD 367–634. London, Penguin.

Alcock, S. 2002. *Archaeologies of the Greek Past: Landscape, Monuments, and Memories. Cambridge*, Cambridge, Cambridge University Press.

Alcock, S. and Osborne, R. (eds) 2007. *Classical Archaeology*. Oxford, Blackwell.

Allison, J.R. 1996. Comments on the impacts of changing variability and population growth on virgin Anasazi cultural development. *American Antiquity* 61(2): 414–18.

Anawalt, P.R. 1996. Aztec knotted and netted capes: colonial interpretations versus Indigenous primary data. *Ancient Mesoamerica* 7: 187–206.

Andah, B.W. 1995. European encumbrances to the development of relevant theory in African archaeology. In Ucko (ed.), 96–109.

Andersson, A.-C., Campbell, F., Gillberg, A., Hansonn, J., Jensen, O.W., Karlsson, H. and Rolöff, M. (eds) 1997. *The Kaleidoscopical Past: Proceedings of the 5th Nordic TAG Meeting, Gothenburg 1997*. Gotarc Serie C: Arkeologiska Skrifter. Dept of Archaeology, University of Gothenburg.

Andrén, A. 1998. *Between Artefacts and Texts: Historical Archaeology in Global Perspective*. New York, Plenum.

Anthony, D.W. 1995. Nazi and eco-feminist prehistories: ideology and empiricism in Indo-European archaeology. In Kohl and Fawcett (eds), 82–97.

Arnold, B. 1990. The past as propaganda: totalitarian archaeology in Nazi Germany. *Antiquity* 64: 464–78. Reprinted in Hodder and Preucel (eds), 549–69.

Arnold, B. and Gibson, D.B. (eds) 1995. *Celtic Chiefdom, Celtic State*. Cambridge, Cambridge University Press.

Arnold, B. and Hassmann, H. 1996. Archaeology in Nazi Germany: the legacy of the Faustian bargain. In Kohl and Fawcett (eds), 70–81.

Arnold, D.E. 1995. *Ceramic Theory and Cultural Process*. Cambridge, Cambridge University Press.

Arnold, J.E. (ed.) 1996. *Emergent Complexity: The Evolution of Intermediate Societies*. Archaeological Series 9. Ann Arbor, International Monographs in Prehistory.

Arnold, J.E., Colten, R.H. and Pletka, S. 1997. Contexts of cultural change in southern California. *American Antiquity* 62(2): 300–18.

Ashman, K.M. and Barringer, P.S. (eds) 2000. *After the Science Wars: Science and the Study of Science*. London, Routledge.

Ashmore, W., Lippert, D. and Mills, B. (eds) 2010. *Voices of American Archaeology: 75th Anniversary of the SAA*. SAA Press.

Assmann, J. 2006. *Religion and Cultural Memory: Ten Studies*. Stanford, Stanford University Press.

Atalay, S. 2006. Indigenous archaeology as decolonizing practice. *American Indian Quarterly* 30(3): 280–310.

Atkinson, J.A., Banks, I. and O'Sullivan, J. 1996. *Nationalism and Archaeology: Scottish Archaeological Forum*. Glasgow, Cruithne Press.

Auel, J. 1980. *Clan of the Cave Bear*. London, Hodder and Stoughton.

Baines, J. and Yoffee, N. 2000. Order, legitimacy and wealth: setting the terms. In Richards, J.E. and Van Buren, M., *Order, Legitimacy, and Wealth in Ancient States*. Cambridge, Cambridge University Press.

Balme, J. and Beck, W. (eds) 1995. *Gendered Archaeology: The Second Australian Women in Archaeology Conference*. Research Papers in Archaeology and Natural History 26. Canberra, Australian National University.

Baker, F., Taylor, S. and Thomas, J. (eds) 1990. *Writing the Past in the Present*. Lampeter, St David's University College.

Bapty, I. and Yates, T. (eds) 1990. *Archaeology After Structuralism: Post-Structuralism and the Practice of Archaeology*. London, Routledge.

Barrett, J.C. 1994. *Fragments From Antiquity: An Archaeology of Social Life in Britain, 2900–1200 BC*. Oxford, Blackwell Publishers.

Barrett, J. and Ko, I. 2009, forthcoming. A phenomenology of landscape: a crisis in British landscape archaeology? *Journal of Social Archaeology*.

Barton, C.M. and Clark, G.A. (eds) 1997. *Rediscovering Darwin: Evolutionary Theory in Archaeological Explanation*. Papers of the American Anthropological Association 7. Arlington, American Anthropological Association.

Bate, L.F. 1998. *El Proceso de Investigación en Arqueología*. Barcelona, Ediciones Crítica.

Baudrillard, J. 1995. *The Gulf War Did Not Take Place*. Bloomington: Indiana University Press.

Bayman, J.M. 2002. Hohokam craft economies and the materialization of poer. Journal of Archaeological Method and Theory 9(1): 69–95.

Beck, L.A. (ed.) 1995. *Regional Approaches to Mortuary Analysis*. New York, Plenum Press.

Beck, R., Bolender, D., Brown, J.A. and Earle, T.K. 2007. Eventful archaeology: the space and place of structural transformation. *Current Anthropology* 48(6): 833–60.

Beer, G. 1996. *Open Fields: Science in Cultural Encounter*. Oxford, Oxford University Press.

Bell, J.A. 1994. *Reconstructing Prehistory: Scientific Method in Archaeology*. Philadelphia, Temple University Press.

Benavides, O.H. 2001. Returning to the course: social archaeology as Latin American philosophy. *Latin American Antiquity* 12(4): 355–70.

Bender, B. 1998. *Stonehenge: Making Space*. Oxford, Berg.

Bender, B., Hamilton, S. and Tilley, C. 2007. *Stone Worlds: Narrative and Reflexivity in Landscape Archaeology*. Walnut Creek, Left Coast Press.

Bentley, A. and Shennan, S.J. 2003. Cultural transmission and stochastic network growth. *American Antiquity* 68(3): 459–85.

Bentley, R.A. 2006. Academic copying, archaeology and the English language. *Antiquity* 80: 196–281.

Bergman, I. 2006. Indigenous time, colonial history: Sami conceptions of time and ancestry and the role of relics in cultural reproduction. *Norwegian Archaeological Review* 39: 151–61.

Berggren, A. and Hodder, I. 2003. Social practice, method, and some problems of field archaeology. *American Antiquity* 68(3): 421–34.

Bernal, I. 1980. *A History of Mexican Archaeology*. London, Thames and Hudson.

Bernbeck, R. 1997 *Theorien in der Archäologie*. Tübingen, Francke Verlag.

Bernstein, R.J. (ed.) 1985. *Philosophy and Modernity*. Cambridge, Polity Press.

Bettinger, R.L. and Eerkens, J. 1997. Evolutionary implications of metrical variation in Great Basin projectile points. In Barton and Clark (eds), 177–91.

Biehl, P.F., Gramsch, A. and Marciniak, A. (eds) 2002. *Archaeologies of Europe: History, Methods, Theories*. Münster, Waxmann.

Binford, L.R. 1962. Archaeology as anthropology. *American Antiquity* 11: 198–200.

Binford, L.R. 1964. A consideration of archaeological research design. *American Antiquity* 29: 425–41.

Binford, L.R. 1967. Smudge pits and hide smoking: the use of analogy in archaeological reasoning. *American Antiquity* 32(1): 1–12.

Binford, L.R. 1972. *An Archaeological Perspective*. New York, Seminar Press.

Binford, L.R. 1977. Historical archaeology: is it historical or archaeological? In Ferguson (ed.), 13–22. Reprinted in Binford 1983b, 169–78.

Binford, L.R. 1978. *Nunamiut Ethnoarchaeology*. New York, Academic Press.

Binford, L.R. 1980. Willow smoke and dog's tails: hunter-gatherer settlement systems and archaeological site formation. *American Antiquity* 45: 4–20. Reprinted in Hodder and Preucel (eds), 39–60.

Binford, L.R. 1981a. Behavioural archaeology and the Pompeii premise. *Journal of Anthropological Archaeology* 37(3): 195–208.

Binford, L.R. 1981b. *Bones: Ancient Men and Modern Myths*. New York, Academic Press.

Binford, L.R. 1983. *Working at Archaeology*. New York, Academic Press.

Binford, L.R. 1983a. *In Pursuit of the Past: Decoding the Archaeological Record*. London, Thames and Hudson.

Binford, L.R. 1987. Data, relativism and archaeological science. *Man* 22: 391–404.

Binford, L.R. 2001. *Constructing Frames of Reference: An Analytical Method for Archaeological Theory Building Using Hunter-Gatherer and Environmental Data Sets*. Berkeley, University of California Press.

Binford, L.R. 2002. *In Pursuit of the Past: Decoding the Archaeological Record*. Berkeley, University of California Press. Second edition.

Blain, J. and Wallis, R.J. 2004. Sacred sites, contested rights: contemporary pagan engagements with the past. *Journal of Material Culture* 9(3): 237–61.

Blain, J. and Wallis, R.J. 2007. *Sacred Sites, Contested Rights: Pagan Engagements with Archaeological Monuments*. Chichester, Sussex Academic Press.

Blakey, M.L. 1995. Race, nationalism, and the Afrocentric past. In *Making Alternative Histories: The Practice of Archaeology and History in Non-Western Settings*. Santa Fe, School of American Research, 213–28.

Blakey, M.L. and Rankin-Hill, L.M. 2004. The New York African Burial Ground Skeletal Biology Final Report Volume I. Electronic document, http://www.nps.gov/afbg/historyculture/index.htm

Blanton, R., Feinman, G.M., Kowalewski, S.A. and Peregrine, P.N. 1996. A dual-processual theory for the evolution of Mesoamerican civilization. *Current Anthropology* 37(1): 1–14.

Bloch, M. 1983. *Marxism and Anthropology*. Oxford, Clarendon Press.

Boivin, N. and Owoc, M.A. (eds) 2004. *Spils, Stones and Symbols: Cultural Perceptions of the Mineral World*. London, UCL Press.

Borofsky, R. 2002. The four subfields: anthropologists as mythmakers. *American Anthropologist* 104: 463–80.

Bourdieu, P. 1977. *Outline of a Theory of Practice*. Cambridge, Cambridge University Press.

Bradbury, M. 1987. *Mensonge*. London, Andre Deutsch.

Bradley, R. 1993. *Altering the Earth: The Origins of Monuments in Britain and Continental Europe*. Edinburgh, Society of Antiquaries of Scotland.

Bradley, R. 2000. *An Archaeology of Natural Places*. London, Routledge.

Bradley, R. and Edmonds, M. 1993. *Interpreting the Axe Trade: Production and Exchange in Neolithic Britain*. Cambridge, Cambridge University Press.

Brantingham, P.J. 2007. A unified evolutionary model of archaeological style and function based on the Price Equation. *American Antiquity* 72(3): 395–416.

Braudel, F. 1980. *On History*. London, Weidenfeld and Nicolson.

Brown, J.A. 1997. The archaeology of ancient religion in the Eastern Woodlands. *Annual Review of Anthropology* 26: 465–85.

Brown, J.A. 2006 Where's the power in mound building? An Eastern Woodlands perspective. In Butler, B.M. and Welch, P.D. (eds.), *Leadership and Polity in Mississippian Society*, Occasional Paper No. 33, Center for Archeological Investigations, Carbondale, Southern Illinois University 197–213.

Brown, M.F. 2008. Cultural relativism 2.0. *Current Anthropology* 49(3): 363–83.

Brück, J. 2005. Experiencing the past? The development of phenomenological archaeology in British prehistory. *Archaeological Dialogues* 12(1): 47–72.

Brück, J. 2007. Landscape politics and colonial identities: Sir Richard Colt Hoare's tour of Ireland, 1806. *Journal of Social Archaeology* 7: 224–49.

Brumbach, H.J. and Jarvenpa, R. 1997. Ethnoarchaeology of subsistence space and gender: a subarctic Dene case. *American Antiquity* 62(3): 414–36.

Brumfiel, E.M. 1992. Distinguished lecture in archaeology: breaking and entering the ecosystem – gender, class and faction steal the show. *American Anthropologist* 94: 551–67.

Brumfiel, E.M. 1996. The quality of tribute cloth: the place of evidence in archaeological argument. *American Antiquity* 61(3): 453–62.

Brumfiel, E. 2003. It's a material world: history, artifacts and anthropology. *Annual Review of Anthropology* 32, 205–23.

Brumfiel, E. and Earle, T.K. (eds) 1987. *Specialisation, Exchange and Complex Societies*. Cambridge, Cambridge University Press.

Brumfiel, E.M. and Fox, J.W. (eds) 1994. *Factional Competition and Political Development in the New World*. Cambridge, Cambridge University Press.

Burke, H., Smith, C., Lippert, D., Watkins, J. and Zimmerman, L. (eds) 2008. *Kennewic Man: Perspectives on the Ancient One*. Walnut Creek, Left Coast Press.

Burtt, F. 1987. 'Man the hunter': bias in children's archaeology books. *Archaeological Review from Cambridge* 6(2): 157–74.

Butler, J. 1990. *Gender Trouble*. London, Routledge.

Butler, J. 1993. *Bodies That Matter: On the Discursive Limits of 'Sex'*. London, Routledge.

Campbell, M. 2006. Memory and monumentality in the Rarotongan landscape. *Antiquity* 80: 102–117.

Carey, J. 1992. *The Intellectuals and the Masses: Pride and Prejudice among the Literary Intelligentsia, 1880–1939*. London, Faber.

Carneiro, R. 2003. *Evolutionism in Cultural Anthropology: A Critical History*. Boulder, Westview Press.

Carr, C. and Neitzel, J.E. 1995. *Style, Society and Person: Archaeological and Ethnological Perspectives*. New York, Plenum.

Cartwright, J. 2000. *Evolution and Human Behaviour: Darwinian Perspectives on Human Nature*. Cambridge, MIT Press.

Casella, E. and Fowler, C. (eds) 2005. *The Archaeology of Plural and Changing Identities: Beyond Identification*. New York, Kluwer.

Chadwick, A. 2003. Post-processualism, professionalisation, and archaeological methodologies. *Archaeological Dialogues* 10: 97–117.

Chakrabarti, D. 1998. *Colonial Indology: Sociopolitics of the Ancient Indian Past*. New Delhi, Munshiram Manoharlal.

Chakrabarti, D. 2003. *Archaeology in the Third World: A History of Indian Archaelogy since 1947*. New Delhi, Printworld.

Chapman, R. 2003. *Archaeologies of Complexity*. London, Routledge.

Chartier, R. 1994. *The Order of Books: Readers, Authors and Libraries in Europe Between the 14th and the 18th Centuries*. Cambridge, Polity.

Childe, V.G. 1929. *The Danube in Prehistory*. Oxford, Oxford University Press.

Childe, V.G. 1936. *Man Makes Himself*. London, Watts.

Childe, V.G. 1942. *What Happened in History*. Harmondsworth, Penguin.

Childe, V.G. 1958. Retrospect. *Antiquity* 32: 69–74.

Childe, V.G. 1958. *The Prehistory of European Society*. Harmondsworth, Penguin.

Childe, V.G. 1979. Prehistory and Marxism. *Antiquity* 53, 93–5.

Christenson, A.L. (ed.) 1989. *Tracing Archaeology's Past: The Historiography of Archaeology*. Carbondale, Southern Illinois University Press.

Claassen, C. (ed.) 1992. *Exploring Gender Through Archaeology*. Madison, Prehistory Press.

Claassen, C. (ed.) 1994. *Women in Archaeology*. Philadelphia, University of Pennsylvania Press.

Clark, G.A. 2003. American archaeology's uncertain future. In Gillespie et al. (eds), 51–68.

Clark, J.G.D. 1952. *Prehistoric Europe: The Economic Basis*. London, Methuen.

Clark, J.G.D. 1982. *The Identity of Man as Seen by an Archaeologist*. London, Methuen.

Clarke, D.L. 1968. *Analytical Archaeology*. London, Methuen.

Clarke, D.L. 1973. Archaeology: the loss of innocence. *Antiquity* 47: 6–18.

Clarke, D.L. 1978. *Analytical Archaeology*. Second edition, revised by Bob Chapman. London, Methuen.

Cobb, C.R. 1993. Archaeological approaches to the political economy of nonstratified societies. In Schiffer, M. (ed.) *Advances in Archaeological Method and Theory 5*. Tucson, University of Arizona Press, 43–100.

Cobb, C.R. 2003. Mississippian chiefdoms: how complex? *Annual Review of Anthropology* 32: 63–84.

Cohen, G.A. 1978. *Karl Marx's Theory of History: A Defence*. Oxford, Clarendon Press.

Cohen, P.S. 1968. *Modern Social Theory*. London, Heinemann.

Coimbra, F. and Dimitriadis, D. (eds) 2008. *Cognitive Archaeology as Symbolic Archaeology: Proceedings of the 15th UISPP World Congress 23*. Oxford, British Archaeological Reports.

Coleman, S.M. and Carlin, L. (eds) 2004. *The Cultures of Creationism: Anti-Evolutionism in English-Speaking Countries*. Aldershot, Ashgate.

Collingwood, R.G. 1939. *An Autobiography*. Oxford, Oxford University Press.

Collingwood, R.G. 1946. *The Idea of History*. Oxford, Oxford University Press.

Conkey, M.W. 1989. The structural analysis of Palaeolithic cave art. In Lamberg-Karlovsky (ed.), 135–54.

Conkey, M.W. and Spector, J. 1984. Archaeology and the study of gender. In Schiffer, M. (ed.) *Advances in Archaeological Method and Theory 7*. New York, Academic Press, 1–38.

Conkey, M. 2005. Dwelling at the margins, action at the intersection? Feminist and Indigenous archaeologies 2005. *Archaeologies: Journal of the World Archaeological Congress* 1: 9–80.

Conkey, M.W. 2007. Questioning theory: is there a gender of theory in archaeology? *Journal of Archaeological Method and Theory* 14: 285–310.

Conkey, M.W. and Gero, J. 1997. From programme to practice: gender and feminism in archaeology. *Annual Review of Anthropology* 26: 411–37.

Cooper, M.A., Firth, A., Carman, J. and Wheatley, D. (eds) 1995. *Managing Archaeology*. London, Routledge.

Cooper, N. 1997. The gentry house in an age of transition. In Gaimster and Stamper (eds), 115–26.

Coudart, A. 1999. Why is there no post-processual archaeology in France? *Antiquity* 73: 161–7.

Coulson, C. 1992. Some analysis of the castle of Bodiam, East Sussex. In Harper-Bill and Harvey (eds), 51–108.

Courbin, P. 1988. *What is Archaeology?* Chicago, Chicago University Press.

Cowgill, G. 1993. Distinguished lecture in archaeology: beyond criticising New Archaeology. *American Anthropologist* 95: 551–73.

Criado Boado, F. and Villoch Vásquez, V. 2000. Monumentalising landscape: from present perception to the past meaning of Galician megalithism (north-west Iberian peninsula). *European Journal of Archaeology* 3(2): 188–216.

Croce, B. 1921. *Theory and History of Historiography*. London, Harrap.

Crossland, Z. 2009. Of clues and signs: the dead body and its evidential traces. *American Anthropologist* 111(1): 69–80.

Crowell, A.L. 1997. *Archaeology and the Capitalist World System: A Study From Russian America*. New York, Plenum.

Crumley, C.L. 1979. Three locational models: an epistemological assessment of anthropology and archaeology. In Schiffer, M.B. (ed.) *Advances in Archaeological Method and Theory* 2. New York, Academic Press, 141–73.

Crumley, C.L. 1987. A dialectical critique of hierarchy. In Patterson and Galley (eds), 155–9.

Crumley, C.L. (ed.) 1994. *Historical Ecology, Cultural Knowledge and Changing Landscapes*. Santa Fe, School of American Research Press.

Crumley, C.L. (ed.) 1995. *Heterarchy and the Analysis of Complex Societies*. Archaeological Papers of the American Anthropological Association 7.

Culler, J. 1997. *Literary Theory: A Very Short Introduction*. Oxford, Oxford University Press.

Cumberpatch, C. and Hill, J.D. (eds) 1995. *Different Iron Ages: Studies on the Iron Age in Temperate Europe*. BAR International Series 602. Oxford, British Archaeological Reports.

Cunliffe, B., Davies, W. and Renfrew, A.C. (eds) 2002. *Archaeology: The Widening Debate*. Oxford, Oxford University Press.

Curta, F. 2001. Pots, Slavs and 'imagined communities': Slavic archaeologies and the history of the early Slavs. *European Journal of Archaeology* 4(3): 367–84.

D'Altroy, T.N. and Hastorf, C.A. (eds) 2001. *Empire and Domestic Economy*. New York, Kluwer.

Damm, C. 2005. Archaeology, ethnohistory, and oral traditions: approaches to the Indigenous past. *Norwegian Archaeological Review* 38(2): 73–87.

Daniel, G.E. 1941. The dual nature of the megalithic colonisation of prehistoric Europe. *Proceedings of the Prehistoric Society* 7: 1–49.

David, B., McNiven, I., Manas, L., Manas, J., Savage, S., Crouch, J., Neiman, G. and Brady, L. 2003. Goba of Mua: archaeology working with oral tradition. *Antiquity* 158–172.

David, D. 1996. Revolutionary archaeology in Cuba. *Journal of Archaeological Method and Theory* 3: 159–88.

Davidson, I. and Noble, W. 1996. *Human Evolution, Language, and Mind: A Psychological and Archaeological Enquiry*. Cambridge, Cambridge University Press.

Davies, P., Robb, J.G. and Ladbrook, D. 2005. Woodland clearance in the Mesolithic: the social aspects. *Antiquity* 79, 280-288.

Davis, W. 1992. The deconstruction of intentionality in archaeology. *Antiquity* 66: 334–47.

Dawkins, R. 1989. *The Selfish Gene*. Second edition. Oxford, Oxford University Press.

De Beaune, S., Collidge, F.L. and Wynn, T. (eds) 2009. *Cognitive Archaeology and Human Evolution*. Cambridge, Cambridge University Press.

Deagan, K. 1983. *Spanish St Augustine: The Archaeology of a Colonial Creole Community*. New York, Academic Press.

Deagan, K. 1991. Historical archaeology's contributions to our understanding of early America. In Falk (ed.), 97–112.

Deetz, J.F. 1972. Archaeology as a social science. In Leone, M. (ed.), 108–17.

Deetz, J.F. 1977. *In Small Things Forgotten: The Archaeology of Early American Life*. New York, Anchor.

Deetz, J.F. 1988. History and archaeological theory: Walter Taylor revisited. *American Antiquity* 55: 13–22.

Delanty, G. 1997. *Social Science: Beyond Constructivism and Realism*. Milton Keynes, Open University Press.

Delle, J. 1998. *An Archaeology of Social Space: Analysing Coffee Plantations in Jamaica's Blue Mountains*. New York, Plenum.

Demarest, A.A. 1989. Ideology and evolutionism in American archaeology: looking beyond the economic base. In Lamberg-Karlovsky (ed.), 89–102.

DeMarrais, E., Gosden, C. and Renfrew, A.C. (eds) 2004. *Rethinking Materiality: The Engagement of Mind with the Material World*. Cambridge, McDonald Institute.

Demoule, J. 1999. Ethnicity, culture and identity: French archaeologists and historians. *Antiquity* 73: 190–8.

Dennett, D.C. 1995. *Darwin's Dangerous Idea: Evolution and the Meanings of Life*. London, Allen Lane.

Derrida, J. 1988. Afterword: toward an ethic of discussion. In Graff, G. (ed), *Limited Inc*. Evanston, Northwestern University Press.

Diamond, J. 1997. *Guns, Germs and Steel: The Fates of Human Societies*. London, Cape.

Diamond, J. 2005. *Collapse: How Societies Choose to Fail or Survive*. London, Allen Lane.

Diaz-Andreu, M. 1993. Theory and ideology in archaeology: Spanish archaeology under the Franco regime. *Antiquity* 67: 74–82.

Diaz-Andreu, M. and Champion, T. (eds) 1996. *Nationalism and Archaeology in Europe*. London, University College London Press.

Diaz-Andreu, M. and Lucy, S. 2005. *Archaeology of Identity*. London, Routledge.

Diaz-Andreu, M. and Sørenson, M.-L. (eds) 1998. *Excavating Women: A History of Women in European Archaeology*. London, Routledge.

Dobres, M.-A. 2000. *Technology and Social Agency*. Oxford, Blackwell.

Dobres, M.-A. and Robb, J. (eds) 2000. *Agency in Archaeology*. London, Routledge.

Dornan, J. 2002. Agency and archaeology: past, present and future directions. *Journal of Archaeological Method and Theory* 9(4): 303–29.

Dowson, T. (ed.) 2000. Queer archaeologies. Special themed edition, *World Archaeology* 32(2).

du Cros, H. and Smith, L. (eds) 1993. *Women in Archaeology: A Feminist Critique*. Occasional Papers in Prehistory 23. Canberra, Australian National University.

Duke, P. 1992. Braudel and North American archaeology. In Knapp (ed.), 99–111. Reprinted in Hodder and Preucel (eds) (1996), 240–57.

Duke, P. and Wilson, M.C. (eds) 1995. *Beyond Subsistence: Plains Archaeology and the Postprocessual Critique*. Tuscaloosa, University of Alabama Press.

Dunnell, R.C. 1980. Evolutionary theory and archaeology. In Schiffer, M. (ed.), *Advances in Archaeological Method and Theory* vol. 3. New York, Academic Press.

Dunnell, R.C. 1989. Aspects of the application of evolutionary theory in archaeology. In Lamberg-Karlovsky (ed.), 35–49.

Eagleton, T. 1991. *Ideology: An Introduction*. London, Verso.

Eagleton, T. 2003. *After Theory*. New York, Basic Books.

Earle, T.K. (ed.) 1993. *Chiefdoms: Power, Economy and Ideology*. Cambridge, Cambridge University Press.

Earle, T.K. 1997. *How Chiefs Come to Power: The Political Economy in Prehistory*. Stanford, Stanford University Press.

Earl, T.K. 2000. Archaeology, property and prehistory. *Annual Review of Anthropology* 29: 39–60.

Earle, T.K. 2002. *Bronze Age Economics: The Beginnings of Political Economies*. Boulder, Westview Press.

Earle, T.K. and Erickson, J.E. (eds) 1977. *Exchange Systems in Prehistory*. New York, Academic Press.

Earle, T.K. and Erickson, J.E. (eds) 1982. *Contexts for Prehistoric Exchange*. New York, Academic Press.

Earle, T.K. and Preucel, R.W. 1987. Processual archaeology and the radical critique. *Current Anthropology* 28(4): 501–38.

Easthope, A. 1993. Romancing the Stone: history-writing and rhetoric. *Social History* 18(2): 235–49.

Easthope, A. 1999. *Englishness and National Culture*. London, Routledge.

Ehrenberg, M. 1989. *Women in Prehistory*. London, British Museum.

Ehrenreich, R.M., Crumley, C.L. and Levy, J.E. (eds) 1995. *Heterarchy and the Analysis of Complex Societies*. Washington, American Anthropological Association.

Eller, J.D. 1997. Anti-anti-multiculturalism. *American Anthropologist* 99(2): 249–58.

Elton, G.E. 1991. *Return to Essentials*. Cambridge, Cambridge University Press.

Embree, L. (ed.) 1992. *Metaarchaeology: Reflections by Archaeologists and Philosophers*. Boston, Kluwer Academic Publishing.

Engels, F. 1972. (first published 1884). *The Origin of the Family, Private Property and the State. In the Light of the Researches of Lewis H. Morgan*. London, Lawrence and Wishart.

Englestad, E. 1991. Images of power and contradiction: feminist theory and post-processual archaeology. *Antiquity* 65: 502–14.

Englestad, E. 2007. Much more than gender. *Journal of Archaeological Method and Theory* 14: 217–34.

Ensor, B. 2000. Social formations, modo de vida, and conflict in archaeology. *American Antiquity* 65(1): 15–42.

Evans, R.J. 2000. *In Defence of History*. Second edition. London, Granta.

Everson, W.K. 1974. *Classics of the Horror Film*. Secaucus, Citadel Press.

Fabian, A.C. (ed.) 1998. *Evolution: Society, Science and the Universe*. Cambridge, Cambridge University Press.

Falck, T. 2003. Polluted places: harbours and bybridity in archaeology. *Norwegian Archaeological Review* 36(2): 105–18.

Falk, D. 1997. Brain evolution in females: an answer to Mr Lovejoy. In Hays-Gilpin and Whitley (eds), 115–37.

Falk, L. (ed.) 1991. *Historical Archaeology in Global Perspective*. Washington, Smithsonian.

Fash, W.L. 1994. Changing perspectives on Maya civilisation. *Annual Review of Anthropology* 23: 181–208.

Faure-Rouesnel, L. 2001. French anthropology and material culture. *Journal of Material Culture* 6: 236–45.

Fawcett, C. Habu, J. and Matsunaga, J. (eds) 2008. *Evaluating Multiple Narratives: Beyond Nationalist, Colonialist, Impreialist Archaeologies*. New York, Springer.

Ferguson, L. (ed.) 1997. *Historical Archaeology and the Importance of Material Things*. Society for Historical Archaeology Special Publications 2.

Ferguson, L. 1992. *Uncommon Ground: Archaeology and Early African America, 1650–1800*. Washington: Smithsonian Institution.

Ferguson, T.J. 1996. Native Americans and the practice of archaeology. *Annual Review of Anthropology* 25: 63–80.

Feyerabend, P. 1988. *Against Method*. Second revised edition. London, Verso.

Feyerabend, P. 1995. *Killing Time: The Autobiography of Paul Feyerabend*. Chicago, University of Chicago Press.

Flannery, K.V. 1972. The cultural evolution of civilisations. *Annual Review of Ecology and Systematics* 3: 399–426.

Flannery, K.V. 1973a. The origins of agriculture. *Annual Review of Anthropology* 2: 271–310.

Flannery, K.V. 1973b. Archaeology with a capital S. In Redman (ed.), 47–58.

Flannery, K.V. (ed.) 1976. *The Early Mesoamerican Village*. New York, Academic Press.

Flannery, K.V. 2006. On the resilience of anthropological archaeology. *Annual Review of Anthropology* 55: 1–13.

Flannery, K.V. and Marcus, E.J. 1976. Formative Oaxaca and Zapotec cosmos. *American Scientist* 64(4): 374–83.

Flannery, K.V. and Marcus, E.J. (eds) 1983. *The Cloud People: Divergent Evolution of the Zapotec and Mixtec Populations*. New York, Academic Press.

Flannery, K.V. and Marcus, E.J. 1993. Cognitive archaeology. *Cambridge Archaeological Journal* 3: 260–70. Reprinted in Preucel and Hodder (eds) (1996), 350–63.

Flannery, K.V. and Marcus, E.J. 2003. The origin of war: new C14 dates from ancient Mexico. *Proceedings of the National Academy of Sciences* 100(20): 11801–5.

Fleming, A. and Johnson, M.H. 1990. The Theoretical Archaeology Group (TAG): origins, retrospect, prospect. *Antiquity* 64: 303–7.

Fleming, A. 2006. Post-processual landscape archaeology: a critique. *Cambridge Archaeological Journal* 16(3): 267–80.

Fleury-Ilett, B. 1993. Identity of France: the archaeological interaction. *Journal of European Archaeology* 1: 169–80.

Fogelin, L. 2007. The archaeology of religious ritual. *Annual Review of Anthropology* 36: 55–71.

Fontein, J. 2006. *The Silence of Great Zimbabwe: Contested Landscapes and the Power of Heritage*. Walnut Creek, Left Coast Press.

Fotiadis, M. 1994. What is archaeology's 'mitigated objectivism' mitigated by? Comments on Wylie. *American Antiquity* 59: 545–55.

Foucault, M. 1977. *Discipline and Punish: The Birth of the Prison*. Harmondsworth, Penguin.

Foucault, M. 1980. *Power/Knowledge*. Brighton, Harvester Wheatsheaf.

Fowles, J. and Brukoff, B. 1980. *The Enigma of Stonehenge*. London Jonathan Cape.

Franklin, M. 2001. A Black feminist-inspired archaeology? *Journal of Social Archaeology* 1(1): 108–25.

Fuller, S. 1992. Being there with Thomas Kuhn: a parable for postmodern times. *History and Theory* 31(3): 241–75.

Funari, P.P.A. 1997a. European archaeology and two Brazilian offspring: classical archaeology and art history. *Journal of European Archaeology* 5(2): 137–48.

Funari, P.P.A. 1997b. Archaeology, history, and historical archaeology in South America. *International Journal of Historical Archaeology* 1(3): 189–206.

Funari, P.P.A., Zarankin, A. and Stovel, E. (eds) 2005. *Global Archaeological Theory: Recent Thoughts*. New York, Kluwer.

Furholt, M. 2008. Pottery, cultures, people? The European Baden material re-examined. *Antiquity* 82: 617–28.

Gaimster, D. and Stamper, P. (eds) 1997. *The Age of Transition: The Archaeology of English Culture 1400–1600*. Oxford, Oxbow.

Galison, P. and Stump, P. (eds) 1996. *The Disunity of Science*. Palo Alto, Stanford University Press.

Gamble, C. 2007. *Origins and Revolutions: Human Identity in Earliest Prehistory*. Cambridge, Cambridge University Press.

Gamble, C. 2008. *Archaeology: The Basics*. London, Routledge.

Gardin, J-C. 1980. *Archaeological Constructs: An Aspect of Theoretical Archaeology*. Cambridge, Cambridge University Press.

Gardin, J.-C. 2002. The logicist analysis of explanatory theories in archaeology. In Franck, R. (ed.) *The Explanatory Power of Models*. New York, Kluwer.

Geertz, C. 1984. Anti anti-relativism. *American Anthropologist* 86: 263–78.

Gell, A. 1992. The technology of enchantment and the enchantment of technology. In Coote, J. and Shelton, A. (eds) *Anthropology, Art and Aesthetics*. Oxford, Clarendon Press, 40–66.

Gell, A. 1998. *Art and Agency: An Anthropological Theory*. Oxford, Clarendon.

Gerding, H. and Ingemark, D. 1997. Beyond Newtonian Thinking – towards a nonlinear archaeology: applying chaos theory to archaeology. *Current Swedish Archaeology* 5: 49–64.

Gero, J. 1985. Socio-politics and the woman-at-home ideology. *American Antiquity* 50: 342–50.

Gero, J. 1988. Gender bias in archaeology: here, then and now. In Rosser (ed.), 33–43.

Gero, J. 1991. Gender divisions of labour in the construction of archaeological knowledge. In Walde and Willows (eds), 96–102.

Gero, J. 1996. Archaeological practice and gendered encounters with field data. In Wright (ed.), 251–80.

Gero, J. and Conkey, M. (eds) 1991. *Engendering Archaeology: Women and Prehistory*. Oxford, Blackwell Publishers.

Gheorgiu, D. 2003. Centres and peripheries amongst archaeologists – archaeological theory after communism. *Antiquity*: 170–1.

Gibbon, G. 1989. *Explanation in Archaeology*. Oxford, Blackwell Publishers.

Giddens, A. 1979. *Capitalism and Modern Social Theory*. Cambridge, Cambridge University Press.

Giddens, A. 1984. *The Constitution of Society: Outline of the Theory of Structuration*. Cambridge, Polity Press.

Giddens, A. 1993. *The Giddens Reader*. Stanford, Stanford University Press.?

Gilbert, S.M. and Gubar, S. 1979. *The Madwoman in the Attic: The Woman Writer and the 19th Century Literary Imagination*. New Haven, Conn., Yale University Press.

Gilchrist, R. 1991. Women's archaeology? Political feminism, gender theory and historical revision. *Antiquity* 65: 495–501.

Gilchrist, R. 1993. *Gender and Material Culture: An Archaeology of Religious Women*. London, Routledge.

Gillespie, S. and Nicholls, D.L. (eds) 2003. *Archaeology is Anthropology*. Archeological Papers of the American Anthropological Association 13. Arlington, American Anthropological Association.

Gimbutas, M. 1989. *The Language of the Goddess*. San Francisco, Harper and Row.

Gimbutas, M. 1991. *The Civilisation of the Goddess: The World of Old Europe*. San Francisco, Harper and Row.

Glassie, H. 1975. *Folk Housing in Middle Virginia: A Structural Analysis of Historic Artefacts*. Knoxville, University of Tennessee Press.

Goffman, E. 1959. *The Presentation of Self in Everyday Life*. New York, Anchor.

Goffman, E. 1971. *Relations in Public: Microstudies of the Public Order*. Harmondsworth, Penguin.

Gonzáles-Ruibal, A. 2006. The past is tomorrow: towards an archaeology of a vanishing present. *Norwegian Archaeological Review* 39: 110–25.

Gonzáles-Ruibal, A. 2006. The dream of reason: an archaeology of the failures of modernity in Ethiopa. *Journal of Social Archaeology* 6(2): 175–201.

Gonzáles-Ruibal, A. (ed.) 2007. Arqueologia Symétrica: Un Giro Teorico sin Revolucion Paradigmática. *Complutum* 18.

Gosden, C. 1992. Endemic doubt: is what we write right? *Antiquity* 66: 803–8.

Gosden, C. 1994. *Social Being and Time*. Oxford, Blackwell Publishers.

Gosden, C. 2001. Postcolonial archaeology: issues of culture, identity and knowledge. In Hodder (ed.), 241–61.

Gosden, C. 2005. What do objects want? *Journal of Archaeological Method and Theory* 12(3): 193–211.

Gosden, C. 1999. *Anthropology and Archaeology: A Changing Relationship*. London, Routledge.

Gould, R. (ed.) 1978. *Explorations in Ethnoarchaeology*. Albuquerque, University of New Mexico Press.

Gould, R. 1980. *Living Archaeology*. Cambridge, Cambridge University Press.

Gould, R. and Schiffer, M. (eds) 1981. *The Archaeology of Us*. New York, Academic Press.

Gould, S.J. 1989. *Wonderful Life: The Burgess Shale and the Nature of History*. New York, Norton.

Gould, S.J. 1997. *The Mismeasure of Man*. Second revised edition. Harmondsworth, Penguin.

Gould, S.J. 2002. *The Structure of Evolutionary Theory*. Cambridge, Harvard University Press.

Gramsch, A. 2000. 'Reflexiveness' in archaeology, nationalism and Europeanism. *Archaeological Dialogues* 7(1): 4–19.

Gramsch, A. and Sommer, U. (eds) forthcoming. *A History of Central European Archaeology: Theory, Methods, Politics*. Bonn, Habelt.

Graves-Brown, P.M. (ed.) 2000. *Matter, Materiality and Modern Culture*. London, Routledge.

Gregory, D. 1994. *Geographical Imaginations*. Oxford, Blackwell Publishers.

Griffin, W. 1991. Review of *Reading the Past* (second edition). *Archaeological Review from Cambridge* 10(1): 124–8.

Gross, P.R. and Levitt, N. 1994. *Higher Superstition: The Academic Left and its Quarrels with Science*. Baltimore, Johns Hopkins University Press.

Guidi, A. 1996. The Italian pluriverse: different approaches to prehistoric archaeology. *The European Archaeologist: Newsletter of the European Association of Archaeologists* 5: 5–8.

Habermas, J. 1970. *Towards a Rational Society: Student Protest, Science and Politics*. London, Heinemann.

Habermas, J. 1975. *Legitimation Crisis*. London, Heinemann.

Hager, L. (ed.) 1997. *Women in Human Evolution*. London, Routledge.

Hall, M. 2000. *Archaeology and the Modern World: Colonial Transcripts in South Africa and the Chesapeake*. London, Routledge.

Hall, M. 2006. Archaeology at the edge: an archaeological dialogue with Martin Hall. *Archaeological Dialogues* 13(1): 55–67.

Halsall, G. 1997. Archaeology and historiography. In Bentley, M. (ed.), 805–27.

Halstead, P. and O'Shea, J. (eds) 1989. *Bad Year Economics: Cultural Responses to Risk and Uncertainty*. Cambridge, Cambridge University Press.

Hamilakis, Y. 1996. Through the looking glass: nationalism, archaeology and the politics of identity. *Antiquity* 70: 975–8.

Hamilakis, Y. 2007. *The Nation and its Ruins: Antiquity, Archaeology and National Imagination in Greece*. Oxford, Oxford University Press.

Hamilakis, Y. and Yalouri, E. 1996. Antiquities as symbolic capital in modern Greek society. *Antiquity* 70: 117–29.

Hamilton, P. 1996. *Historicism*. London, Routledge.

Hamilton, S. and Whitehouse, R. 2006. Phenomenology in practice: towards a methodology for a 'subjective' approach. *European Journal of Archaeology* 9(1): 31–71.

Hänsell, B. and Harding, A.F. (eds) 1998. *Towards Translating the Past: Georg Kossack – Selected Studies in Archaeology. Ten Essays Written From the Years 1974 to 1997*. Rahden, Verlag Marie Leidorf.

Hansonn, M. 2006. *Aristocratic Landscape: The Spatial Ideoology of the Medieval Aristocracy*. Stockholm, Almqvuist & Wiksell.

Harding, J. 2005. Rethinking the great divide: long-term structural history and the temporality of event. *Norwegian Archaeological Review* 38(2): 88–101.

Harding, S. ed. 2004. *The Feminist Standpoint Theory Reader: Intellectual and Political Controversies*. New York, Routledge.

Härke, H. (ed.) 2000. *Archaeology, Ideology and Society: The German Experience*. Frankfurt, Lang.

Härke, H. and Wolfram, S. 1993. The power of the past. *Current Anthropology* 34: 182–4.

Harper-Bill, C. and Harvey, R. (eds) 1992. *Medieval Knighthood IV: Papers from the Fifth Strawberry Hill Conference 1990*. Woodbridge, Boydell.

Harrison, R. 2003. 'The magical virtue of these sharp things': colonialism, mimesis and knapped bottle glass artefacts in Australia. *Journal of Material Culture* 8(3): 311–36.

Harvey, D. 1989. *The Condition of Postmodernity: An Enquiry into the Origins of Cultural Change*. Oxford, Blackwell Publishers.

Hastorf, C.A. 1988. The use of palaeoethnobotanical data in prehistoric studies of crop production, processing, and consumption. In Hastorf and Popper (eds), 119–44.

Hastorf, C.A. 1992. *Agriculture and the Onset of Political Inequality before the Inka*. Cambridge, Cambridge University Press.

Hastorf, C.A. and Johanessen, S. 1991. Understanding changing people/plant relationships in the prehispanic Andes. In Preucel (ed.), 140–55. Reprinted in Hodder and Preucel (eds) (1996), 61–78.

Hastorf, C.A. and Popper, V.S. (eds) 1988. *Current Palaeoethnobotany: Analytical Methods and Cultural Interpretations of Archaeological Plant Remains*. Chicago, University of Chicago Press.

Hawkes, C. 1954. Archaeological theory and method: some suggestions from the Old World. *American Anthropologist* 56: 155–68.

Hawkes, J. 1968. The proper study of mankind. *Antiquity* 42: 255–62.

Hawkes, T. 1976. *Structuralism and Semiotics*. London, Methuen.

Hays-Gilpin, K. and Whitley, D.S. (eds) 1998. *Reader in Gender Archaeology*. London, Routledge.

Hedeager, L. 2006. Scandinavia and the Huns: an interdisciplinary approach to the migration era. *Norwegian Archaeological Review* 40: 42–58.

Hegel, G.W.F. 1956. *The Philosophy of History*. New York, Dover.

Hegmon, M. 2003. Setting theoretical egos aside: issues and theory in North American archaeology. *American Antiquity* 68(2): 213–43.

Held, D. and Thompson, J.B. (eds) 1989. *Social Theory of Modern Societies: Anthony Giddens and His Critics*. Cambridge, Cambridge University Press.

Hensel, W., Tabaczyński, S. and Urbańczyk, P. (eds) 1998. *Theory and Practice of Archaeological Research. Vol. III: Dialogue with the Data: The Archaeology of Complex Societies and its Context in the 90s*. Warsaw, Insitute of Archaeology and Ethnology, Polish Academy of Sciences.

Herva, V.P. and Ikäheimo, J. 2002. Defusing dualism: mind, materiality and prehistoric art. *Norwegian Archaeological Review* 35(2): 95–108.

Hill, J.D. and Cumberpatch, C.G. (eds) 1995. *Different Iron Ages: Studies on the Iron Age in Temperate Europe*. BAR International Series 602. Oxford, British Archaeological Reports.

Hill, J.N. 1970. *Broken K Pueblo: Prehistoric Social Organisation in the American Southwest*. Tucson, University of Arizona Press.

Hillman, G. 1984. Interpretation of archaeological plant remains: the application of ethnographic plant models from Turkey. In Zeist and Casparie (eds), 1–42.

Hills, C. 2003. *Origins of the English*. London, Duckworth.

Hingley, R. 2005. *Globalising Roman Culture: Unity Diversity and Empire*. London, Routledge.

Hinsley, C.M. 1989. Revising and revisioning the history of archaeology: reflections on region and context. In Christenson (ed.), 79–96.

Hinton, D.A. 2005. *Gold and Gilt, Pots and Pins: Possessions and People in Medieval Britain*. Oxford: Oxford University Press.

Hodder, I. 1982a. *The Present Past*. London, Batsford.

Hodder, I. 1982b. *Symbols in Action: Ethnoarchaeological Studies of Material Culture*. Cambridge, Cambridge University Press.

Hodder, I. (ed.) 1987. *The Archaeology of Contextual Meanings*. Cambridge, Cambridge University Press.

Hodder, I. (ed.) 1991a. *Archaeological Theory in Europe: The Last Thirty Years*. Oxford, Blackwell Publishers.

Hodder, I. (ed.) 1991b. *Archaeological Theory in Europe: The Last Three Decades*. London, Routledge.

Hodder, I. 1997. 'Always momentary, fluid and flexible': towards a reflexive excavation method in archaeology. *Antiquity* 71: 691–700.

Hodder, I. 1999. *The Archaeological Process: An Introduction*. Oxford, Blackwell Publishers.

Hodder, I. (ed.) 2001. *Archaeological Theory Today*. Cambridge, Polity Press.

Hodder, I. 2006. Triggering post-processual archaeology and beyond. In Williamson and Bisson (eds) 16–24.

Hodder, I. and Hutson, S. 2003. *Reading the Past: Current Approaches to Interpretation in Archaeology*. Cambridge, Cambridge University Press.

Hodder, I., Karlsson, H. and Olsen, B. 2008. 40 years of theoretical engagement: a conversation with Ian Hodder. *Norwegian Archaeological Review* 41(1): 26–42.

Hodder, I. and Orton, C. 1976. *Spatial Analysis in Archaeology*. Cambridge, Cambridge University Press.

Hodder, I., Shanks, M., Alexandri, A., Buchli, V., Carman, J., Last, J. and Lucas, G. (eds) 1995. *Interpreting Archaeology: Finding Meaning in the Past*. London, Routledge.

Hodge McCoid, C. and McDermott, L.D. 1996. Towards decolonising gender: female vision in the Upper Palaeolithic. *American Anthropologist* 98(2): 319–26.

Hodges, R. 1982. *Dark Age Economics*. London, Duckworth.

Hollinger, R. 1994. *Postmodernism and the Social Sciences*. London, Sage.

Holt, J.Z. 2009. Rethinking the Ramey state: was Cahokia the centre of a theatre state? *American Antiquity* 74(2): 231–54.

Holtorf, C. 2000. Review – Matthew Johnson: *Archaeological Theory: An Introduction*. *Norwegian Archaeological Review* 33: 125–30.

Holtorf, C. 2002. Notes on the life history of a pot sherd. *Journal of Material Culture* 7(1): 49–71.

Holtorf, C. 2007. *Archaeology is a Brand! The Meaning of Archaeology in Contemporary Popular Culture*. Walnu Creek, Left Coast Press.

Holtorf, C. and Karlsson, H. (eds) 2000. *Philosophy and Archaeological Practice: Perspectives for the 21st Century*. Göteborg, Bricoleur Press.

Hrobat, K. 2007. Use of oral tradition in archaeology: the case of Ajdovščina above Rodik, Slovenia. *European Journal of Archaeology* 10(1): 31–56.

Hubert, J. (ed.) 2000. *Madness, Disability and Social Exclusion: The Archaeology and Anthropology of Difference*. London, Routledge.

Humm, M. (ed.) 1992. *Feminisms: A Reader*. London, Harvester.

Hunt, L. (ed.) 1989. *The New Cultural History*. Berkeley, University of California Press.

Huntley, J.P. and Stallibrass, S. (eds) 2000. *Taphonomy and Interpretation*. Oxford, Oxbow.

Hurst, H. and Owen, S. (eds) 2005. *Ancient Colonisations: Analogy, Similarity and Difference*. London, Duckworth.

Hutson, S. 2002. Gendered citation practices in *American Antiquity* and other journals. *American Antiquity* 68(2): 213–43.

Immonen, V. 2005. Defining a culture: the meaning of Hanseatic in medieval Turku. *Antiquity* 81: 720–32.

Ingold, T. 2000. *The Perception of the Environment: Essays on Livelihood, Dwelling and Skill*. London, Routledge.

Ingold, T. 2005. Comments on Christopher Tilley: *The Materiality of Stone: Explorations in Landscape Phenomenology*. *Norwegian Archaeological Review* 38(2): 122–9.

Ingold, T. 2007. Materials against materiality. *Archaeological Dialogues* 14(1): 1–16.

Ingold, T. and Vergunst, J.L. (eds) 2008. *Ways of Walking: Ethnography and Practice on Foot*. Aldershot, Ashgate.

Insoll, T. 2007. 'Natural' or 'human' spaces? Tallensi sacred groves and shrines and their potential implications for aspects of northern European prehistory and phenomenological interpretation. *Norwegian Archaeological Review* 40(2): 138–58.

Insoll, T. (ed.) 2007. *The Archaeology of Identities: A Reader*. London, Routledge.

Jencks, C. 1977. *The Language of Postmodern Architecture*. New York, Pantheon.

Jenkins, K. 1995. *On 'What is History?': From Carr and Elton to Rorty and White*. London, Routledge.

Jenkins, K. (ed.) 1997. *The Postmodern History Reader*. London, Routledge.

Johnson, A.G. 1995. *The Blackwell Dictionary of Sociology: A User's Guide to Sociological Language*. Oxford, Blackwell Publishers.

Johnson, A.L. (ed.) 2004. *Processual Archaeology: Exploring Analytical Strategies, Frames of Reference, and Culture Process*. Oxford, Praeger.

Johnson, M.H. 1989. Conceptions of agency in archaeological interpretation. *Journal of Anthropological Archaeology* 8: 189–211.

Johnson, M.H. 1993. *Housing Culture*. London, University College London Press.
Johnson, M.H. 1996. *An Archaeology of Capitalism*. Oxford, Blackwell Publishers.
Johnson, M.H. 1999. *Archaeological Theory: An Introduction*. Oxford, Blackwell.
Johnson, M.H. 2002. *Behind the Castle Gate*. London, Routledge.
Johnson, M.H. 2006 On the nature of theoretical archaeology and archaeological theory. *Archaeological Dialogues* 13(2): 117–32.
Johnson, M.H. 2007. *Ideas of Landscape*. Oxford, Blackwell Publishers.
Jones, A.M. 2001. *Archaeological Theory and Scientific Practice*. Cambridge, Cambridge University Press.
Jones, A.M. and Macgregor, G. (eds) 2002. *Colouring the Past*. Oxford, Berg.
Jones, G. 1984. Interpretation of archaeological plant remains: ethnographic models from Greece. In Zeist and Casparie (eds), 43–62.
Jones, L. 1997. Conquests of the imagination: Maya-Mexican polarity and the story of Chichen Itza. *American Anthropologist* 99(2): 275–90.
Jones, M. 2007. *Memory and Material Culture*. Cambridge, Cambridge University Press.
Jones, S., Graves-Brown, P. and Gamble, C.S. (eds) 1996. *Cultural Identity and Archaeology: The Construction of European Communities*. London, Routledge.
Joyce, P. 1995. The end of social history? *Social History* 20(1): 73–85.
Joyce, R.A. 1994. Dorothy Hughes Popenhoe: Eve in an archaeological garden. In Claassen (ed.), 51–66. Reprinted in Preucel and Hodder (eds) (1996), 501–16.
Joyce, R.A. with Preucel, R.W., Lopiparo, J., Guyer, C. and Joyce, M. 2002. *The Languages of Archaeology: Dialogue, Narrative, and Writing*. Oxford, Blackwell.
Karlisch, S.M. (ed.) 1997. *Vom Knochenmann zur Menschenfrau. Feministische Theorie und archäologische Praxis [in Stralsund 1996]*. Münster, Agenda-Verlag.
Karlsson, H. (ed.) 2000. *It's About Time: The Concept of Time in Archaeology*. Göteborg, Bricoleur Press.
Keay, S. and Terrenato, N. (eds) 2001. *Italy and the West: Comparative Issues in Romanisation*. Oxford, Oxbow.
Kelley, J.H. and Hanen, M.P. 1988. *Archaeology and the Methodology of Science*. Albuquerque, University of New Mexico Press.
Kelly, R.L. 2000. Elements of a behavioural ecological paradigm for the study of prehistoric hunter-gatherers. In Schiffer (ed.), 63–78.
Kelly, R.L. 2000. *Warless Societies and the Origin of War*. Ann Arbor, University of Michigan Press.
Kepecs, S. and Kolb, M.J. (eds) 1997. New approaches to combining the archaeological and historical records. *Journal of Archaeological Method and Theory* 4.
Klejn, L.S. 1977. A panorama of theoretical archaeology. *Current Anthropology* 18(1): 1–42.
Klejn, L.S. 1993a. It's difficult to be a god. *Current Anthropology* 34: 508–11.
Klejn, L.S. 1993b. To separate a centaur: on the relationship of archaeology and history in Soviet tradition. *Antiquity* 67: 339–48.

Klejn, L.S. 1993c. Is German archaeology atheoretical? *Norwegian Archaeological Review* 26(1): 49–54.

Kluckholn, C. 1939. The place of theory in anthropological studies. *Philosophy of Science* 6: 328–44.

Knapp, B. (ed.) 1992. *Archaeology, Annales and Ethnohistory*. Cambridge, Cambridge University Press.

Knapp, B. 1996. Archaeology without gravity: postmodernism and the past. *Journal of Archaeological Method and Theory* 3: 127–58.

Knappett, C. 2005. *Thinking Through Material Culture: An Interdisciplinary Perspective*. Philadelphia, University of Pennsylvania Press.

Knutson, K. 2007. Comment on Ingela Bergman: Indigenous time, colonial history: Sami conceptions of time and ancestry and the role of relics in cultural reproduction. *Norwegian Archaeological Review* 40: 103–7.

Kobyliński, Z. (ed.) 2001. *Quo Vadis Archaeologia? Whither European Archaeology in the 21st Century?* Warsaw, Polish Academy of Sciences.

Kohl, P. 1987. The use and abuse of world systems theory: the case of the pristine West Asian state. *Advances in Archaeological Method and Theory* 11: 1–35.

Kohl, P. and Fawcett, C. (eds) 1995. *Nationalism, Politics and the Practice of Archaeology*. Cambridge, Cambridge University Press.

Kohler, T.A. 1993. News from the Northern American southwest: prehistory on the edge of chaos. *Journal of Archaeological Research* 1(4): 267–321.

Kohn, M. and Mithen, S. 1999. Handaxes: products of sexual selection? *Antiquity* 73, 518–26.

Kohring, S. and Wynne-Jones, S. (eds) 2007. *Socialising Complexity: Structure, Interaction and Power in Archaeological Discourse*. Oxford, Oxbow.

Kolb, M.J. 1994. Monumentality and the rise of religious authority in precontact Hawai'i. *Current Anthropology* 45: 521–33.

Kowalewski, S.A. 1990. The evolution of complexity in the Valley of Oaxaca. *Annual Review of Anthropology* 19: 39–260.

Kristiansen, K. 1988. The black and the red: Shanks and Tilley's programme for a radical archaeology. *Antiquity* 62: 473–82.

Kristiansen, K. 1998. *Europe Before History*. Cambridge, Cambridge University Press.

Kristiansen, K. 2004. Genes versus agents: a discussion of the widening theoretical gap in archaeology. *Archaeological Dialogues* 11(2): 77–99.

Kristiansen, K. 2008. Do we need the 'archaeology of Europe'? *Archaeological Dialogues* 15(1): 5–25.

Kristiansen, K. and Larsen, M. (eds) 1987. *Centre and Periphery in the Ancient World*. Cambridge, Cambridge University Press.

Kristiansen, K. and Larsson, T.B. 2005. *The Rise of Bronze Age Society: Travels, Transmissions and Transformations*. Cambridge, Cambridge University Press.

Kroeber, A.L. 1948. *Anthropology*. London, Harrap.

Kuhn, T. 1962. *The Structure of Scientific Revolutions*. Chicago, University of Chicago Press.

Kuna, M. and Venclova, N. (eds) 1995. *Whither Archaeology? Papers in Honour of Evzen Neustupný*. Prague, Institute of Archaeology.

LaCapra, D. 1987. *History, Politics and the Novel*. Ithaca, Cornell University Press.

Lampeter Archaeology Workshop 1997. Relativism, objectivity and the politics of the past. *Archaeological Dialogues* 2: 164–98.

Larson, D.O. and Michaelsen, J. 1990. Impacts of climatic variability and population growth on Virgin Branch Anasazi cultural developments. *American Antiquity* 55: 227–49.

Larson, D.O., Neff, H., Graybill, D.A., Michaelsen, J. and Ambos, E. 1996. Risk, climatic variability, and the study of southwestern prehistory: an evolutionary perspective. *American Antiquity* 61(2): 217–41.

Latour, B. 1987. *Science in Action*. Milton Keynes, Open University Press.

Latour, B. 2005. *Reassembling the Social: An Introduction to Actor-Network Theory*. Oxford, Oxford University Press.

Le Goff, J. and Nora, P. 1985. *Constructing the Past: Essays in Historical Methodology*. Cambridge, Cambridge University Press.

Le Roy Ladurie, E. 1974. *The Peasants of Languedoc*. London, Scolar Press.

Le Roy Ladurie, E. 1978. *Montaillou: Cathars and Catholics in a French Village, 1294–1324*. London, Scolar Press.

Le Roy Ladurie, E. 1979. *The Territory of the Historian*. London, Harvester.

Lech, J. 1996. A short history of Polish archaeology. *World Archaeological Bulletin* 8: 177–95.

Lechte, J. 1994. *Fifty Key Contemporary Thinkers*. London, Routledge.

Legendre, J.-P., Olivier, L. And Schnitzler, B. (eds) 2007. *L'Archaeologie Nationale-Socialiste dans les Pays Occupés a L'Ouest du Reich*. Gollion, Infolio.

Leonard, R.D. 1993. The persistence of an explanatory dilemma in Contact Period studies. In Rogers and Wilson (eds), 31–42.

Leone, M.P. (ed.) 1972. *Contemporary Archaeology: A Guide to Theory and Contributions*. Carbondale, Southern Illinois University Press.

Leone, M.P. 1984. Interpreting ideology in historical archaeology: using the rules of perspective in the William Paca Garden in Annapolis, Maryland. In Miller and Tilley (eds), 25–36.

Leone, M.P. 2005. *The Archaeology of Liberty in an American Capital: Excavations in Annapolis*. Berkeley, University of California Press

Leone, M.P. and Potter, P. 1984. *Archaeological Annapolis: A Guide to Seeing and Understanding Three Centuries of Change*. Annapolis, Historic Annapolis Foundation. Reprinted in Preucel and Hodder (eds) (1996), 570–98.

Leone, M.P. and Potter, P. 1988. *The Recovery of Meaning: Historical Archaeology in the Eastern United States*. Washington, Smithsonian Institution.

LePage, M. 2008. Evolution: a guide for the not-yet-perplexed. *New Scientist* 2652, 19 April: 24–5.

Lightfoot, K., Martinez, A. and Schiff, A.M. 1998. Daily practice and material culture in pluralistic social settings: an archaeological study of culture change and persistence from Fort Ross, California. *American Antiquity* 63(2): 199–222.

Lippert, D. 2005. Remembering humanity: how to include human values in a scientific endeavour. *International Journal of Cultural Property* 12(2): 275–80.

Lippert, D. 2006. Building a bridge to cross a thousand years. *American Indian Quarterly* 30: 431–40.

Little, B. 2007. *Historical Archaeology: Why the Past Matters*. Walnut Creek, Left Coast Press.

López Austin, L. and López Luján, L. 2001. *Mexico's Indigenous Past*. Norman, University of Oklahoma Press.

Lubbock, J. 1865. *Pre-historic Times, as Illustrated by Ancient Remains, and the Manners and Customs of Ancient Savages*. London, Williams and Northgate.

Lucas, G. 2001. *Critical Approaches to Fieldwork: Contemporary and Historical Archaeological Practice*. London, Routledge.

Lucas, G. 2005. *The Archaeology of Time*. London, Routledge.

Lucas, G. and Hall, M. 2006. Archaeology at the edge: an archaeological dialogue with Martin Hall. *Archaeological Dialogues* 13(1): 55–67.

Lumbreras, L.G. 2005. *Arqueología y Sociedad*. Lima, Instituto de Estudios Peruanos.

Lyman, R.L. and O'Brien, M.J. 2006. *Measuring Time with Artifacts: A History of Methods in American Archaeology*. Lincoln, University of Nebraska Press.

Lyman, R.L., O'Brien, M.J. and Dunnell, R.C. 1997a. *The Rise and Fall of Culture History*. New York, Plenum.

Lyman, R.L., O'Brien, M.J. and Dunnell, R.C. (eds) 1997b. *Americanist Culture History: Fundamentals of Time, Space and Form*. New York, Plenum.

Lyman, R.L., O'Brien, M.J. and Schiffer, M.B. (eds) 2005. Publishing archaeology in *Science* and *Scientific American*, 1940–2003. *American Antiquity* 70(1): 157–67.

Lyotard, J.-F. 1984. *The Postmodern Condition: A Report on Knowledge*. Manchester, Manchester University Press.

McAnaney, P.A. and Yoffee, N. (eds) 2009. *Questioning Collapse: Human Reselience, Ecological Vulnerability, and the Aftermath of Empire*. Cambridge, Cambridge University Press.

McClure, S.B. 2007. Gender, technology and evolution: cultural inheritance theory and prehistoric potters in Valencia, Spain. *American Antiquity* 72(3): 485–508.

Mace, R., Holden, C.J. and Shennan, S. (eds) 2005. *The Evolution of Cultural Diversity: A Phylogenetic Approach*. London, UCL Press.

McGhee, R. 2008. Aboriginalism and the problems of Indigenous archaeology. *American Antiquity* 73(4): 579–97.

McGuire, K. and Hildebrandt, W. 2005. Re-thinking Great Basin foragers: prestige hunting and costly signaling during the Middle Archaic period. *American Antiquity* 70(4): 695–712.

McGuire, R.H. 1983. Breaking down cultural complexity: inequality and heterogeneity. In Schiffer, M.B. (ed.) *Advances in Archaeological Method and Theory* 8. New York, Academic Press, 91–142.

McGuire, R.H. 1992. *A Marxist Archaeology*. San Diego, Academic Press.

McGuire, R. 1993. Archaeology and Marxism. In Schiffer, M. (ed.) *Archaeological Method and Theory* 5. Tucson, University of Arizona Press, 101–58.

McGuire, R.H. 2008. *Archaeology as Political Action*. Berkeley, University of California Press.

McGuire, R.H. and Paynter, R. (eds) 1991. *The Archaeology of Inequality*. Oxford, Blackwell Publishers.

McGuire, R.H. and Saitta, D.J. 1996. Although they have petty captains, they obey them badly: the dialectics of Prehispanic Western pueblo social organisation. *American Antiquity* 61: 197–216.

Machin, A. 2008. Why handaxes just aren't that sexy: a response to Kohn and Mithen. *Antiquity* 82: 761–9.

Mackenzie, I. (ed.) 1994. *Archaeological Theory: Progress or Posture?* Aldershot, Avebury.

McLellan, D. (ed.) 1977. *Karl Marx: Selected Writings*. Oxford, Oxford University Press.

McNairn, B. 1980. *The Method and Theory of V. Gordon Childe*. Edinburgh, Edinburgh University Press.

McNay, L. 1992. *Foucault and Feminism: Power, Gender and the Self*. Oxford, Polity Press.

McNiven, I.J. and Russell, L. 2005. *Appropriated Pasts: Indigenous Peoples and the Colonial Culture of Archaeology*. Lanham, AltaMira.

Malina, J. and Vasicek, Z. 1990. *Archaeology Yetserday and Today: The Development of Archaeology in the Human Sciences*. Cambridge, Cambridge University Press.

Marcus, J. 2008. The archaeological evidence for social evolution. *Annual Review of Anthropology* 37: 251–316.

Marshall, Y. (ed.) 2002. Community archaeology. Special issue, *World Archaeology* 34(2).

Maschner, H.D.G. 1996. *Darwinian Archaeologies*. New York, Plenum Press.

Mauss, M. and Schlanger, N. 2006. *Techniques, Technology and Civilisation*. Oxford, Berghahn Books.

Mellars, P. and Gibson, K. (eds) 1997. *Modelling the Early Human Mind*. Cambridge, Cambridge University Press.

Mellor, A.K. 1988. *Mary Shelley: Her Life, Her Fiction, Her Monsters*. London, Routledge.

Meltzer, D. 1979. Paradigms and the nature of change in American archaeology. *American Antiquity* 44: 644–57.

Mertens, E. M. (ed.) 1993. Feministische Archäologie. In *Bericht zur Archäologinnentagung 1992 in Kiel [1. Tagung des Netzwerks archäologisch arbeitender Frauen 1992 in Kiel]*, edited by E. M. Mertens, J. K. Koch and J. E. Fries, Kiel, Selbstverlag, 17–23.

Meskell, L. 1999. *Archaeologies of Social Life: Age, Sex, Class, etc. in Ancient Egypt*. Oxford: Blackwell Publishers.

Meskell, L. (ed.) 2002. *Private Life in New Kingdom Egypt*. Oxford, Princeton University Press.

Meskell, L. 2004. *Object Worlds in Ancient Egypt: Material Biographies Past and Present*. Oxford, Berg.

Meskell, L. (ed.) 2005. *Archaeologies of Materiality*. Oxford, Blackwell.

Meskell, L. and Preucel, R. (eds) 2004. *A Companion to Social Archaeology*. Oxford, Blackwell.

Midgley, M. 1985. *Evolution as a Religion: Strange Hopes and Stranger Fears*. London, Methuen.

Miksicek, C.H. 1987. Formation processes of the archaeobotanical record. *Advances in Archaeological Method and Theory* 10: 211–47.

Miller, D. 1987. *Material Culture and Mass Consumption*. Oxford, Blackwell Publishers.

Miller, D. (ed.) 1995. *Acknowledging Consumption: A Review of New Studies*. London, Routledge.

Miller, D. (ed.) 2005. *Materiality*. Durham, Duke University Press.

Miller, D. and Tilley, C. (eds) 1984. *Ideology, Power and Prehistory*. Cambridge, Cambridge University Press.

Milner, G.R. 1998. *The Cahokia Chiefdom*. Washington, Smithsonian.

Mirza, M.N. and Dungworth, D.B. 1995. The potential misuse of genetic analyses and the social construction of 'race' and 'ethnicity'. *Oxford Journal of Archaeology* 14(3): 345–54.

Mitchell, P. 1981. *The Open Book of the Prehistoric World*. London, Hodder and Stoughton.

Mithen, S. 1989. Ecological interpretations of Palaeolithic art. *Proceedings of the Prehistoric Society* 57: 103–14. Reprinted in Preucel and Hodder (eds) (1996), 79–96.

Mithen, S. 1990. *Thoughtful Foragers: A Study of Prehistoric Decision Making*. Cambridge, Cambridge University Press.

Mithen, S. 1991. 'A cybernetic wasteland'? Rationality, emotion and Mesolithic foraging. *Proceedings of the Prehistoric Society* 57(2): 9–14.

Mithen, S. 1997. *The Prehistory of the Mind: The Cognitive Origins of Art, Religion and Science*. London, Thames and Hudson.

Mithen, S. (ed.) 1998. *Creativity in Human Evolution and Prehistory*. London, Routledge.

Mithen, S. 2005. *The Singing Neanderthals: The Origin of Music, Language, Mind and Body*. London, Weidenfeld and Nicholson.

Mithen, S. 2008. 'Whatever turns you on', a response to Anna Machin, 'Why handaxes just aren't that sexy'. *Antiquity* 82: 766–9.

Mobley-Tanaka, J.L. 1997. Gender and ritual space during the pithouse to pueblo transition: subterranean mealing rooms in the North American Southwest. *American Antiquity* 62(3): 437–48.

Mooney, C. 2005. *The Republican War on Science*. New York, Basic Books.

Moore, H.L. 1987. *Space, Text and Gender*. Cambridge, Cambridge University Press.

Moore, H.L. 1988. *Feminism and Anthropology*. Oxford, Polity Press.

Moreland, J. 2001. *Archaeology and Text*. London, Duckworth.

Moreland, J. 2006. Archaeology and texts: subservience or enlightenment. *Annual Review of Anthropology* 35, 136–228.

Morris, I. 2004. Classical archaeology. In Bintliff (ed.), 253–71.

Moser, S. 1996. Science, stratigraphy, and the deep sequence: excavation vs regional survey and the question of gendered practice in archaeology. *Antiquity* 70: 813–23.

Moser, S. 1998. *Ancestral Images: The Iconography of Human Origins*. Ithaca, Cornell University Press.

Moser, S. 2007. On disciplinary culture: archaeology as fieldwork and its gendered associations. *Journal of Archaeological Method and Theory* 14(3): 235–63.

Moser, S., Glazier, D., Phillips, J.E., Nasser el Nemr, L., Saleh Mousa, M., Nasr Aiesh, R., Richardson, S., Connor, A. and Seymour, M. 2002. Transforming archaeology through practice: strategies for collaborative archaeology and the

Community Archaeology Project at Quseir, Egypt. *World Archaeology* 34(2): 220–48.

Moss, M. 2005. Rifts in the theoretical landscape of archaeology in the United States: a comment on Hegmon and Watkins. *American Antiquity* 70(3): 581–7.

Muller, J. 1997. *Mississippian Political Economy*. New York, Plenum.

Murray, T. 1995. On Klejn's agenda for theoretical archaeology. *Current Anthropology* 36: 290–2.

Neiman, F.D. 1997. Conspicuous consumption as wasteful advertising: a Darwinian perspective on spatial patterns in Classic Maya terminal monument dates. In Barton and Clark (eds), 267–90.

Neiman, F.D. 2008. The lost world of Monticello: an evolutionary perspective. *Journal of Anthropological Research* 64(2): 161–94.

Nelson, M.C., Nelson, S.M. and Wylie, A. (eds) 1994. *Equity Issues for Women in Archaeology*. Archaeological Papers No.5. Washington, American Anthropological Association.

Nelson, M.C., Hegmon, M., Kulow, S. and Schollmeyer, K.G. 2006. Archaeological and ecological perpectives on reorganization: a case study from the Mimbres region of the US Southwest. *American Antiquity* 71(3): 403–32.

Nelson, S.M. (ed.) 2007. *Women in Antiquity: Theoretical Approaches to Gender and Archaeology*. Lanham, AltaMira Press.

Neustupný, E. 1993. *Archaeological Method*. Cambridge, Cambridge University Press.

Nicholas, G.P. 1994. On the Goddess Myth and methodology. *Current Anthropology* 35: 448–9.

Nottveit, O.-M. 2006. The kidney dagger as a symbol of masculine identity – the Ballock dagger in Scandinavian context. *Norwegian Archaeological Review* 39(2): 138–50.

O'Brien, M.J. (ed.) 1996. *Evolutionary Archaeology: Theory and Application*. Salt Lake City, University of Utah Press.

O'Brien, M. and Lyman, R.L. 2000. Darwinian evolution is applicable to historical archaeology. *International Journal of Historical Archaeology* 4(1): 71–112.

O'Brien, M.J., Lyman, R.L. and Schiffer, M.B. (eds) 2005. *Archaeology a Process: Processualism and its Progeny*. Salt Lake City, University of Utah Press.

O'Keeffe, T. 2007. *Archaeology and the Pan-European Romanesque*. London, Duckworth.

Olivier, L. 2000. L'impossible archéologie de la mémoire: à propos de *W ou le souvenir d'enfance* de Georges Perec. *European Journal of Archaeology* 3(3): 387–406.

Olivier, L. 2008. *Le Sombre Abîme du Temps: Memoire et Archéologie*. Paris, Seuil.

Olsen, B. 2003. Material culture after text: re-membering things. *Norweigan Archaeological Review* 36: 87–104.

Orme, B. 1981. *Anthropology for Archaeologists: An Introduction*. Ithaca, Cornell University Press.

Orser, C. 1996. *An Historical Archaeology of the Modern World*. New York, Plenum.

Orser, C. 2004. *Race and Practice in Archaeological Interpretation*. Philadelphia, University of Pennsylvania Press.

Oyuela-Caycedo, A. (ed.) 1994. *History of Latin American Archaeology*. Aldershot, Avebury.

Oyuela-Caycedo, A., Anaya, A., Elera, C.G., and Valdez, L.M. 1997. Social archaeology in Latin America? Comments to T.C. Patterson. *American Antiquity* 82(2): 365–76.

Parcero Oubiña, C. 2003. Looking forward in anger: social and political transformations in the Iron Age of the North-western Iberian peninsula. *European Journal of Archaeology* 6(3): 267–99.

Parsons, K. 2003. *The Science Wars: Debating Scientific Knowledge and Technology*. New York, Prometheus Press.

Patrik, L.E. 1985. Is there an archaeological record? In Schiffer, M.B. (ed.) *Advances in Archaeological Method and Theory* 8. New York, Academic Press, 27–62.

Patterson, O. 1982. *Slavery and Social Death: A Comparative Study*. Cambridge, Harvard University Press.

Patterson, T.C. 1986. The last sixty years: towards a social history of Americanist archaeology. *American Anthropologist* 88: 7–26.

Patterson, T.C. 1990. Some theoretical tensions within and between the processual and the postprocessual archaeologies. *Journal of Anthropological Archaeology* 9(2): 189–200.

Patterson, T.C. 1994. Social archaeology in Latin America: an appreciation. *American Antiquity* 59: 531–7.

Patterson, T.C. 1995. *Towards a Social History of Archaeology in the United States*. Fort Worth, Harcourt Brace.

Patterson, T.C. and Galley, C.W. (eds) 1987. *Power Relations and State Formation*. Washington, American Anthropological Association.

Pauketat, T.R. 2001. Practice and history in archaeology. *Anthropological Theory* 1(1): 73–98.

Pauketat, T.R. 2004. *Ancient Cahokia and the Mississippians*. Cambridge, Cambridge University Press.

Pauketat, T.R. 2007. *Chiefdoms and Other Archaeological Delusions*. Lanham, AltaMira.

Peregrine, P.N. 2001. Cross-cultural comparative approaches in archaeology. *Annual Review of Anthropology* 30: 1–18.

Pickering, A. 1984. *Constructing Quarks: A Sociological History of Particle Physics*. Edinburgh, Edinburgh University Press.

Piggott, S. 1968. *Ancient Europe*. Edinburgh, Edinburgh University Press.

Piontek, J. 2006. Origin of the Slavs as a pretext for discussion. *Archaeologia Polona* 44: 317–31.

Piotrowska, D. 1997–98. Biskupin 1993–1996: archaeology, politics and nationalism. *Archaeologia Polona* 35–6: 255–85.

Platt, C. 1981. *The Parish Churches of Medieval England*. London, Secker and Warburg.

Platt, C. 2007. Revisionism in castle studies: A caution. *Medieval Archaeology* 51: 83–102.

Pluciennik, M. 1996. Genetics, archaeology and the wider world. *Antiquity* 70: 13–14.

Pluciennik, M. 2005. *Social Evolution*. London, Duckworth.

Politis, G. 2001. On archaeological praxis, gender bias and Indigenous peoples in South America. *Journal of Social Archaeology* 1: 90–107.

Politis, G. 2002. South America: in the garden of forking paths. In Cunlifee et al. (eds), 193–244.

Politis, G. and Alberti, A. 1999. *Archaeology in Latin America*. London, Routledge.

Pollard, A.M. and Bray, P. 2007. A bicycle made for two? The integration of scientific techniques into archaeological interpretation. *Annual Review of Anthropology* 36: 245–59.

Potter, P. 1994. *Public Archaeology in Annapolis: A Critical Approach to History in Maryland's Ancient City*. Washington, Smithsonian Institution.

Pratap, A. 2009. *Indigenous Archaeology in India: Prospects of an Archaeology of the Subaltern*. BAR International Series 1927. Oxford, British Archaeological Reports.

Pratezellis, A. 2000. *Death by Theory: A Tale of Mystery and Archaeological Theory*. New York, Altamira.

Preucel, R.W. 1991a. The philosophy of archaeology. In Preucel (ed.), 17–29.

Preucel, R.W. (ed.) 1991b. *Processual and Postprocessual Archaeologies: Multiple Ways of Knowing the Past*. Southern Illinois University at Carbondale Occasional Paper No. 10. Carbondale, Southern Illinois University Press.

Preucel, R.W. 1995. The postprocessual condition. *Journal of Archaeological Research* 3(2): 147–75.

Preucel, R.W. 2006. *Archaeological Semiotics*. Oxford, Blackwell.

Preucel, R. and Hodder, I. (eds) 1996. *Contemporary Archaeology in Theory: A Reader*. Oxford, Blackwell Publishers.

Pyburn, K.A. (ed.) 2003. *Ungendering Civilisation: Rethinking the Archaeological Record*. London, Routledge.

Raab, L.M. and Larson, D.O. 1997. Medieval climatic anomaly and punctuated cultural evolution in coastal southern California. *American Antiquity* 62(2): 319–36.

Rainbird, P. and Hamilakis, Y. (eds) 2001. *Interrogating Padagogies: Archaeology in Higher Education*. BAR International Series 948. Oxford, British Archaeological Reports.

Rathje, W.L., Hughes, W.W., Wilson, D.C., Tani, M.K., Archer, G.H., Hunt, R.G. and Jones, T.W. 1992. The archaeology of contemporary landfills. *American Antiquity* 57(3): 437–47.

Redman, C. (ed.) 1973. *Research and Theory in Current Archaeology*. New York, Wiley.

Redman, C.L. 1978. *The Rise of Civilisation: From Early Farmers to Urban Society in the Ancient Near East*. San Francisco, Freeman.

Redman, C.L. 1991. Distinguished lecture in archaeology: in defence of the seventies. *American Anthropologist* 93: 295–307.

Reisch, G.A. 1991. Chaos, history, and narrative. *History and Theory* 30(1): 1–20.

Renfrew, A.C. 1973a. *Before Civilisation: The Radiocarbon Revolution and Prehistoric Europe*. Harmondsworth, Penguin.

Renfrew, A.C. (ed.) 1973b. *The Explanation of Culture Change*. London, Duckworth.

Renfrew, A.C. 1982. Socio-economic change in ranked societies. In Renfrew et al. (eds), 1–8.

Renfrew, A.C. 1984. *Approaches to Social Archaeology*. Edinburgh, Edinburgh University Press.

Renfrew, A.C. (ed.) 1986. *Peer Polity Interaction and Socio-Political Change*. Cambridge, Cambridge University Press.

Renfrew, A.C. 1993. Cognitive archaeology: some thoughts on the archaeology of thought. *Cambridge Archaeological Journal* 3(2): 248–50.

Renfrew, A.C. 2005. Cognitive archaeology. In Renfrew and Bahn (eds), 41–5.

Renfrew, A.C. 2007. *Prehistory: Making of the Human Mind*. London, Weidenfeld and Nicholson.

Renfrew, A.C. and Bahn, P. 2004. *Archaeology: Theories, Methods and Practice*. Fourth revised edition. London, Thames and Hudson.

Renfrew, A.C. and Bahn, P. (eds) 2005. *Archaeology: The Key Concepts*. London, Routledge.

Renfrew, A.C. and Bahn, P. 2008. *Archaeology: Theories, Methods and Practice*. Fifth edition. London, Thames and Hudson.

Renfrew, A.C. and Cooke, K. (eds) 1979. *Transformations: Mathematical Approaches to Culture Change*. London, Academic Press.

Renfrew, A.C. and Shennan, A. (eds) 1982. *Ranking, Resource and Exchange*. Cambridge, Cambridge University Press.

Renfrew, A.C. and Zubrow, E. 1994. *The Ancient Mind: Elements of Cognitive Archaeology*. Cambridge, Cambridge University Press.

Renfrew, A.C., Frith, C. and Malafouris, L. (eds) 2009. *The Sapient Mind: Archaeology Meets Neuroscience*. Oxford, Oxford University Press.

Revell, L. 2009. *Roman Imperialism and Local Identities*. Cambridge, Cambridge University Press.

Reyman, J. (ed.) 1992. *Rediscovering Our Past: Essays on the History of American Archaeology*. Aldershot, Avebury.

Richerson, P.J. and Boyd, R. 2005. *Not By Genes Alone: How Culture Transformed Human Evolution*. Chicago, University of Chicago Press.

Ridley, M. (ed.) 1997. *Evolution: An Oxford Reader*. Oxford, Oxford University Press.

Rindos, D. 1989. Undirected variation and the Darwinian explanation of cultural change. *Archaeological Method and Theory* 1: 1–45.

Robbins, R. (ed.) 1972. *Sir Thomas Browne: Religio Medici, Hydriotaphia, and the Garden of Cyrus*. Oxford, Oxford University Press.

Robin, C. 2006. Gender, farming, and long-term change: Maya historical and archaeological perspectives. *Current Anthropology* 47(3): 409–33.

Rogers, J.D. and Wilson, S.M. (eds) 1993. *Ethnohistory and Archaeology: Approaches to Postcontact Change in the Americas*. New York, Plenum.

Ronnes, H. 1999. *Architecture and Elite Culture in the United Provinces, England and Ireland, 1500–1700*. Amsterdam University Press.

Rorty, R. 1989. *Contingency, Irony and Solidarity*. Oxford, Blackwell Publishers.

Rorty, R. and Engel, P. 2007. *What's The Use of Truth?* New York, Columbia University Press.

Roscoe, P.B. 1995. The perils of 'positivism' in cultural anthropology. *American Anthropologist* 97(3): 492–504.

Rosser, S.V. (ed.) 1988. *Feminism within the Science and Health Care Professions: Overcoming Resistance*. New York, Pergamon.

Rouseeau, J. 2006. *Rethinking Social Evolution: The Prespective from Middle-Range Societies*. Montreal, McGill-Queen's University Press.

Rubertone, P.E. 2000. The historical archaeology of native Americans. *Annual Review of Anthropology*: 425–46.

Russell, P. 1993. The Palaeolithic mother-goddess: fact or fiction? In du Cros and Smith (eds), 93–7. Reprinted in Hays-Gilpin and Whitley (eds) (1998), 261–8.

Sabloff, J. 1990. *New Archaeology and the Ancient Maya*. New York, Scientific American.

Sabloff, J. 2008. *Archaeology Matters: Action Archaeology in the Modern World*. Walnut Creek, Left Coast Press.

Sahlins, M. 1995. *How 'Natives' Think: About Captain Cook, For Example*. Chicago, University of Chicago Press.

Saitta, D. 1992. Radical archaeology and middle-range theory. *Antiquity* 66: 886–97.

Santley. R.S. and Alexander, R.T. 1992. The political economy of core-periphery systems. In Schortman and Urban (eds), 23–49.

Saunders, A.D. 1977. Introduction to five castle excavations. *Archaeological Journal* 134: 1–10.

Scarry, J.F. (ed.) 1996. *Political Structure and Change in the Prehistoric Southeastern United States*. Gainesville, University of Florida Press.

Scheinsohn, V. 2003. Hunter-gatherer archaeology in south America. *Annual Review of Anthropology* 32: 339–61.

Schiffer, M.B. 1976. *Behavioural Archaeology*. New York, Academic Press.

Schiffer, M.B. 1987. *Formation Processes of the Archaeological Record*. Albuquerque, University of New Mexico Press.

Schiffer, M.B. 1995. *Behavioral Archaeology: First Principles*. Salt Lake City, University of Utah Press.

Schiffer, M.B. 1996. Some relationships between behavioural and evolutionary archaeologies. *American Antiquity* 61: 643–62.

Schiffer, M.B. (ed.) 2000. *Social Theory and Archaeology*. Salt Lake City, University of Utah Press.

Schiffer, M.B. 2002. *Behavioral Archaeology*. Second edition. New York, Percheron.

Schiffer, M.B. and Miller, A.R. 1999. *The Material Life of Human Beings: Artifacts, Bahviour and Communication*. London, Routledge.

Schmidt, M. 2001. Untitled review. *European Journal of Archaeology* 4: 273–8.

Schmidt, P.R. and Patterson, T.C. (eds) 1995. *Making Alternative Histories: The Practice of Archaeology and History in Non-Western Settings*. Santa Fe, School of American Research Press.

Schmidt, P.R. and Walz, J.R. 2007. Re-presenting African pasts through historical archaeology. *American Antiquity* 72(1): 53–70.

Schnapp, A. 1993. *The Discovery of the Past*. Paris, Editions Carré.

Shnirelman, V.A. 1995. Alternative prehistory. *Journal of European Archaeology* 3: 1–20.

Schortman, E.M. and Urban, P.A. (eds) 1992. *Resources, Power, and Regional Interaction*. New York, Plenum.

Schortman, E.M. and Urban, P.A. 1994. Living on the edge: core/periphery relations in ancient southeastern Mesoamerica. *Current Anthropology* 35: 401–13.

Schrire, C. 1995. *Digging Through Darkness: Chronicles of an Archaeologist*. Charlottesville, University of Virginia Press.

Schulke, A. 2000. 'Die Mittel- und Osteuropäische Ür und Frühgesichtsforschung in den Jahren 1933–1945', Berlin, 19–23 November 1998. *Journal of European Archaeology* 3(3): 417–29.

Schwartz, G.M. and Nichols, J.J. (eds) 2006. *After Collapse: The Regeneration of Complex Societies*. Tucson, University of Arizona Press.

Schwyzer, P. 2007. *Archaeologies of English Renaissance Literature*. Oxford, Oxford University Press.

Sebastian, L. 1996. *The Chaco Anasazi: Sociopolitical Evolution in the Prehistoric Southwest*. Cambridge, Cambridge University Press.

Segal, D.A. and Yanagisako, S.J. 2005. *Unrapping the Sacred Bundle: Reflections on the Disciplining of Anthropology*. Durham, Duke University Press.

Seifert, D. (ed.) 1991. Gender in historical archaeology. *Historical Archaeology* 25(4): 1–155.

Shakespeare, T. 2006. *Disability Rights and Wrongs*. London, Routledge.

Shalin, D.N. 1992. Critical theory and the pragmatist challenge. *American Journal of Sociology* 98(2): 237–79.

Shanks, M. 1992. *Experiencing the Past*. London, Routledge.

Shanks, M. 1996. *Classical Archaeology of Greece: Experiences of the Discipline*. London, Routledge.

Shanks, M. and Pearson, M. 2001. *Theatre/Archaeology*. London, Routledge.

Shanks, M. and Tilley, C. 1987. *Social Theory and Archaeology*. Oxford, Polity Press.

Shanks, M. and Tilley, C. 1992. *Re-Constructing Archaeology: Theory and Practice*. Second edition. London, Routledge.

Shanks, M. and McGuire, R. 1996. The craft of archaeology. *American Antiquity* 61(1): 75–88.

Shennan, S.J. (ed.) 1988. *Archaeological Approaches to Cultural Identity*. London, Routledge.

Shennan, S.J. 2001. Demography and cultural innovation: a model and its implications for modern human culture. *Cambridge Archaeological Journal* 11: 5–16.

Shennan, S.J. 2002. *Genes, Memes and Human History*. London, Duckworth.

Shennan, S.J. 2008. Evolution in archaeology. *Annual Review of Anthropology* 37: 75–1.

Shepherd, N. 2002. The politics of archaeology in Africa. *Annual Review of Anthropology* 31: 189–209.

Silliman, S. 2005. Culture contact or colonialism? Challenges in the archaeology of native North America. *American Antiquity* 70(1): 55–74.

Singleton, T. (ed.) 1985. *The Archaeology of Slavery and Plantation Life*. Orlando, Academic Press.

Singleton, T. 1995. The archaeology of slavery in North America. *Annual Review of Anthropology* 24: 119–40.

Skibo, J.M. and Schiffer, M. 2008. *People and Things: A Behavioural Approach to Material Culture*. New York, Springer.

Skibo, J.M., Walker, W.H. and Neilsen, A.E. 1995. *Expanding Archaeology*. Salt Lake City, University of Utah Press.

Smail, D.L. 2008. *On Deep History and the Human Brain*. Berkeley, University of California Press.

Smith, A.T. 2003. *The Political Landscape: Constellations of Authority in Early Complex Societies*. Berkeley, University of California Press.

Smith, C. and Ward, G.K. (eds) 2000. *Indigenous Cultures in an Interconnected World*. London, Allen and Unwin.

Smith, C. and Wobst, M. 2005a. Decolonising archaeological theory and practice. In Smith and Wobst (eds), 5–16.

Smith, C. and Wobst, M. (eds) 2005b. *Indigenous Archaeologies: Decolonising Theory and Practice*. London, Routledge.

Smith, J. 2009. *Charles Darwin and Victorian Visual Culture*. Cambridge, Cambridge University Press.

Smith, L. 1994. Heritage management as postprocessual archaeology. *Antiquity* 88: 300–9.

Smith, M.E. 2004. The archaeology of ancient state economies. *Annual Review of Anthropology* 33: 73–102.

Snead, J.E. 2008. *Ancestral Landscapes of the Pueblo World*. Tucson, University of Arizona Press.

Sofaer, J. 2006. *The Body as Material Culture: A Theoretical Osteoarchaeology*. Cambridge, Cambridge University Press.

Sofaer Derevenski, J. (ed.) 2000. *Children and Material Culture*. London, Routledge.

Sokal, A. 2008. *Beyond the Hoax: Science, Philosophy and Culture*. Oxford, Oxford University Press.

Sokal, A. and Bricmont, J. 1998. *Fashionable Nonsense: Postmodern Intellectuals' Abuse of Science*. New York, Picador.

Sommer, U. 2000. Theory and tradition in German archaeology. *Archaeological Dialogues* 7: 160–8.

Sørensen, M.L.S. 1992. Gender archaeology and Scandinavian Bronze Age studies. *Norwegian Archaeological Review* 25(1): 31–49.

Sørensen, M.L.S. 2000. *Gender Archaeology*. Oxford, Polity.

South, S. 1997a. *Method and Theory in Historical Archaeology*. New York, Academic Press.

South, S. (ed.) 1997b. *Research Strategies in Historical Archaeology*. New York, Academic Press.

Spector, J. 1993. *What This Awl Means: Feminist Archaeology at a Wahpeton Dakota Village*. St Paul, Minnesota Historical Society Press.

Spencer, C.S. 1997. Evolutionary approaches in archaeology. *Journal of Archaeological Research* 5: 209–64.

Spencer, C.S. and Redmond, E. 2004. Primary state formation in Mesoamerica. *Annual Review of Anthropology* 33: 173–99.

Spender, D. 1980. *Man Made Language*. London, Routledge.

Staecker, J. 2005. The concepts of imitation and translation: perceptions of a Viking Age past. *Norwegian Archaeological Review* 38(1): 3–28.

Stanish, C. 2001. The origin of state societies in south America. *Annual Review of Anthropology* 30, 41–64.

Steward, J. 1955. *Theory of Culture Change: The Methodology of Multilinear Evolution.* Chicago, University of Illinois Press.

Steward, J. 1977. *Evolution and Ecology.* Chicago, University of Illinois Press.

Stout, A. 2008. *Creating Prehistory: Druids, Ley Hunters and Archaeologists in Pre-War Britain.* Oxford, Blackwell.

Sturt, F. 2006. Local knowledge is required: a rhythm analytical approach to the late Mesolithic and early Neolithic of the East Anglian fenland. *Journal of Maritime Archaeology* 1: 119–39.

Tabaczyński, S. 1993. The relationship between history and archaeology: elements of the present debate. *Medieval Archaeology* 37: 1–14.

Tabaczyński, S. 2006. Archaeology – anthropology – history: unconscious foundationsn and conscious expressions of social life. *Archaeologia Polonia* 44: 15–39.

Tabaczyński, S. 2007. Polish archaeology in my lifetime. *Antiquity* 81: 1074–82.

Tainter, J. 1990. *The Collapse of Complex Societies.* Cambridge, Cambridge University Press.

Tainter, J. 2006. Archaeology of overshoot and collapse. *Annual Review of Anthropology* 35: 59–74.

Tarlow, S. and West, S. (eds) 1998. *The Familiar Past? Archaeologies of Late Historic Britain.* London, Routledge.

Taylor, C.C., Everson, P. and Wilson-North, R. 1990. Bodiam Castle, Sussex. *Medieval Archaeology* 34: 155–7.

Taylor, W. 1948. *A Study of Archaeology. Memoirs of the American Anthropological Association* 69.

Teltser, P.A. 1995. *Evolutionary Archaeology: Methodological Issues.* Tucson, University of Arizona Press.

Terrenato, N. (ed.) 2000. Archaeologia Teorica: X Ciclo di Lezioni Sulla Richercha Applicata in Archaeologia Certosa di Pontignano (Siena), 9–14 Augusto 1999. Firenze, Insegna del Giglio.

Thomas, D.H. 1998. *Archaeology.* Third edition. Orlando, Harcourt Brace.

Thomas, D.H. 2000. *Skull Wars: Kennewick Man, Archaeology, and the Battle for Native American Identity.* New York, Basic Books.

Thomas, D.H. and Kelly, R.L. 2006. *Archaeology.* Belmont, Wadsworth.

Thomas, J. 1988. Neolithic explanations revisited: the Mesolithic–Neolithic transition in Britain and south Scandinavia. *Proceedings of the Prehistoric Society* 54: 59–66.

Thomas, J. 1991. A reply to Steven Mithen. *Proceedings of the Prehistoric Society* 57(2): 15–20.

Thomas, J. 1999. *Understanding the Neolithic.* London, Routledge.

Thomas, J. 1999. *Time, Culture and Identity: An Interpretative Archaeology.* London, Routledge.

Thomas, J. 2004. The great dark book: archaeology, experience, and interpretation. In Bintliff (ed.), 21–36.

Thomas, J. 2004. *Archaeology and Modernity.* London, Routledge.

Thompson, E.P. 1978. *The Poverty of Theory and Other Essays.* London, Merlin Press.

Tilley, C. 1991. *Material Culture and Text: The Art of Ambiguity.* London, Routledge.

Tilley, C. 1994. *A Phenomenology of Landscape*. London, Routledge.

Tilley, C. 2004. *The Materiality of Stone: Explorations in Landscape Phenomenology*. Oxford, Berg.

Tilley, C. 2005. Phenomenology. In Renfrew and Bahn (eds), 201–7.

Tilley, C. 2008. *Body and Image: Explorations in Landscape Phenomenology*. Walnut Creek, Left Coast Press.

Tilley, C., Keuchler-Fogden, S., Keane, W., Rowlands, M. And Spyer, P. (eds) 2006. *Handbook of Material Culture*. London, Sage.

Tomášková, S. 2006. Yes, Virginia, there is gender: shamanism and archaeology's many histories. In Williamson and Bisson (eds), 92–113.

Tomášková, S. 2007. Mapping a future: archaeology, feminism, and scientific practice. *Journal of Archaeological Method and Theory* 14: 264–84.

Toynbee, A.J. 1934. *A Study of History*. Oxford, Oxford University Press.

Trigger, B.G. 1980a. *Gordon Childe: Revolutions in Archaeology*. London, Thames and Hudson.

Trigger, B.G. 1980b. Archaeology and the image of the American Indian. *American Antiquity* 45: 662–76.

Trigger, B.G. 1984. Archaeology at the crossroads: what's new? *Annual Review of Anthropology* 13: 275–300.

Trigger, B.G. 1989. Hyperrelativism, responsibility and the social sciences. *Canadian Review of Sociology and Anthropology* 26: 776–91.

Trigger, B.G. 1991. Distinguished lecture in archaeology: constraint and freedom – a new synthesis for archaeological explanation. *American Anthropologist* 93: 551–69.

Trigger, B.G. 1993. Marxism in contemporary Western archaeology. In Schiffer, M. (ed.) *Advances in Archaeological Method and Theory* 5. Tucson, University of Arizona Press, 159–200.

Trigger, B.G. 1995a. Expanding middle-range theory. *Antiquity* 69: 449–58.

Trigger, B.G. 1995b. Romanticism, nationalism, and archaeology. In Kohl and Fawcett (eds), 263–79.

Trigger, B.G. 1997. *Sociocultural Evolution*. Oxford, Blackwell Publishers.

Trigger, B.G. 2000. Roger Beefy's primer. *Cambridge Archaeological Journal* 10(2): 367–91.

Trigger, B.G. 2006. *A History of Archaeological Thought*. Second edition. Cambridge, Cambridge University Press.

Tringham, R. 1991. Households with faces: the challenge of gender in prehistoric architectural remains. In Conkey and Gero (eds), 93–131.

Trinkaus, E. and Shipman, P. 1992. *The Neandertals: Changing the Image of Mankind*. New York, Knopf.

Tuhiwai Smith, L. 1999. *Decolonising Methodologies: Research and Indigenous Peoples*. Dunedin, University of Otago Press.

Turnbaugh, W.A. 1993. Assessing the significance of European goods in 17th century Naragansett society. In Rogers and Wilson (eds), 133–57.

Tusa, N. and Kirkinen, T. (eds) 1992. *Nordic TAG: The Archaeologist and His/Her Reality. Report from the 4th Nordic TAG Conference*. Helsinki, University of Helsinki.

Ucko, P. 1989. *Academic Freedom and Apartheid*. London, Duckworth.

Ucko, P. (ed.) 1995. *Theory in Archaeology: A World Perspective*. London, Routledge.

Unstead, R.J. 1953. *Looking at History 1: From Cavemen to Vikings*. London, Black.

Van Dyke, R. and Alcock, S. (eds) 2003. *Archaeologies of Memory*. Oxford, Blackwell.

Van Dommelen, P. 2000. Material concerns and boundless diversity. *European Journal of Archaeology* 3(3): 409–16.

Veit, U. 1988. Ethnic concepts in German prehistory: a case study in the relationship between cultural identity and archaeological objectivity. In Shennan (ed.), 35–56.

Virágos, G. 2006. *The Social Archaeology of Residential Sites: Hungarian Noble Residences and Their Social Context From the 13th Through to the 16th Century: An Outline for Methodology*. BAR International Series 1583. Oxford, British Archaeological Reports.

Voss, B. 2008a. Sexuality studies in archaeology. *Annual Review of Anthropology* 37: 317–36.

Voss, B. 2008b. Gender, race and labor in the archaeology of the Spanish colonial Americas. *Current Anthropology* 49(5): 861–93.

Voss, B. 2008c. *The Archaeology of Ethnogenesis: Race and Sexuality in Colonial San Fransisco*. Berkeley, University of California Press.

Walde, D. and Willows, N.D. (eds) 1991. *The Archaeology of Gender. Proceedings of the 22nd Annual Chacmool Conference*. Calgary, University of Calgary Press.

Wall, D.Z. 1994. *The Archaeology of Gender: Separating the Spheres in Urban America*. New York, Plenum.

Wallerstein, I. 1974. *The Modern World-System*. New York, Academic Press.

Walsh, K. 1992. *The Representation of the Past: Museums and Heritage in the Postmodern World*. London, Routledge.

Warnier, J.-P. 1999. Construire la Culture Materielle: l'homme qui pensait avec ses doigts. Paris, Presses Universitaires de France.

Warnier, J.-P. 2001. A praxeological approach to subjectivation in a material world. *Journal of Material Culture* 6(1): 5–24.

Washburn, D.K. (ed.) 1983. *Structure and Cognition in Art*. Cambridge, Cambridge University Press.

Wason, P.K. 1994. *The Archaeology of Rank*. Cambridge, Cambridge University Press.

Watkins, J. 2000. *Indigenous Archaeology: American Indian Values and Scientific Practice*. Walnut Creek, AltaMira Press.

Watkins, J. 2003. Beyond the margin: American Indians, First Nations, and archaeology in north America. *American Antiquity* 68: 273–85.

Watson, P.J. 1991. A parochial primer: the new dissonance as seen from the midcontinental United States. In Preucel (ed.), 265–76.

Watson, P.J. 1995. Archaeology, anthropology and the culture concept. *American Anthropologist* 97(4): 683–94.

Watson, P.J., LeBlanc, S.A. and Redman, C.L.R. 1971. *Explaation in Archaeology: An Explicitly Scientific Approach*. New York, Columbia University Press.

Watson, P.J., LeBlanc, S.A. and Redman, C.L.R. 1984. *Archaeological Explanation: The Scientific Method in Archaeology*. New York, Columbia.

Watson, R.A. 1990. Ozymandias, king of kings: post-processual radical archaeology as critique. *American Antiquity* 41: 410–15.

Watson, R.A. 1991. What the New Archaeology has accomplished. *Current Anthropology* 32: 275–91.

Webmoor, T. 2007. What about 'one more turn after the social' in archaeological reasoning? Taking things seriously. *Word Archaeology* 39(4): 369–78.

Webmoor, T. and Witmore, C.L. 2008. Things are us! A commentary on human/things relations under the banner of a 'social' archaeology. *Norwegian Archaeological Review* 41(1): 53–70.

Wheatley, D., Earl, G.P. and Poppy, S. (eds) 2002. *Contemporary Themes in Archaeological Computing*. Oxford, Oxbow.

White, H. 1987. *The Content of the Form: Narrative Discourse and Historical Representation*. Baltimore, Johns Hopkins University Press.

White, L. 1949. *The Science of Culture: A Study of Man and Civilisation*. New York, Farar, Stroux and Giroux.

Whitley, D.S. (ed.) 1998. *Reader in Archaeological Theory: Post-Processual and Cognitive Approaches*. London, Routledge.

Whitley, J. 2002. Too many ancestors. *Antiquity* 76: 119–26.

Wilcox, M. 2010. NAGPRA and Indigenous peoples: the social context, controversies and the transformation of American archaeology. In Ashmore et al. (eds).

Wilkie, L. 2010. *The Lost Boys of Zeta Psi: A Historical Archaeology of Masculinity in a University Fraternity*. University of California Press, Berkeley.

Wilks, R.R. 1985. The ancient Maya and the political present. *Journal of Anthropological Research* 41(3): 307–26.

Willey, G.R. and Sabloff, J. 1993. *A History of American Archaeology*, Third edition. New York, Freeman.

Williams, R. 1988. *Keywords: A Vocabulary of Culture and Society*. London, Fontana.

Williamson, R.F. and Bisson, M.S. (eds) 2006. *The Archaeology of Bruce Trigger: Theoretical Empiricism*. Montreal, McGill-Queen's Press.

Williamson, T. and Bellamy, E. 1983. *Ley Lines in Question*. London, Heinemann.

Wilson, E.O. 2006. *From So Simple a Beginning: The Four Great Books of Charles Darwin*. New York, Norton.

Wilson, S. 1999. *The Emperor's Giraffe And Other Stories of Cultures in Contact*. New York, Basic Books.

Witmore, C.L. 2006. Vision, media, noise and the perception of time: symmetrical approaches to the mediation of the natural world. *Journal of Material Culture* 11(3): 267–92.

Wolpert, L. 1992. *The Unnatural Nature of Science*. London, Faber.

Woodward, I. 2007. *Understanding Material Culture*. London, Sage.

Wright, R. (ed.) 1996. *Gender and Archaeology*. Philadelphia, University of Pennsylvania Press.

Wylie, A. 1985. The reaction against analogy. *Advances in Archaeological Method and Theory* 8: 63–111.

Wylie, A. 1992a. On scepticism, philosophy, and archaeological science. *Current Anthropology* 33: 209–13.

Wylie, A. 1992b. The interplay of evidential constraints and political interests: recent archaeological research on gender. *American Antiquity* 57: 15–35. Reprinted in Preucel and Hodder (eds), 431–59.

Wylie, A. 1992c. On 'heavily decomposing red herrings': scientific method in archaeology and the ladening of evidence with theory. In Embree (ed.) (1992), 269–88.

Wylie, A. 1993a. A proliferation of new archaeologies: 'Beyond Objectivism and Relativism'. In Yoffee and Sherratt (eds), 20–6.

Wylie, A. 1993b. Workplace issues for women in archaeology: the chilly climate. In du Cros and Smith (eds), 245–60.

Wylie, A. 1996. The constitution of archaeological evidence: gender politics and science. In Galison and Stump (eds), 311–43.

Wylie, A. 2002. *Thinking From Things: Essays in the Philosophy of Archaeology.* Berkeley, University of California Press.

Wylie, A. 2006. Moderate relativism, political objectivism. In Williamson, R.F. and Bisson, M.S. (eds), 25–35.

Yarrow, T. 2003. Artefactual persons: the relational capacities of persons and things in the practice of excavation. *Norwegian Archaeological Review* 36(1): 65–73.

Yentsch, A. 1991. The symbolic divisions of pottery: sex-related attributes of English and Anglo-American household pots. In McGuire and Paynter (eds), 192–230. Reprinted in Preucel and Hodder (eds) (1996), 315–48.

Yentsch, A.E. 1994. *A Chesapeake Family and Their Slaves.* Cambridge, Cambridge University Press.

Yentsch, A.E. and Beaudry, M.C. (eds) 1992. *The Art and Mystery of Historical Archaeology: Essays in Honour of James Deetz.* Boca Raton, CRC Press.

Yoffee, N. 1979. The decline and rise of Mesopotamian civilisation: an ethnoarchaeological perspective on the evolution of social complexity. *American Antiquity* 44: 5–35.

Yoffee, N. 2005. *Myths of the Archaic State: Evolution of the Earliest Cities, States and Civilisations.* Cambridge, Cambridge University Press.

Yoffee, N. and Cowgill, G.L. (eds) 1988. *The Collapse of Ancient States and Civilisations.* Tucson, University of Arizona Press.

Yoffee, N. and Sherratt, A. (eds) 1993. *Archaeological Theory: Who Sets The Agenda?* Cambridge, Cambridge University Press.

Zeist, W.V. and Casparie, W.A. (eds) 1984. *Plants and Ancient Man: Studies in Palaeoethnobotany.* Rotterdam, Balkema.

Index